Proceedings of the Institution of Mechanical Engineers

Conference

Sizewell 'B'— The First of the UK PWR Power Stations

13-14 September 1989
Ramada Renaissance Hotel
Manchester

Sponsored by
Power Industries Division of the Institution of Mechanical Engineers

In association with
British Nuclear Energy Society
Institution of Electrical Engineers
Institute of Energy

IMechE Conference 1989-8

Published for the Institution of Mechanical Engineers by
Mechanical Engineering Publications Limited

The Publishers are not responsible for any statement made in this publication. Data, discussion and conclusions developed by authors are for information only and are not intended for use without independent substantiating investigation on the part of potential users.

Printed by Waveney Print Services Ltd, Beccles, Suffolk.

Contents

C388/025   Sizewell 'B' power station − engineering and construction   1
A Walker

C388/020   Safety philosophy and implications on plant design of Sizewell 'B'   7
V S Beckett and J Kirk

C388/011   Diversity: safety system design against common mode failure   13
D B Boettcher and S J Cereghino

C388/013   Sizewell Nuclear Island fluid systems design   21
A C Hall

C388/033   Functional specification for Sizewell 'B' systems   31
D P Luckhurst and A B H Chevalier

C388/010   Radioactive waste management at Sizewell 'B'   39
K Rutter

C388/016   A proven technology for boron and liquid waste treatment systems of
Sizewell 'B' PWR   49
G Vallee, B Fabre, P Maury and A D McKay

C388/030   Steam turbine generators for Sizewell 'B' nuclear power station   55
J A Hesketh and J Muscroft

C388/031   Heat exchange equipment for the Sizewell 'B' turbine generators   67
W J Torrance

C388/026   Development of the Sizewell 'B' station automatic control system   75
A R Maccabee and I G Palfreyman

C388/014   Distributed digital processing technology applied to commercial
nuclear power station controls   87
G W Remley

C388/038   The life cycle benefits of an integrated system approach to
control and instrumentation   99
J C Higgs

C388/041   Inspection of the Sizewell 'B' PWR   113
P Johnson

C388/042   Sizewell 'B' PWR reactor pressure vessel pre-service and
in-service inspection requirement   119
A C Ashton, P D Kelsey and G C Shand

C388/047   Validation of inspections for Sizewell 'B'   131
G J Lloyd

C388/023   Sizewell 'B' steam generator design builds upon the Westinghouse
Model F to meet United Kingdom safety case   143
R L Sylvester, J P Fogarty and J L Thomson

C388/007   Test facility for pressurized water reactor coolant pumps   155
I S Paterson and G C Mulholland

C388/024   Primary system pipework for Sizewell 'B'   173
H Stigter and J Haentjens

C388/027   Development of improved methods for seismic design and pipe break protection   179
G D T Carmichael and P T George

C388/018   Safety and relief valve testing   197
S Bryant, P T George and D R Airey

C388/008   Valve operability testing and stellite replacement   205
G P Airey, S Bryant and D J W Richards

C388/001   Equipment qualification for Sizewell 'B'   215
A H Fox, and J C Catlin

C388/021   Application of seismic requirements to the Sizewell 'B' nuclear power station   225
D J Shepherd, C R Smith and R M White

C388/037   Development of the environmental qualification profile for Sizewell 'B'   237
K T Routledge and D B Utton

C388/029   Sizewell 'B' PWR − structural design of the primary containment   245
R Crowder and D W Twidale

C388/022   Design and analysis of the containment liner   257
J B Shaw

C388/045   The Sizewell 'B' containment airlocks   267
S C Davis, P Leslie and W O Livsey

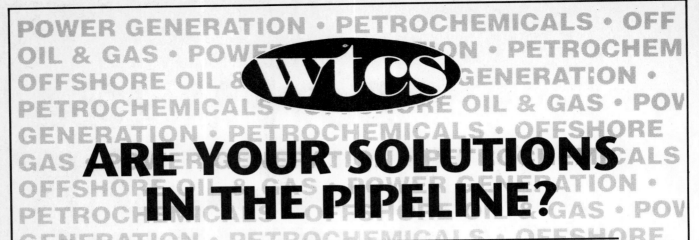

C388/025

Sizewell 'B' power station—engineering and construction

A WALKER, BSc, CEng, MIMechE
PWR Project Group, National Power Division of CEGB, Knutsford, Cheshire

SYNOPSIS   The Sizewell 'B' design is based on the Callaway PWR station in Missouri, USA.   There
have been many papers describing the additional criteria covering safety, operational experience
and design and manufacturing practices which were applied to the Callaway reference design and
which led to the Sizewell 'B' design concept.   This paper describes the implementation of some
of these design criteria leading to the layout related design features.   Comparisons are drawn
with the reference design.   This paper concludes by describing various aspects of the design
and construction process and the progress which has been made on the Sizewell site.

1   INTRODUCTION

The Sizewell 'B' power station uses the
standard Westinghouse four loop PWR with
the station layout being based on the arrangement developed by the Bechtel Corporation
for the SNUPPS plants as built at Callaway
and Wolf Creek in the USA.   The SNUPPS station
design concept was adapted to enable British
requirements on safety, electrical grid
conditions, standards and practices to be
incorporated.   The station reference design
drawn up by NNC on behalf of the CEGB in
1982 included an early assessment of the
impact of these requirements.   This was
used as the design basis for the Public
Inquiry which lasted from 1983 to 1985.
In parallel with the Public Inquiry and
subsequent to it, the detailed design of
the station has been developed by the Sizewell
'B' Project Management Team, a CEGB organisation
comprised of staff from CEGB and NNC.   As
the system and component designs were clarified
it has been possible to see more clearly
the impact that the British requirements
on safety and other features are having
on the overall station design for Sizewell 'B'.
This paper outlines the progression from
the SNUPPS basic design to the current Sizewell
'B' arrangement, comments upon the design
process and describes the current state
of construction.

2   SNUPPS DESIGN

An outline plan of the SNUPPS power block
is shown on Figure 1.   This includes the
containment building, auxiliary and control
building, the turbine hall, the fuel building
and separately the radwaste building.   The
following factors were important in determining
the size and shape of the SNUPPS power block.
There is a single 1200 megawatt 1800 r/min
turbine.   As a result the turbine hall is
comparatively narrow.   Also since it is
not necessary to spread out the steam pipework
as is required with multi-turbine designs,
it is possible to do without a mechanical

annexe.   The pre-stressed concrete containment
building is 42.6m diameter.   The safeguard
systems have been designed on the basis
of having two trains of equipment to achieve
hot and cold shutdown conditions.   The
emergency power supplies for these trains
are provided by two diesel generators,
housed in a building which forms part of
the power block, located next to the control
building.   An important feature of the
SNUPPS style of power block layout is the
construction access which is afforded to
the containment building.   This is achieved
by having the auxiliary building offset
subtending approximately 240° of arc of
the containment building plan, enabling
handling devices to be located on the ground
close to the periphery of the remainder
of the containment and providing direct
access by way of a temporary opening through
the containment wall.

3   SIZEWELL 'B' REFERENCE DESIGN

The Sizewell 'B' reference design prepared
by NNC on behalf of the CEGB in 1982, used
the designs which had been developed for
the SNUPPS wherever this was   judged to
be practicable and acceptable bearing in
mind UK requirements.

Key factors of the SNUPPS layout incorporated in the reference design included:

°   the general arrangement of the primary
     circuit

°   the disposition of main components
     within the reactor containment building
     and fuel building

°   the design basis of the reactor containment
     including the general location of
     penetrations

°   access to the containment for construction

○ the general arrangement of buildings forming the nuclear island. In particular, the relation in elevation between the primary circuit and the auxiliary building containing the reactor safeguard pumps was retained.

However, although the philosophy, adopted by the CEGB and NNC, was to minimise change from the SNUPPS concept the following fundamental changes were adopted:-

(a) Two 625 megawatt, 3000 r/min main turbine generators.

(b) All electrical equipment was based on the UK standard frequency and voltages. This led to a number of alterations in the layout because the UK equipment was generally larger than comparable equipment in the USA.

(c) An increase in the containment building diameter from 42.6m to 45.7m to accommodate increased plant sizes and to improve access for maintenance.

(d) A secondary containment is provided.

(e) The capacity of the emergency core cooling system was increased by having four rather than two high head safety injection pumps and by increasing the size of the four accumulators, located inside the primary containment by 50 per cent.

(f) The reliability and diversity of the auxiliary feed system was improved by using two turbine driven feed pumps to back up the electrically driven pumps, rather than one as provided in the SNUPPS design.

(g) An emergency boration system was included as a secondary method of shutting down the reactor, involving a further four tanks inside the primary containment building each with its own piping and valves.

(h) An emergency charging system employing steam driven pumps, separate from the chemical and volume control charging system was introduced, located in the steam and feed cell.

(i) In line with the significant system change of having four trains of safeguard equipment for shutting down the reactor and maintaining it at hot shutdown conditions, four 100 per cent capacity diesel generators provided power for the four principal safety separation groups. The two additional diesels were located in the auxiliary shutdown building separate from the power block and on the side remote from the two diesel generators included in the SNUPPS design.

In addition to being incorporated in the layout of the reference design (see Figure 2) all of these changes were included in the specifications for mechanical, electrical and control and instrumentation systems. These form the basis of the enquiry specifications covering the detailed design, manufacture and construction of major plant items and systems. The reference design layout was used as the basis of the first issue of the Pre-Construction Safety Report in April 1982 (ref 1).

4   DESIGN FOR CONSTRUCTION

The evolution of the layout from that of the reference design depicted in Figure 2 was carried out systematically in accordance with a carefully prepared design change procedure. This ensured that the detailed design documentation specifying manufacture and construction remained consistent with the safety case.

The overall arrangement of plant within the primary containment has not changed during the design development phase. The 3.1m increase in containment diameter compared with SNUPPS which was decided upon in 1981 had been made primarily to accommodate the increase in size of the reactor coolant pump motor resulting from the change in electrical parameters and also to accommodate the 50 per cent increase in the volume of the accumulators. The resulting increase in containment building volume has proved sufficient for the additional pipework and cabling resulting from the four trains of safeguard equipment whilst retaining satisfactory access for maintenance.

It was in June 1984 that the Project Management Team (PMT), staffed jointly by CEGB and NNC, was set up to carry out the architect engineering and to manage the Sizewell 'B' project.

Up until 1984 the work on the 1/20 scale design model of the main buildings of the nuclear island had been concentrated on locating main items of mechanical equipment and on the routing of the critical large diameter high energy pipe runs. In the period from 1985 until Section two Consent was granted in March of 1987, the PMT carried out an intensive exercise aimed at identifying the space requirements for the remainder of the equipment notably the electrical equipment and HVAC. In conjunction with this exercise the smaller diameter pipes were being modelled on the 1/20 scale model and multi-disciplined reviews were being carried out to take account of the safety design basis of systems taking account of postulated hazards such as fire and earthquakes. As this work proceeded it became obvious that the impact of the four trains of safety equipment involving the introduction of additional fire barriers, the separation of cabling and of the HVAC was considerable both in the auxiliary building and in the control building. Early in 1985 it was decided to introduce a further floor onto the auxiliary building to house the HVAC plant. A year later in February 1986 a relatively major realignment of the Sizewell 'B' power block layout was initiated. The purpose of this realignment which is described below was to ensure that there would be ample space for equipment, much of which had still to be designed in detail by the contractors.

(a) The two diesel generators previously located in the power block were installed in a separate building on the eastern side of the site.

(b) The water treatment plant which had been located between the two turbines was housed in a separate building on the southern end of the site.

(c) The control building was extended to cover the area vacated by the diesels.

(d) The decontamination workshop was extended.

(e) A system of service tunnels with inter-connections between the power block and the peripheral buildings was designed. This was provided to enable the electrical and pipework services to be easily installed avoiding the need for extensive trenches and disruption to the construction site access which these would entail. The tunnel structures provided the necessary fire barriers to achieve the separation group philosophy.

The radwaste building volume has also been considerably increased partly to enable the processed waste drum store to be increased in capacity from one year in the reference design to between 7 and 10 years of arisings. This change has been incorporated to give more time for NIREX to provide a long term storage repository.

Figure 3 shows a plan view of the station with the revised layout of the peripheral buildings which represents the design now being constructed. Figure 4 shows the service tunnels.

From the submission of the first issue of the Pre Construction Safety Report until the granting of the site licence in June 1987, there was a dialogue with the NII to ensure that all of the required licencing commitments were clearly identified and understood. One aspect which received considerable attention was the bearing capacity of the soil particularly in view of having to design for a seismic event. The variation in the levels of the undersides of the basemats of the main buildings making up the power block and the sandy composition of the soil led to a decision to increase the depth of excavation basically under all of the power block to provide a simpler excavation profile and also to replace the soil with mass fill concrete. On lighter buildings with relatively shallow

foundations a process of soil stablisation by vibration was specified. Figure 5 shows some of the mass fill concrete under the power block and also shows the profile of the structural concrete under the reactor containment and fuel buildings which is substantially the same as the SNUPPS stations.

5   DETAILED DESIGN AND CONSTRUCTION

Although a small number of contracts had been placed in the period from 1984 to 1986 mainly in order to get information regarding key items of plant such as the primary circuit, it was only after Section two Consent was given in March of 1987 that it became possible to place the majority of contracts and start to get the detailed design information necessary to confirm the layout. It also had not been possible to build up the civil engineeiring design team prior to Section two Consent. During the initial period on site when the diaphragm wall contractor was constructing the underground wall which was to make dewatering such a straight forward operation and the main civil contractor was carrying out the preliminary works involving the excavation and the pouring of the mass fill concrete, the civil engineering design team had to begin the preparation of the drawings for the permanent buildings. This progressive process has involved not only the structural analysis which in this case has to include seismic events and the subsequent preparation of general arrangement and detail drawings of reinforcement but also the design of many hundreds of embedments. A decision had been taken to use embedments cast in the concrete structure for mounting equipment rather than surface mounted plates. This has necessitated a high level of co-operation between the contractors carrying out the detailed design, the central layout team, who have to process the information and assure its compatibility, and the civil engineering designers.

As the detailed equipment design information is received from the mechanical and electrical contractors it appears that the decisions taken three years ago to modify the layout to provide more space have been justified. The changes involved increases in the amount of civil works and, in the case of the service tunnels, introduced a significant additional quantity of work to be carried out early in the construction programme. At the time of writing the stuctural concrete basemats of most of the buildings have been cast and a start has been made on the walls of the auxiliary and control buildings. The system of service tunnels is well advanced and backfilling has largely taken place. This has been accomplished in line with the 63 month target programme and it should provide a good basis for erection of cabling and pipework later this year.

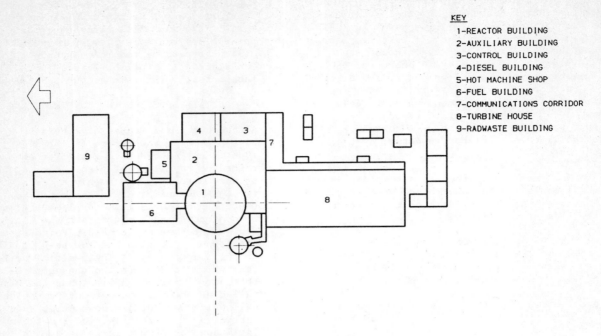

Fig 1   SNUPPS power block

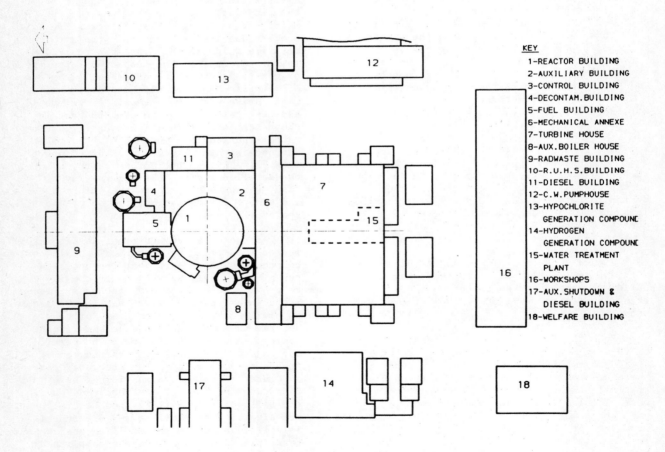

Fig 2   The Sizewell 'B' original reference design

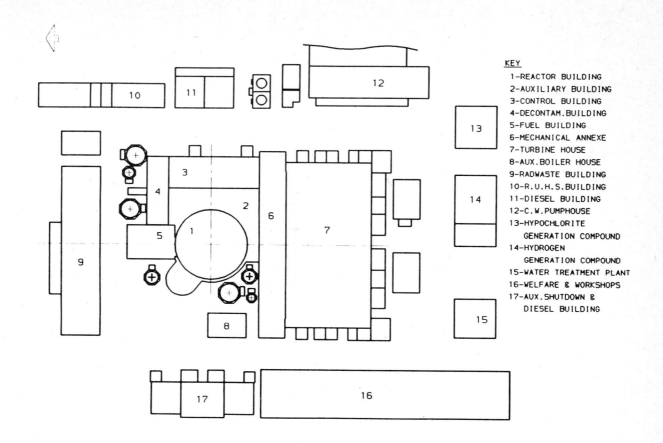

KEY
1-REACTOR BUILDING
2-AUXILIARY BUILDING
3-CONTROL BUILDING
4-DECONTAM.BUILDING
5-FUEL BUILDING
6-MECHANICAL ANNEXE
7-TURBINE HOUSE
8-AUX.BOILER HOUSE
9-RADWASTE BUILDING
10-R.U.H.S.BUILDING
11-DIESEL BUILDING
12-C.W.PUMPHOUSE
13-HYPOCHLORITE
    GENERATION COMPOUND
14-HYDROGEN
    GENERATION COMPOUND
15-WATER TREATMENT PLANT
16-WELFARE & WORKSHOPS
17-AUX.SHUTDOWN &
    DIESEL BUILDING

Fig 3   Sizewell 'B' design for construction

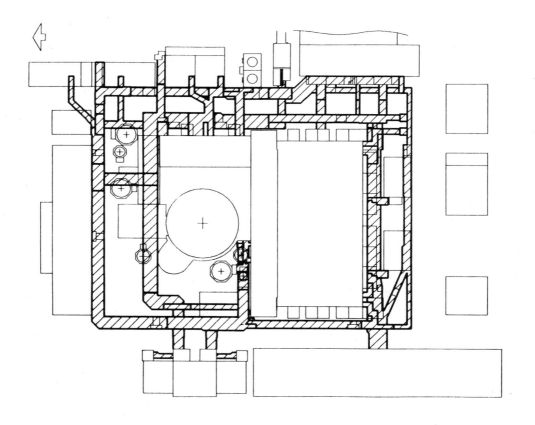

Fig 4   Sizewell 'B' service tunnels

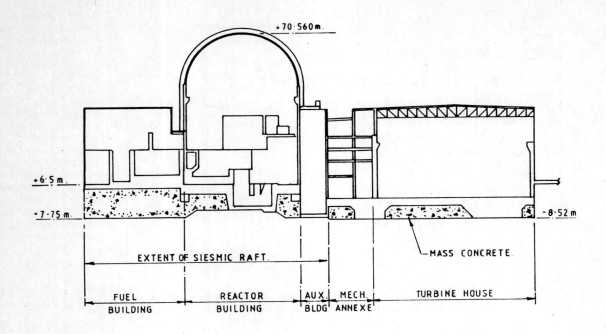

Fig 5   Sizewell 'B' power block elevation

Safety philosophy and implications on plant design of Sizewell 'B'

V S BECKETT, BSc and J KIRK, BSc
PWR Project Group, National Power Division of CEGB, Knutsford, Cheshire

This paper briefly describes the CEGB approach to achieving safety of its nuclear power stations and the way in which this safety approach is translated into design provisions on Sizewell 'B' is illustrated. The two examples chosen are:

-        protection against fire

-        engineering a safe shutdown

The first of these is the internal hazard that has the greatest effect on the detailed internal building layout because of the resulting segregation requirements for the safety trains of equipment. The second example shows how the safety targets are achieved by engineering sufficient redundancy and diversity into the systems required to safely shutdown the reactor.

APPROACH TO SAFETY

The Central Electricity Generating Board has a direct responsibility for the safety of Sizewell 'B'. Under the privatisation proposals this responsibility will pass to the National Power Company. In discharging this responsibility the Board's fundamental approach is that the designers have a lead responsibility for safety in the way they develop the design. They are also responsible for producing the safety documentation which justifies the adequacy of their plant. For Sizewell 'B' this responsibility rests with the Project Management Team at Knutsford. As an added assurance that this reponsibility is being effectively discharged the Board has a separate and independant body called the Health and Safety Department which oversees the design and construction activities. In addition this department is responsible for formally submitting the safety case for the station to the Nuclear Installations Inspectorate (NII) and authorising ministries as appropriate to enable those bodies to review the safety of the plant and to exercise their consents by the issue of construction and operating licenses.

To ensure a rigorous and consistent approach to safety the Board set down design safety criteria which are consistent with the NII safety assessment principles. These top level criteria are amplified and interpreted in design safety guidelines for a specific reactor system such as the Sizewell 'B' PWR.

The standards embodied in the criteria and guidelines are based on the fundamental principle requirement that the risk presented by a power station must be as low as reasonably practicable (ALARP).

From this base, guidance is given to the designers on the standards of design and construction to be adopted. This includes deterministically based rules such as single failure criteria and in addition numerical targets are set which relate to the reliability of the plant and its protection systems. The overall target is that when all accident sequences that could lead to an uncontrolled release of radioactivity to the environment are considered the summated effect should be that the likelihood of such a release would be less than one in a million per year of reactor operation.

Rather than elaborate further on the details of the safety criteria and design safety guidelines we will turn to specific implementation in Sizewell 'B' of safety protection provisions. Two examples are given, firstly the way of mitigating the effects of internal plant hazards such as fire and secondly the way in which the reactor is shutdown should a fault occur.

FIRES

Fire is the internal hazard that has the greatest impact on the detailed internal building layout. With respect to nuclear safety there are three main elements in the design approach for protection against fires.

1.   The first is prevention. This involves systematic consideration of the use, nature and disposition of combustible materials: the potential for plant/maintenance operations to provide ignition sources: and the relative location of combustible materials and potential ignition sources. In particular, cable insulation materials have been developed that are fire retardant and, compared with PVC, produce less toxic smoke and corrosive gas.

2.   The second element is to limit the severity of fires that could start, principally by the provision of a comprehensive fire detection and suppression system.

3.	The third element involves the limitation of the consequences of fires assumed to start and not rapidly extinguished. The principal means of providing such plant protection is that of segregation. Segregation is provided to limit the maximum spread of credible fire. Some segregation is incorporated in the overall layout by separation between buildings and major plant locations. Mainly, however, segregation is provided by subdividing buildings into a number of smaller areas by the use of fire barriers.

One of the principal criteria that determines the segregation requirements is the single failure criterion. This requires that safe shutdown is achieved following a hazard (in this case fire damage to equipment) in combination with single failure of a further item of equipment and another item unavailable due to maintenance. In order to ensure that the appropriate plant is available following a postulated fire, this leads directly to the provision of the four trains of safety classified equipment required to achieve and maintain hot and intermediate shutdown appropriately segregated from each other.

To ensure reliable reactor tripping and initiation of safeguard system action the reactor primary protection system is also fourway segregated. The reactor secondary protection system is fourway segregated where it is routed together with the primary protection system and two-way segregated elsewhere. Such segregation is provided by fire barriers, which are three-hour rated.

Hot or intermediate shutdown are states for which the plant can be maintained indefinitely following a fire. It is desirable to secure the option of cold shutdown as soon as possible, although there is no specific time limit. A design target of 72 hours has been adopted for Sizewell 'B'.

Two-way segregation by means of principal fire barriers is provided for equipment required for cold shutdown. Thus, given fire damage coincident with outage for maintenance and single failure, it would be necessary to effect repair or reinstatement of plant, or manual plant actuations before proceeding to cold shutdown. In practice, the pumps required for cold shutdown and associated 11kV power supplies are fourway segregated and hence any repair/reinstatement is applicable to lower voltage circuits only.

The auxiliary building is divided into two halves by a fire barrier, each half containing one train of hot shutdown equipment (electric-driven auxiliary feed and charging pumps) and two trains of cold shutdown equipment. The steam and feed annexe is separated by a principal fire barrier from the auxiliary building and is divided vertically by a further fire barrier. Each subdivision contains one steamdriven feed and emergency charging pump, together with the mainsteam feed pipework, main steam isolating valve and steam generator pressure relief provision associated with two steam generators. This

four fold segregation, as well as that for the control building and diesel houses, is shown in Fig. 1.

The principal fire areas are subdivided into smaller fire areas to provide additional segregation. Such subdivision of principal fire areas is done to reduce further the amount of safety classified equipment affected by a fire, to protect personnel and to improve economic security.

The buildings and principal fire areas are connected to each other through a cable tunnel and riser system, which permits principal fire areas associated with the same train of hot-intermediate shutdown equipment to be connected by power, control and instrumentation cabling via segregated routes, thereby preserving the required segregation of safety trains.

In a limited number of areas, it is not always possible to provide physical fourway segregation by three-hour rated fire barriers. Examples are within the reactor building itself, which is discussed below, and the main control room. In such cases, other measures are taken to ensure that the overall station risk is acceptable.

Fire Protection within the Reactor building

The reactor building is designed to withstand high internal pressures and temperatures and is classed as a principal fire barrier which protects the equipment in it from fires outside and vice-versa.

It is not possible to sub-divide the areas within the reactor building by physical barriers in the same way as that provided in, for example, the auxiliary building. This is because of the compartment venting and hydrogen mixing requirements after a LOCA. There are also a significant number of cases where sensors associated with each of the separation groups are necessarily located in relatively close proximity on the same equipment item.

The approach taken inside the primary containment is to achieve the maximum segregation reasonably practicable between the four separation groups by means of one or more of the following measures:

(i)	Partial structural barriers such as the secondary shield walls;

(ii)	separation by distance;

(iii)	local protection of cabling, for example, with durasteel enclosures or similar cable protection.

In addition to providing this segregation particular emphasis is placed on limiting the quantities of fixed combustibles and sources of fire risk such as pumps and motors, and on the careful control to be applied to transient combustibles and their removal from the containment prior to reactor startup. There are no significant fixed combustibles apart from cable insulation, containment atmosphere cleanup charcoal filters and the RCP lube oil.

Fixed fire fighting systems are provided over principal cable tray routes. The charcoal filters are also provided with a fixed fire suppression system.

To limit the possibility of RCP lubricating oil spillage leading to fire, the design includes provisions for detecting and collecting leaking oil. The provisions include primary and secondary leak collection system.

REACTOR SHUTDOWN

The approach adopted to ensure safe shutdown of the reactor is a good illustration of how the principles of defence in depth, redundancy, diversity and failsafe features are incorporated into the Sizewell 'B' design. A combination of inherent reactor characteristics and engineered safety features including passive systems provides extremely high assurance that, should a fault occur, the reactor will be promptly and automatically brought to a sub-critical condition.

Engineered Systems

The principal engineered method by which this initial shutdown is achieved is by the rapid insertion into the reactor core of the rod control cluster assemblies (RCCAs), which are normally used to effect short-term adjustments in reactor power as the station output varies. The other main method is to increase the concentration in the primary coolant of the soluble neutron absorber boron.

There are 53 RCCAs arranged in nine groups (six shutdown and three control). Each RCCA consists of a cluster of stainless-steel clad, silver-indium-cadmium alloy rods that move up and down within selected fuel assemblies distributed evenly over the core cross-section. Each RCCA is suspended from a drive rod controlled by a series of electromagnetic latches located above the reactor vessel.

During normal operation, all the shutdown RCCAs are withdrawn from the core and are held stationary by continuous energization of the latches. Should the holding current be interrupted, either deliberately or inadvertently, all the latches are released and the RCCAs fall into the core under gravity to shut-down the fission process.

Failure of sufficient RCCAs to enter the core when required is extremely unlikely due to the reliable and fail-safe nature of the mechanisms used. However, a completely separate engineered system is provided to overcome the effects of such an anticipated transient without trip (ATWT). This is the emergency boration system (EBS), which, as its name implies, is arranged to increase the level of boron (as boric acid) in the coolant when needed.

Both tripping of the RCCAs and initiation of the EBS are examples of the operation of engineered safety features - the name given to equipment which is provided either exclusively for safety or, in some cases, for combined operational and safety purposes. Such features have to be carefully optimized by the designers to achieve the necessary balance between availability and safety at a reasonable level of cost and complexity.

However, in addition to these features the Sizewell 'B' reactor, in common with other PWRs, has important inherent characteristics that help to ensure safe shut down in the event of certain types of fault. These are the negative moderator temperature coefficients of reactivity and the effect of moderator voiding. The first effect is important for faults where the primary circuit remains intact, whereas the second effect is important should there be a significant loss of coolant from the reactor.

The engineered safety features, which provide protection against all types of postulated fault, are arranged to come into action promptly and automatically when needed to shut down and to cool the reactor and contain any potential escape of radioactive material. They do this under the control of the reactor protection system (RPS), which is the general name given to the equipment which detects the actual or potential onset of plant faults and initiates the necessary actions, such as reactor tripping, starting up of safety plant item, and warning the plant operators.

The Reactor Protection System

The RPS actually comprises two entirely separate but complementary systems - the primary protection system (PPS) and the secondary protection system (SPS). Each has its own reactor trip and engineered safety features actuation sub systems. The PPS is capable of dealing with almost all postulated faults: the SPS deals with the remainder and also provides extra reliability to deal with those faults that are postulated to occur relatively frequently, and for which the PPS alone cannot provide the very high reliability required.

Both the PPS and the SPS monitor selected important plant parameters, such as coolant temperature and pressure, continuously during normal plant operation.

Each parameter is measured by four sensors, each of which is associated with one of four separately-powered groups of logic equipment.

Each logic group, known as a "guardline", independently detects any deviation of the measured parameters from pre-determined values. Such a deviation indicates that a fault may have occured or be imminent.

If two or more guard lines indicate a fault conditions, the reactor is tripped by interrupting the power supplies to the RCCA holding coils. Signals are also sent to the appropriate safety and supporting systems.

To ensure maximum reliability of the functions of reactor tripping and engineered safety features actuation, the PPS and SPS not only employ separate sensors, wiring, power supplies, logic units and trip circuit breakers, but also rely on different principles to achieve the complex decision-making processes required.

The PPS uses microprocessors to perform signal selection, comparison and logical combination functions. The SPS uses magnetic logic elements known as "laddics", which were developed for use in gas-cooled reactor protection systems. In each system, the two-out-of-four voting logic is maintained throughout, from the plant sensors to the trip breakers and output circuitry.

The Emergency Boration System

The PPS also actuates the EBS to provide rapid boration of the primary coolant in the unlikely event that more than one RCCA fails to enter the core following a trip demand. Additionally, following certain cooldown faults the EBS would be automatically triggered to augment control-rod action and to provide additional shutdown margin.

The EBS consists of four tanks containing concentrated boric acid solution (about 7000 ppm of boron), each connected by pipes to the inlet and outlet of one of the primary reactor-coolant pumps. The tanks, which are located as close as possible to the primary circuit, are isolated in normal operation by a closed valve in each pipe.

A schematic of the EBS is shown in Fig.2.

When the appropriate signal is generated by the PPS, the power supplies to the valve actuators are removed and the valve opens automatically by spring action.

The contents of the tanks are then forced into the reactor coolant pumps suction lines under the action of the pump head. This is a passive safety feature in the sense that there is no requirement for active safeguard pumps to start up. The concentrated boric-acid solution mixes with the coolant as it passes through the pumps towards the core, which it reaches within a few seconds. Successful discharge of any three of the four EBS tanks provides sufficient boric acid to raise the average concentration of boron in the primary coolant by about 300 ppm which is sufficient to shutdown the reactor.

Conclusion

The UK safety design requirements lead to the need to provide redundant plant and diverse systems for the protection and safeguard of the reactor. Further the necessity to consider hazards, particularly fire, leads to segregation of plant items within these systems.

The result of applying these safety requirements to specific plant items and buildings for SXB has been demonstrated in this paper.

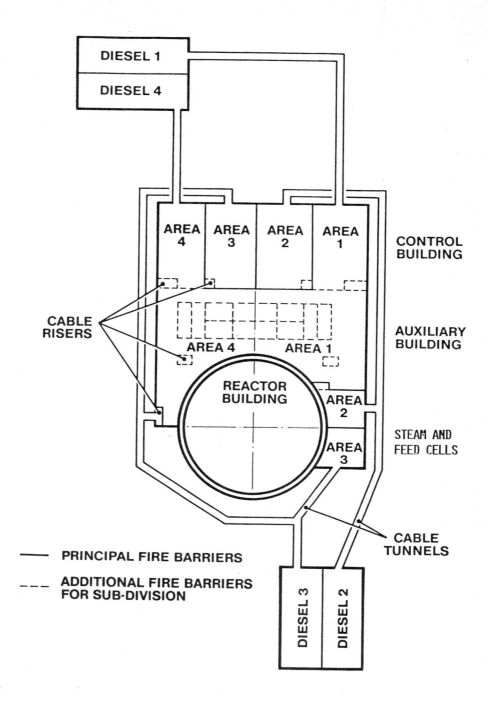

Fig 1   Schematic arrangement of segregation

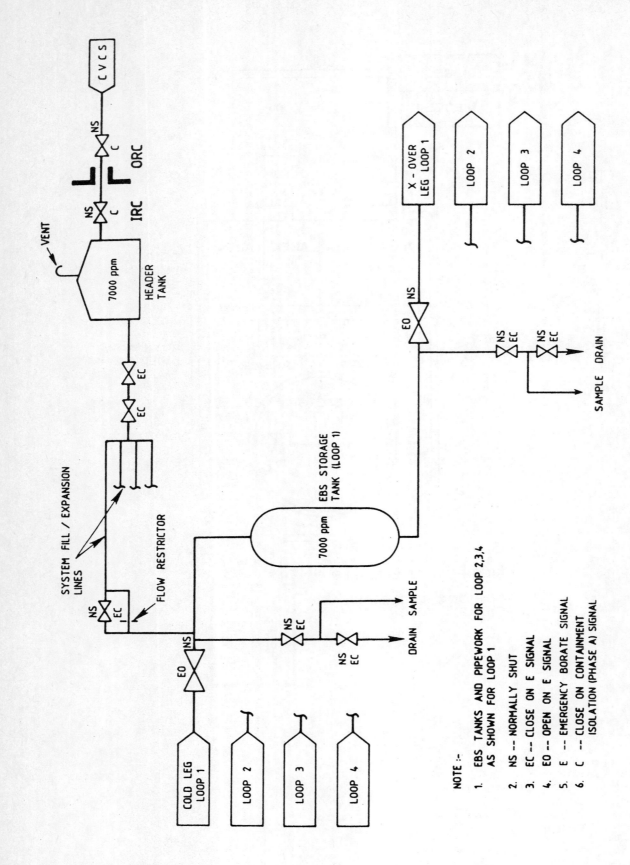

Fig 2   Emergency boration system

NOTE :-

1. EBS TANKS AND PIPEWORK FOR LOOP 2,3,4
   AS SHOWN FOR LOOP 1

2. NS -- NORMALLY SHUT

3. EC -- CLOSE ON E SIGNAL

4. EO -- OPEN ON E SIGNAL

5. E -- EMERGENCY BORATE SIGNAL

6. C -- CLOSE ON CONTAINMENT
        ISOLATION (PHASE A) SIGNAL

C388/011

Diversity: safety system design against common mode failure

D B BOETTCHER, BSc
PWR Project Group, National Power Division of CEGB, Knutsford, Cheshire
S J CEREGHINO, BS, MBA, PE
Bechtel Limited, CEGB, Knutsford, Cheshire

SYNOPSIS: Safety systems for Nuclear Power Stations are composed of redundant sets of equipment. Common mode effects mean that increasing redundancy may not obtain more reliability and hence diversity is introduced. Diversity is the provision of dissimilar means of achieving the same objective. This paper overviews the diversity strategy utilised in the design of Sizewell B.

1 INTRODUCTION

The safety systems of nuclear power plants are composed of multiple (redundant) sets of similar equipment. The degree of redundancy is determined by deterministic and probabilistic criteria. For example, the single failure criterion used in the US leads to two-way redundancy, while the UK criteria lead to more than two-way redundancy for selected safety equipment. However, such criteria do not address common mode failure of equipment. The Nuclear Installations Inspectorate's Safety Assessment Principles and the Central Electricity Generating Board's Design Safety Guidelines take account of this shortcoming, noting that more and more redundancy does not necessarily obtain more and more reliability. For this reason, diversity is incorporated into the design of selected systems for Sizewell B.

Diversity is the provision of dissimilar means of achieving the same objective by the use of features that differ in design or operation. The Sizewell B implementation of diversity involves the application of a hierarchy of dissimilarity. The highest level of diversity is functional, where fundamentally different systems achieve the objective. Next is component diversity where similar systems utilise components with dissimilar designs. Lastly, diversity may be introduced into similar systems with similar components by procuring the components from different manufacturers or different manufacturing routes.

This paper overviews the diversity strategy utilised in the design of Sizewell B. It describes the methodology employed by the design team to review the design implementation and confirm that adequate diversity has been delivered. It summarises the major unique features of the Sizewell 'B' design that arise due to the implementation of diversity. Finally, the paper briefly examines the advantages, disadvantages and cost-benefits of diversity.

2 BACKGROUND

To prevent the release of radioactive material to the environment, nuclear power stations are provided with safeguards systems. These systems are composed of a mixture of passive and active devices. Passive devices perform their function without physical movement whereas active devices require some change involving physical movement to achieve their function. An example of a passive device would be a reactor pressure vessel, which retains the radioactive material associated with the operation of the reactor. An example of an active device would be a pump which supplies feed after a reactor trip to remove decay heat.

It has been recognised that no single safeguard system can be one hundred percent reliable. This recognition has spawned a number of acceptance criteria and design bases which are applied to the design of safeguards systems. For example, the single failure criterion is used to ensure that a minimum level of redundancy of active and/or passive components has been achieved. The possibility that an event such as a flood or other hazard, or the interaction of two systems, might simultaneously affect several redundant safeguards systems is also recognised and is addressed by physically separating redundant plant or the introduction of intervening barriers.

To reduce further the possibility of a single event defeating several mutually redundant systems, diversity is introduced as a design basis. Diversity is a term used to denote that two systems which achieve the same end do so in different ways or use different equipment. The shutdown rods and boron steel balls used on the steel pressure vessel Magnox reactors are diverse means of achieving reactor shutdown, the boron balls being provided to overcome the potential common mode failure of the shutdown rods in the event of a severe depressurisation accident.

The boron ball shutdown devices illustrate a non-prescriptive application of the principle of diversity; they were provided to address an identified common mode failure mechanism. Equivalent devices were not fitted on the magnox reactors with pre-stressed concrete pressure vessels because catastrophic failure of the pressure vessel was outside the design basis for those stations. In more recent years, diversity has begun to become a prescriptive design basis of safeguards systems to be applied when high reliability is required, even where no common mode failure mechanism has been identified.

The Sizewell B reference plants, the PWR stations at Wolf Creek and Callaway in the United States, do not have diversity built into their safeguards systems as a fundamental design basis in its own right. The reference plants do have diversity built in where this has been found necessary to address specific common mode failure concerns. For example, a steam driven auxiliary feed pump is supplied to address concerns over loss of electrical power. On Sizewell B Nuclear Power Station, diversity has been implemented as a prescriptive safeguards system design basis and therefore a number of changes have been made to the reference plant design.

The changes to the reference design have increased the capital cost and complexity of the plant and will increase the maintenance burden on the station staff throughout the life of the station. This paper identifies the significant changes to the reference plants, discusses the impact on the design of the plant of providing this additional diversity and estimates the additional capital cost and cost-benefits involved.

2.1 Industry Practice

Diversity has been employed on previous UK power stations. The application of diversity on early generation stations was generally in response to a specific concern over the performance of a system or item of plant under fault conditions and, because these concerns usually came to light during the construction or early operational life of the station, this tended to result in backfits. The boron ball shutdown devices of the Magnox stations are diverse from the shutdown and control rods and were supplied to respond to concerns over potential common mode failure of the shutdown rods in the event of a severe depressurisation accident. The concern became significant only after the plants were operating and hence the boron ball shutdown devices had to be back-fitted.

The first UK nuclear power station on which the principle of diversity was adopted as a fundamental safety system design basis was Heysham B. The basis for determining that diversity was required was that well-engineered systems or barriers typically exhibit a reliability of the order of 10-4 failures per demand (Ref 1). Higher reliabilities of up to 10-5 failures per demand could be justified individually, but where the required reliability was better than 10-5 failures per demand, then diversity was introduced. The net result was that for the less frequent faults, a redundant mitigation system provided adequate reliability, whereas for the more frequent faults, independent and diverse mitigation systems were required.

Diversity is also employed on US nuclear power stations. For each fault which is within the station's design basis, there are typically two parameters monitored by the reactor protection system, either of which alone would be sufficient to detect the fault. These parameters are selected to be as different from each other as practicable (ie diverse). There is no requirement to use different equipment to monitor, process or initiate safeguard actuation signals from the diverse parameters.

Design features of safeguards plant which may be regarded as diverse also appear in US plants, but they are not provided against a prescriptive diversity requirement. Examples of these features are the steam driven auxiliary feedwater pump and the anticipated transient without trip mitigation features. Each of these has been added to the generic PWR design in response to a specific licensing issue, for example the steam driven auxiliary feedwater pumps allow a station to withstand a 'station blackout', that is a loss of normal and emergency ac electric power.

2.2 Sizewell B Design Approach

The approach which the Sizewell B project management team adopted towards the provision of diversity was a prescriptive one similar to that adopted for Heysham B. As before, it was taken that a redundant and well-engineered safeguard system of the standard and quality encountered at a nuclear power station would typically exhibit a reliability limited by common mode failure effects to the order of 10-4 failures per demand. Because the target frequency for an individual fault/failure sequence leading to an uncontrolled radioactive release was 10-7 per annum, a single redundant mitigation system would provide adequate reliability to mitigate faults of frequency less than or equal to 10-3 per annum, whereas for the more frequent faults, two independent and diverse mitigation systems were required. The degree of diversity required, that is the degree of the difference between the two systems, was taken as being related to the level of reliability required. For faults with frequencies only slighter greater than 10-3 per annum, less diversity was required than for faults of higher frequency.

The means of ensuring that diversity was incorporated into the design consisted of written project procedures, which ensured that the need for diversity was considered at an early design stage and that the implications were recognised throughout the

14

detailed design of the station. The 1982 reference design for the Sizewell B power station included the major design features which the designers found necessary to meet the UK requirements. These features are discussed in more detail in the following section. To ensure that the requirements for diversity were comprehensively considered, a strategy document was prepared to identify faults which were sufficiently frequent to require diverse means of mitigation and to identify the major systems involved in their mitigation.

3 DIVERSE DESIGN FEATURES

The most significant changes made to the reference SNUPPS plant design because of diversity considerations are discussed below. Other detailed changes have been made for diversity reasons, but those summarised below are the most significant in terms of cost, impact on the reference design and effect on the safety case.

3.1 Secondary Protection System

The functions of fault detection, reactor trip demand and initiation of the necessary safeguards systems are achieved by the reactor protection system. The reactor protection system is comprised of two diverse sub-systems, the primary protection system and the secondary protection system.

The primary protection system is a computer based system being developed by Westinghouse in the US. The system makes use of microprocessor technology to provide the features of a traditional solid state protection system, together with comprehensive and reliable self checking.

The secondary protection system is diverse from the primary protection system and provides similar trip and safeguards features actuations for the most frequent plant faults. The system is based on Laddics, ferrite modules which carry out the voting logic, together with solid state trip amplifiers and relays to actuate the safeguards features. The secondary protection system monitors reactor conditions via its own sensors. The parameters used by the secondary protection system to detect a condition requiring it to act are, wherever possible, different from those used by the primary protection system. In addition, the sensors used by the secondary protection system are as different as practicable from those of the primary protection system, for instance thermocouples are used instead of resistance temperature devices.

3.2 Emergency Boration System

In the US, the possibility of failure of the reactor trip function has received significant attention since the events at Salem and San Onofre when the trip breakers failed to open. For PWR plants, this attention has focused on the reactor trip breakers and has resulted in plants fitting diverse trip breakers and anticipated

transient without trip (ATWT) mitigation systems, which make use of the PWR's inherent negative temperature coefficient of reactivity. The Sizewell B design incorporates several features to make the likelihood of an ATWT very low. The primary protection system and the secondary protection system are redundant and diverse means of detecting faults and initiating a reactor trip. These two systems utilise diverse means of interrupting the power supplies to the control rod drive mechanisms which allows the control rods to fall into the reactor core. To accommodate the remote possibility that common mode failure might result in the control rods not falling into the core once their power supply is interrupted, a diverse system, the Emergency Boration System (EBS) has been incorporated into the Sizewell B design. The EBS is a passive injection system comprising four tanks filled with concentrated boric acid solution, one per loop of the reactor coolant system. Each tank is connected to its coolant loop at two points which span the reactor coolant pump of the loop. Each tank is normally isolated from the reactor coolant system but, on a demand from the primary protection system following detection of two or more rods failing to insert or a rundown of the reactor coolant pumps, fast acting valves are opened and the head of the reactor coolant pump purges the tanks contents into the reactor coolant system. The actuation on reactor coolant pump rundown allows the EBS to function without requiring pumped injection.

3.3 Emergency Charging System

The Chemical and Volume Control System (CVCS) is used to recycle reactor coolant system fluid during normal operation and, following a reactor trip, to add boron to the reactor coolant system, offsetting the increase in reactivity which results from the decay of fission product poisons. Boration is also required before the reactor coolant system may be cooled down to cold shutdown or refuelling conditions to offset the increase in reactivity which accompanies the cooldown. The CVCS also provides reactor coolant pump seal protection by injecting fluid into the reactor coolant pump seal package. The CVCS comprises two electric motor driven centrifugal pumps together with associated storage tanks, heat exchangers, pipework and valves. The Emergency Charging System (ECS) is capable of providing the same basic functions as the CVCS and is diverse from it. The ECS injects borated water into the RCS via the reactor coolant pump seals to provide reactivity control and pump seal protection. Although makeup to the RCS to maintain inventory is of secondary importance because the letdown routes can be isolated, the ability of the ECS to protect the reactor coolant pump seals is important because it prevents damage to the seals which might give rise to a loss of coolant accident (LOCA). The ECS comprises two turbine driven positive displacement pumps together with a storage tank, associated pipework and valves. Because the ECS does not recycle RCS fluid, no heat exchangers are required. The ECS has no letdown connections to the RCS and injects only into the reactor coolant pump seals. The system is therefore considerably simpler than the CVCS and it plays no role in the normal operation of the station.

3.4 Secondary DC and Battery Charging Diesels

Electrical power is required both to operate equipment and to power instrumentation. The principal source of electricity is the offsite grid and, during normal operation, the station's turbine generators. An alternative supply is available from four essential diesel generators. These are started automatically and re-energise the essential 3.3kV and 415V busbars. To provide instrumentation and control supplies during the short period while the diesel generators are being started, there are batteries and chargers, with inverters for instrument ac supplies. Because control and instrument power is required by the diverse primary and the secondary protection systems and their associated plant, there are corresponding diverse primary and secondary battery systems. The chargers, batteries and inverters of these systems are of diverse manufacture.

The diverse safeguards plant itself does not require electrical supplies to provide power, being either steam, pneumatic or spring powered. However, control and instrument supplies are required for operation and monitoring. To provide battery charging in the event of the four essential diesels failing, two battery charging diesel generators which are diverse from the essential diesel generators are provided. These battery charging diesel generators are each approximately one sixteenth of the power output of an essential diesel and will be of different manufacture to the essential diesels. To reduce the possibility that a bad batch of fuel oil might affect several diesel generators simultaneously, fuel oil for the battery charging diesels will be obtained from a different source to that for the essential diesels.

3.5 CVCS Relief Path

The reactor pressure vessel plays an important role in the maintenance of nuclear safety. It supports the reactor core, maintaining its geometry and directing the flow of cooling water over it. It is also one of the principal barriers to a release of radioactivity. Because of these important roles, special precautions are taken to ensure that the reactor coolant system is not exposed to pressures beyond its design limits. Two diverse means of relieving excess pressure are provided for the operating modes where an overpressurisation event is within the design basis.

During normal operation the diverse means of preventing overpressurisation of the reactor coolant system are the spring loaded safety relief valves required by the American Society of Mechanical Engineers (ASME) Boiler and Pressure Vessel design code (code safety valves) and three pilot operated safety relief valves (POSRVs). The POSRVs are hydraulically actuated valves, opened and closed by the RCS pressure acting on a stepped piston actuator. The hydraulic pressure is switched away from the larger side of the stepped piston to open the valve and returned to close it. During normal operation this switching is done by a spring loaded pilot valve which responds to reactor coolant system pressure.

When the reactor is shutdown for refuelling, it is necessary to limit possible overpressure to lower values. The design of the POSRVs incorporates a feature which permits reduction of the pressure at which they open. This is done by forcing open the spring loaded pilot valve by means of a dc solenoid actuator. In this mode of operation, the POSRVs are under the control of the primary protection system which monitors the reactor coolant system temperature and pressure, actuating the pilot valves if the pressure exceeds that allowed at a given temperature. Because the setpoint of the code safety valves cannot practically be changed to allow for the reduced pressure which is acceptable under these circumstances, an alternative relief route is provided. This alternative relief route is normally provided via spring loaded safety relief valves attached to the suction pipework of the Residual Heat Removal System (RHRS).

However, a number of incidents have been recorded on operating plants where the RHRS, and hence the suction path relief valves, has become inadvertently isolated from the reactor coolant system during the shutdown period. Under these conditions, the decay heat from the fuel can cause reactor coolant temperatures and pressures to rise quite quickly while the reactor vessel remains cool due to its thermal inertia. Although the POSRVs will provide a relief path under these circumstances, it was decided that a second diverse relief path was required due to the frequency of the reported events. Because of this a new relief path attached to the CVCS letdown line is provided. This path is isolated during normal operation and is only connected to the RCS when the operators open remotely controlled valves during the shutdown. Relief of excessive pressure is then provided by spring loaded safety relief valves.

3.6 Boron Dilution Block

Because soluble boron is used in the primary coolant to control reactivity, the concentration of boric acid in the reactor coolant system must be controlled to ensure that unplanned reactivity excursions do not take place. Control of the boron concentration of the RCS is normally effected via the CVCS and hence the CVCS has the ability to achieve reductions in concentration by the addition of unborated water.

Between the point at which unborated water is added to the CVCS and the suction of the charging pumps are a set of valves. These valves are closed automatically on a reactor trip to terminate planned dilution operations which might be underway at the time of the trip, and are also closed automatically on a source range flux high or doubling time low when at shutdown. Once the valves are closed, the charging pumps take their suction from the refuelling water storage tank which is maintained at a high boric acid concentration. To make this boron dilution block fully effective, the design of the CVCS on the reference plants has been changed for Sizewell B to eliminate pipework connections downstream of the boron dilution block valves which might carry unborated water.

Because experience feedback had indicated that dilution incidents were relatively frequent, and sometimes occurred at shutdown or during reactor startup, additional protection channels were added to the secondary protection system, including new source range flux monitoring chambers, and two valves additional to the two present in the reference plant were also added. The additional valves are diverse from the original valves, using pneumatic instead of motor actuators and being of a different mechanical type, and are closed by the secondary protection system.

4 SIZEWELL B DIVERSITY REVIEW

To confirm the inclusion of diversity into the appropriate safeguards systems in line with the criteria adopted, the Sizewell B Project Management Team conducted a systematic review of the design. Two key documents formed the basis for organizing and conducting the review. Firstly, the design strategy document for diversity requirements was consulted to determine the scope of the review and the guidelines for the implementation of diversity. Secondly, a technical memorandum was prepared, defining the specific working methods of the diversity review.

The Diversity Requirements strategy document systematically identified the necessary safety functions for those initiating faults with a frequency greater than 10-3 per annum. It also provided the next tier of detailed information by identifying the systems or portions of systems that perform a given safety function following these faults (frontline systems). While not identifying the systems that support the frontline system, it stated that diversity of support systems is necessary to preclude potential common mode failure of the frontline systems. Furthermore, the strategy document defined three acceptable means of implementing diversity:

Functional Diversity

The application of different concepts, physical principles or modes of operation to the means of achieving a given safety function.

Component Diversity

Functionally equivalent components of diverse systems are of dissimilar design.

Manufacturing Diversity

Functionally equivalent components of diverse systems are produced by different manufacturers or different manufacturing and inspection routes.

Given this scope and guidance, a technical memorandum was prepared, extending the systematic approach of the strategy document to the review of the design. The memorandum established a review team with members drawn from the Safety and Technology and Project Engineering Branches of the PMT, thereby providing diversity of technical experience and judgment to the review itself.

The systems and components necessary to detect and mitigate frequent faults were grouped under eight functional topics:

o   Control of Reactivity.
o   Maintenance of Hot/Intermediate Shutdown.
o   Decay Heat Removal at Cold Shutdown and from Spent Fuel.
o   Reactor Coolant System Inventory Control.
o   Main Steam/Feed Isolation.
o   Reactor Coolant and Main Steam System Overpressure Protection.
o   Fault Detection and Reactor Trip.
o   Containment Isolation.

In addition, because of the important role of electrical supplies and the need for diversity between the primary and secondary dc systems, the Electrical System was also reviewed.

When reviewing the systems and components, the review methodology required that the three types of diversity be viewed as a hierarchy with functional diversity as the most desirable. Finally, the memorandum required the production of a report, reviewed by appropriate members of the PMT, that summarised the review process and documented the adequacy of the diversity provided in the design.

4.1 Review Process

The first step undertaken was to determine for each safety function under consideration, the specific items of plant within each of the frontline and support systems that were required to mitigate frequent faults. The active components within each system were then examined. Passive components were not considered because either the failure frequency of such items is so low that similar components are considered acceptable in systems required to be diverse, or because the failure modes of such components involves gradual, detectable loss of function. Then, based upon piping and instrumentation drawings and logic diagrams, simplified functional sketches were prepared. The functionally equivalent components in the two systems (frontline and support) were juxtaposed and their level of diversity assessed. The review process is shown in Figure 1 and a typical functional sketch and comparison table are shown in figures 2 and 3.

The Diversity Review found that functional and component diversity had been designed into the Sizewell B Power Station. In the main, the frontline systems operate with fundamentally different principles or significantly different component designs. Because of the diversity in the frontline systems, it generally followed that the support systems were also diverse (eg ac electrical power versus steam; air versus motor operated valves; component cooling water versus self-cooled or process cooled; ac powered heating, ventilation and cooling equipment (HVAC) versus dc powered HVAC or no HVAC required).

In some cases, a lack of diversity at the component level in systems which appeared to be diverse on initial inspection was encountered. In the majority of cases this was corrected by specifying different components for one of the systems. In a few situations it was necessary to accept minimal diversity of the hardware or different manufacturers of similar devices as the means of achieving diversity; in these cases, close attention was paid to the safety role of the components concerned and justifications were provided that were based upon the degree of diversity required, operating experience of similar components or significant differences in the utilisation of the equipment.

5   COST OF IMPLEMENTATION AND CONTRIBUTION TO SAFETY

The most significant elements in the cost of implementing diversity on Sizewell B are the additional systems not typically found on a PWR. Modifications to existing systems involve costs approximately an of order magnitude lower than the additional systems. Collectively, the two additional fluid systems, the secondary protection system, the battery charging diesels and the secondary electrical system, the boron dilution block modifications and the diverse CVCS relief path contribute approximately L8M - L10M of additional hardware costs. Changes to effect component diversity or manufacturing diversity of equipment already included in the design have an insignificant direct impact on capital costs.

The figure of L8M to L10M does not include the (more difficult to quantify) indirect costs associated with: additional space to house the equipment, commodities such as concrete, rebar and supports, raceway components and cabling, engineering effort, contract management of additional contracts, increased construction craft manhours, diverse spare parts, increased maintenance manhours, etc. When these factors are included, the incremental cost of the additional diversity in the Sizewell B design will be significantly greater than the simple hardware costs.

It is difficult to quantify the overall cost to benefit ratio realised by the introduction of diversity. Some features provide clear benefits in terms of safety; these are the additional systems introduced to respond to specific concerns. For example, it is recognised that the continuity of reactor coolant pump seal injection flow provided by the emergency charging system results in an appreciable reduction in the potential risk due to small LOCAs. The battery charging diesels and the secondary electrical system significantly improve the plant's ability to cope with station blackout. These features respond to specific concerns which are currently receiving industry wide attention.

On the other hand, the imposition of a common mode failure limit on reliability has resulted in changing valve operators from motor to air, changing valve types from gate to globes, and adding systems and components such as the EBS and the CVCS pressure relief line. Some of these changes result in relatively minor increases in cost but for others the costs are quite significant. The improvement in safety gained by the addition of these features is dependent on the common mode failure limit assumed in the probabilistic safety assessment.

Because there is not universal agreement on the magnitude of the common mode failure limit, or even that a fixed limit is appropriate, it is unrealistic to attempt to assess the cost benefit ratio of such modifications. The high levels of separation and segregation supplied on modern power stations, together with good design practice, experience feedback evaluation programmes and in-service testing, may in reality provide a more effective way of systematically addressing common mode failures than the prescriptive application of diversity.

6   CONCLUSIONS

Diversity, on a selective basis, is an important design basis for safeguards systems. The greatest quantifiable gains in safety are made when the design process takes account of experience feedback and examines the design of systems and components to identify plausible, mechanistic, common mode failures and then supplies specific, diverse features to target these concerns. The addition of diverse systems or components to respond to unidentified common mode failures may not provide significant improvements in safety.

Ref 1.   HM Nuclear Installations Inspectorate - Safety Assessment Principles for Nuclear Power Reactors. April 1979.

Acknowledgment: This paper is published by permission of the Sizewell B Project Management Team of the Central Electricity Generating Board.

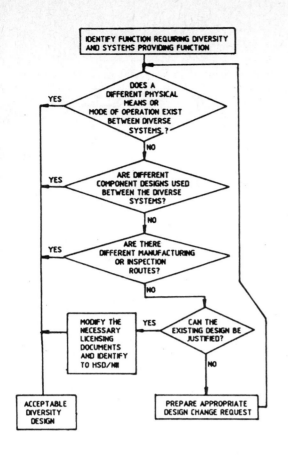

POTENTIAL BASES FOR JUSTIFICATION

- Timing and duration of safety or service function requirement.

- Magnitude of reliability target and safety significance.

- Special design features included to address specific identified failure modes.

- Scenario causes gradual, detectable degradation in component performance.

- Scenario causes limited degradation such that safety functions can be accomplished.

- Other Systems can maintain safe shutdown, integrity of RCPB or mitigate fault until lost function can be restored.

- Normal operation of system/component permits assessment of operability.

- Special training, surveillance or maintenance features included to address specific identified failure modes.

Fig 1   Assessment of diversity

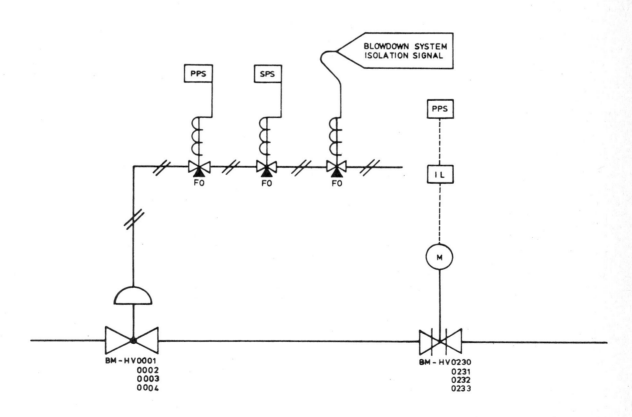

Fig 2   Steam generator blowdown isolation

Duty	X System	Y System	Type of Diversity
Isolation Valve	Parallel Slide Gate Valve BM-HV-0230 HV-0231 HV-0232 HV-0233	Globe Valve BM-HV-0001 HV-0002 HV-0003 HV-0004	Component
Valve Operator	Motor operation Normally open - fail as is	Air operator with series solenoid actuated pilot valves. Normally open - fail shut	Component
Automatic Actuation Signals	PPS	SPS PPS	Component
Power Source	Essential ac power system	Spring closure following release of air from actuator	Functional
HVAC	Auxiliary Building	Auxiliary Building	Valve qualified for further environment than loss of HVAC

Fig 3   Steam generator blowdown isolation diversity

C388/013

Sizewell Nuclear Island fluid systems design

A C HALL, BSc
PWR Power Projects, Knutsford, Cheshire

SYNOPSIS   The Sizewell Nuclear Island fluid systems design has been based on that of an operating American reference plant. The principal changes which have been introduced in order to meet British requirements are discussed, as is the structured review process which has been set up in order to assure that these changes fulfil their design objective, and that they are effectively integrated into the overall design.

NOTATION

Q	volumetric flow rate (m^3/sec)
ρ	density of fluid (Kg/m^3)
d	characteristic dimension (m)
g	gravitational acceleration (m/sec^2)
ν	kinematic viscosity (m^2/sec)
Ri	Richardson number
Re	Reynolds number

1.0   INTRODUCTION

The Pressurised Water Reactor design has evolved over a period of more than thirty years. Since the start up of Shippingport in the United States in 1957 about 210 further plants have been ordered in the Western world and in 20 countries. The principal reason for the concepts adoption in the United Kingdom has been its proven capability of being safely and economically implemented by a wide variety of electricity generating utilities.

Apart from experimental and prototype reactors, previous civil nuclear power plants in the United Kingdom have relied exclusively on gas reactor technology. For this, and other reasons, the United Kingdom has developed safety and operating requirements which, in some instances, differ significantly from those which are applied elsewhere in the world.

The Sizewell challenge has been to produce a detailed design which fully satisfies British requirements, whilst capitalising to the maximum extent possible on the vast operating experience and research and development programmes which are available world wide. The approach adopted has been to take as a starting point an established 'reference plant', and to introduce the changes necessary to meet British requirements. The reference plant selected was the Callaway unit owned by The Union Electric Company of St Louis, Missouri and commissioned in 1985. Callaway itself is one of a small family of essentially identical plants which are collectively referred to as SNUPPS (Standard Nuclear Power Plants Systems).

This paper discusses the principal fluid systems design changes which have been required for Sizewell, and the steps taken to assure that new or modified systems will operate with the same high level of reliability as the more traditional systems.

2.0   NUCLEAR ISLAND FLUID SYSTEMS FUNCTIONS

The basic concept of the PWR is well known and is simple. It consists of a primary circuit which transports heat from the reactor core to a number of steam generators utilising high pressure sub-cooled water. The steam generators are used to boil water in a separate secondary loop which contains the power generating turbine. In addition to its power conversion function the primary circuit plays a central role in plant safety and in reactivity control. (The latter is effected by varying the concentration of dissolved boric acid, which is a neutron absorber). In order to perform these functions, the primary circuit requires a number of nuclear auxiliary fluid systems. These systems are basically used to control the temperature, pressure and chemistry of the primary loop. In addition to those fluid systems interfacing directly with the primary loop, others are needed for, for example, the cooling of components, the containment and the spent fuel pond, and for post accident fission product clean up in the reactor containment building. The main Nuclear Island fluid systems are listed in table 1 which also provides an indication as to whether significant changes have been required and the reasons for these changes.

Table 1. Principal Nuclear Island fluid systems changes.

System	Magnitude of change	Reason for change
Reactor coolant	None	-
Residual heat removal	(b)	(1)
Chem. and vol. control	(b)	(2)(3)
Safety injection	(a)	(1)
Containment spray	(a)	(1)
Reserve ultimate heat sink	New System	(2)
Emergency boration	New System	(2)
Emergency charging	New System	(2)
Main feedwater	(a)	(1)
Main steam	None	-
Auxiliary feedwater	(a)	(1)
Component cooling water	(a)	(1)
Boron Thermal Regeneration	Deleted	(3)

Notes (a) Significant detailed change. No new technology.
       (b) Relatively minor detail change.

       1   Reliability requirement
       2   Licensing requires new function to be provided.
       3   Simplification

3.0   NOVEL SYSTEMS AND SYSTEM FUNCTIONS

The major system level changes with reference to SNUPPS are discussed below. Changes at a component level and in equipment qualification are discussed elsewhere (1, 2, 3) as is the plant's instrumentation and control system (4,5).

3.1   Reactor Coolant System

The Reactor Coolant System (RCS) is considered to consist of the Reactor Pressure Vessel, the four primary loops (each containing a Steam Generator, a Reactor Coolant Pump and Primary Pipework) and the Pressuriser.

At a system level the system remains unchanged in any direct sense. It is, however, the vehicle by which other revised or new systems interact with the core. This, together with revised requirements for accident studies has significantly modified the transients against which its constituent components have to be mechanically designed (6).

3.2   Emergency Boration System

3.2.1 Background

This is a new system. Its function is to provide a rapid secondary shutdown capability by boration of the primary loop in the event of failure of the control rods to insert when demanded. (Elsewhere in the world a slower shutdown using the reactors normal boron control systems is accepted). The background to the requirements for the system are discussed in reference 7.

The functional requirements are:-

1. Departure from nucleate boiling in the core must be prevented.
2. The reactor conditions must remain stable until the operator can control reactivity by use of the Chemical and Volume Control System (CVCS).
3. The physical parameters of the primary coolant should remain within the range of applicability of the appropriate computer codes.
4. The RCS pressure should be limited to acceptable levels.

The system bears some resemblance to systems considered for other plants to provide for the rapid boration of the primary loop during accidental cooldown events. However, requirement 4 above when applied to a loss of 11KV power supplies coupled with a failure to insert rods, and using British assumptions, means that very rapid boration is required. For this reason a new design is being implemented.

3.2.2 System Design

As indicated in Figure 1 the system consists of four tanks each of which is connected across one of the four reactor coolant pumps. The tanks, which contain a minimum of 7000 ppm boric acid, are normally cold and depressurised and are connected to a single header tank. When the system is actuated, fast acting valves isolate the tanks from the header tank, and the single inlet and outlet valves open allowing the reactor coolant pump head to flush the contents of the tanks into the reactor coolant system.

The inertia of the reactor coolant pumps assures proper functioning of the system even after a loss of power supplies to the pumps. (The inertia is artificially increased by large flywheels in order to ameliorate the core thermohydraulic transient associated with a loss of reactor coolant flow).

3.2.3 Design Substantiation - Hydraulic Performance

Effective functioning of the system requires that the contents of the tanks should be rapidly discharged into the reactor coolant system, where they should be mixed with reactor coolant. Once the system valves have been aligned, the systems performance will be defined by flow rate and tank mixing characteristics.

The flow rate can be calculated with confidence and verified during commissioning. The optimum performance would be obtained if there were no mixing in the tank, that is if slug flow occurred. The reactor coolant fluid is about 75% of the density of that in the EBS tank as a result of their relative temperatures and boron concentrations. Since the incoming reactor coolant fluid enters the top of the EBS tank, buoyancy forces will tend to maintain separation. (Domestic hot water tank effect). However, the relatively high velocity of about 8 m/sec in the inlet pipe will tend to promote mixing.

Fault studies for the safety analysis report were performed on the basis of a mixing model which was considered to be conservative. In order to verify this, a one third scale test was performed by NNC at Whetstone. (8). The tests used pure water and brine to simulate density differences and the inlet water was stained with methyl violet to permit visualisation of the mixing. Exit concentrations were inferred from an electrical conductivity meter.

The appropriate dimensionless numbers when considering hydraulic similarity for this configuration are the Richardson number (ratio of intertial to buoyancy forces) and Reynolds number (ratio of intertial to viscous forces).

$$\text{Richardson number, } Ri = \frac{\rho \, Q^2}{\Delta \rho \, d^5 \, g}$$

$$\text{Reynolds number, } Re = \frac{4Q}{\pi \nu \, d}$$

The values for the actual EBS are respectively 7×10^{-3} and 1.48×10^6. The significance of these values is firstly that, because the Richardson number is very much less than unity, buoyancy forces dominate over inertial forces in the tank itself and, secondly, the Reynolds number is well into the turbulent region where hydrodynamic parameters change only slightly with Reynolds number.

Tests were performed over a range of density differences in order to verify lack of sensitivity to this parameter (i.e. density difference).

In order to understand system performance and to verify the conservatism of the computer modelling techniques used in fault studies, test runs were made with and without Reactor Coolant Pump coast down and for a variety of initial tank flow rates. Tests were also performed to assess the advantages to be gained by introducing a baffle into the tank to reduce mixing. The results indicated that only marginal improvements were to be gained by the latter. Since the baffle significantly exacerbated the thermal stresses produced in the storage tank by actuation of the system, the option was discarded.

The tests verified the conservatism of the mixing assumptions used in safety analysis and it therefore remains only to confirm the system flow rate during plant commissioning in order to fully demonstrate the efficacy of the hydraulic design.

3.2.4 Mechanical Performance

It is evident that the system must not jeopardise the integrity of the primary pressure boundary under accident conditions or following spurious actuation. For this reason the systems pressure boundary is qualified as ASME III Class 1.

Actuation of the system results in a very rapid pressure increase, and subsequently in a thermal shock. For this reason it has been necessary to subject the tank to very careful analysis. In particular, in addition to the normal analyses required by the code, the tank has been subjected to extensive fatigue analyses, and to a rigorous fracture mechanics analysis.

3.3 Emergency Charging System

3.3.1 Background

This is a new system. Its primary function is to provide seal injection to the Reactor Coolant Pumps in the event of a complete loss of a.c. power. (Station blackout coupled with failure of all four emergency diesels). It also plays a role in the provision of make up and boration capability in the event of loss of a.c. power.

The controlled leakage Reactor Coolant Pump utilises a concept where water is normally injected into the seal assembly by the Chemical and Volume Control System (CVCS). Some of this water escapes via the seals and is recycled to the CVCS. The remainder passes down the pump shaft and into the Reactor Coolant System. This arrangement assures that the seal assembly is normally operating in cool water. In the event that seal injection ceases for any reason, there is a flow reversal along the pump shaft and reactor coolant liquid passes directly through the seals. A heat exchanger referred as the 'thermal barrier' surrounds the pump shaft below the seal assembly. This normally cools the reactor coolant flow to the seals in the event of loss of seal injection, using the Component Cooling Water System (CCWS).

Both the CVCS and the CCWS rely on the stations a.c. power supplies. A total loss of all a.c. power will result in uncooled primary water passing to the reactor coolant pump seals. This could ultimately lead to increased leakage at a time when no make up capability exists. The Emergency Charging System has been introduced to prevent this situation from arising.

The safety case in other countries is built on the low probability of the event, coupled with the limited nature of seal degradation which, with appropriate emergency procedures permits the plant to be held in a safe condition until power supplies can be restored.

In Belgium a somewhat similar system is provided in the 'bunker' used to provide vital services in the event of a severe external accident This system, however, is electrically powered using supplies from the bunker's diesels.

3.3.2 System Design

The conceptual design of the ECS is shown in Figure 2. The system comprises a batching tank for preparation of borated water, a storage tank, two positive displacement pumps and all associated pipework and valves.

The ECS storage tank contains borated water at the required concentration. This is supplied as required via a transfer pump from a dedicated boric acid batching tank. The two positive displacement pumps are steam turbine driven, steam being supplied from the main steam lines. Turbine exhausts are direct to atmosphere.

The two pumps take suction from the ECS borated water storage tank and discharge via separate delivery lines. Relief valves are provided to protect the pumps in the event of inadvertent operation against closed discharge valves. Each pump's discharge line includes a flow meter and a filter assembly. These lines connect to a distribution header within the reactor building.

One normally closed power operated isolation valve and one non-return valve are provided in each pump discharge line to meet containment isolation requirements.

Recirculation lines are provided to enable periodic testing of the pumps and filters to be carried out, without disrupting normal operation of the CVCS seal injection system.

Within the reactor building the system delivers to each of the four CVCS seal delivery lines via individual connections from the ECS distribution header. Each of the four ECS delivery lines includes a locked-in-position flow control valve which together with the flow measuring orifices on the common ECS/CVCS delivery lines is used for initial flow balancing. The ECS delivers into the CVCS seal injection lines via non-return valves, one per line, which together with the containment isolation non-return valve isolates the ECS from the CVCS when the latter is at high pressure and the ECS is inoperative.

Similarly, back flow into the CVCS during ECS operation is prevented by non-return valves in the CVCS seal injection lines.

The storage tank is external to the auxiliary building in an area remote from the storage tanks associated with the CVCS, (i.e. the boric acid tanks, the reactor make-up water tanks and the refuelling water storage tank). The ECS pumps, steam turbines and associated filters are located under the feed and steam cell in a region of the auxiliary building which is segregated from the region containing the CVCS components.

The ECS is specifically designed to be independent of off-site and on-site a.c. power and of the CCWS. Secondary d.c. supplies are used for all associated control and instrumentation, including operation of the steam supply valves to the steam turbine drives. Steam supplies are taken from the main steam system, upstream of the Main Steam Isolation Valves. All cooling services required by the ECS, (e.g. pump and turbine bearing cooling) are similarly provided independently of the CCWS.

The flow from a single pump is adequate to meet the requirements of the four Reactor Coolant Pump seals and those for make-up during cooldown or for boration purposes. Initiation of the system therefore requires the start of only one pump. The second pump is aligned ready for actuation, but is started only in the event of failure of the first pump.

3.3.3 Design Substantiation

At a system level no new technology is used. Positive displacement charging pumps have been used before to provide normal seal injection in earlier designs of the CVCS. Substantial experience exists in designing such systems and, for example, the application of dampners to reduce system pulsations originating in the reciprocating pump.

The use of a self regulating turbine driver for a positive displacement pump is novel, but involves no new technology as such. Turbine drivers exhausting to atmosphere have been used in PWR Auxiliary Feedwater Systems for many years, and considerable experience exists in designing turbines and inlet systems to accept rapid automatic initiation from a cold condition.

The main task of the system reviewers is, therefore, to assure themselves that all of the identified functional requirements are met by the system under all design conditions.

3.4 Pressuriser Relief System

3.4.1 Background

The Reactor Coolant System pressure is normally maintained within acceptable limits by the pressuriser and its associated control circuits. The pressuriser is a $51m^3$ tank connected to the primary loop by an 350mm surge line. Under normal operating conditions it is about 60% full of water at the saturation temperature.

Positive pressure surges are controlled by spraying water at a subcooling of about 60°C into the steam phase. Negative pressure surges are controlled by heaters immersed in the water phase.

Under more extreme conditions of positive surge, it is necessary to relieve steam from the Pressuriser into the Pressuriser Relief System in order to maintain the system pressure within acceptable limits. The more severe faulted conditions result in the lifting of the code safety valves. Operating transients on the SNUPPS Plants are dealt with by power operated relief valves.

On SNUPPS, the code safety valves are sized on the basis of a turbine trip without reactor trip, taking credit for the operation of only safety grade devices. The resulting system performance is then shown to be adequate for other events considered in the safety case.

For Sizewell, the formal design basis of the system has been expanded to accommodate those transients for which credit has been taken in the preparation of the safety case. A full discussion of this is beyond the scope of this paper. However, the following four cases scope the requirements for the system.

1. Normal hot over pressure protection based on a turbine trip with delayed reactor trip. This results in a discharge of steam from the pressuriser.

2. Cold over pressure mitigation where the system pressure is increased by either a net heat or mass addition when the primary circuit and pressuriser are cold and water solid. Under these conditions the acceptable pressure is limited by brittle failure considerations, and the pressure response (with a very incompressible system) is very rapid. The limiting case is the spurious starting of the high head safety injection system. This case results in a rather large discharge flow rate of subcooled water.

3. Feed and bleed. Although not a part of the formal safety case, it has been claimed that in the event of unavailability of the steam generator heat removal path, whilst the plant is at hot conditions, cooling may be effected by feeding the RCS with the Safety Injection System and bleeding via the pressuriser relief system. This implies filling the Pressuriser and then discharging hot flashing water through the relief system.

4. Loss of offsite power with failure of the reactor to trip. (Most limiting of the 'anticipated transients without trip'). For a SNUPPS plant this results in discharge of liquid water through the relief system and a relatively severe over pressure transient. For Sizewell, operation of the Emergency Boration System limits the transient to such an extent that it is less severe than the case discussed in 1 above.

The above cases require that the system should be able to safely accommodate defined discharge rates of steam, subcooled water or flashing water.

3.4.2 System Design

The Sizewell system utilises two conventional spring loaded safety valves to provide the code safety valve function. The actuation pressure of these valves is set mechanically, and is not adjustable during operation. Spring loaded safety valves are prone to leak after operation and, therefore it is operationally very desirable to prevent their opening except under fault conditions. This is one of the reasons for the provision of power operated relief valves in the SNUPPS reference plant design. For Sizewell the three relief valves have been replaced by elegant pilot operated valves of French design (SEBIM valves).

The SEBIM valve is held closed by a hydraulic piston subjected to system pressure. The pilot valve is a spring loaded device which operates in condensed and cooled process fluid. When the pilot valve reaches its mechanically preset pressure, it vents fluid from the actuator of the main valve and allows it to open. When the pressure falls, the pilot valve re admits fluid to the hydraulic piston and causes it to close the main valve. The stem of the pilot valve has an extension piece to which a solenoid actuator is fitted. The solenoid can be used to open the valve at pressures lower than the mechanical set point (9).

The SEBIM valves will be mechanically set to operate at the pressure required for their function during normal power operation. The set pressure is of the order of 10 bars below that of the spring loaded valves, and the valves are sized to prevent the system pressure reaching the reactor trip set point for the most limiting operational transient. (A complete loss of station load).

When the plant is shut down and at a reduced temperature. The reactor protection system provides over pressure protection by generating a signal which actuates the solenoid operators on the SEBIM valves. The pressure set point is a function of temperature and is calculated to prevent the Reactor Pressure Vessel from being taken into a forbidden operating regime.

In France, the SEBIM valves are used as code safety valves, as well as relief valves. Their use on Sizewell can, therefore, be considered to provide valuable backup to the code valves.

The system arrangement of the Pressuriser Relief System is shown in Figure 3. The safety and relief valves discharge into a ring header from which a discharge line leads to the Pressuriser Relief Tank sparger. The relief tank contains water and nitrogen gas and is sized to accept 110% of the normal full load steam inventory of the Pressuriser.

The system downstream of the safety and relief valves does not play a direct safety role and is provided to prevent contamination of the reactor building. The Pressuriser Relief Tank is provided with bursting disks to prevent over pressurisation for beyond design basis events. The discharge piping may be required to accept steam, flashing water or subcooled water, and has been designed to accept the mechanical and thermal loadings which these cases can produce.

3.4.3 Design Substantiation

The SEBIM pilot operated relief valves have been used extensively in reactor systems in France and Belgium for the relief of steam, saturated water and subcooled water. They are also in the process of undergoing an exhaustive series of tests at the CEGB's Marchwood Laboratories (10).

The design bases of the system reflect rather severe accident conditions and so preclude on line testing of the system.

However, the thermal, hydraulic and mechanical responses of the system have been extensively modelled using a variety of established computer codes. It has been shown that the various parameters remain within acceptable limits. (11).

3.5 Reserve Ultimate Heat Sink

3.5.1 Background

The Component Cooling Water System (CCWS) provides a series of vital cooling functions for the plant, under a variety of conditions. These include, amongst others; cooling of safety and non-safety grade equipment; providing cooling to the thermal barriers of the Reactor Coolant Pumps; decay heat removal via the Residual Heat Removal Heat Exchangers for normal cold shutdown and following a loss of coolant accident.

The CCWS is itself cooled by the Essential Service Water System (ESWS) during normal conditions. The ESWS draws water directly from the sea.

The Reserve Ultimate Heat Sink (RUHS) is required to provide a backup cooling capability for a variety of low probability scenarios involving failure of some aspect of the plants first line of cooling. The main conditions requiring its functioning are:

1. Loss of the Essential Service Water System, for example, as a result of blockage of the intake screens, whilst the balance of the systems function normally.

2. Loss of the normal Component Cooling Water System capability, for example, as a result of multiple pump failures.

3. Loss of coolant accident and loss of Essential Service Water as a result of a safe shutdown earthquake.

Requirements for the Reserve Ultimate Heat Sink are discussed in more detail in reference 7.

3.5.2 System Design and Operation

The system consists of two separate but identical trains. The main features of this design are illustrated in Figure 4. The main components are the main and auxiliary heat exchangers, two circulating pumps, a surge tank and associated piping and valves. The system is capable of being aligned in different ways depending on the nature of the emergency requiring its use. The RUHS heat exchangers utilise air cooling in order to provide diversity from the sea water cooling of the Essential Service Water System. Each RUHS heat exchanger incorporates two banks of fans, each of which is powered from a separate electrical separation group.

When used in a scenario where the Essential Service Water System is lost, the system is aligned so that the main RUHS heat exchanger replaces the Component Cooling Water Heat Exchanger in the Component Cooling Water System. The latter system operates in essentially the same manner as during normal operation except that the essential low temperature loads, such as safeguard pump coolers, are isolated from the main Component Cooling Water System loop and valved into a loop with the RUHS pumps and auxiliary heat exchanger. This alignment is effected automatically upon loss of ESWS flow.

For the second scenario where there is a complete loss of capability of the Component Cooling Water System, for example as a result of loss of all pumps, the system is manually aligned. The system can be manually realigned so that one train cools the reactor building fan coolers and associated low temperature loads, with the other train aligned in order to provide cooling to the essential low temperature loads so as to permit reactor make up and boration to be effected. If only one train is available then it is normally aligned to the fan coolers; but from time to time reactor building cooling is terminated in order that the train may be realigned to permit make up and boration.

For the third scenario, the RUHS must be capable of rejecting the heat loads placed on the Component Cooling Water system by either a large loss of primary coolant or a main steam line break within the containment, following an earthquake. It is of interest to note that since the primary loop and safety grade portions of the main steam system are designed to sustain seismic loadings, this combination is outside the original design basis for the plant. It has, however, been addressed because of concerns expressed by the Safety Authorities. The system would for this scenario normally be aligned as for the first scenario. Given the low probability of the event, a less extreme ambient air temperature has been assumed.

3.5.3 Design Substantiation

The rather large seismically qualified air cooled heat exchangers are being used in a novel application but involve no new technology as such.

3.6 Changes in other Systems

Changes have been made in other systems in order to meet, for example, specific British reliability or separation requirements. In most instances these changes have been minor in nature. However, in the case of the Safety Injection System and Auxiliary Feedwater System, the design deviates substantially from the SNUPPS reference plant both in terms of sizing and of the number of

components (Redundancy). In none of these cases, however, are the designs novel, in the sense that they require either new technology or an unusual application of existing technology.

4.0 DESIGN ASSURANCE

Viewed against the totality of the station design, the above system changes are limited in nature. Experience, however, has shown that even minor 'improvements' can, if not properly verified, result in significant problems. Further, the British separation philosophy has resulted in fairly significant layout changes in some areas of the plant. Such changes can impact system performance and require the reevaluation of hazards such as high energy line breaks.

Prior to the release of the approved design documents, the various design organisations have, of course, performed their own internal reviews and checking in line with their quality assurance programmes. In addition to this, the station design has been subjected to a structured review process which has made the maximum use of available expertise and experience.

4.1 Interface Engineering Reviews

For Sizewell, the Primary Circuit is being supplied by the Westinghouse Electric Company. The remainder of the systems have been designed and supplied by other organisations in the United Kingdom. As indicated above, the Primary Circuit itself has not been the subject of any system level changes. However, as part of its contract Westinghouse has been required to perform reviews of the key interfacing systems.

These reviews are now essentially complete. Although they yielded a number of useful recommendations, no major issues were uncovered.

4.2 Specialist Reviews

The Project Management Team have set up a number of specialist review groups with the objective of performing 'lateral' reviews for particular topics encompassing a number of systems. In many instances these review activities have been greatly facilitated by the 1/20 scale plastic model. This model is located at Booths Hall at Knutsford, where the bulk of the systems design activities are taking place. It models all components, cable trays, piping and tubing, including instrument lines. Colour coding is used to identify the various separation groups, and safety classes.

System reviews are conducted around the model to assess the impact of the actual, layout and environment on the systems functionality.

Hazards reviews are conducted to assess the systems' potential vulnerability to internal hazards including fire, flooding and high energy line breaks, and to external hazards such as seismic, extreme winds and aeroplane crash. The utility of the model for this purpose, particularly in terms of assessing the impact of consequential failures in adjacent equipment, is evident.

Reviews are performed to assess operator radiation doses as part of the commitment to ALARP (As low as reasonably practicable radiation doses). These reviews assess systems and components design, operating procedures and layout utilising the existing data bases of operating experience with respect to radiation sources.

Diversity reviews are performed to assess the vulnerability of the integrated systems to common cause failures.

4.3 Project Director's Reviews

The CEGB Sizewell Project Director has initiated a series of reviews of selected aspects of the plant design, using groups of independent experts drawn from across the nuclear industry. The first of these reviews dealt with the 'Control of Reactivity' and has already presented its conclusions to the Project Director. The second which addresses 'Hazards and Equipment Qualification' is underway at the moment. These reviews are broadly based but have probed in depth in areas of potential concern.

5.0 CONCLUSIONS

The Nuclear Island fluid systems' design for Sizewell is based on an operating reference plant. The changes necessary to meet British requirements have been subjected to a structured review process. As a consequence the Sizewell design is able to take full profit of the world PWR experience.

REFERENCES

(1) SYLVESTER, R. L. FOGERTY, B. E. THOMPSON, J. L. Sizewell 'B' Steam Generator builds upon the Westinghouse Model F to meet the U.K. safety case. I.Mech.E 388. Manchester 1989.

(2) STIGTER, H. Primary system pipework. I.Mech.E. C388. Manchester 1989.

(3) JOHNSON, P. Inspection of the Sizewell 'B' PWR. I.Mech.E. C388. Manchester 1989.

(4) REMLEY, G. PEPPER, J.W. Distributed digital processing technology applied to commercial nuclear power station contracts. Lessons learned, and future direction. I.Mech.E. C388. Manchester 1989.

(5) HIGGS, J. C. The life cycle benefits of an integrated system approach to C and I. I.Mech.E. C388. Manchester 1989.

(6) LUCKHURST, D. P. CHEVALIER, A. Functional specification of the Sizewell 'B' systems. I.Mech.E. C388. Manchester 1989.

(7) BOETTCHER, D. CEREGHINO, S. Diversity: Safety system design for common mode failure. I.Mech.E. C388 Manchester 1969.

(8) RIPPON, J. P. SMEDLEY, C. Assessment of the performance of an emergency boration system for anticipated transients without trip faults. ANS conf. Anticipated and abnormal transients in nuclear power plants. Atlanta U.S.A. 1987.

(9) OLIVON, G. CABANNES, J. L. PETITE, R. Improving French PWR over pressure protection with SEBIM valves. Nuc. Eng. Int. May 84

(10) LUNG, F. K. K. One dimensional quasi-steady-state model for cold water discharge prediction of a pilot operated relief valve. I.Mech.E C373 Southampton 1989.

(11) Sizewell 'B' PWR pre-construction safety report 1987, Chapter 15 (PMT, CEGB, Booths Hall).

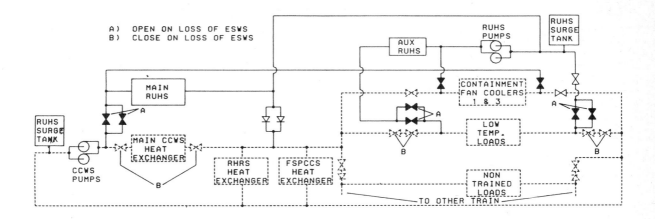

A) OPEN ON LOSS OF ESWS
B) CLOSE ON LOSS OF ESWS

Fig 1   Emergency boration system outline design

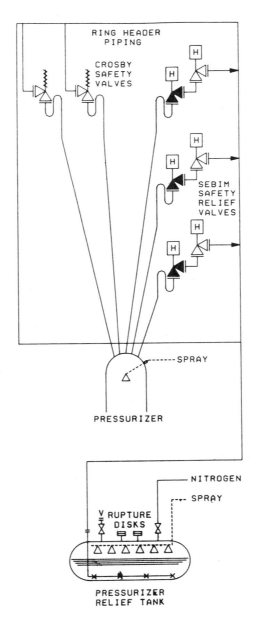

Fig 2   Emergency charging system outline design

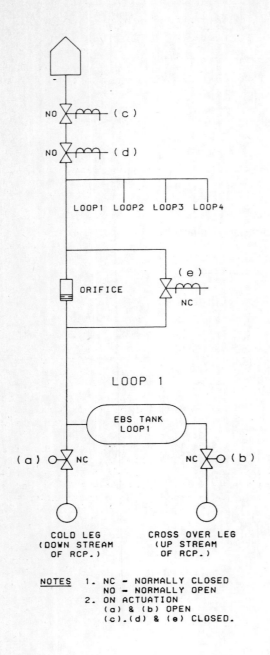

Fig 3   Pressurizer relief system outline design

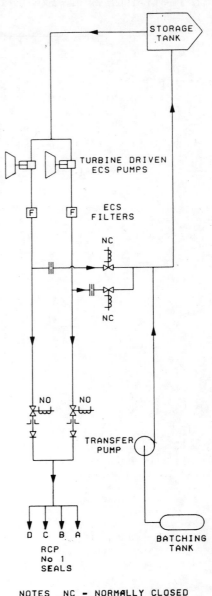

Fig 4   Reserve ultimate heat sink outline design

C388/033

Functional specification for Sizewell 'B' systems

D P LUCKHURST, BEng and **A B H CHEVALIER**, MSc
National Nuclear Corporation Limited, Knutsford, Cheshire

SYNOPSIS The functional specifications for the Sizewell 'B' Power Station establish the conceptual design for each system and identify the requirements arising from the safety case. The principal safety requirements and their impact on the conceptual design are described in this paper.

The reliability requirements which comprise both numerical targets and deterministic requirements, such as the single failure criterion, have a major impact on the design. The application of the single failure criterion is examined, using detailed examples, to illustrate the impact on the conceptual design of systems and therefore on the functional specifications.

1 INTRODUCTION

The Sizewell 'B' Power Station has made extensive use of functional specifications in the development of its design. Individual system functional specifications have been prepared for virtually all systems. These specify the safety role of the system, the functional requirements arising from the safety case and a conceptual design from which the design work can proceed. The UK reliability requirements have had a major impact on the conceptual design of the plant systems. Detailed safety assessment is carried out to confirm that the Sizewell 'B' design acceptably meets the UK safety requirements. Single Failure Analyses are an example of such safety assessments and their impact on the plant via the system functional specifications is described.

2 SYSTEM FUNCTIONAL SPECIFICATIONS

A system functional specification has been produced for systems either with a nuclear safety role or which contribute significantly to nuclear safety on the Sizewell 'B' Power Station. The prime purpose being to convey to the plant designers the specific system requirements arising from the contribution of that system to the safety of the plant. The majority of systems on Sizewell 'B' have had their functional requirements addressed in this manner. The small number of remaining systems for which no functional specification exists have been assessed to ensure that they do not contribute to safety in any meaningful manner.

This document, being a detailed definition of safety requirements, serves to translate the commitments implicit in the safety case into a specification for the detailed design of both safeguard systems and systems having relatively minor safety implications alike. To this extent the concept of system functional specifications has been more fully applied for Sizewell 'B' than for other previous UK nuclear stations.

The format and content which has been developed for Sizewell 'B' provides a consistent framework for identifying and justifying safety requirements to be met by plant designers. The justification is an important ingredient in that it provides the necessary explanation for what may otherwise be obscure limitations or restrictions. Providing the answer to the question 'why' is particularly important as it is the intention to build a series of PWR power stations based on the Sizewell 'B' design; of course it is necessary to distinguish clearly between the functional requirements and the material which is presented as back-up or explanatory information.

Each system functional specification contains a statement of the system role; a summary of relevant guidelines, principles and standards; a description of the conceptual design of the system and the specific system requirements.

The system role is identified with regard to the overall objectives for preventing or reducing the frequency of faults or in achieving fault mitigation. It is derived from consideration of the following basic safety functions which are defined in the Pre-Construction Safety Report for Sizewell 'B'.

(i)   Control of reactivity
(ii)   Decay heat removal

(iii) Control of radioactive release.
(iv) Maintenance of plant within safe limits.
(v) Support of safeguards system operations.

The guidelines, principles and standards of particular relevance to the system design are composed of three parts. The CEGB Design Safety Guidelines for PWR is a key reference as it is the document to which the plant is to be designed for safety. Secondly the Nuclear Installations Inspectorate (NII) Safety Assessment Principles describe the principles which are used to assess the safety of the station and the adequacy of the detailed system design. Note that the Design Safety Guidelines reflect the Safety Assessment Principles. Lastly, reference is made to specific US requirements of relevance to the system. These are included because they represent a valuable collection of experience and guidance specifically related to the design of light water reactors. They also provide the basis of the design for the reference plant for Sizewell 'B', the SNUPPS units in the USA.

A brief description of a conceptual design and system operation is provided. The functional specification is not a system description document and therefore the level of detail is merely sufficient for a proper understanding of a system concept which, when further developed, will satisfy the safety and licensing requirements. A description of the conceptual design is also necessary to allow the subsequent specification of individual component requirements.

The specific system requirements include coverage of the following aspects.

(a) Performance Requirements (for both the system and individual components

A quantitative statement is given of the performance requirements necessary to satisfy the safety role of the system in all relevant modes of operation. Specific items may include pump duty points or pump flow, heat exchanger performance, tank sizing, valve opening/closing times, fail safe states and filter efficiency.

(b) Reliability and Integrity Requirements

Where possible target reliabilities for specific system performance capabilities associated with particular faults or fault categories are identified. Those features of the conceptual design which contribute to, or are important in, meeting the system target reliabilities are also identified, including requirements for diversity.

Where appropriate, the text includes a clear statement of these features which enable the single failure criterion to be met.

Requirements which contribute to the integrity of the system are identified. These may include categorisation (including safety classification), quality assurance classification, material specification, process fluid chemistry specifications and requirements to operate within specified limits.

(c) Control and Instrumentation

The system functional specification sets out all of the requirements for automatic or manual controls and instruments and alarms necessary for the system to perform its safety functions; e.g. pump start/stop, opening/closing of isolation valves and the operation of flow control valves. Requirements for instrumentation arising from the need to monitor the achievement of these functions or to confirm that the plant is being maintained in a safe state are also included.

Requirements for manual control capability are specified in full, including the location(s) from which each operation is to be performed; e.g. main control room, auxiliary shutdown room, or local to plant or switchgear. Note that any operator action that may be necessary for the successful mitigation of faults or hazards is not claimed in the safety case to be carried out in less than 30 minutes following the fault or hazard.

(d) Service Requirements

The system functional specification identifies all requirements for services from other systems which enable the subject system to carry out its safety role. This may include a.c. and/or d.c. power supplies, cooling water, compressed air and HVAC.

(e) Radiological Protection Requirements

Any aspects of the design or layout which are required to limit the radiation exposure of operators or members of the public to levels which are as low as reasonably practicable (ALARP) are identified. The system functional specification considers system operation, maintenance, testing and inspection in addition to the consequences of normal leakages from the system in terms of both the total exposure and the maximum individual exposure of station staff or of the public both during normal operation and during or following faults. Particular attention is paid to those features which are required to achieve the individual dose limits during normal operation and following faults.

(f) Hazard Protection Requirements

Design features which are necessary for the system to perform its role (e.g. retain its integrity, retain its functional capability) in the event of plant hazards are identified. Such features include segregation, fire barriers, structural protection, sumps/drains for flood protection, and so on.

The seismic categorisation that is appropriate for components of the system is stated, having regard to the role of the system during and following a safe shutdown earthquake.

(g) Monitoring, Testing and Maintenance

Any requirements for testing and maintenance of the system components during normal operation and following faults in relation to their safety role are included. Restrictions on maintenance frequency, duration etc, arising from reliability or man-rem considerations are identified.

It should be noted that the frequency at which components are tested affects the component failure rate that is used in the probabilistic assessment of reliability.

(h) System Design and Environmental Conditions

The purpose of this item is to specify those steady-state or transient loadings which are experienced by the system during all relevant operational states of the plant and which the system must be designed to withstand in order to remain capable of performing its designated safety role.

Requirements arising from the role of the station in producing electricity efficiently and economically are outside the scope of the system functional specification as this is a matter for the plant designer to address directly.

The major safety requirements are the performance requirements which stem from transient analysis, the reliability and integrity requirements (particularly in the area of NSSS component integrity), the radiological protection requirements derived from the application of the ALARP principle and the hazard protection requirements where fire and earthquake tend to dominate. Of these safety requirements the UK reliability requirements have the greatest impact on the conceptual design of the plant systems. They have led directly to the increase in provisions from the SNUPPS units to those for Sizewell 'B' and are more fully examined in the subsequent section of this paper. The other aspects are addressed in other papers to be presented at this Conference.

3 UK RELIABILITY REQUIREMENTS

The UK reliability requirements broadly consist of probabilistic targets and a deterministic criterion. Probability targets are used to ensure that a disciplined approach is made to the design of systems and that adequately reliable systems are developed. However, numerical/probability treatment can only form part of the safety case. In particular, regardless of numerical targets the plant should also be assessed in a deterministic way.

3.1 Probabilistic Targets

The CEGB Design Safety Guidelines define targets for the maximum frequency of fault sequences which have the potential to lead to a large uncontrolled release of radioactivity to the environment. The targets are:

(i)   for any single accident which could lead to a large uncontrolled release of radioactivity, the accident frequency should be less than 10^{-7} per year. This is interpreted to mean that the product of the initiating fault frequency and the probability of failure to control the accident should be less than 10^{-7} per year

(ii)   the total frequency of all accidents leading to an uncontrolled release of radioactivity as in (i) above, should be less than 10^{-7} per year.

The Design Safety Guidelines also specify that dependent, or common mode, failures of similar plant items must be considered. The probability of such a common mode failure affecting plant items of one type must not be assumed to be less than 10^{-5} failures per demand. A common mode failure limit of 10^{-4} failures per demand is more generally assumed for a single set of similar plant items, which may be mechanical, electrical, instrumentation or protection.

The application of the above guidelines has two major impacts on the design. Firstly, diverse systems must be provided which are individually capable of fulfilling the safety functions which are necessary after each frequent initiating fault (i.e. those faults whose frequency is greater than approximately 10^{-3} per year). Secondly, the redundancy of plant items within each system must be sufficient to ensure that the reliability of the system is consistent with the overall targets.

The following systems, additional to the US reference plant, have been provided for Sizewell 'B' to improve diversity.

(i)   Two reactor protection systems, based on different operating principles have been provided. The primary protection system (PPS) is based on microprocessors and the secondary protection system (SPS) is based on solid state logic elements.

Both protection systems provide signals for initiation of Reactor Trip and Engineered Safety Features following all frequent initiating faults. Either PPS or SPS provides protection following infrequent faults.

(ii)   An Emergency Boration System provides a reactor shutdown capability for faults in which it is assumed that three or more Rod Cluster Control Assemblies (RCCAs) fail to enter the core following a reactor trip demand (ATWT). This system is also required following certain cooldown faults involving less than three RCCAs failing to insert into the core following reactor trip.

(iii) Two diverse sets of auxiliary feedwater pumps supply water to the steam generators, via separate nozzles on each steam generator, when the main feedwater system is not available either as a result of the fault or as a result of subsequent system failure. One set of pumps is motor driven and the other set is driven by steam turbines.

(iv) A route is provided for rejection of heat, after reactor trip, to the atmosphere. This route operates in the event of failure of the normal heat rejection route to the sea.

(v) An Emergency Charging System supplies borated water for protection of the RCP seals and control of reactivity in the long term after reactor trip. This system is driven by steam turbines and is diverse from the Chemical and Volume Control System which normally fulfills these functions.

(vi) A Battery Charging Diesel System is provided which is different to, and separate from, the main diesel generators. In the event of loss of offsite power supplies and failure of all the main diesel generators, this system provides charging supplies to the batteries which support operation of the steam turbine driven auxiliary feedwater and emergency charging systems.

The topic of diversity is more fully treated in another paper to be presented at this Conference.

3.2 Deterministic Criterion

Safety considerations other than the probabilistic targets also influence the redundancy of plant items provided in the system design and therefore the functional specification for each of the systems. In particular, the deterministic 'single failure' criterion requires that, following a fault (or hazard) any necessary safety function can be performed despite the loss of equipment as a consequence of the fault (or hazard), the unavailability of equipment owing to maintenance and the failure of any single other item of equipment (active or passive).

The aim of this overriding requirement is to make the credible failure of any plant item tolerable, even though systems may be shown to meet the probabilistic targets given above. This is regarded as part of the basic safety philosophy.

The main difference between the UK single failure criterion and the US single failure criterion is that the UK criterion specifically includes consideration of maintenance. In simple terms the UK criterion can be described as being equivalent to N-2 rather than N-1 (where N is the number of redundant plant items).

The implication of the UK single failure criterion in general, leads to a design with additional redundancy of plant items.

The numbers of High Head Safety Injection pumps, Essential Service Water pumps, Fuel Storage Pond Cooling pumps and main Diesel Generators have been increased from two to four.

The capacity of each of the four accumulators has been increased such that each accumulator provides half the required inventory rather than a third. In effect this increases the redundancy of the accumulators since failure of one of the accumulators to inject is now acceptable in addition to the loss of the accumulator associated with the breached loop of the reactor coolant system. The accumulators, being purely passive, are not normally assumed to be subject to a single failure.

Comparable design changes have been necessary in the associated services systems such as HVAC and power supplies.

Similarly the approach to single failure following hazards results in 4-way redundancy and segregation of equipment needed to establish or maintain hot or intermediate shutdown, including protection system equipment which ensures automatic tripping of the reactor and actuation of engineered safeguard systems. For equipment required to establish and maintain cold shutdown it is assumed that repair or restoration of unavailable equipment (other than that damaged by fire) will be possible so that 2-way segregation is sufficient.

Notwithstanding the additional redundancy of major plant items provided for Sizewell 'B' at the outset, detailed analyses have been performed throughout the design stage in order to ensure that the design is consistent with the above criterion. These analyses have resulted in a limited number of further minor modifications to the design.

4 DETAILED SAFETY ANALYSIS AND ITS IMPACT ON THE DESIGN

Single failure analysis is an example of the detailed safety analysis necessary to demonstrate compliance with UK safety requirements. It also serves to illustrate the iterative process of specifying functional requirements.

Individual system single failure analyses have been performed for all safeguard systems and their necessary services as well as for a number of other lesser important systems. A total of 35 different systems have been separately assessed as well as more general assessments of single failure withstand capability following selected hazards (fire and earthquake). The overall conclusion of this work, recently completed, is that the level of redundancy provided on Sizewell 'B' is satisfactory with regard to single failure considerations.

The system assessments have generally been prepared to standard formats. These provide; the safety role of the system, a brief description (including details of any necessary services), a summary of faults requiring operation of the system, the success states applicable to each safety role, the effect of maintenance and an analysis of both active and passive failures within the system. Any potential exceptions which may be identified are discussed and either a case is presented that the current design position is acceptable or, in a very limited number of instances, a design change to improve the capability of the system is referred to.

The more recent analyses has been carried out to the accepted interpretation of NII Safety Assessment Principle 112. In summary, this requires that for each fault situation (including fault combinations) the system should still meet its required safety duty performance in the presence of any single failure. The failures considered should include both passive and active components. The above should ideally still be met where a maintenance or test procedure requires part of the system to be placed in a state where it cannot perform its safety duty. Exceptions may be permitted where a reasoned case is made, in particular for maintenance considerations and failure of passive components.

The NII criterion differs in detail from the criterion specified in the CEGB Design Safety Guidelines. The differences between these two documents were generally referred to at the Sizewell 'B' Public Inquiry. Subsequently, the two criteria have been reviewed and it is anticipated that a common criteria will be adopted which will be based on the NII position. However, during the initial period of single failure analysis the differences in interpretation between the two criteria led to the need for a limited amount of re-analysis and design modifications.

One difference is that the CEGB single failure criterion refers to performance of the overall safety function whereas the NII criterion is to be applied separately to each system providing a 'protective action'. The significance of this is that where diverse systems are provided to meet the probabilistic targets the CEGB criterion can be interpreted to apply to both systems together, whereas in the case of the NII criterion this is to be applied separately to each system.

Another difference is that whereas the CEGB criterion is interpreted to be applied following a single initiating fault, the NII criterion clearly specifies that it should also be applied following fault combinations for which the system is required to act.

As an example, the Emergency Charging System, referred to in section 3, is only required to act following fault combinations (specifically multiple equipment failures). This system together with the Chemical and Volume Control System, which normally provides the functions of RCP seal protection and long term boration, have sufficient redundancy to meet the single failure criterion. However, when considering the Emergency Charging System alone, the original design shown on Figure 1 was susceptible to single failures by virtue of common pipework and equipment downstream of the two redundant steam driven pumps. In order to improve this capability and hence satisfy the NII criterion, the design of the Emergency Charging System was modified to eliminate the potential for such failures disabling the whole system, Figure 2.

However, it is not only systems that are new to Sizewell 'B' that have been modified as a result of single failure assessment. As a further example, the Component Cooling Water System, a demineralised water system which forms part of the heat rejection route, is selected. This system is similar in principle to that provided on the SNUPPS units (the major differences being due to the fact that Sizewell 'B' is a coastal site). For this system, the general redundancy and disposition of plant was determined to be acceptable with one particular exception. The Component Cooling Water System, whilst having two separate trains of equipment, has interconnections between these two trains to allow the cooling of certain non-redundant components to be achieved from either train, see Fig 3. It was determined that the failure of the pressure boundary of the normally shut train isolation valve on the suction side of the pumps could jeopardise both trains of the system by draining both surge tanks prior to 30 minutes (the time at which manual intervention could be claimed). A simple design change, the re-arrangement of these valves and the adjacent non-return valves, has been made to the design preventing the failure leading to loss of the whole system. This re-arrangement is illustrated in Fig 3.

The Fuel Storage Pond Cooling System provides a final example. The safety role of this system is to remove heat from the fuel storage pond by means of closed loop cooling of the pondwater. The system is similar in principle to that of the SNUPPS units but on Sizewell 'B' the system comprises four 100% pumps rather than two i.e. two pumps in each of two separate trains, see Fig 4. Nonetheless, a limiting passive failure in the suction line of one of the trains was determined to lead to a loss of inventory from the fuel storage pond affecting both trains of the Fuel Storage Pond Cooling System

as well as disabling by flooding one of the
safety means of providing make-up water to the
pond situated adjacent to this train (the
flask preparation bay water transfer system).
Providing make-up water to the pond is a back-
up means (independent from the cooling system)
of adequately protecting spent fuel in the
event of loss of normal cooling.

A way of limiting the consequences of
this failure was determined and is being
adopted for Sizewell 'B'. This consists of
altering the relative position of the suction
lines of the two trains within the fuel
storage pond such that the consequences of
the passive failure are limited to no worse
than:

(i)   the loss of both trains of the
        cooling system

(ii)   the loss of one train of the cooling
        system and the adjacent make-up
        provisions.

The results of ongoing detailed safety
assessments, such as the single failure
analyses discussed above, are fed through to
the system designers via updates of the
initial system functional specifications. In
the main this provides for a more complete
justification of existing requirements rather
than new requirements.

This process of updating functional
requirements extends up to the
Pre-Operational Safety Report (POSR). At
this stage a fully complete and verified set
of functional requirements, consistent with
the POSR, is available which confirms the
adequacy of the detailed design
implementation.

In the event of a safety assessment
showing the need to modify the plant design,
as in the above examples for the Emergency
Charging System, the Component Cooling Water
System or the Fuel Storage Pond Cooling
System, the design modification has to be
separately endorsed as necessary and sufficient.
This is the subject of a carefully controlled
change procedure.

5   CONCLUSIONS

A satisfactory safety case has been presented
for the Sizewell 'B' Power Station and the
necessary licensing clearances have been
obtained to enable construction to proceed.
System Functional Specifications are produced
to ensure that the detailed design
implementation is consistent with the safety
case. Safety analyses having the potential to
impact the plant design are largely completed.
In particular, the system single failure analyses
have recently been completed. Updating of system
functional specifications is carried out to take
account of such analyses. It is firmly
anticipated that any future safety analysis will
confirm the adequacy of the Sizewell 'B' design.

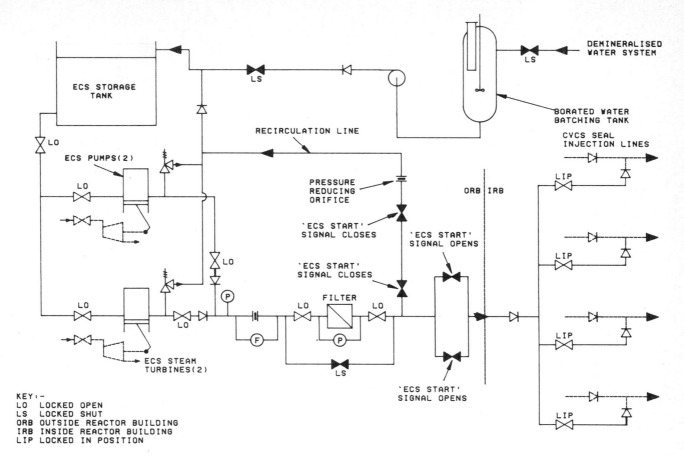

KEY:-
LO   LOCKED OPEN
LS   LOCKED SHUT
ORB OUTSIDE REACTOR BUILDING
IRB INSIDE REACTOR BUILDING
LIP LOCKED IN POSITION

Fig 1   Original emergency charging system (ECS)

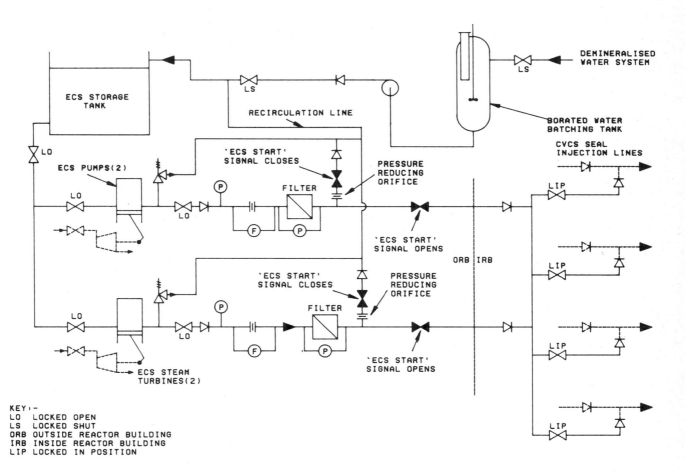

KEY:-
LO   LOCKED OPEN
LS   LOCKED SHUT
ORB OUTSIDE REACTOR BUILDING
IRB INSIDE REACTOR BUILDING
LIP LOCKED IN POSITION

Fig 2   Emergency charging system (ECS)

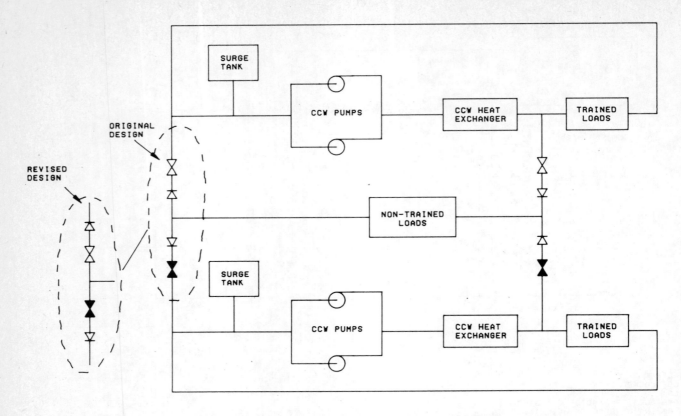

Fig 3   Component cooling water (CCW) system — simplified schematic

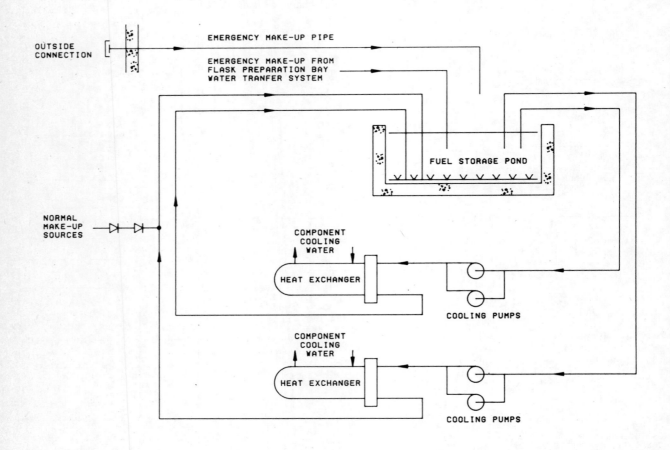

Fig 4   Fuel storage pond cooling system

C388/010

Radioactive waste management at Sizewell 'B'

K RUTTER, BSc
PWR Project Group, National Power Division of CEGB, Knutsford, Cheshire

SYNOPSIS This paper outlines the CEGBs approach to radioactive waste management at Sizewell 'B'. The methods proposed by the CEGB to limit the volume of radioactive waste arisings are discussed and the design and the proposed methods of operation of the radwaste plant are presented.

1 INTRODUCTION

This paper describes the CEGBs proposal for radioactive waste (radwaste) management at Sizewell 'B'. The radwaste systems have been designed to satisfy the requirements of both the National and the CEGB radioactive waste management strategies. These strategies require that; waste arisings are minimised, disposal of low level (LLW), and intermediate level (ILW) solid wastes is effected as early as possible, and that discharges to the environment are maintained as low as reasonably practicable (ALARP).

The minimisation of waste arisings takes two forms, firstly, at source by the appropriate selection of materials and operating conditions in the primary circuit, and secondly, during operation by limiting the volumes of waste sent to the radwaste plant for processing.

The radwaste plant operator is provided with processing facilities such that he can select the most appropriate liquid waste treatment process to meet the ALARP commitment and that solid waste arisings can be packaged into a form suitable for early disposal off-site.

2 THE LIMITATION OF RADIOACTIVE WASTE ARISINGS

2.1 Introduction

The design and the proposed mode of operation of Sizewell 'B' will have a significant effect on the amount of activity which arises from reactor operations. It should be noted however that the majority of these measures have been adopted primarily with the aim of reducing radiation doses to operators, rather than reducing the volume of radwaste arisings.

2.2 Sources of Radioactivity

The radioactivity which arises from station operation can be divided into three classes:

(a) Fission products; which arise principally as leakage from any failed fuel in the reactor, or as an impurity from the fissioning of 'tramp uranium dioxide' present on the outside of the fuel pins.
(b) Activation products; which arise as a result of the activation of the constituents of the coolant.
(c) Corrosion products; which arise from the activation of corrosion products released from the internal surfaces of the reactor primary circuit.

The important radioactive species are those which are assumed to be circulating at high temperature and pressure in the primary circuit and which could be routed to the radwaste plant during station operation. Each radionuclide is separately assessed for its contribution to off-site doses. Those radionuclides that contribute significantly to off-site doses can be given special attention to minimise their impact. For Sizewell 'B' the major contributor to the off-site dose is from the liquid discharge stream, which is dominated by corrosion products.

2.3 Principal Sources of Liquid and Solid Wastes

The operation of the Chemical and Volume Control System (CVCS) to control the reactor coolant chemistry leads to the removal of significant amounts of radioactivity from the primary circuit via the filters and demineralisers in the CVCS system. These filters and demineralisers also capture large quantities of corrosion products released from the primary circuit into the coolant during the period when the reactor is being bought to cold shutdown. The CVCS filter cartridges and demineraliser resins become solid waste when they are replaced.

If primary to secondary leakage occurs in the steam generators radioactive species present in the primary circuit coolant will be released into the secondary circuit.

Ultimately these leaked radioactive species will lead to the production of radioactively contaminated resins and cartridge filters associated with the control of secondary circuit conditions. They may also contaminate any sludges present in the base of the steam generators.

2.4 Limitation of Arisings

2.4.1 Fission Products

The integrity of the cladding which surrounds the irradiated fuel is of paramount importance in reducing the release of fission products from the fuel during both reactor and refuelling operations. The incidence of fuel defects has shown a marked decline, as a result of improvements in manufacturing techniques (1).

Another cause of fission product releases is the failure of fuel in service due to an incipient defect in the reactor plant. The most notable failure of this type is due to 'baffle jetting' which causes the fuel cladding to fail due to fatigue as a result of jet impingement. A redesign incorporated for Sizewell 'B' will remove this potential defect.

A further cause of fuel failure is erosion by foreign bodies within the primary circuit fluid. A rigorous policy of primary circuit cleanliness, during all phases of reactor operation, will be implemented at Sizewell 'B' to minimise the potential for this type of fuel failure.

2.4.2 Corrosion Products

Corrosion products within the primary circuit arise from two sources; firstly, the direct release from in-core surfaces, and secondly, from the deposition, activation and re-release from in-core surfaces.

Three principal methods of reducing the production of corrosion products have been adopted at Sizewell 'B'. These are; firstly the careful selection of materials, both in-core and within the primary circuit to ensure that corrosion product release is minimised, secondly, the adoption of a reducing chemistry regime for the primary circuit fluid, and thirdly, pre-operational and pre-commissioning practices.

2.4.2.1 Material Selection

Cobalt is the major contributor to activity in corrosion products and as a result a major programme of cobalt reduction has been applied to Sizewell 'B'. Cobalt in the primary circuit arises from two sources; firstly, as an impurity in components such as piping, reactor internals and steam generator tubing, and secondly, as the principal constituent in hard facing alloys (such as Stellites), used in applications where a combination of good wear and corrosion resistance is required.

The steam generator tubing represents by far the greatest area of metal exposed to the coolant, and the potential for the release of corrosion products is very large. Much effort has been expended, by the CEGB to reduce the various forms of corrosion of steam generator tubes, and the alloy to be employed at Sizewell 'B' exhibits reduced corrosion compared with the alloy most widely used at present.

The use of Inconel 690 steam generator tubing rather than Inconel 600 will result in a reduction in the overall material release to the primary circuit, and a reduction in cobalt release from the steam generator tubing by a factor of up to two.

The CEGB have committed to undertake a programme to qualify non cobalt containing alloys for hard facings, particularly for valve applications, although alternate alloys have not been qualified in time for application at Sizewell 'B'.

2.4.2.2 Primary Circuit Chemistry

The overriding requirements for the primary circuit coolant are that it should perform the function of heat transfer and it should contribute to core reactivity control without prejudice to the integrity of structural materials, components and fuel cladding.

For structural materials (stainless steel, and Inconel) general corrosion is unlikely to be a significant issue. Environmentally assisted cracking of Inconel 600 steam generator tubes has been reported, however, Inconel 690, which has been selected for Sizewell 'B', is much less susceptible to such failure.

For fuel cladding material, a chemistry regime which restricts general corrosion is required in order to prevent the formation of thick oxide films which would impair heat transfer to the fuel and eventually lead to fuel failure.

The CEGB have recognised that radiation levels around the primary circuit are influenced by the composition of the primary circuit and much effort has been devoted to evaluating the primary circuit chemistry which leads to the least activation. A 'high pH' chemistry appears to lead to reductions of up to an order of magnitude in the primary coolant activity with the consequent benefit of reductions in the specific activity of liquid radwaste arising. Worldwide experience has shown that reductions in primary circuit activity as a result of 'high pH' operation have occurred and it is expected that a primary circuit chemistry regime giving these improvements will be adopted for Sizewell 'B'.

2.4.2.3 Pre-operation

The importance of pre-operational cleanliness and of careful operation during plant

40

commissioning has been clearly demonstrated by French PWR operational experience where significant circuit contamination has occured (Fessenheim) as a result of inappropriate plant commissioning procedures. The French now take great care to establish clean conditions in the primary circuit prior to operation and significant benefits in operator dose reduction have accrued from this programme.

It is intended that a similarly rigorous control over plant commissioning and pre-operation procedures will be exercised at Sizewell 'B' to ensure that clean conditions are maintained in the primary circuit right up to power raise.

2.4.3 Activation Products

The activation products carbon 14 and tritium are produced by direct activation of the coolant and nothing realistically can be done to limit their production. Tritium is a ternary fission product of the fuel and diffuses into the coolant through the fuel cladding walls.

2.4.4 Steam Generator Primary/Secondary Leakage

There have been numerous instances of primary to secondary leakage associated with steam generator tube degradation in operating PWRs. The factors that contribute to this tube degradation, in particular operating chemistry and design considerations, have been identified and steps taken to reduce tube degradation and the associated primary to secondary leakage.

Tighter control has been imposed on secondary circuit chemistry and this has resulted in a reduction in the number of forced outages due to steam generator tube degradation. The chemistry control to be applied at Sizewell 'B' will be at least as strict as that currently applied to operating PWRs, and the benefits associated with improved water chemistry will be applicable to Sizewell 'B'.

In addition to improved operating chemistry, the Sizewell 'B' steam generator design (Model F) has been modified to reduce the possibility of tube degradation. Specific modifications include:

(a) broached quatrafoil alloy steel (Type 405) tube support plates replace the previously used drilled circular hole carbon steel configuration, to mitigate against tube 'denting'
(b) full depth hydraulic expansion of the tubes into the tubesheet to prevent concentration of an aggressive environment within the tubesheet and the resultant possibility of tube degradation
(c) selection of a more corrosion resistant tube material
(d) stress relief annealing of the small radius U bends to prevent stress corrosion cracking from the primary side

(e) modification of flow distribution to reduce sludge accumulation on top of the tubesheet

The effectiveness of these measures has been demonstrated by the fact that to date there have been no reported unforced outages associated with primary to secondary leakage in Model F steam generators.

3 GASEOUS RADWASTE MANAGEMENT

The design of the Gaseous Radwaste System (GRWS) includes the following specific functions; to delay short lived radionuclides to allow for decay prior to release to the environment such that radiation doses to the operating staff and the public are As Low As Reasonably Achievable (ALARA), to exercise appropriate control of the GRWS in order to reduce to a very low level the risk of an internal hydrogen explosion and to maintain the system boundary.

3.1 Gaseous Radwaste System Design

The primary source of influent gas to the GRWS is via the continuous purge of the volume control tank with hydrogen. The continuous operation of the GRWS serves to reduce the fission gas concentration in the reactor coolant system which, in turn, reduces the escape of fission gases during maintenance operations or through equipment leakages. Smaller quantities are received, via the vent connections from the boron recycle evaporator gas stripper, the reactor coolant drain tank, the pressuriser relief tank, and the boron recycle hold-up tanks.

During the Tender stage for the radwaste plant, it was proposed that the CEGB should consider an alternative method of radwaste gas treatment to that adopted for SNUPPS. The alternative process involves the use of activated charcoal to delay the discharge of noble gas isotopes to achieve the required discharge levels. Charcoal bed delay systems (CBDS) have been adopted worldwide for the treatment of gaseous radwaste arisings at both PWR and BWR stations.

The CBDS proposed for Sizewell 'B' consists of two identical trains of process equipment, with sufficient interconnections such that any component in either train can operate with other system components in either train. Facilities are provided to purge any system component, with nitrogen, back to the input of the operating process train. The design provides for maximum system availability under envisaged operating conditions of the CBDS.

The design and operation of the CBDS is based on the use of activated charcoal in the guard and main bed vessels to delay the passage of fission product gases through the charcoal beds by selective adsorption and desorption. The delay time between adsorption and desorption of the fission product gases is sufficient to allow for a substantial decay, thus minimising active gaseous discharges.

The Sizewell 'B' CBDS is designed to provide a minimum of 45 days for xenon 131m under all envisaged operating regimes. The 45 days delay period allows for the xenon 131m activity (12 days half life) to decay to an acceptable level. Krypton 85 the other major constituent of the GRWS flow has a half life of 10.8 years and is therefore unaffected by delays of this magnitude.

An analysis of the anticipated operating cycles of the GRWS has concluded that a design target delay time of 65 days for xenon 131m, at normal operating temperature (18°C) will ensure that the minimum of 45 days delay will be achieved under all envisaged operating conditions.

The amount of charcoal required for the main adsorber beds in order to achieve the design minimum delay time of 65 days of Xenon isotopes is calculated using the method presented in section 2.2.13 of NUREG 0017 'The PWR Gale Code'(2). The value of the dynamic adsorption coefficient recommended in (2) has been adopted for Sizewell 'B'. Table 1 presents a comparison between the operating parameters selected for Sizewell 'B' and existing CBDS installations at other operating PWR stations.

The main flowpath of the CBDS consists of a single pass through a cooler condenser, gas reheater, charcoal guard bed, charcoal main adsorber bed, and a high efficiency particulate (HEPA) filter. The cooler condenser has two refrigeration units, one being on standby. A second, complete redundant train of process equipment is provided. Each process train is provided with oxygen content and moisture content monitoring instrumentation, to alert the radwaste plant operator to malfunction of the process equipment.

After treatment in the CBDS the gas is discharged to atmosphere via a dedicated stack. The gaseous discharge is continuously monitored. Should the level of activity in the discharge stream rise above that authorised for discharge, an isolation valve in the discharge line is automatically closed to terminate the discharge.

3.2 Gaseous Radwaste System Operation

Two process trains of equipment are provided, the selection of the duty train being via manually operated isolation valves, the stand-by train being protected by locked shut valves. It is intended that one process train will be on permanent stand-by used only if a failure occurs on the duty train, and except under exceptional circumstances the stand-by main bed will be kept clean at all times.

3.2.1 Normal Operation

In the planned mode of normal operation fresh hydrogen gas is continuously introduced into the volume control tank where it mixes with fission gases, stripped from the reactor coolant by the action of the volume control tank letdown line spray nozzle. The gas is continually vented from the volume control tank at the desired pressure and flow rate via a pressure control valve, into the inlet manifold of the carbon bed delay system. The hydrogen pressure acts as the driving force to maintain flow through the system.

The CBDS also accepts flows on an intermittent basis from a number of other plant items. These intermittent flows are operator accepted.

The moist incoming gas is cooled to approximately 4°C in the cooler condenser. The process gas is cooled in a coil near the bottom of the tank and the water that is condensed is removed in a separator vessel inside the tank. The condensate drains by gravity to the drain collection tank.

Gas leaving the cooler condenser goes through a section of piping heated by electric tracing. Heating the gas to approximately ambient temperature lowers its relative humidity, thereby reducing the equilibrium moisture level of the activated charcoal and raising its delay coefficient.

The dehumidified warm gas then passes through the guard bed, adsorber bed and HEPA filter, ultimately discharging to the environment, via a single line.

Start-Up

At plant start-up the operator selects the stream to be used, and manually sets all valves in the system in the correct position.

Cooling the glycol in the cooler condensers is initiated, to speed the cooling operation, both refrigerators can be used. Once the glycol has reached normal operating temperature the system will be nitrogen purged. The purge gas is discharged via the normal flow discharge line.

Final start-up is effected by initiating gas flow from source.

Shutdown

The system is shutdown by simply stopping the flow. The outlet valve is closed to prevent oxygen from entering the system.

3.2.2 System Faults

(a) Moisture Ingress

If remedial measures fail to prevent excessive moisture being carried over to the guard bed, the guard bed will absorb the moisture and the operator will be alerted to the problem by the moisture analysers.

The alarm level of the moisture analyser will be set such that moisture carryover to the guard bed will be minimised. Should the moisture content alarm be activated, the operator has a number of options available to him; he can switch to the standby cooler condenser; he can switch

to the standby guard bed purging the 'wet'
guard bed with dry nitrogen to drive off
the excess moisture (the purge flow being
routed to the inlet of the operational
process stream); or he can, if the moisture
level of the influent gas is such that
the integrity of the main bed is at risk,
isolate the GRWS whilst the source of
the moisture ingress is investigated and
isolated.

(b) Oxygen Ingress

The GRWS normally operates with a hydrogen
atmosphere, the only other process gas
routinely handled by the system is
nitrogen, used for system purging. The
ingress of oxygen to the GRWS could, if
undetected, lead to the formation of a
potentially explosive mixture within the
GRWS. The GRWS incorporates features
to limit the potential for, and minimise
the consequence of, oxygen ingress to
the GRWS.

Duplicate oxygen analysers are provided
downstream of the cooler condensers, these
will alert the operators to the presence
of oxygen in the process stream. The
alarm level of the analyser will be set
at a significant margin above the Higher
Flammability Limit (HFL) for oxygen in
hydrogen mixtures to give the operator
time to identify and isolate the oxygen
source before a hazardous condition
occurs.

The GRWS is designed to withstand the
effects on an internal hydrogen explosion.
The GRWS is not designed against the von
Neumann spike as it is of such short
duration that vessels and pipes of typical
engineering dimensions do not have
sufficient time to respond to the spike
(approx 10^{-6} seconds). The GRWS is however
designed against the more important
Chapman-Jouget pressure level, which has
a time duration of the same order of
magnitude as the natural breathing
oscillations of vessels and pipes. In
addition during the detonation the maximum
stress levels in elements such as flanges
are functions of the elements natural
frequency. This concept allows the
calculation of a dynamic loading factor
for each component in the system. The
dynamic loading factor is dependent on
the components actual configuration.

To ensure that no pressure boundary
violations occur during a hydrogen
detonation, the calculated stress levels
must be within values which permit
pressure containment without significant
oversizing of components.

Dependent upon the particular component,
its geometry and its operating pressure,
the actual pressure experienced during
the transient will vary. The resulting
calculated stress is approximately twice
the code allowable static stress level.
This is less than the dynamic yield limit

of the material, which is approximately
three times the code allowable (static)
stress.

The main function of the GRWS is to prevent
the unauthorised discharge of gaseous activity
from the plant. Even if, due to multiple
plant failures in the GRWS, both main delay
beds were unable to provide the design delay
period the automatic discharge isolation valves
would close on the detection of high discharge
activity by the duplicated discharge radiation
monitors and terminate the discharge.

The loss of the GRWS does not lead to an
unauthorised discharge and also it does not
have an effect on the principal upstream
source, the Volume Control Tank. The reactor
can continue to operate and can be brought
to cold shutdown conditions, if required,
without the GRWS being in service.

4   LIQUID RADWASTE MANAGEMENT

The Liquid Radwaste System (LRWS) must be
designed to ensure; satisfactory integrity
of containment isolation, where it interfaces
with the LRWS; that radiation doses to station
staff and members of the public are 'As Low
As Reasonably Achievable' (ALARA) and that
discharges to the environment comply with
the requirements of the Department of the
Environment (DoE) and the Ministry of
Agriculture Fisheries and Food (MAFF).

4.1 Liquid Radwaste System Design

The LRW processing facilities proposed for
Sizewell 'B' consist of a number of discrete
process routes. The selection of treatment
route for a liquid waste arising depends upon;
the source of the waste, the processing
required, and the ultimate destination of the
processed fluid.

Facilities for radio-chemical and
conventional chemical sampling are provided
by the Radwaste Sampling System and all
discharge paths are monitored for activity
by the Process Radiation Monitoring system.
The LRWS is divided into subsystems so that
the different drain streams can be processed
separately dependent on the nature and activity
of the various influents. The subsystems
are manually initiated.

Each subsystem consists of accumulation
tanks, transfer pumps, filters and with the
exception of the chemical drains sub-system,
monitor tanks and associated discharge pumps.

Drain Channel 'A' contains the radwaste
evaporator and the distillate demineraliser,
whilst Drain Channel 'B' contains the radwaste
monitor tank demineraliser and the radwaste
charcoal absorber.

4.1.1 Drain Channel 'A'

Drain channel 'A' normally collects clean
tritiated waste from the reactor coolant

system via the equipment drains system, the gaseous waste system and the reactor coolant drain tank. It can also collect effluents from the radwaste evaporator distillate filter for reprocessing.

4.1.2 Drain Channel 'B'

The influents to this system may be contaminated with boric acid, chromates and organics. Some of the influents are potentially active from the radioactive floor and equipment drains subsystem (DRW) which collects miscellaneous leakage from systems within the controlled areas of the auxiliary and containment buildings. Generally, the amount of reactor coolant leakage in these areas is very small, the bulk of the leakage being from non-radioactive or only slightly radioactive systems. Drain Channel 'B' also collects decontamination water used for routine area wash downs, spent fuel flask wash downs and laboratory equipment decontamination rinses. The chemical solutions used to clean the walls and floor of the refuelling pool are also collected by the floor drains subsystem and processed as necessary. The active floor drains tanks have provision for pH adjustment.

Facilities for oil interception and separation are not provided for the floor drains system. This is in line with the experience gained from the French and US operating stations where oil separators are not provided on floor drains systems.

4.1.3 Laundry and Hot Shower Subsystem

The Laundry and Hot Shower Subsystem (LHSS) collects waste water from, the personnel showers and handbasins in the main changeroom, and from the active laundry. The LHSS process fluid contains detergent, but is low in activity and does not normally require treatment prior to discharge.

Effluent from the showers and handbasins in the main changerooms passes through a radiation monitor prior to entering the LHSS accumulation tank, and if the activity is low it is routed to the Secondary Liquid Waste System for discharge.

4.1.4 Chemical Drains Subsystem

The CDT subsystem receives spent samples composed of chemically contaminated tritiated water from the plant sample stations.

Chemically contaminated decontamination wastes from the decontamination centre, or decontamination wastes from local decontamination operations may also be received by the radwaste chemical drain tank if they are not suitable for processing.

4.1.5 Radwaste Discharge Main

The radwaste discharge main is double contained throughout its length and leakage detection facilities are provided. Here the effluent is mixed with the discharge from the Circulating Water (CW) system, prior to the discharge to the sea via the CW outfall.

The dilution of the effluent from the radwaste building by the CW discharge flow will give an equivalent Dilution Factor of approximately 3500.

4.2 Liquid Radwaste System Operation

The LRWS provides the plant operator with the maximum possible flexibility with regard to processing options. The operator having sampled the appropriate LRWS inlet collection tank, can select, based on the results of the sample analysis, the most appropriate process and discharge route. The selected route is then set up by making the appropriate manual adjustments to the plant operating valves. All important process valves are provided with limit switches which indicate process routing on a mimic display in the radwaste control room. The limit switches also provide input to the LRWS programmable logic controller (PLC), which provides both permissive and plant protection interlocks to prevent hazard to the plant, or the operators, due to inappropriate process routing. The cross connections, which provide alternative process routes between the main process channels are protected by locked shut valves, under administrative control.

Operation of the LRWS is essentially the same during all phases of normal reactor plant operation; the only differences are in the load on the system. The LRWS is not required for safe reactor shutdown.

4.2.1 Drain Channel 'A' Operation

Normally waste is accumulated in the radwaste hold-up tank and when the level reaches a pre-set value the waste is sampled, pH adjusted if necessary, and pumped via a filter to monitor tank 'A'.

After sampling in monitor tank 'A' the liquid, if acceptable for discharge, is discharged via the radwaste discharge line to the CW surge chamber, via the on-line radiation monitor and the flow proportional sampler.

If the waste is unsuitable for direct discharge, the waste evaporator is aligned to the radwaste evaporator feed pumps and the evaporator is started. The distillate is then pumped continuously to monitor tank 'A' for discharge. If, however, it is desired to recover the water, the evaporator distillate may be processed further. First by passing through the distillate demineraliser, and then if necessary through the liquid radwaste charcoal adsorber to the radwaste evaporator distillate tank. This tank is fitted with a diaphragm to prevent oxygen ingress into the water.

When it is desired to reduce tritium levels in the plant, distillate from the BRS evaporator will be directed to monitor tank 'A' for discharge. At such times, the waste from drain channel 'A' may be discharged to monitor tank 'B', either directly or after processing.

4.2 Drain Channel 'B' Operation

Normally, one active floor drains tank is aligned to receive the discharge from the floor and equipment drains system while the other tank is being used as a hold-up tank. This procedure allows the waste to be sampled and pH adjusted (if necessary). The waste is filtered prior to discharge, when the effluent is transferred to monitor tank 'B', mixed and again sampled.

If the radioactivity is too high for direct discharge and the total dissolved solids are low (25ppm) the effluent is returned to the active floor drains tank for treatment in the radwaste monitor tank demineraliser before disposal.

If the radioactivity is high and the total dissolved solids are also high, the effluent may be transferred to drain channel 'A' for processing either directly by the radwaste evaporator or to the radwaste hold-up tank for hold-up and subsequent processing by the radwaste evaporator if necessary.

4.2.3 Laundry and Hot Shower Subsystem Operation

The effluent from the plant laundry is collected in the laundry and hot shower system drain tank, located in the mechanical annexe, from where it is transferred, on level control, to the active laundry and hot shower tank in the radwaste building. When this tank is full, a batch of liquid is transferred to the selected monitor tank, via a filter, where it is mixed, sampled and then discharged to the CW surge chamber via the radwaste discharge main.

A second monitor tank is provided for the laundry and hot shower system and under high in-flow conditions, one monitor tank may be filled as the other is being discharged.

4.4 Chemical Drains Systems Operation

Spent radioactive samples and chemical waste from the plant sample stations are collected in the chemical drains tank when the nuclear laboratories are in use. Normally one tank is used to accumulate the waste while the second is heldup for delay or for discharge at a convenient time. Before discharging, the contents of the selected tank are mixed by recirculation, sampled and pH adjusted (if necessary). The tank contents are then discharged to the environment via the chemical drains tank filter.

However, small quantities of radioactive waste may be transferred to the solid radwaste management system for solidification if necessary.

4.3 Liquid Discharge Monitoring

All liquid treatment systems have a radiation monitor located in their discharge manifold.

The monitor takes a constant-mass fraction of the liquor being discharged into a lead shielded counting chamber, the shielding being required to reduce background. Positioned in the chamber is a sodium iodide scintillator detector assembly, chosen because its sensitivity is sufficient to detect the predicted gamma activity levels.

A flow proportional liquid effluent sampler is provided to extract a fully representative sample, including particulates, from the liquid radwaste stream, prior to entering the CW outfall pipe.

The sampler operates by drawing effluent continuously from the main effluent pipeline, through a sample loop, and returning it to the line. The liquid running through this loop is sampled by testing small, frequent aliquots, using a linear acting shuttle valve. The frequency of valve operation is controlled by an electromagnetic flowmeter installed in the effluent line; sample rate being directly proportional to effluent discharge rate.

The sampler is interlocked with a final discharge valve which prevents radwaste discharge when the sampler is not switched on or fails in service. In the latter case provision is made to administratively override the interlock so that the discharge can proceed.

4.4 Liquid Radwaste System Discharge Levels

Treatment facilities exist within the LRWS to reduce the level of activity discharge from any of the influent streams. A cost benefit study carried out on the treatment of liquid wastes concluded that even for Drain Channels 'A' and 'B' the additional processing cost was grossly disproportionate to the monentary value of the reduction in discharge. The source of this additional processing cost is the increase in solid waste arisings concomitant with the use of the LRWS processing facilities.

The increased usage of the demineralisers or the radwaste evaporators will lead to increased volumes of spent resins and evaporator concentrates that will have to be processed by the SWMS.

Table 2 presents, in ranking order, the predicted reductions in liquid activity discharge based on the treatment of Drain Channels 'A' and 'B', the increase in solid waste arisings as a result of this treatment, and the calculated increase in operator dose.

From Table 2 it can be seen that the treatment of Drain Channel 'A' is the most beneficial single option (in terms of discharge reduction) followed by the treatment of Drain Channels 'A' and 'B' together. The use of demineralisation only for Drain Channels 'A' and 'B' should provide the most beneficial mode of operation as it provides a significant reduction in liquid discharge activity (approx. 83%), whilst keeping the increase in both operator dose and solid waste arising to a minimum.

The treatment of discharge streams other than Drain Channels 'A' and 'B' has been shown to be impractical on a regular basis. However should full treatment of Drain Channels 'A' and 'B' be undertaken, these other discharge streams become the dominant contributors to the level of liquid discharge, and the selective treatment of 'higher than normal' activity batches will yield a reduction in liquid activity discharged and will not incur significant penalties in terms of either solid waste arisings or operator dose.

5 SOLID WASTE MANAGEMENT

The Solid Waste Management System (SWMS) collects, processes and packages radioactive wastes generated as a result of plant operation in normal and fault conditions, and accumulates this packaged waste in a safe manner prior to transport off-site for disposal.

The levels of radionuclides present in the arisings to the SWMS depend mainly on the activity in the reactor coolant system and the decontamination factors achieved in the chemical and volume control system, the boron recycle system and the fuel pool clean-up system.

In addition the levels of radionuclides present in the floor drains system, the steam generator blowdown system and the decontamination factors achieved in the liquid radwaste management system also have an impact on SWMS arisings.

The SWMS is designed to accumulate spent resins and evaporator concentrates for up to two years before processing, and the associated accumulation area is large enough to hold those wastes for a further period after packaging. For dry wastes, a post processing accumulation area is available to hold drummed low level wastes for one year. Both the drummed medium active waste store and the low/medium active large item wastestore are sized for station lifetime accumulation.

5.1 The Solidification System

The solidification system consists of a resin concentrating system, an encapsulation machine with both cement and polymer filling stations, a solids metering system, a new drum store, an active waste store and means of handling both new and filled drums.

The solidification system operates on a batch basis to solidify evaporator concentrates, chemical wastes, spent resins and spent activated charcoal. It can also be used to permanently encapsulate spent radioactive cartridge filters in drums.

The resin concentrating system transfers spent resin and charcoal from the appropriate storage tank to a hydrocyclone. Here the solids to water ratio is adjusted to provide the water content necessary to assure complete solidification when the slurry is mixed with solidification agent. The spent resin is then fed into a conical resin hopper where the resin settles providing a 100% flooded feedstock for the resin metering pump. From here the settled waste in the resin hopper is metered into the encapsulation machine.

At the encapsulation machine, empty drums (shielded as appropriate) are transferred from the new drum store to the first station within the encapsulation machine. The solidification agents may be either monomer or cement, however, it is anticipated that most wastes will be encapsulated in cement. Pre-set quantities of monomer/catalyst mixture or cement will be added at different stations within the machine. The active wastes i.e. resins, concentrates and chemical drains waste are also delivered directly into the drum at the various stations. Additional chemicals required for the solidification process may be added at either the active waste addition stations or the solidification agent stations. The drum contents are mixed during material addition using the sacrificial paddle which is located in the drum prior to entering the encapsulation machine.

The drums are then transferred to curing stations where they remain immobilised for the required curing period. The cured solid matrix is then subject to remotely controlled Quality Assurance checks. The drum is then capped and the lid (shielded as appropriate) is replaced. Radioactive spent filter cartridges may also be loaded into clean drums and encapsulated in a similar manner.

Upon completion of the encapsulation process, the drum surface is monitored for external contamination, which if found is removed by dry brushing and vacuuming techniques. Radiation levels are then recorded, this information will be passed directly to the drum data bank for inclusion on the drum identifying code. The drum is weighed, labelled and transferred remotely to the waste store.

5.2 Solid Waste Store

The store is divided into a conditioned waste store, a medium active drummed waste store, a low activity drummed waste store, and a medium/low activity large item waste store where used equipment and non standard packages are held. The active areas are shielded and means are provided for remote handling of the radioactive packages. In addition, a local buffer store is provided for the reception of low active dry waste.

The conditioned waste (ILW) will be disposed of in drums 1.2 metres high by 0.8 metres diameter, appropriately shielded internally to achieve 0.5 mGy/hr dose rate. The maximum weight of such drums is less than 5 tonne. Low active waste will be packaged in 200 litre steel drums for disposal without shielding.

The shielded storage area for the conditioned waste drums has a capacity of approximately 2400 drums. The low level storage area has a capacity of about eight hundred 200 litre drums. The area provided for the low/medium active store is where used equipment and non-standard packages will be stored. A further area of 4000 m^3 gross volume exists within the radwaste building which could be used as an additional accumulation area if required.

5.3 Solid Waste System Operation

The encapsulation machine is used when sufficient resins, filters or concentrates have accumulated. Resin from the selected resin storage tank is transferred to the hydrocyclone and after dewatering the resulting slurry is pumped in measured amounts into the drum under PLC control. The appropriate amount of monomer or cement is added at a separate filling station. Dependent on the process, further chemicals are added and the drum contents are mixed for a prescribed time. The drum is then transferred to the curing station.

The operator by directing the PLC, adjusts the amount and type of chemicals, and the mixing time to suit the activity and type of waste being encapsulated. After the appropriate quality assurance checks the drum surface activity is monitored and if found to be satisfactory the drum is capped and the lid replaced. The drum is then transferred to the conditioned waste store.

Evaporator concentrates are encapsulated in drums in a similar way except that they are transferred directly to the drum. When the concentrate transfer is complete, all lines are flushed with reactor make-up to prevent precipitation. Used filters are inserted into empty drums which are then filled with cement.

On completion of processing of all solid wastes the filled drums are accumulated in the appropriate store. Every year, or more frequently if desired, the drums are transferred to the despatch bay and loaded on to the transport vehicle. All solid waste is transported in approved containers.

Low level wastes are transported without the use of shielding because the levels of radioactivity are sufficiently low to meet the specified radiation limits for transport. Shielding of the more active wastes is achieved by the design of the drum, and the dose rates limited further by controlling the gamma radioactive contents in each package.

An assessment of drum radiation, made at the time of despatch of any radioactive waste material, ensures that all containers leaving the site are within prescribed limits. Similarly, external drum surface contamination measurements are made to ensure compliance with transport regulations.

The SWMS ensures that the radiation doses to both the station staff and members of the public are reduced to ALARA by employing on the station well proven methods and plant for handling waste, a versatile encapsulation machine which can use a variety of solidification matrices to ensure an adequate encapsulation of the radioactive species and by providing equipment to ensure that the volume of solid waste is minimised by best practicable means.

6   CONCLUSIONS

The paper presents the CEGBs proposals for the management of radioactive waste at Sizewell 'B'. The report also advances the case that the Board has satisfied the 'best practical means' approach to the limitation of radioactive waste arisings.

The limitation of radioactive waste arisings can be achieved by two distinct means, firstly by reducing the potential waste arisings at source by the prudent design and operation of both primary and secondary circuit plant and secondly by the judicious treatment of those arisings which cannot be stopped at source.

The paper also details the measures that have either, already been adopted for Sizewell 'B', or are under active consideration for adoption, to limit radioactive waste arisings at source. The measures adopted at the design stage are; the careful selection of filter sizes for the primary circuit, the selection of an appropriate primary circuit chemistry regime, the reduction of cobalt in primary circuit components (particularly the steam generator tubing, and the primary circuit pipework and rector internals), and the adoption of measures to prevent primary to secondary circuit leakage (such as; full depth tube expansion, increased corrosion resistance of steam generator tubes).

Measures that can be adopted during operation are; a strict policy of failed fuel management and the limitation of the volume of wastes sent to the liquid radwaste system during station operation (particularly in the period immediately post shutdown).

The design of the three principal radwaste treatment systems is presented. It is also demonstrated that; by the appropriate choices of processing equipment, provision of standby plant and of alternative processing routes for liquid wastes sufficient flexibility has been provided in the radwaste treatment systems to ensure that the authorised levels of activity discharge can be met under all normal and fault operational modes.

The case presented above for the management of gaseous, liquid and solid waste arisings at Sizewell 'B' satisfies the requirements of both the National and CEGB strategies for radioactive waste management. This is achieved with respect to minimisation of waste arisings, early disposal of LLW and ILW solid wastes, the flexibility of plant operability, and the control of discharges to the environment to as low as reasonably practicable.

It is concluded that the plant as designed is capable of managing wastes in accordance with Government strategy and Regulatory requirements.

REFERENCES

(1) Light Water Reactor Performance, American Nuclear Society - Topical Meeting, April 1988, Williamsburg, Virginia, USA

(2) NUREG 0017 'Calculation of Releases of Radioactive' Materials in Gaseous and Liquid Effluents from Pressurised Water Reactors (PWR - Gale Code), US NRC, April 1976.

Table 1 Comparison of CBDS Operating Parameters

STATION	OPERATING TEMPERATURE $^{\circ}$C	DEW POINT $^{\circ}$C	RELATIVE HUMIDITY %	FLOW RATE M^3 HR^{-1}	DYNAMIC ADSORPTION COEFF CM^3 $GRAM^{-1}$		XENON DELAY DAYS	CHARCOAL MASS kg
					XENON	KRYPTON		
VANDELLOS 2	18 - 40	4	40	1.7	300	17	45	6400
SOUTH TEXAS PROJECT	25 - 30	6	-	1.7	330	18.5	67.5	9755
KOREA 7 & 8 (TWIN UNIT)	40	-	-	3.4	284	16	77.2	19056
MILLSTONE 3	40	2	-	1.5	240	15	60	12550
SIZEWELL 'B' (OPERATING)	18	4	40	1.7	460	22	91	8125
SIZEWELL 'B' (DESIGN)	40	4	11	1.7	330	18	65	8125

Table 2 Treatment Options For Drain Channels A and B

TREATMENT OPTION	DCA GBq/yr	DCB GBq/yr	Other Streams GBq/yr	Total GBq/yr	Reduction GBq/yr	Additional Solid Waste Drums/yr	Additional Operator Dose (man-sv)
Minimum Treatment	629	233	56	918	-	-	-
DCA Demin	63	233	56	352	566	9	1×10^{-2}
DCA Evap & Demin	2.6×10^{-2}	233	56	289	629	17	4×10^{-2}
DCA & DCB Demin	63	35	56	154	764	17	2×10^{-2}
DAC & DCB Evap & Demin	0.26	1.1×10^{-2}	56	56	862	65	1.6×10^{-1}
DCB Demin	629	35	56	720	198	17	4×10^{-2}
DCB Evap & Demin	629	1.1×10^{-2}	56	685	233	48	1.2×10^{-1}

Note 1. Tritium not included
      2. Minimum treatmnt is hold-up, filter and discharge

C388/016

A proven technology for boron and liquid waste treatment systems of Sizewell 'B' PWR

G VALLEE, B FABRE and **P MAURY**
Stein Industrie, Velizy Villacoublay, France
A D McKAY, BSc, CEng, MIMechE
Davy McKee Nuclear Limited, Stockton-on-Tees, Cleveland

This paper concerns the design of the boron recycle and liquid radwaste treatment systems for SIZEWELL B nuclear power plant. The purpose of these two main systems is discussed with emphasis on the performance to be achieved. Processing into recyclable solutions of the borated water discharged from the reactor coolant circuit is described in detail with information on the selected equipment and operating procedures. Liquid radwaste treatment is also covered including the possible operating connections between these two main systems. The involvement of these systems in the radwaste treatment plant is summarized. Special attention is paid to the physical processes involved, namely degassing, evaporation and decontamination. The author shows ways in which the design has been optimized to improve decontamination performance in order to minimize discharge to the environment. This paper is based on the positive experience of STEIN INDUSTRIE - a subsidiary of the French Company ALSTHOM - in the design, supply and operation of about one hundred similar units since 1976.

In a pressurized water nuclear plant, special attention is paid to waste management in order to avoid hazardous material being released into the environment.

Every effort is therefore made in the RADWASTE TREATMENT PLANT to recycle reusable fluids after processing and to concentrate not directly reusable active material as much as possible before encapsulation and storage.

Different processes are necessary for liquid treatment : evaporation, gas-stripping and chemical.

STEIN INDUSTRIE -a subsidiary of the French Company ALSTHOM- has for over fourteen years been designing, manufacturing and operating liquid treatment systems by the evaporation and gas-stripping processes, under respectively Unitech/OTV licence.

The authors examine the boron recycle and liquid radwaste treatment systems for SIZEWELL B

SCHEME N° 1

I - PURPOSE OF THE TWO MAIN SYSTEMS

The primary use of these systems concerns the treatment of the reactor coolant discharge.

Reactor coolant contains boron -a neutron absorber- in the form of boric acid (H_3BO_3). The boron dilution is adjusted with the passage of time to compensate for the aging of the core, enabling the thermal power to be controlled (rapid and fine variation of the power is ensured by the rod cluster control assembly).

Boron content varies from a few tens of p.p.m. at the end of the fuel cycle to 1200 ppm at the start of a new cycle. Boron content is raised to a safety level of at least 2000 ppm during a re-fuelling period.

The boron content of the reactor coolant circuit is controlled by injection of make up water or concentrated boron solution (7000 ppm as boron) from the Chemical and Volume Control System.

The boron recycle evaporator processes the reactor coolant discharge and can operate in two modes : recycling (the most frequently used) or non-recycling.

In recycling operation, the reactor coolant is separated into two fluids :

- degassed deborated water of quality suitable for reinjection into the reactor coolant circuit

- concentrated boric acid solution (7000 ppm as boron) for reinjection into the Volume Control System.

In non-recycling operation, the evaporation is continued to obtain a boric acid concentration of 42 000 ppm as boron compatible with the encapsulation process. The concentrate is then drained to the radwaste concentrate tank prior to encapsulation.

Concentration by water evaporation is a general process. It is used for reactor coolant treatment as well as for liquid radwaste treatment.

In SIZEWELL B, as in all P.W.R. power plants, wastes are present in various auxiliary circuits : blowdown, vents and drain lines, chemical waste and floor washing detergent headers. These fluids form, the not directly reusable fluids because of their activity level and/or their chemical quality. Therefore it is stored in hold-up tanks for processing.

A function of the liquid waste treatment circuit is to separate the waste by evaporation into two constituents :

- a concentrate containing the activity of the solids and dissolved salts, which is drained to the Radwaste Concentrate Tank for encapsulation

- a distillate that can be discharged after monitoring or returned to the reactor circuit if suitable chemically and radiologically.

II - BORON RECYCLE EVAPORATOR SYSTEM

II.1 - Outline of boron recycle evaporator system

After storage in hold-up tanks, the reactor coolant is sent to an EVAPORATOR unit which separates the deborated water (distillate) from the concentrated boric acid solution.

The deborated water is then degassed in a GAS-STRIPPER unit to separate out the gaseous fission products and the hydrogen.

The degassed deborated water is suitable after demineralisation for reinjection into the reactor coolant. Recycling the distillate to the evaporator is possible if the required quality has not been achieved.

The expected performance data are :

- treatment capacity of 3.5 m^3/h

- stripping factor -i.e. the ratio between the gaseous activity concentration of the liquid before and after gas stripping-above 10^5

- boron concentration capacity of 7000 ppm or 42000 ppm

- decontamination factor -i.e. the ratio between the non-volatile radionuclide volumetric activity of the concentrate and of the distillate- greater than 10^6 for 42 000 ppm boron concentration mode.

SCHEME N° 2

II.2 - Description of boron recycle evaporator system

The boron recycle evaporator system includes two main sections : the concentrate and the distillate.

The concentrate section includes the EVAPORATOR unit formed by the following main components operating as a forced circulation loop :

- a heater (straight tube heat exchanger)

- an evaporator vapour vessel

- an axial flow circulating pump.

The volume of the concentrate loop is about 5 m^3 and the flowrate of the circulating pump about 1000 m^3/h.

The reactor coolant to be treated is pumped from a hold-up tank at an average flowrate of 3.5 m^3/h.

The evaporator vapour vessel separates the concentrate and the distillate sections.

The distillate section includes the decontamination column associated with evaporator vapour vessel together with the GAS STRIPPER unit formed by the following main components :

- a stripping column

- a distillate condenser (U tube type with free distillate level).

Various connections are associated with the Evaporator and Gas-stripping units such as :

- liquid feed

- concentrate discharge

- distillate recirculation

- distillate discharge

- concentrate and distillate sampling circuits

- active and non-active gas discharge

- services such as heating steam, cooling wate etc.

The materials used for this system are :

- Incoloy 825 for concentrate circuits

- Stainless steel 316 L for other process circuits

- Carbon steel for main services circuits.

II.3 - Operation of boron recycle evaporator system

When sufficient liquid has accumulated in the boron recycle storage tanks, the boron recycle evaporator system runs on a cycle basis. The operator selects the operating mode -recycling (7000 ppm boron) or non-recycling (42 000 ppm boron)-and the system runs automatically.

In the 7000 ppm boron mode, the operation of the system is cyclic with alternate distillate production and boron concentrate discharge.

By circulation through the heater, the temperature of the reactor coolant to be concentrated is increased. The vapour is produced by flashing in the vapour body, allowing concentration of the remaining liquid in the concentrate loop.

A constant level in the concentrate loop is maintained by injection of preheated coolant feed into the vapour vessel.

The vapour produced in the vapour vessel contains boron concentrate droplets which are separated from the vapour in two stages :

- gravity separation in the vapour vessel

- final separation in the decontamination column.

The final separation of the remaining concentrate droplets is achieved by contact of the vapour with clean distillate through venturi trays and a demister.

At this stage the vapour is deborated and needs to be condensed and degassed.

Degassing is the physical process of extracting dissolved gases from a liquid. Thermal gas stripping needs to be completed by diffusion gas-stripping, where the gas is desorbed from the liquid into the vapour phase. This is performed through systems allowing the transfer surface area between both the liquid and the gaseous phases to be increased.

SIZEWELL B gas-stripper is equipped with two sets of perforated trays.

The deborated vapour goes through the upper trays before condensing in the distillate condenser. The distillate obtained is first degassed by diffusion with the deborated vapour in the upper trays of the gas-stripper. A final degassing is performed in the lower trays by diffusion with clean vapour produced by reboiling of clean distillate at the bottom of the gas-stripper.
The clean vapour charged with active gas at the lower trays outlet joins the deborated vapour going to the condenser.

Non-condensible active gases are separated from the vapour in the condenser and sent to the gaseous radwaste system.

The distillate is pumped out from the bottom of the gas-stripper and sent to the storage tanks after cooling.

When the required boron concentration is reached in the concentrate loop, the distillate is recycled into the concentration loop while the concentrate is partially discharged for about ten minutes to the boron concentrate tanks. At the end of this cycle, the unit returns automatically to the distillate production mode for about 30 minutes to 2 hours, depending on the boron concentration of the reactor coolant feed, etc.

The operating procedure in the 42 000 ppm boron mode is similar to the 7000 ppm mode procedure, except for the boron concentrate discharge. When the 42000 ppm boron concentration is reached in the loop, the unit stops automatically and the loop is completely discharged by nitrogen pressure to the waste concentrate tanks under operator control.

III - RADWASTE EVAPORATOR SYSTEM

III.1 - Outline of radwaste evaporator system

The radwaste evaporator system concentrates :

- the liquid radwaste to 42 000 ppm boron concentration compatible with the encapsulation process or to 300 g/l dry solids

- the reactor coolant to a 42 000 ppm boron concentration for encapsulation.

The radwaste evaporation system can also process the reactor coolant to 7000 ppm acting as a back-up to the Boron Recycle System. For this duty, the evaporator system must be flushed and cleaned to remove all remaining hazardous materials resulting from the radwaste duty.

The expected performance data are similar to these of the boron recycle evaporator system.

III.2 - Description of radwaste evaporator system

The radwaste evaporator design is similar to the boron recycle evaporator design. The system is completed with two large 20 m^3 capacity radwaste concentrate tanks allowing about 2 years storage before encapsulation. These tanks are provided with air sparging to avoid hazardous material settling at the bottom.

The material used for radwaste concentrate circuits for evaporators and tanks is Inconel 625 instead of Incoloy 825.

III.3 - Operation of radwaste evaporator system

For reactor coolant treatment, operation of the radwaste evaporator system is identical to the operation of the boron recycle evaporator system.

For radwaste treatment, the operation is similar to 42000 ppm boron operation and the main differences being as follows:

- generally, radwaste do not carry any active gas, and so the gas-stripper is by-passed in the process operation

- therefore the distillate is directly pumped from the condenser instead of from the gas-stripper

- non-condensible gases separated in the condenser are sent directly to the HVAC instead of to the gazeous radwaste sytem.

PHOTO

IV - INTEGRATION OF THESE SYSTEM INTO THE RADWASTE TREATMENT PLANT

Both the boron recycle and liquid radwaste evaporator systems are located in the south-east of the Radwaste Treatment Building. Space for a third evaporator has been allowed for in a future extension.

These two systems occupy 300 m^2 on 4 levels, representing about 15 % of the volume of the radwaste plant.

The largest items of equipment are :

- the two concentrate tanks (h 5.8 m dia. 3.2 m)
- the vapour vessel (h 3.4 m dia. 1.7 m)
- the heater (h 5.7 m dia. 0.8 m)
- the decontamination column (h 4.4 m dia 1.3 m)
- the gas-stripper (h 4.8 m dia. 0.9 m)
- the concentrate loop pipe (dia. 0.6 m)

Each component in contact with the concentrate is located in individual shielded concrete cells. Active pipes run in special corridors. Active valves are located in valve rooms or valve boxes controlled by extended spindles or remote devices.

V - A PROVEN TECHNOLOGY

SIZEWELL B evaporator and gas-stripping systems are based on the experience and knowledge acquired by STEIN INDUSTRIE from the worldwide supply of about 100 treatment systems over the last fourteen years. The first units have been in operation for the last ten years.

SIZEWELL B treatment systems are designed on the basis of this proven technology and include the latest developments such as :

- integrated evaporator and gas stripper system. This design has been chosen for the 1500 MW N4 French PWR boron recycle system, which is an improvement over the 900 MW French PWR operating with an intermediate storage tank between the gas-stripper and the evaporator systems.

- decontamination column separate from the vapour vessel. The 900 MW French PWRs were initially provided with radwaste decontamination trays included in the vapour vessel. Fouling problems developed on these trays after a few years of operation, as the evaporators were treating some fluids not foreseen at the design stage. Separate decontamination columns were developed and have been in operation for the last three years.

- venturi trays for decontamination column. The use of such venturi trays is the result of cooperation with the French Company S.G.N.. Tricastin 900 MW French PWR is provided with these trays ensuring a high decontamination factor.

The design of a combined boron recycle and radwaste treatment in the same system, as required for SIZEWELL B, is the main difference compared with the French Unit. However, a combined system has been supplied for TIHANGE 2 (Belgium PWR) 8 years ago.

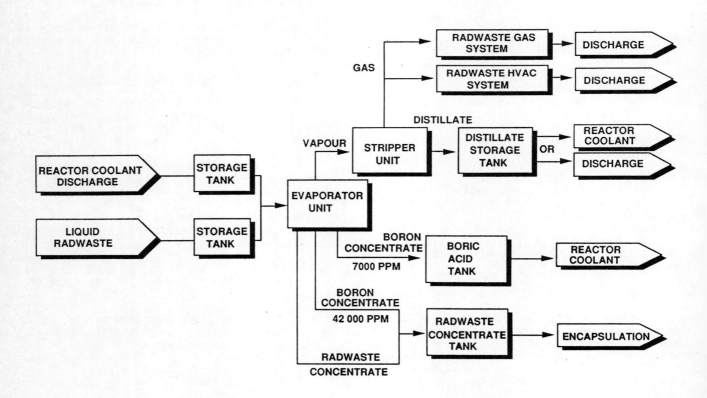

Fig 1   Sizewell 'B' radwaste evaporator system

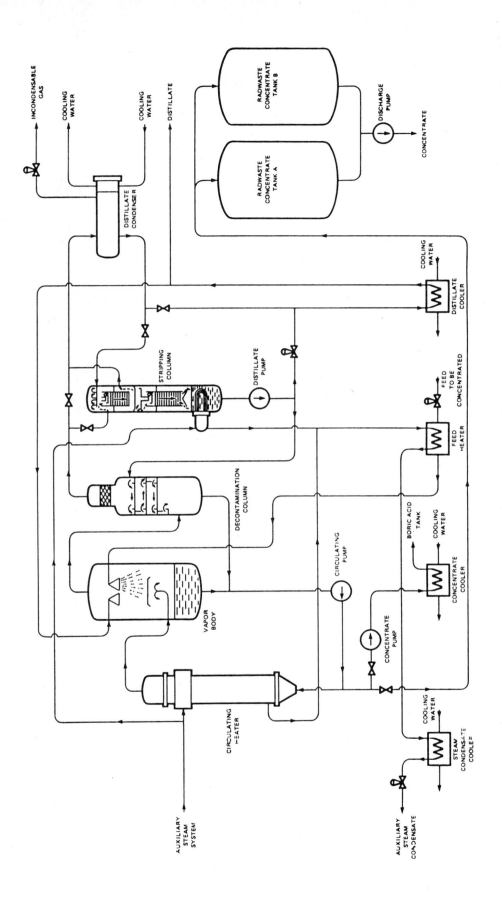

Fig 2 Radwaste evaporator system

Fig 3

C388/030

Steam turbine generators for Sizewell 'B' nuclear power station

J A HESKETH, BSc(Eng), CEng, MIMechE and **J MUSCROFT**, MA, CEng, MIMechE
GEC Alsthom Turbine Generators Limited, Rugby, Warwickshire

SYNOPSIS   The thermodynamic cycle of the modern 3000 RPM steam turbine as applied at Sizewell 'B' is presented. Review is made of the factors affecting thermal efficiency including the special nature of the wet steam cycle and the use of moisture separation and steam reheating.   Consideration is given to the optimisation of the machine and cycle parameters, including particular attention to reheating and to the provision of feedheating, in order to achieve a high overall level of performance.   A modular design approach has made available a family of machines suitable for the output range 600-1300 MW.   The constructional features of the 630 MW Sizewell 'B' turbine generators from this range are described in detail.   The importance of service experience with wet steam turbines and its influence on the design of modern turbines for pressurised water reactor applications is discussed.

1   INTRODUCTION

The power plant industry has, over the past 25 years, gained considerable experience in operating large turbines in wet steam nuclear applications.   The first such GEC machines entered service in 1963 and a number have now achieved over 100 000 hours of service.   These machines are associated with a variety of types of water cooled reactors, some turbines running at half speed (1800 RPM) on 60 Hz systems and some at full speed (3000 RPM) on 50 Hz systems with individual machine outputs up to 985 MW. The overall power train at Sizewell 'B' incorporates two turbine-generator units, each of 630 MW nominal output and each machine draws one half of the steam flow generated by the 3425 MW(Th) PWR reactor.   The Sizewell 'B' turbine-generators are presently under construction.   The general design features of these machines are described below against the background of earlier experience.

2   THERMODYNAMIC CYCLE

2.1   General thermodynamic requirements

Thermodynamic considerations dictate the basic design of the turbine and associated plant for water cooled reactors and this has led to modern plant arrangements shown in simplified form in Figure 1a.   The expansion of steam through the various components of the turbine cycle is illustrated in Figure 1b.   The live steam conditions are moderate compared with modern fossil fuelled plant but the mass and volumetric flow rates are correspondingly increased for the same electrical rating.   Live steam, initially at saturated or slightly wet condition, is expanded in the high pressure cylinder with increase in wetness during expansion.   An external water separator is applied after the HP cylinder outlet to remove moisture from the wet steam flow and to produce virtually dry saturated steam.   This is followed by steam-to-steam reheating using either live steam or both live and bled steam in order to avoid excessive wetness in the low pressure expansion.   Expansion of superheated steam ensues in the low pressure cylinders and the lower wetness levels achieved as a result of reheating reduce blading losses and improve overall thermal efficiency.   Suitable provision is made in the turbine feedheating system for utilisation of the high temperature water drained from the water separator and from live and bled steam reheaters to maximise efficiency.

The moisture separation, reheating and feedheating equipment is described in detail in a companion paper (ref. 1).

2.2   Turbine terminal conditions

Turbine stop valve pressures in modern PWR's are typically 60-70 bar with steam wetness values at turbine inlet of the order 0.25-0.40%.   Final feedwater temperatures required for return to the Steam Generator are generally in the range 220-230°C, requiring extraction pressures of about 25 to 30 bar for steam tapped to the top heater.

2.3   Moisture separator reheater

Wet steam cycles for modern large turbines employ external moisture separation.   This is conventionally followed by live steam reheating which leads to lower LP expansion wetness, to reduced blading losses and so to improved overall performance.   The resulting low pressure expansion which, at the thermodynamically optimum level of pressure for water separation, gives an expansion line close to that used in a typical high temperature reheat cycle as shown in Figure 1b.

The additional use of a bled steam reheater is governed by economic factors. The position of the low pressure expansion line is not affected and the issue is one of efficiency and output improvement, against additional cost; the degree of improvement being dependent on factors which can be selected by the turbine supplier. Principal factors are the HP cylinder exhaust pressure, the bled steam pressure from the appropriate stage of the HP cylinder and the terminal temperature differences in the reheater. The bled steam reheater improves the cycle efficiency by sharing the heating duty and so reducing the amount of steam taken by the live steam reheater. Nowadays it is generally found that a bled steam reheater is economically attractive.

2.4 Cycle arrangement

A typical cycle arrangement applicable to PWR turbines incorporates three or four LP feedwater heaters, a deaerator and either two or three HP feedwater heaters. The particular arrangement used with the Sizewell 'B' turbines, with four LP and three HP feedwater heaters, is shown in Figure 2. This has evolved, as described below, from the basic arrangement of Figure 1 to yield high levels of cycle efficiency.

In the Sizewell 'B' cycle the drains from the first two low pressure heaters, mounted in the neck of the condenser to save space, are cascaded to the condenser via a drains cooler. The third and fourth low pressure heaters have their drains pumped forward, not only improving heat rate but also avoiding the necessity to flash their drains up to heaters in the condenser neck. The forward pumping of drains also removes the need for integral drains coolers on the low pressure heaters.

With the reheat pressures at a relatively low level (5.9 bar abs) it has been found possible to apply three high pressure heaters and so obtain further improvement in performance. The hot drain water from the live steam reheater is utilised in a drains cooler installed after the final heater and this gives performance improvement compared with the more conventional method of routing the drain directly to the final heater. Employment of this relatively large number of feedheaters has been found to be economic for Sizewell 'B' where high value has been placed on improvements in overall efficiency.

2.5 Selection of reheat pressure

For turbines operating at 3000 RPM, it is mechanically possible to provide a high pressure double-flow cylinder with sufficient staging to expand steam efficiently to reheat pressures down to 5 bar or less. The low pressure cylinders can be designed to accommodate a wide range of inlet pressures, with higher reheat pressures necessarily resulting in shorter, less efficient, blades in the early stages. The optimum reheat pressure for best cycle efficiency, taking account of such changes in blading efficiency, is in the region of 5 to 8 bar. The variation of cycle efficiency against reheat pressure is very small over this range, so that small departures from the thermodynamic optimum do not involve too great a penalty. The thermodynamically optimum reheat pressure is somewhat lower for two-stage reheat than for single-stage reheat.

Existing designs of GEC turbines for PWR application at 3000 RPM typically have five HP stages and five LP stages. As indicated earlier the optimised pressure is such that the resulting LP expansion line is closely similar to that used on conventional high temperature turbines. It follows that the same LP cylinders can be used on either kind of turbine without change, and will be subjected to the same steam conditions, and to last stage blade erosion rates at which vast experience has already been gained.

2.6 Factors influencing cycle efficiency

The overall cycle efficiency and corresponding heat rate is influenced by many factors including those mentioned above and others related to internal parameters associated with plant components. On a cycle with large volumetric flows and low pressure levels it is particularly important to reduce pressure losses in the main steam circuit by generous sizing and careful design of steam transfer components (inlet and outlet casings, pipework, valves, etc).

The effect on heat rate of such improvements include:-

i) Addition of live steam reheating after the moisture separation process will improve performance by about 1.5%.

ii) Addition of bled steam reheating to moisture separation and live steam reheating will give benefit of about 0.5%.

iii) Addition of an extra stage of feedheating (from 7 heaters to 8) will usually give an improvement of about 0.3%.

iv) Reduction of pressure drop through the steam side reheater circuit by one percentage point will reduce the heat rate by 0.1%.

v) Improvement of terminal temperature differences for bled and live steam reheaters by 10°C will improve heat rate by 0.1% and 0.2% respectively.

vi) Pumping forward LP external heater drains is worth about 0.1%.

vii) Provision of a drains cooler for live steam reheater drains gives a gain of about 0.08%.

viii) Improvement due to terminal temperature differences change of 1°C in all feedheaters and drain coolers is about 0.15%.

Each of these parameters can be modified so as to increase efficiency, but in each instance only at additional cost. Whether such improvements are worthwhile can only be determined by an economic assessment. Because in each application different evaluation factors may apply, the optimised values may differ from case to case. Improvements of this type have been incorporated in the Sizewell 'B' cycle. The overall effect of present day economics has generally led to elaborate steam cycles which yield thermal efficiencies, depending on condenser pressures, in the range of 34.5% to 37.0%.

3 TURBINE DESIGN AND ARRANGEMENT

3.1 Modular cylinder design concept

The organisation of the design of a series of machines covering a wide output range from a number of standard cylinder modules is discussed in detail for high temperature turbines at 3000 RPM in reference 2. A similar approach is adopted to the design of cylinder modules for nuclear wet steam turbines for both 50 Hz and 60 Hz systems as discussed in reference 3. The 50 Hz modular family of nuclear wet steam turbines is designed for three power levels (600-700, 900-1000, 1200-1300 MW) in the range of outputs from 600 MW up to 1300 MW.

Essentially a particular cylinder module has a fixed rotor geometry and fixed outer casing scantlings. Stationary and moving blade heights are varied, usually over only the early stages, to match the flow requirements over the range of output considered. In the case of LP cylinders adjustments to the sizes of rotor journals and couplings are made to suit the transmitted machine torque.

The high pressure and the low pressure cylinder modules for machine outputs and condenser pressures similar to those adopted at Sizewell 'B' are shown in Figures 3a and 3b respectively.

3.1 High pressure cylinder

The HP cylinder consists of two flows, each with five stages of blading. Because the inlet pressure and temperature are only moderate the casing is essentially of single shell construction, with diaphragms mounted in diaphragm carriers to permit ease of extraction of bled steam. With an inlet pressure of 66.8 bar and an optimised exhaust pressure of 5.9 bar, the economic assessment showed that three high pressure feedheaters could be justified, with bled steam taken after the second, third and fourth stages of blading. Bled steam for the reheater is also taken after the second stage. Bled steam quantities and general cylinder design considerations led to the bled steam being taken symmetrically from both flows after stage two but asymmetrically from the rear flow after stage three and from the front flow after stage four. The four steam inlet pipes are attached directly to the casing. Steam exhausts through eight exhaust pipes, located symmetrically in top or bottom halves, with four outlets at each end of the casing.

As on high temperature cylinders, disc and diaphragm type of construction is employed. The moving blades are shrouded and are attached to the monobloc rotor using pinned roots. The HP rotor is a stiff design having its major critical speed above the running speed. The diaphragms, containing the fixed blades, are kinematically supported in the diaphragm carriers so as to maintain concentricity whilst permitting relative thermal expansion. The diaphragms carry the rotor interstage spring-backed glands and also, on an extension ring, the tip seals which co-operate with cylindrical ribs on the moving blade shrouding. This type of construction ensures that small effective radial clearances are maintained over long periods of operation.

Water, appearing progressively and in substantial quantities as a result of expansion in the wet region, is removed after each stage to reduce the potential for erosion and give a drier, more efficient, subsequent expansion. Tapped bled steam flow provides the most effective vehicle for water removal and in this respect on the Sizewell 'B' application two bled belts are employed in each of the opposed flows of blading. At stages where bled belts are not present alternative arrangements are made to effect internal moisture separation by application of an extension to the diaphragm mounted tip seal which is appropriately slotted to permit extraction of water collecting on the outer flow boundary.

3.2 Low pressure cylinders

The current design of the standard GEC 3000 RPM LP cylinder module with 945mm last row blades, as shown in fig. 3b, will be used on Sizewell 'B'. This module is identical to that used on a large number of high temperature machines over a wide range of outputs.

The five stages of blading in each opposed flow are carried on a monobloc rotor. The standard LP rotor has its first major critical speed below the running speed. The diaphragms are mounted in a single shell inner casing supported in a fabricated outer casing. Steam is admitted through two inlets in the top half and exhaust steam discharges downwards to an underslung condenser. At Sizewell the condenser is spring mounted at the basement floor level and has a rigid connection at the turbine exhaust.

The average cooling water temperature at Sizewell 'B' is 13°C and this will yield good condenser vacua and relatively high exhaust volumetric flowrates. For the standard 945mm blade LP module, an evaluation study showed that for an optimised back pressure of 43 mbar the economic exhaust area would be provided by using three LP cylinders.

3.3 Turbine arrangement

A sectional arrangement through the turbine as designed for Sizewell 'B' is shown in Figure 4.

Each rotor is supported on two bearings which are mounted in pedestals supported directly on the low tuned foundation block. The rotor system thrust bearing is mounted in the bearing pedestal between the HP and the first LP cylinder.

The moisture separator and reheater vessels are mounted horizontally at the turbine floor level on each side of the turbine alongside the low pressure cylinders. Detail design aspects of the moisture separator reheaters are discussed in detail in reference 1. The arrangement adopted for the Sizewell 'B' Turbine-Generator, as supported by steel foundations, is shown in Figure 5.

4 ELECTRICAL GENERATOR

A range of standard GEC 50Hz generators is available to complement the standard range of steam turbines and machines up to 985 MW are currently under construction.

The generators and exciters to be supplied for Sizewell 'B' are of established standard GEC 3000 RPM design and at 660MW rating are entirely suitable for the power level of two turbine-generator units per reactor. The standard 660MW frame has previously been used on many fossil-fired and AGR units in the UK and 600/660MW units have been widely applied abroad; no special conditions are imposed by the PWR plant at Sizewell 'B'.

The arrangement of the generator plus exciter is shown in Figure 6 and an application is shown on the Torness AGR plant in Figure 7.

The generator employs a single-piece steel rotor carrying axial field windings which are cooled by hydrogen forced to flow through ducts within the copper conductors. The stator laminations are also cooled by hydrogen flowing in radial ducts across the cylindrical core. The hydrogen at a pressure of 5.15 bara is circulated by centrifugal fans at each end of the rotor and is re-cooled in vertical heat exchangers within the gas-tight stator frame. The stator conductors and all connections and terminals are cooled by demineralised water flowing within the hollow copper conductors in a closed circuit. The generator voltage is 23.5 kV.

The excitation current supply to the rotating field is provided by a directly driven rotating-armature type A.C. exciter with rotating rectifiers (diodes). Its excitation is in turn supplied by a constant-voltage 400 Hz A.C. permanent-magnet pilot exciter. Regulation of the generator excitation is carried out using a thyristor type automatic excitation regulator, which controls the output current of the pilot exciter.

Further details of the standard generator are given in reference 4.

5 CONTROL REQUIREMENTS AND VALVE ARRANGEMENTS

5.1 Governing and control

The speed and load control of the Sizewell B turbine will be performed by an electro-hydraulic governor of advanced design, based on the use of microprocessor technology. The use of up-to-date electronic hardware and techniques will enable a wide range of speed/load controls, protection functions and fully controlled unit start-up programmes to be achieved with high reliability.

Since nuclear units generally operate at high levels of base load, throttle control is used in all cases, with the governing valves opening in unison. To prevent large volumes of steam and flashing water stored in the reheaters from causing high machine overspeed under loss of electrical load, interceptor valves are required in the hot reheat pipes between the reheater outlets and the LP cylinder inlets.

5.2 High pressure valves

The main stop and governing valves used for present PWR applications are similar in design to those used for reheat valves on high temperature turbines with appropriate material changes. Each machine employs four stop and four governing valves. A piloted stop valve, surrounded by a strainer, and a single seated balanced governing valve are arranged coaxially opposed in a single chest as shown in Figure 8a. These chests are mounted horizontally on flexible supports, two on each side of the HP cylinder, with short loop pipes connecting to turbine inlets. The chests are stacked in pairs vertically, one above the other, as can be seen in Figure 5.

5.3 Low pressure valves

The large volumetric flow at LP cylinder inlet requires that the interceptor valves are of necessity very large in size, with diameters of the order of 1m. Butterfly valves as shown in Figure 8b are well suited to this application, having the advantage of producing very low pressure drop in the normal operating fully-open position. They are used for both stop and governing valves, one stop and one governing valve being combined in a single chest located in each hot reheat pipe. Substantial operating experience now exists with valves of this design.

6 MATERIAL SELECTION AND OPERATING EXPERIENCE

6.1 Wet steam erosion

Since steam conditions in the LP cylinders of GEC turbines for PWR applications with moisture separation and live steam reheating are very similar to those in high temperature turbines it is evident that there are no special LP erosion problems. However, in the HP cylinder conditions are completely different from those in high temperature turbines. The progressive increase in wetness through the cylinder at relatively high pressures has a powerful potential for causing erosion damage. With the velocities of entrained moisture droplets and main steam not differing significantly in the blade path at the relatively high steam densities applying, coupled with the use of stainless steel for the whole steam path, blade path erosion is not a significant problem. Potential for erosion damage is highest in the casings and associated pipework and valves, either where there are changes in flow direction or across joint surfaces of pressure seals.

6.2 Operating experience with nuclear wet steam turbines

It follows from the above that experience with nuclear wet steam turbines has greatest relevance to the design of the HP cylinder, valves and pipework, with particular reference to erosion problems on stationary components due to steam wetness. In considering these problems for full speed 3000 RPM PWR turbines, experience with wet steam turbines running at both full and half speed and operating with different types of reactor is fully relevant. Service experience with 17 GEC turbines with ratings up to 1200MW, including PWR, BWR, CANDU and SGHWR applications amounts to more than 170 machine years, with individual machine operating times up to 150 000 hours.

Earliest experience was with a small machine of 22MW rating running at 3600 RPM with a CANDU reactor. This was followed by two larger machines, a 100MW machine running at 3000 RPM using SGHWR steam and a 220MW machine running at 1800 RPM with a CANDU reactor. A number of erosion problems were initially encountered on these units, for which design solutions were evolved and changes made in material selection, and these were proved by subsequent service.

Later machines incorporating these features have now achieved considerable service experience. A machine of 54MW rating at 3000 RPM for a BWR station in Holland has run for 130 000 hours. At 3000 RPM two further machines for BWR application, of 400MW output, have each been in operation for more than 70 000 hours. The HP cylinders of these 400MW machines are of single flow type, so the experience is equivalent to that of a double flow cylinder on a machine of up to 800MW output. These machines are in service at Ringhals Nuclear Power Station in Sweden where a single reactor supplies steam to the two turbine-generators in the same manner as will be applied at Sizewell 'B'. At 1800 RPM a 600MW turbine for PWR application in Korea has reached over 60 000 hours of operation. Inspection of the HP cylinders of all these machines has shown them to be in very good condition.

At the larger outputs two 1200MW PWR turbines running at 1800 RPM are in service at San Onofre in the USA. A similar 1200MW unit, but for BWR application, is in service at Enrico Fermi Power Station, also in the USA. Two 1000MW PWR turbines, also running at 1800

RPM but of later design, are in service in Korea. The machine arrangement of these 1000MW turbines is generally similar to that of large 3000 RPM turbines and is shown in Figure 9.

6.3 Material selection

The above experience allows confident selection of materials for components in wet steam environments (Ref.5). The selection depends on steam pressure and wetness and the nature of the steam flow associated with the particular design features of the components involved.

At the very low levels of wetness at turbine inlet, carbon steel is used for steam pipework and valve chests. For the HP casings and diaphragm carriers, where the level of wetness is greater, a low chromium alloy steel is used. The same material is also used for cold reheat pipes.

For welded diaphragms a fully stainless steel blade path is employed, including the nozzle blades and spacer bands forming the nozzle annulus boundaries at inner and outer diameters. Low alloy steel is adequate for diaphragm rims and centres.

On the faces of all joints sustaining pressure differences a deposit of stainless steel cladding is applied to prevent any significant wire drawing erosion. Such faces include bolted joints between top and bottom half casings and diaphragm carriers, and axial contact faces at diaphragm carrier and diaphragm supports. Figure 10 shows a typical HP cylinder horizontal joint incorporating stainless steel weld inlays. In addition to the application of protective cladding on the horizontal joint faces of diaphragm inner and outer rings, the top and bottom half diaphragms are bolted together across the outer rings to assist in joint protection.

No special protection is applied to the body of the low alloy steel HP rotor, nor to the interstage gland regions. However, because of the high degree of exhaust wetness, the rotor end glands are packed with dry steam obtained by throttling live steam.

7 CONCLUDING REMARKS

A family of modern 3000 RPM turbine generators in the output range 600-1300 MW has been developed, matching standard reactor capacities, for application in PWR power stations on 50 HZ electrical systems. The turbine designs are based on substantial operating experience with machines associated with a variety of water cooled reactors. The generator designs are also based on substantial operating experience.

The 630 MW turbine generators currently under construction for Sizewell 'B' are typical of the range and will benefit from the soundly based standard features evolved from the wide experience on earlier machines.

REFERENCES

1. W.J. Torrance - Heat exchange Equipment for Sizewell 'B' Turbine Generators . I.Mech.E. Conference 1989 "Sizewell B - The first of the UK PWR Stations".

2. D. Kalderon - Design of large steam turbines for fossil and nuclear power stations. I.Mech.E. Conference 1979 "Steam turbines for the 1980's".

3. G. Hobson and J. Muscroft - Design of large steam turbines for pressurised water reactor power stations. I.Mech.E. Conference 1983 "Steam plant for pressurised water reactors".

4. F.R. Harris and R.B. Bennett - Design features of the turbine generator plant for Castle Peak 'B' power station, Hong Kong. I.E.E. Proceedings Part C 1983.

5. D.V. Thornton - Materials for turbine plant operating with wet steam. B.N.E.S. Conference 1988 "Technology of turbine plant operating with wet steam".

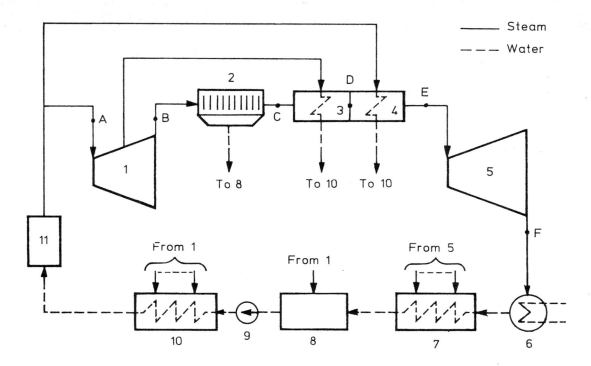

1. HP Turbine Cylinder
2. Moisture Separator
3. Bled Steam Reheater
4. Live Steam Reheater
5. LP Turbine Cylinder
6. Steam Condenser
7. LP Heaters
8. Deaerator
9. Feed Pump
10. HP Heater
11. Steam Generator

(a) Cycle components

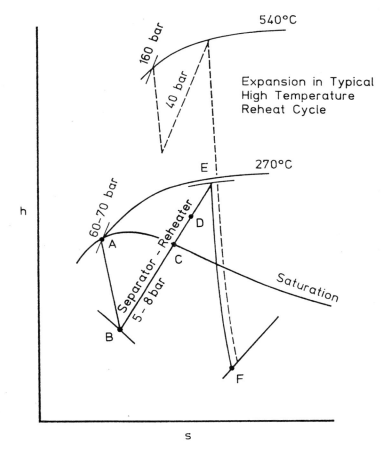

(b) Expansion lines for typical
PWR and high temperature
reheat turbines

Fig 1   Steam cycle simplified

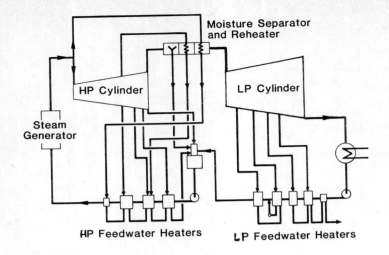

Fig 2   Sizewell PWR cycle arrangement

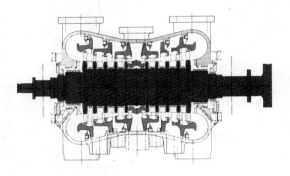

(a)   600 – 700 MW HP cylinder module

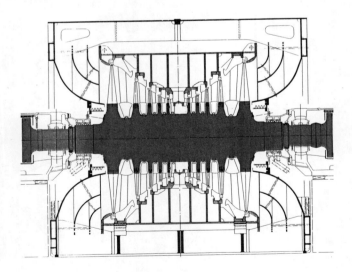

(b)   Standard LP cylinder module

Fig 3   3000 r/min turbine cylinder module

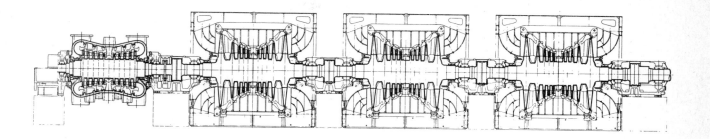

Fig 4   630 MW turbine for Sizewell 'B' power station

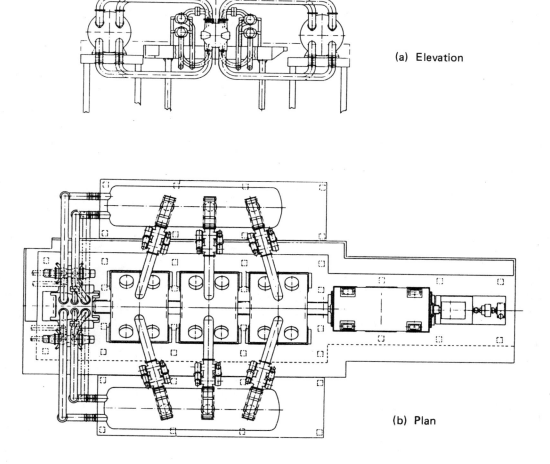

(a) Elevation

(b) Plan

Fig 5   General arrangement of Sizewell 'B' turbine with moisture
separator and reheater vessels

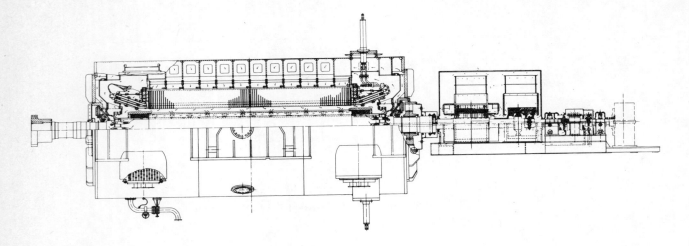

Fig 6   Sectional arrangement of the electrical generator for the Sizewell 'B' power station

Fig 7   660 MW generator application at Torness power station

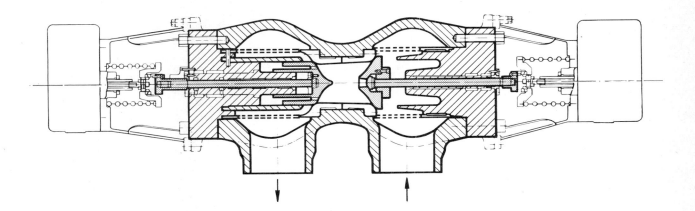

(a) High pressure stop and governing valve

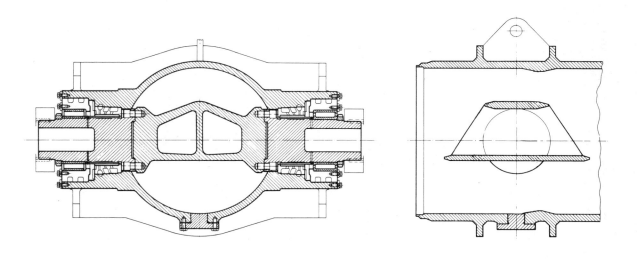

(b) Low pressure valve

Fig 8   Valve arrangements

Fig 9   1000 MW 1800 r/min turbine in PWR power station

Fig 10   Stainless steel weld inlay on typical HP cylinder horizontal joint

C388/031

Heat exchange equipment for the Sizewell 'B' turbine generators

W J TORRANCE, BSc
GEC Alsthom Turbine Generators Limited. Manchester

SYNOPSIS

The Heat Exchange Equipment associated with the Sizewell 'B' Turbine Generators embodies features specific to the wet steam cycle of the PWR.

In comparison with fossil fuelled plant, steam conditions are considerably lower and so for a given electrical output, steam and feed water flows are of necessity much higher. In addition, the plant must embody measures to combat wet steam erosion and to accommodate substantial quantities of draining separated condensate.

The paper describes key features of design, layout and material selection on the Sizewell 'B' heat exchange equipment which address these problems.

1   INTRODUCTION

The design of the heat exchange equipment (condensers, feed water heaters and moisture separator reheaters) for the Sizewell 'B' Turbine Generators draws heavily on well established and proven designs used for modern fossil fired plant of similar capacity. A number of key differences are incorporated however to suit the special needs and characteristics of PWR plant, and to reflect up-to-date design practice for such plants.

This paper describes these differences and highlights the significant features of the design of the plant. The design of the Moisture Separator Reheaters (MSRs), plant items peculiar to wet steam cycles, is discussed in some detail.

2   OVERALL DESCRIPTION OF PLANT

The steam and feed cycle for Sizewell 'B' is shown diagrammatically in figure 1. The plant design and system arrangement are selected by economic analysis of capital and lifetime operating costs, based on evaluation factors declared by the customer.

During such analysis, consideration is given to -

(for the Condensers)

(a)   Variation of overall surface area for condensation, yielding variations in the turbine back pressure.

(b)   Variations in the number of tubes and condenser length between tubeplates (LBTP) which may result in variations in the cooling water flow and in the power consumption of the cooling water pumps.

(for the Feed Heaters)

(a)   Variations in the number of stages of feed heating.

(b)   Variations in the surface area provided in each feed heater, resulting in variations in performance and terminal temperature difference (TTD).

(c)   Provision of drain cooling.

(d)   Sizing and routing of steam lines to the heaters.

(e)   Sizing and routing of condensate lines from the heaters.

(for the MSR's)

(a)   Sizing of heating tube nests.

(b)   Sizing and routing of steam lines.

(c)   Routing of separated water.

(d)   Routing of condensate.

After consideration of the above major criteria and numerous other less significant factors the cycle shown was chosen.

The turbine train includes 3 low pressure cylinders each with a twin nest transverse underslung single pass condenser.

The low pressure feed train comprises a Drains Flash Condenser (DFC) four stages of low pressure (LP) heater, and a deaerating heater/storage vessel.

The high pressure train comprises three stages of high pressure (HP) heater and separate high pressure drains cooler to cool condensate from the live steam section of the MSR's.

3 THE CONDENSERS

The condensers are of basically carbon steel construction, and comprise a series of drilled tube support plates, arranged to provide self draining of the tubes during shutdown, and a fabricated steel plate shell and plate and section neck.

The water tubes are 1" O/D x 0.7mm wall titanium roller expanded into a double tubeplate arrangement. The outer (water side) tubeplates are in aluminium bronze and the inner (steam side) in carbon steel. This arrangement provides the necessary corrosion resistance to the sea water on the tube side and prevents harmful possible contamination of the steam cycle by copper. The narrow interspace between them is completely filled with demineralised water maintained at a pressure higher than either that of the steam space or of the cooling water by being fed from an elevated header tank. In the unlikely event of a leakage through either expanded joint, such leakage is of the demineralised water and is detected by a fall in level in the header tank.

The necks of the condenser are arranged to hold the combined first two stages of LP feed heater and the turbine bypass diffusers.

The condensers are rigidly connected to the LP turbine exhausts and are supported from the basement floor on a series of packs of coil springs.

The condenser waterboxes are of approximately half conical shape to minimise air entrapment and to ensure optimum water flow distribution.

4 THE LOW PRESSURE FEED HEATERS

The Drain Flash Condenser (DFC) and the third and fourth stages of low pressure feed heaters are simple single shell tubeplate heaters with stainless steel type 304L tubes, roller expanded into carbon steel tubeplates. This type of heater is illustrated in figure 2.

The function of the DFC is to recover additional heat from the drains from the combined LP1/2 heater described below by flashing the drains at a pressure lower than that in the heater and condensing the vapour over tubes containing the feed flow.

The combined LP1/2 heaters in the condenser necks are so arranged to minimise the space occupied and to minimise the length (and hence pressure drop) of the bled steam piping supplying them. This type of heater is illustrated in figure 3.

The first stage heater comprises a D shaped cross section nest of stainless steel U-tubes, the feed water in which is heated by the lowest pressure bled steam tapping.

The LP2 heater is also of D shaped cross section and is totally enclosed within a correspondingly D-shaped shell. This heater receives steam from a higher pressure tapping.

The LP2 stage is isolated completely from LP1 on the steam side by the use of metallic bellows seals at shell penetrations.

Steam inlets and shell drains are accommodated within generously sized wrap-around belts. Impingement baffles protect the tube nests from incoming steam flow.

5 THE DEAERATOR HEATER/STORAGE VESSEL

This item, hereinafter termed the "Deaerator", is mounted at an elevated position in the plant. The deaerator heads are of the compact spray type to Stork design, comprising a series of stacked stainless steel discs which, under the effect of pressure of incoming feed water separate slightly to discharge a fine mist spray of water droplets. These droplets impinge on a series of splash baffles above stored water level.

Heating steam is fed into the storage/heater vessel via a pair of longitudinal manifold pipes from which vertical pipes, perforated at their lower end, protrude into the stored water. Steam is thus admitted initially at low level and rises through the stored water to be finally fully condensed on the relatively cooler droplets of incoming feed water. A vent to the condenser carries away incondensable gases.

A consistently high level of deaeration is maintained by virtue of the fact that the stored water is maintained at the saturation temperature corresponding to the vessel pressure. This is achieved by distribution of heating steam which is as near uniform as possible throughout the vessel. This uniform distribution of heating steam also minimises gross axial transport of steam above water level and thus avoids the possibility of harmful wave formation and consequential surges. The high elevation of the deaerator, together with its selected size and control system ensures that the required reactor feed pump NPSH is maintained during all anticipated operating conditions including load rejection and all predicted operational transients. The deaerator is generally fabricated from carbon steel, with the spray devices, the steam distribution piping, the incoming feed water and reactor feed pump leak-off diffusers being of stainless steel to prevent erosion damage.

A part illustration of a deaerator is shown in figure 4.

6 THE HIGH PRESSURE FEED WATER HEATERS

The high pressure (HP) feed water heaters are provided in 2 50% flow lines. By comparison with the equivalent feed heaters in modern fossil fired subcritical steam power plant the PWR feed pressure is much lower, typically 120 bar g rather than 220 bar g. The feed flow is approximately double that of a fossil fired plant of equivalent electrical output. The consequence of this is the need for proportionately much larger units.

The Sizewell HP heaters have outside diameters of 1.8m are 13.5m long and have a fabricated weight of around 65 tonnes. A typical HP heater is shown in figure 5.

Instead of the heating steam having superheat, as in typical modern fossil fired plant, at entry to the HP heaters on a PWR it has a high moisture content and special measures must be taken to eliminate the risk of erosion damage. Specific attention is paid to the steam inlet design, the condensing and drain cooling zones operating in conditions not dissimilar to those of the superheated cycle. The steam inlet nozzles are of an enlarged swept design to reduce steam velocity at entry. The inlet connection itself and the adjacent shell surfaces are protected with a roll-clad liner of austenitic stainless steel.

A stainless steel baffle arrangement at the inlet connection prevents direct steam impingement on the tube nest assembly. The HP heater tubes themselves are of type 439 (18 per cent Chromium) ferritic stainless steel. The tubes are seal welded, using a very reliable automatic process, into the carbon steel tubeplate, the welding being done autogenously into a layer of Inconel weld deposit on the front face of the tubeplate.

The comprehensively baffled drain cooler is fabricated from carbon steel.

A fabricated cylindrical barrel and hemispherical end of carbon manganese steel is used on the water side header in place of the more usual cast hemisphere used on fossil fired plant. This is necessary as post weld heat treatment, required for the thickness of material used, could cause embrittlement of the heater tubes. The tubeplate and cylindrical barrel are therefore post weld heat treated as an assembly prior to tube end welding, and the final closing seam between the barrel and the hemispherical end receives only a local heat treatment after welding, avoiding harmful overheating of the tube material.

The tubes are expanded into the tubeplate after welding to close the interspace crevice.

7   THE MOISTURE SEPARATOR REHEATERS

In PWR plant the steam supplied to the turbine is saturated, and after expansion in the high pressure cylinder, contains approximately 12-16 per cent water. Most or all of this water must be removed before expansion can continue in the low pressure cylinder. It is now also common practice to provide reheating of the steam to evaporate such residual moisture as remains and to superheat the steam to prevent excessive moisture in the later stages of low pressure expansion. Such excessive moisture is of course detrimental to the efficiency of the turbine and increases its susceptibility to erosion damage in the later stages. A single stage reheater reduces turbine specific steam consumption by around 1.5 per cent and a two stage by a further 0.5 per cent.

The Sizewell 'B' Turbine Generator sets are provided with combined moisture separator/reheater (MSR) vessels, with two per turbine generator set, arranged at engine room floor level parallel to and on either side of the machine.

An MSR is shown in figure 6. The MSR comprises an outer pressure vessel into which is fitted a frame containing the separator elements and two reheater tube nests.

Steam is admitted via the four inlet nozzles in the vessel head, passes around the outside of the central frame and enters the moisture separator panels which are arranged in the bottom of the frame.

The separator panels comprise an outer plate with varying perforations to admit steam uniformly to the separator elements which are fixed to it. The separator elements are stacks of thin corrugated stainless steel blades. The water droplets in the steam impinge on the blades and the resulting film is carried away by a combination of gravity and the inclination of the corrugations promoting downward flow of the film. From each level in each separator panel a drainage trough leads via drainage downpipes to a system of closed segregated draining channels in the bottom of the frame, which discharge into a drainage pot incorporating a manometric seal to prevent steam leakage. Into this pot is also discharged water draining from the shell of the vessel.

The MSR drainage system is so designed as to limit the inventory of water present in the vessel to minimise the effects of the drains flashing in the event of load reduction causing depressurisation of the MSR.

Each separator panel discharges partially dried steam into a separate chamber from where it passes to the first stage tube nest, alternate tube support plates of which correspond with the edges of the panels. There is thus no axial flow of steam. Good uniform distribution of flow is effected by virtue of the pressure drop through the tube nests. Considerable model testing has taken place in the author's Company to enable the selection of separator front plate perforations so as to further improve steam distribution along the length of the MSR and to ensure even steam loading in each segment of the MSR irrespective of the outside approach velocity.

The steam then enters the two horizontal tube nests. The first stage tube nest is fed with heating steam bled from the HP cylinder, and the second stage with live steam tapped from the flow to the turbine from the steam generator. Since the heat transfer coefficient on the inside of the tube (in condensing steam) is much greater than that on the outside to the dry steam, extended surface externally finned tubes are used in both nests.

The tubes are supported in drilled plates pitched to avoid potentially damaging tube vibration. The square profile bends of the tubes are in the steam flow in order to contribute to heat transfer, and because of the span of the outermost tubes, would be more susceptible to vibration than the straight lengths. Additional drilled support plates are therefore provided in the bend area, together with flow restriction devices to control the maximum possible steam velocity in the bend area to an acceptable value.

The plenum area above the live steam tube nest is provided with a double skinned construction, employing a relatively thin inner shell fixed to the outer in such a way as to permit differential expansion. The stagnant interspace between the skins provides effective thermal insulation preventing undue heat loss from the heated steam to the cold reheat steam outwith the frame.

The outlet connections embody a flexible metallic bellows seal between the top of the frame and the vessel shell. This is to segregate the steam flows and to permit axial differential expansion of the frame and shell.

The horizontal reheater tube bundles referred to above each consist of a nest of the integrally finned tubes welded and expanded into circular tubeplates with attached headers. The tube material is type 439 stainless steel as in the HP heaters. Again as in the HP heaters the tubes are welded to an Inconel layer weld deposited onto the front face of the tubeplate. The type 439 material has a thermal expansion coefficient similar to that of the carbon steel used for the tube supports and the nest frame, thereby avoiding undue differential expansion.

As the steam being heated passes through the tube nests the temperature difference between it and the heating steam varies. This can result in the variation in condensation of the heating steam, leading potentially to flooding of the lower legs of the outermost tubes of each nest. This flooding, if permitted, tends to be intermittent in any one tube, with "slugs" of condensate being formed and ejected from the affected tubes. This condensate will tend to be sub-cooled by the flow of relatively cool steam outside the tube. Two effects result from this phenomenon. The first is mechanical effects on the tube, both from the fluctuating flow of steam and condensate, the second is from fluctuating sub-cooling of the affected tubes causing distortion of the tube nest, and increasing the risk of fatigue failure of the tube to tubeplate connection due to the thermal cycling.

This whole problem is overcome by the following measures:

a) Arranging gravity drainage of the tube nest by having the 'U' tubes in the vertical plane with downward flow of the heating steam and small but positive drainage slopes.

b) Allowing a flow of 2 to 3 per cent of the full load steam flow to vent to a feed heater operating at a lower pressure. This vent flow is proportionately greater at lower loads and it ensures positive steam flow through the tubes at all conditions.

c) Fitting perforated steam distribution plates at the inlet to the tubes, calibrated to ensure correct distribution of the heating steam.

It is known that even very slight leaks or bypassing of the steam being heated is extremely detrimental to reheater performance. Great care is therefore taken to ensure adequate sealing of all possible leakage or bypass paths.

The frame is of fully welded construction. The heating tube nests are fitted through the frame by way of packed glands around the peripheries of the tubeplates. Peripheral metallic seals are fitted around each tube nest to prevent steam flow bypassing the tube nests.

Equally, bypassing of the heating steam can be very harmful to MSR performance. The header division plates are therefore fully welded around their periphery, with the exception of small areas at the tubeplate edges, which are carefully sealed by an unwelded close fitting seal plate. This avoids undue restraint in this relatively highly stressed area.

Erosion of component parts of the MSR due to contact with high velocity wet steam flow is prevented by the use of stainless steel in susceptible areas. The outer skin of the central frame is made from 12 per cent Chromium ferritic stainless steel, and the inlet end and entire straight length of the vessel is protected by a series of overlapping austenitic stainless steel "tiles".

The type 439 stainless steel selected for the reheater tubes is inherently resistant to the two phase steam/water flow.

The predicted performance of the MSR is such that

a) The steam leaving the separators will have a residual moisture content less than 0.25 per cent.

b) The pressure drop of the heated steam flow through the MSR will be less than 3 per cent of the inlet pressure.

c) The outlet temperature difference between heating and heated steam will be around 8.3 degrees Celsius.

8   THE SYSTEMS

8.1   Bled Steam System

The bled steam system is sized and arranged to avoid significant erosion by use of suitable steam flow velocities. All bled steam tappings except those to the combined LP1 and LP2 feed heaters incorporate non-return and isolating valves, preventing reverse flow and permitting isolation of feed heaters from the turbine. The combined LP1 and LP2 feed heaters are provided with normal and emergency manometrically sealed drains, sized to prevent flooding of the heater.

All bled steam lines, except that to the elevated deaerator are arranged with continuous drainage fall to the heaters. The line to the deaerator, taken from the cold reheat line, rises continuously.

During normal operation, any condensate not carried forward by steam flow drains back to the cold reheat line which has continuous drains.

Bled steam supply to all feed heaters is under level control from the heater. In the event of high condensate level in the heater, the isolating valve closes and a powered actuator closes the non-return valve.

The piping and in-line equipment on the bled steam lines to the HP heaters and the deaerator are in 2.25 per cent Chromium/1 per cent Molybdenum alloy steel to resist wet steam erosion.

The corresponding piping to the LP heaters is in carbon steel, the velocities being sufficiently low that erosion is not a concern.

8.2   Drains System

Drains from the combined LP1/LP2 feed heater are passed to the Drains Flash Condenser which itself drains to the Turbine Condenser.

The Number 4LP heater drains to the Number 3 Drains Receiver from where condensate is pumped forward into the Deaerator.

The High Pressure heater drains cascade down to the Number 6, the drain flow from which is passed to the Deaerator.

The MSR live steam tubenest drains pass into the High Pressure Drains Cooler, and thence to the HP drains.

The MSR bled steam nest drains to the Number 8 HP heater.

Separated moisture from the MSR is pumped to the Deaerator.

The system is designed to maximise the energy recovery from the drains flows and to provide the highest degree of integrity and protection from water ingress into the Turbine.

8.3   Turbine Bypass System

A turbine Bypass System is provided to fulfil the following functions:-

1.   To permit the operation of the Turbine Generator with an excess steam supply for example during start-up.

2.   To permit safe disposal of cycle steam in the event of an turbine trip, thus permitting continued operation of the reactor.

3.   To permit safe disposal of steam generated after a total plant trip, due to continued evolution of heat in the reactor.

Under such conditions the excess steam is passed to pressure let down and desuperheating devices mounted in the necks of the condensers.

9   CONCLUSION

The Heat Exchange Equipment for the Sizewell 'B' Turbine Generators embodies many well proven design features from fossil fired and other nuclear plant, as well as several specific provisions for the special needs of the PWR cycle.

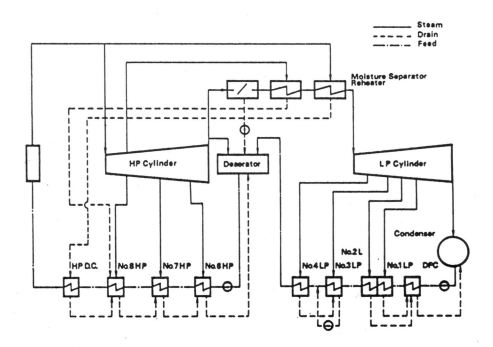

Fig 1   Steam feed cycle for 630 MW turbine Sizewell nuclear power station

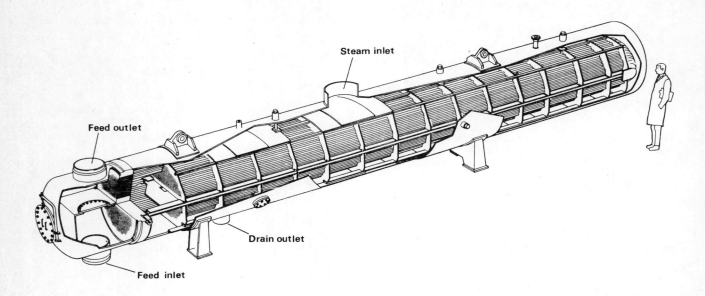

Fig 2   Single stage LP feedheater

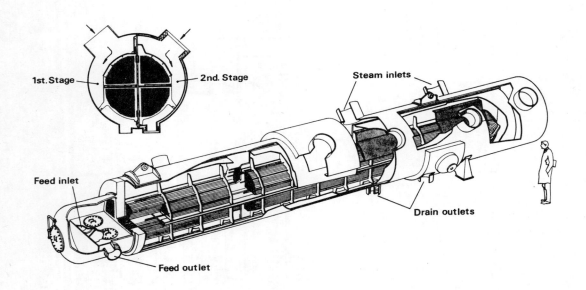

Fig 3   Two stage LP feedheater

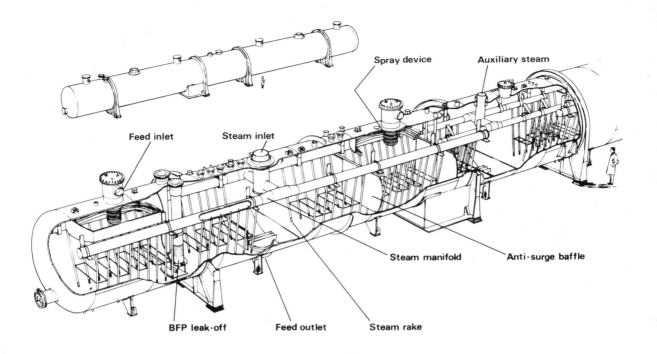

Fig 4   Spray type deaerator

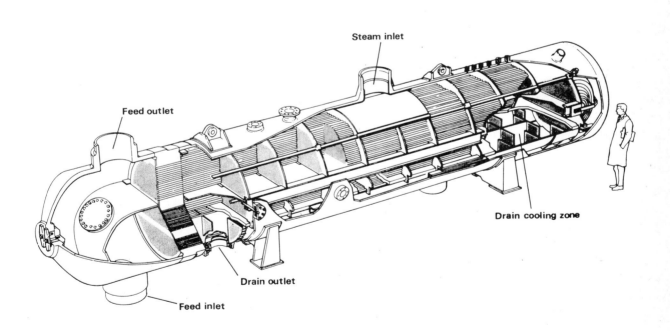

Fig 5   Wet steam HP feedheater

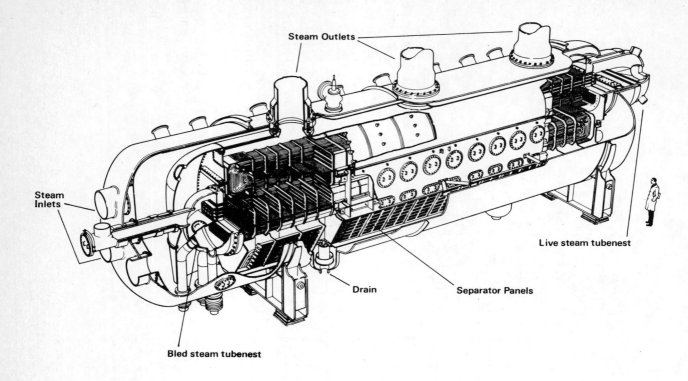

Steam Outlets

Steam Inlets

Live steam tubenest

Drain

Separator Panels

Bled steam tubenest

Fig 6   Moisture separator/reheater

C388/026

Development of the Sizewell 'B' station automatic control system

A R MACCABEE, BSc and **I G PALFREYMAN**, BA
National Nuclear Corporation Limited, Knutsford, Cheshire

SYNOPSIS   Although Sizewell 'B' is based on the Westinghouse SNUPPS PWR design, differences in plant design, instrumentation and CEGB requirements are identified. These differences introduced the need for major changes from the SNUPPS control system.

The programme of analysis undertaken to develop the Sizewell 'B' control system was required to conform to the key dates of the parallel control and instrumentation development. The analytical route adopted, described in some detail, also inevitably involved the development of theoretical methods.

The first stage of analysis was the development of a total plant dynamic model (SIBDYM) over a period of some five years. This model, with the SNUPPS analogue control system, was validated against test records of existing PWR plant and applied in the early stages of examination of the control system design.

Further development allowed a linear approximation to the total plant dynamic model to be established. This linear model was used to identify plant interactions and consolidate a control system structure.

The developed control system was modelled and has been tested to demonstrate conformity with the identified roles of the control system in normal operation and in support of plant safety, the requirements of the CEGB and the UK grid system and all identified plant constraints.

1 INTRODUCTION

The Sizewell B PWR design is based on the Westinghouse Standardised Nuclear Unit Power Plant System (SNUPPS). Although the major components of the nuclear steam supply system retain the SNUPPS design, changes have been made to other plant items and systems for a number of reasons. In particular, significant development of the Station Automatic Control System (SACS) has been necessary to meet CEGB requirements for Sizewell B, whilst maintaining an overall design concept similar to the original SNUPPS design.

Of the total range of factors which made the SACS development necessary, the most significant were:

(i)   the Sizewell B specification was for digital control using distributed microprocessors, consistent with recent CEGB practice, instead of the SNUPPS analogue system

(ii)   Sizewell B has twin turbines, while SNUPPS has a single turbine. The twin turbines are required to be capable of asymmetric operation and the plant is expected to run through the loss of one of two operating turbines

(iii)   in line with Westinghouse design development, the loop bypass measurement of outlet temperature from the reactor vessel was eliminated. Reactor power signals to the control and protection systems are derived from measurements of N^{16} activation in each outlet leg

(iv)   development of the safety case has led to some extensions to the protection system and modifications to instrumentation.

This paper describes the programme of analysis carried out by NNC to develop the SACS performance specification to accommodate the above factors, under contract to the CEGB.

2 DEVELOPMENT PROGRAMME

The development programme undertaken in support of design was in four phases:

(i) the specification of a dynamic
mathematical model representing
those plant items affected by or
having some impact on the
operation of the control system
in normal plant operation, in
departures from normal conditions
not intended to result in a
reactor trip, or followig a
reactor trip

(ii) the development of a method to
derive a reduced order, linear
model approximation to the
non-linear model developed above

(iii) the application of multivariable
control theory methods to the
responses generated from the
linear model approximation to the
plant

(iv) testing the derived control
algorithms in the non-linear
dynamic model to demonstrate
compliance with the operational
requirements of the plant.

The phasing of other contracts was such
that indications of the control system
structure affecting instrumentation
requirements and microprocessor
capacity were required at an early
stage. This early information was
obtained from analogue control studies
in parallel with item (ii) and part of
item (iii) of the above programme.

3 THE DYNAMIC PLANT MODEL

The Sizewell B dynamic model SIBDYM was
a joint NNC/CEGB development with
responsibilities broadly defined as:

(i) NNC to produce a dynamic model of
the plant in modular form, using
professional judgement to
simplify the representation
wherever justified, such that the
developed model is an economical
design aid but sufficiently
representative of the plant
behaviour to be used in control
system studies

(ii) CEGB to produce benchmark modules
of plant items, interchangeable
with the NNC modules, with
minimum simplification and
without undue consideration of
running time and cost.

With interchangeable modules, the main
behavioural characteristics of the
plant can be cheaply assessed, with the
ability to carry out more detailed
assessments of selected components.
The remainder of this paper
concentrates on the NNC version, as
used in the control system studies.

The SIBDYM code makes use of the CEGB's
Plant Modelling System Program (PMSP),
(1). This developed package is a
powerful modelling aid, reducing the

programming element of the task by
allowing physical processes to be
presented as ordinary differential or
algebraic equations, to robust solution
routines within the package. In
addition, the output from the PMSP
calculations includes the state space
matrix representation of the equivalent
linear model which is itself derived
from small perturbations about the
steady state solution. This output was
essential to the multivariable control
analysis described later.

The SIBDYM model includes
representation of the following plant
components and systems:

(i) Primary cirucit

Coolant loops and reactor coolant
pumps; reactor vessel, including
the inlet nozzles, downcomer,
reactor inlet plenum, reactor
core, reactor outlet plenum and
outlet nozzles. The neutronics
of the reactor core are
represented by an axial
one-dimensional model, with
models of the control and
shutdown rod banks and the
control rod drive equipment.

Chemical and volume control
system - the letdown path from
and charging path to the reactor
coolant system.
Pressuriser vessel, pressuriser
spray, proportional and back-up
heaters and relief valves.

Steam generator primary side.

(ii) Secondary circuit

Steam generator secondary side,
feed nozzles and rings,
separators, outlet nozzle and
relief valves.

Steam mains, steam isolation
valves and steam header.

Turbines HP and LP stages,
governor and interceptor valves,
condensate system.

Steam dump system.

Deaerators.

Feed pumps, feed heaters, feed
lines and feed header.

Feed regulating valves.

(iii) Control systems, either the
SNUPPS - based analogue system or
its digital replacement.

(iv) Protection system.

The models of the primary circuit loops
can be run in three modes:

Single loop   when all four loops are
              assumed to be operating
              symmetrically

Two loop   when any one loop is
              perturbed relative to the
              other three

Four loop   when all four loops can
              operate or be perturbed
              asymmetrically.

Of these options, the single loop
representation was used to produce the
state space matrices for the control
theory applications, to limit the scale
of the problem, leaving the asymmetric
representation for subsequent proving
of the derived control system.

Validation of the NNC version of SIBDYM
has consisted of code-to-code
comparisons and code simulations of
test transients on operating PWRs. The
simulation of test transients on
operating plant provided the more
reliable validation and examples of
comparisons between the plant data and
model results are provided in Fig 1 to
3. These are from the simulation of a
single plant test involving a rapid
reduction of 50% load from full load,
initiated at the turbine. This
simulation is of particular importance
to Sizewell B, because of the
similarity to the loss of one of two
turbines from full load.

The comparisons of Fig 1 to 3 and the
other validation material demonstrated
that simulations by the NNC version of
SIBDYM were adequate for the purposes
of control system design.

4 ANALOGUE CONTROL STUDIES

Reference to Fig 4 should be made in
this and subsequent sections.

The early analogue control studies
using the SIBDYM model concentrated on
areas of difference from SNUPPS already
identified. In particular, the twin
turbine design had an impact not only
on the load control system but also on
the feed control systems and on the
turbine bypass (steam dump) control
systems.

SIBDYM simulations were used to
investigate possible control strategies
for the steam dump system and the feed
pump control system in the presence of
large turbine-to turbine asymmetries,
including the extreme of trip of one
turbine.

The preferred solution arising from
this study was that the feed pumps
(normally two in operation per turbine)
should be controlled to a master speed
demand, to maintain a desired value of
steam generator pressure drop. In
asymmetric turbine operation, the water
levels in the two deaerators (one per

turbine) would diverge. This
divergence of deaerator levels was used
to offset the feed pump speed demands,
so that the speed of the feed pumps
drawing on the deaerator with higher
level was increased by the offset and
the speed of the other feed pumps was
reduced by the same offset. The mean
speed of the four feed pumps normally
operating still matched the master
speed demand. In the original study,
only proportional control of the level
mismatch between deaerators was
considered. Further analysis showed
that the incorporation of integral
control could improve the performance
in sustained asymmetric operation,
given suitable performance
characteristics of the deaerator level
instrumentation.

The arrangement of steam dump valves
with a twin turbine configuration also
differs from SNUPPS. There are two
banks of valves exhausting to the
condensers and a further bank
exhausting to atmosphere for each
turbine. To accommodate asymmetric
loss of load from the two turbines, a
load partitioning algorithm was
simulated, working on the principle
that condensers accept dumped steam in
proportion to the loss of load
sustained by the associated turbine.
In the particular case of a single
turbine trip, the partitioning
algorithm only directs dumped steam to
the condenser of the tripped turbine.
Note, however, that interlocks are
provided to inhibit the dumping of
steam to a failed condenser.

Additional early analogue control
studies investigated the steam
generator level control at low power.
Problems had been identified on other
PWR plant with level control
instabilities in low power operation,
which could be exacerbated by the
requirement on Sizewell B to provide
automatic changeover between control on
the bypass feed regulating valves and
control on the main feed regulating
valves. The analysis led to the
conclusion that some, if not all, of
the reported unstable behaviour
resulted from the design of the bypass
feed regulating valves in that:

(i)   the valve C_v was too low by a
      factor of 2 to 3

(ii) the valve characteristic, the
      variation of C_v with valve lift,
      was highly non-linear, with an
      increase in gain by a factor of 9
      occurring at about 50% valve lift.

This conclusion resulted in a
recommendation that linear feed valve
characteristics should be specified for
Sizewell B, with a more appropriate
sizing of the feed bypass regulating
valves. This revised specification
allowed the automatic valve changeover

facility to be defined on the principle of simultaneous adjustment of the main and bypass regulating valves, one opening and the other closing at pre-determined rates, resulting in minimum perturbation to the feed flow at the the steam generators.

5 DIGITAL CONTROL STUDIES

5.1 Method development

In parallel with the analogue control studies described above, the calculation route selected for the digital control analysis was being developed and assessed.

It would have been possible to convert the analogue control algorithms to 'backward difference' digital algorithms, include the latter in the SIBDYM model and then attempt to stabilise and optimise the resulting system, largely by trial and error using time response techniques. This option was rejected on the grounds that the resource required is unpredictable and the process would not provide the necessary insight into the important plant dynamics affecting control behaviour.

The strategy selected was to base the control system design on an understanding of the plant dynamics, allowing the SNUPPS design to influence the final control system design, but not to the exclusion of any significant variations derived from the analysis. In outline, the method adopted was:

(i)   linearise the plant model about selected steady-state operating conditions

(ii) using a Computer Aided Design (CAD) package, generate frequency response matrices relating plant outputs (measurements) to plant inputs (control actuators)

(iii) using a CAD package, attempt to reduce any significant interactions between control loops

(iv) having reduced interaction to acceptable levels, design controllers using single input – single output (SISO) methods

(v)   provide a simple sample-data control model for initial time response evaluation of the controllers

(vi) provide a detailed sample-data control model for longer term proving and final optimisation studies in the full scope non-linear simulation model, SIBDYM.

The CAD package selected for the frequency response analysis was the

CEGB package ALADDIN (2), which is a development of CLADP (3). This was designed to accept input of the plant model either in transfer function or state matrix form. The latter option was consistent with the output produced by the PMSP lineariser, using the SIBDYM model. However, while the linearised model derived from the smallest symmetric SIBDYM model contained nearly 200 state variables, the maximum order acepted by the ALADDIN package was 50 so that significant model reduction was required to match the model to the CAD package. A model reduction method was developed in an NNC code MERLIN, which carried out three distinct functions:

(i)   translation of the state matrices from the PMSP output into diagonal form

(ii) reduction of the model by:

(a) removing those modes of the system which respond sufficiently rapidly to disturbances to be deemed to respond instantaneously

(b) removing those modes of the system which contribute least to the responses between the system inputs and the system outputs

(iii) since the diagonalised matrix is invariably complex, the final stage of the code translates the diagonal matrix of the reduced system into a real tri-diagonal form suitable for input to ALADDIN.

To check the adequacy of the reduced models obtained by application of the MERLIN technique, step disturbances were applied in turn to the system inputs and the resulting time responses compared with those arising from equivalent disturbances applied to the original non-linear model. From this comparison, it was judged that any reduced model of order less than about 70 would no longer be representative of the full model. A 'stretched' version of ALADDIN was therefore derived, capable of accepting up to 100 states.

Some preliminary analysis was carried out using the stretched version of ALADDIN, operating on the state matrix form of the reduced SIBDYM model. However, when applied to a system of this order, the process was too slow to be considered acceptable for interactive use. One of the main shortcomings was the length of time required to generate frequency responses from the state matrix model.

This setback was overcome when a relatively minor development of the MERLIN code was shown to be capable of rapid generation of frequency responses from the diagonalised form of the state matrices of the full-order model. Further modification of the ALADDIN package enabled direct input of the frequency responses calculated 'off-line' using MERLIN. For all subsequent frequency response analysis, the frequency responses relating outputs to inputs of the original plant model were generated by MERLIN and the need for model reduction was eliminated.

5.2 Frequency domain

The input vector chosen to define the state space form of the plant model consisted of the elements:

- normalised feed regulating valve area

- boron concentration in the primary coolant

- normalised feed pump speed

- pressuriser proportional heater bank power

- normalised turbine governor valve area

- normalised control bank insertion

- charging flow from chemical and volume control system to primary coolant.

The output vector consisted of the elements:

- reactor inlet water temperature

- reactor outlet water temperature

- normalised reactor power

- steam pressure at steam generator outlet

- normalised steam flow from steam generator

- feed pump discharge pressure

- turbine power

- steam generator water level

- normalised feed flow to steam generator

- pressuriser water level

- pressuriser pressure.

The 7 x 11 matrix of frequency responses was obtained using MERLIN. At this stage only symmetrical operation was being considered, leaving turbine to turbine and steam generator to steam generator interactions for later analysis. The frequency responses were derived initially from the continuous linear model; this was a

reasonable approach, since the degree of control loop interaction is largely independent of whether the control is implemented in continuous or discrete time.

The 7 x 11 matrix of frequency responses was reduced to 6 x 6 by:

(i)   omitting the boron concentration input, since this system is much slower acting than any other

(ii) omitting the outputs for reactor power, feed flow and steam flow, forming an arithmetic mean of the inlet and outlet temperatures and forming a difference of the feed pump discharge pressure and steam pressure.

This 6 x 6 combination of inputs and outputs coresponded essentially to the principal elements of the SNUPPS analogue design.

After appropriate re-ordering of the inputs and outputs so that logical associations of actuators and measurements should appear on the leading diagonal of the frequency response matrix, some scaling of inputs and outputs was performed to make the ALADDIN displays of Nyquist plots adequately visible for the subsequent column and row manipulations required to reduce interactions.

Significant interaction was found within the sub-system involving the feed regulating valve, feed pump speed, steam generator water level and feed to steam differential pressure. By manipulations to the columns of the frequency response matrix, the level of interaction in this 2 x 2 sub-system was significantly reduced. The manipulations were equivalent to forming two pseudo-actuators, each consisting of a different linear combination of the individual actuators, feed regulating valve area and feed pump speed.

Interaction was also deduced from examination of the coupling between the average coolant temperature and the pressuriser level, which could be removed by appropriate row manipulations in the matrix. Such manipulations were equivalent to forming a pseudo-output from a linear combination of average coolant temperature and pressuriser level, but a more meaningful interpretation, once a control loop had been closed around such a psuedo-output, was that the pressuriser level demand should be scheduled linearly with respect to the average coolant temperature. This result was consistent with the physical behaviour of the system and the SNUPPS analogue design, serving to reinforce the approach being adopted for Sizewell B.

5.3 Time domain

Following the frequency response analysis, wholly for continuous time systems, described above, it was necessary to determine appropriate sample times for the control loops, in order to change to discrete time systems. For the six loops being considered, a sample time of 1 second was selected initially, the choice being influenced by the following considerations.

(i) Many of the plant outputs required by the control system would be routed via the Primary Protection System and would be subject to an inherent dead time of the order of 1 second. Sampling at a faster rate offered no obvious benefit, while a control system designed for a faster sampling rate without taking account of such a dead time could be prone to instability.

(ii) The effects of an external disturbance on the plant must not cause unacceptable transients to occur prior to detection and controlling action. The dynamics of the PWR were shown to be such that sampling rates much slower than once per second were judged to be unaccceptable.

At this stage, although a significant proportion of the analysis was outstanding, a detailed specification of the control system performance requirements was required, so that preparation of design documents could proceed before putting the control system implementation out to tender. The specification concentrated on those areas which had an impact on the computer hardware provision and although control algorithms were specified, these were for indications of the likely number of arithmetic and logical operations to be performed at the selected sampling rates.

The control analysis continued with an assessment of provisional controller gains from consideration of the gain and phase margins of the open loop frequency responses. To test these controllers using time response input to ALADDIN, a PMSP model was prepared that could integrate the complex differential equations described by the diagonalised linear SIBDYM model. Included in this model was an idealised and simplified representation of a sample data control system derived from the matrix manipulations described above, that is, the manipulations were translated into the control system as simple gain changes in the controllers, as cross links between controllers to form pseudo-actuator demands, or as links between measurements to provide reference scheduling. The loops were closed with discrete proportional plus integral control algorithms.

Time domain analysis of 10% step disturbances in load using this simplified model identified a number of important factors:

(i) for the pressuriser controllers, the controller gains chosen from considerations of stability were far in excess of those that could be obtained from considerations of the relevant actuator capabilities. This was because the scope of the linear analysis could only represent the pressuriser proportional heater bank, used for trimming actions in steady-state operation, while significant pressure transients require actuation of the back-up heaters or the pressuriser spray. Pending further analysis, the control constants for the pressuriser pressure and level controllers were set at the values defined for the SNUPPS analogue system

(ii) There was instability in the turbine load behaviour and in the feed to steam pressure drop behaviour. In both cases the speed of response of these outputs to the associated inputs rendered the sampling rate too slow to adequately describe the transient behaviour. Since there was little scope for reducing the sampling period, the problem was eliminated by including a simple lag filter operating on the two outputs, to slow down the output response as seen by the controller.

(iii) although the steam generator level and feed to steam pressure drop had been decoupled, there was still interaction between the load control system and the steam generator level, causing excessive movement of the feed regulating valve. Further examinaton of the frequency response matrix suggested that this interaction could probably be reduced by additional row manipulations on the matrix, equivalent to scheduling the steam generator level demand against turbine load. This scheduling was not considered desirable, but a similar transient effect could be achieved by use of a steam flow signal (closely equivalent to turbine load), offset by a feed flow signal, responding more slowly, to return the level demand to its original position.

 C388/026

This solution results in a system similar to the SNUPPS three-element analogue controller.

Having completed a preliminary full-load design by the methods described above, the process was repeated for a range of part-load conditions. These further studies identified the need to schedule some controller gains with the measured load, but no other changes.

The final item was consideration of the effect of the absence of a reactor outlet temperature measurement in the Sizewell B design. The analysis described above assumed that an average coolant temperature signal could be provided directly from both inlet and outlet temperature measurements. Examination of the frequency response matrix using only reactor inlet temperature as the plant output and control bank insertion as the associated plant input showed that no row or column manipulations could adequately reduce the interaction levels.

Effort was originally aimed at simulating an average temperature output from a combination of the inlet temperature and reactor power outputs, but there was uncertainty in the steady-state accuracy of such a system. Further examination identified that manipulation of the differential equation representing the average temperature controller would allow the system to be respecified as proportional plus integral control acting on the inlet temperature together with proportional only control acting on a reactor power to turbine power mismatch signal.

It should be noted that the SNUPPS analogue control system used a reactor power to turbine power mismatch signal in addition to average temperature control. For Sizewell B, the power mismatch signal was derived as a part of, but not in addition to, the average temperature control. However, this was a conclusion derived from small perturbation analysis and the gain of the power mismatch term could be increased, if analysis of larger disturbances indicates a need.

6 CONTROL SYSTEM VERIFICATION

Analysis of a range of transients on the full non-linear SIBDYM model with the digital control system represented has revealed no unexpected control system response characteristics.

This analysis was extended to include an assessment of turbine to turbine and steam generator to steam generator interactions by running the four loop version of SIBDYM with both turbines represented. The level of interaction

between the turbine load controllers was sufficiently low to avoid the complexity of cross-coupling between the two controllers. In the case of the steam generators, the major source of interaction between the steam generator levels and feed to steam pressure drop had been removed in the symmetrical control system design phase and no other interactions were identified.

The current version of the SIBDYM model includes a detailed model of the digital control system which:

(i)   recognises the distributed nature of the system so that individual controllers are not generally synchronised one to another

(ii)   includes delay times associated with plant measurements routed through the Primary Protection System

(iii) includes delays associated with signal scanning and processing of other measurements

(iv)   includes all other non-linear features such as actuator rate limits and end-stops.

This model has been and continues to be used to evaluate and optimise the plant and control system behaviour. This analysis will continue up to the time at which the plant is commissioned, culminating in the provision of SACS parameters and predictions of the control and plant behaviour during the setting-to-work of the controllers and the related commissioning tests.

7 CONCLUDING REMARKS

(i)   Considerable effort has been expended on the development of a detailed mathematical model of the Sizewell B plant. The effort has been justified by the results of subsequent validation exercises, giving confidence that the dynamic characteristics of the plant are well represented by the model. Without this confidence, any application to control system design would be of limited value.

(ii)   A sound understanding of the plant dynamic characteristics and the interaction between loops within the Station Automatic Control System has been acquired. At all stages of the linear analysis, the most accurate representation of the plant was retained, since there was ultimately no need to further approximate the model dynamics.

(iii) Analysis using the full non-linear model incorporating a

representation of the developed
digital control system has
confirmed the conclusions derived
from the linear analysis.

(iv) Application of the methods
developed has demonstrated the
benefits of some additions to the
SNUPPS control system for
Sizewell B, while confirming the
basic features of the SNUPPS
system.

REFERENCES

1   STIRRUP J F and MANN A J S.
     Plant Modelling System Program
     Reference Manual
     CEGB/CISD/CC/P732, 1985

2   THOMPSON M A. ALADDIN – Analysis
     and Design of Linear Control
     Systems
     CEGB/CISD/N924, 1983

3   EDMUNDS J M. CLADP – Cambridge
     Linear Analysis and Design
     Package, 3rd version
     Cambridge University Engineering
     Department, 1981

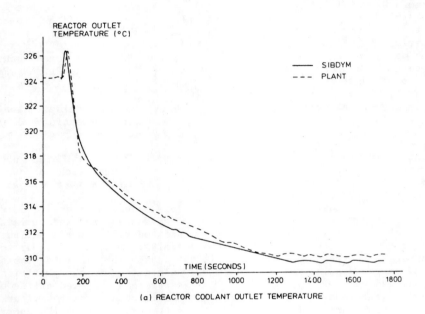

(a) REACTOR COOLANT OUTLET TEMPERATURE

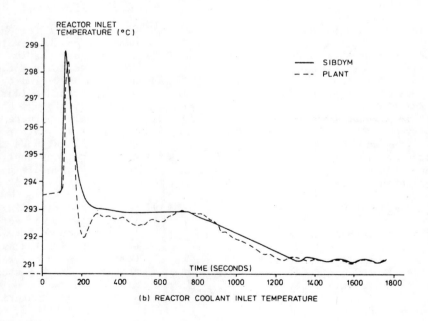

(b) REACTOR COOLANT INLET TEMPERATURE

Fig 1   Simulation of rapid 50 per cent power reduction from full power;
         variation of reactor inlet and outlet temperatures

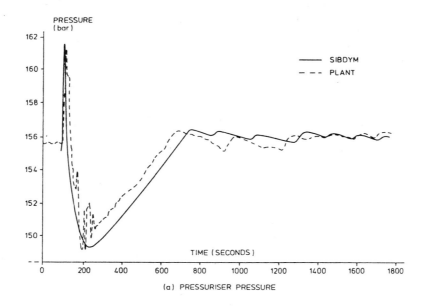

(a) PRESSURISER PRESSURE

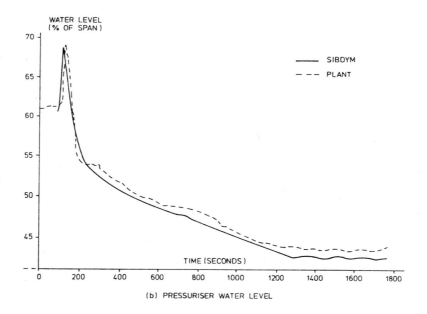

(b) PRESSURISER WATER LEVEL

Fig 2   Simulation of rapid 50 per cent power reduction from full power;
variation of pressurizer pressure and water level

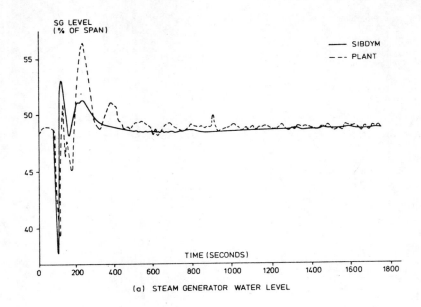

(a) STEAM GENERATOR WATER LEVEL

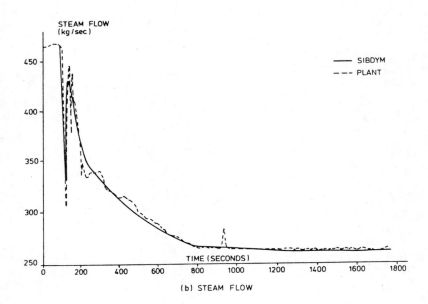

(b) STEAM FLOW

Fig 3   Simulation of rapid 50 per cent power reduction from full power;
variation of steam generator water level and steam flow

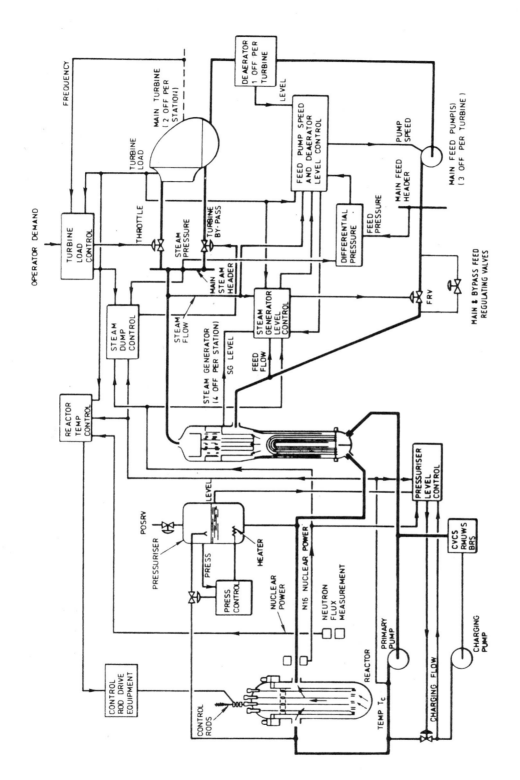

Fig 4   PWR basic station control system

C388/014

Distributed digital processing technology applied to commercial nuclear power station controls

G W REMLEY, BS Physics
Westinghouse Electric Corporation, Pittsburgh, Pennsylvania

INTRODUCTION

In any commercial nuclear power plant, the functions of control, protection, and monitoring are required to keep the plant operating efficiently and safely. Due to the criticality of these functions, the C&I systems performing the functions must meet stringent reliability and failure tolerance criteria.

Over the thirty or more years that commercial nuclear power plants have been operating, the C&I systems have evolved from analog amplifier and relay-based control circuits monitoring a moderate number of plant parameters to distributed digital processing systems monitoring a large number of plant parameters and performing complex control operations.

The basis for this change has been the needs or desires associated with plant control and safety, evaluated against the capabilities of C&I technology based on distributed digital processing. In general, the results have been successful, but particular applications and the evolutionary path have had some difficulties.

Westinghouse Electric has had significant experience with distributed digital processing C&I systems for commercial nuclear power stations. This experience is associated with two distinct areas of application. In the United States, it has been over ten years since a contract for a new nuclear power station has been issued. However, the demand for replacement systems and upgrade systems for plants in operation and plants under construction has been growing steadily. These new systems are based on digital technology. New plant experience is based on the application of Westinghouse designs and through international relationships such as licensing agreements and joint development programs. In particular, the Westinghouse Integrated Protection System (IPS) is the state-of-the-art culmination of all the previous reactor protection system practices. The IPS in a slightly modified form is the Primary Protection System (PPS) for the Sizewell B nuclear power plant. Because of the significant processing capability of the multi-processor system, the IPS is able to handle more plant parameters than ever before and to perform more complex logic functions.

The IPS is part of a complete distributed digital C&I architecture for new commercial nuclear power plants. Other C&I systems that are part of this architecture are the station autocontrol system, special plant monitoring systems, the alarm system, the operation display system, the station computer system, and balance-of-plant control systems (or interfaces). These systems are interconnected with a communication network of data links and data highways that utilize fiber optic technology. The man-machine interface associated with the distributed digital equipment is organized into a modern control room arrangement.

This paper will focus on the design of the IPS that has undergone intensive review in several countries, including the United Kingdom and the United States. Specifically, the focus will be on the IPS architecture, the structure of the embedded software, the diagnostic software and hardware including the application of fail-safe design principles, and the requirements for data management in a distributed microprocessor system. Based on experiences to date, the application of the lessons learned from the IPS design process will be applied to a completely distributed digital I&C architecture for new nuclear power plants.

ARCHITECTURE

Integrated Protection System Architecture

The IPS architecture contains several different types of redundancy to meet its high reliability and availability goals.

Overall, the IPS is a two-out-of-four system. The details of two-out-of-four logic take into account the safety application of operational bypasses for maintenance and test.

Within one of the trains (channel sets or guard-lines), there is additional redundancy and separation of functions. There are two-out-of-three auctioneered voter elements, one-out-of-two elements that are based on detection and control of failures, and groupings of functions such that independent functions that operate on the same event are separated.

The IPS is a four train system in which each train receives inputs from one plant sensor for each variable to be used in the protective functions. The four trains are completely independent electrically and physically. Thus each train receives a measurement of each process variable which is completely independent of the values received by the other three trains.

Each train of the IPS uses two independent microprocessor systems for generating the reactor partial trips and two more for generating the engineered safety features partial actuation signals. All of the more probable faults can be detected by two or more diverse process variables. These diverse variables are allocated to the independent microprocessors in such a way that independent functions that operate on a single event are separated.

The partial trip status corresponding to each measured parameter is communicated from each train to the other three trains over optical data links which convey the signals while maintaining electrical isolation between the trains. Each train thus receives four independent partial trip signals for each process variable: one derived from its own field instrumentation, and three via the other three trains of the IPS.

The partial reactor trip signals generated in each train of the IPS are combined with each other and with those received from the other three trains such that in normal operation, all protective functions operate on the basis of a two-out-of-four voting logic on the four independent partial trip signals.

Dedicated microprocessors in the Engineered Safety Features Actuation Subsystem (ESFAS) of the IPS combine the partial actuation signals to determine whether protective action is required. The partial actuation signals generated in each train are combined with the partial actuation signals from the other three trains in the same logical manner as the partial reactor trip signals.

Integrated Logic System Architecture

The system level outputs from each of the redundant ESFAS are communicated to the Integrated Logic System (ILS) over two independent optical data highways which carry redundant copies of the same data. The data highways are arranged in a star configuration and permit two-way communication so that actuation commands can be transmitted to the ILS from the ESFAS, and equipment status information can be transmitted in the reverse direction.

In order to reduce the amount of cabling between the IPS and the plant control rooms, the majority of manual control signals and status indication signals are transmitted over redundant data highways. Each train has separate data highways to the control rooms, and all data messages are sent accompanied by error checking data so that any failure of the link is immediately detected and, even if left uncorrected, only affects one train. A few signals, notably the manual reactor trip and system level manual actuation and block signals, are hard wired from the control room to the IPS.

The ILS portion of the IPS performs the logic for controlling individual items of plant equipment and is divided into four independent and separated trains. The ILS is further divided within each train into a number of subsystems which can be distributed around the plant close to groups of components to be actuated. The ILS receives the system level actuation signals over redundant optical data highways from the ESFAS and combines them with manual actuation signals and interlocks to determine whether a component should be actuated.

Each ILS cabinet contains three identical microprocessor systems, each of which receives data over one of the three redundant data highways.

Manual actuation signals are received from the control rooms over redundant multiplexed data links. The actuation signals for each component generated in the three separate logic paths are finally combined in a two-out-of-three voting logic to produce the final actuation signal to the component. It should be noted that the component level manual actuation logic is not performed in the ILS on Sizewell B, the CEGB having decided to separate the manual and automatic actuation routes for safeguards components.

Applicability to Other C&I Systems

All of the IPS architectural features carry over to the other systems of the distributed digital C&I architecture. The ILS two-out-of-three logic is directly applicable to the nuclear control logic and the balance-of-plant control logic if the reliability requirements warrant. The one-out-of-two configuration is based on the detection and control of failures. That is, the one-out-of-two configuration is not voted but configured with an active control elements and active standby element. This configuration has the widest application. Examples of such configurations are the modulating control functions of the Integrated Control System (ICS), the ICS process data highway, the ICS logic data highway, the Plant Process Data System (PPDS), and the Alarm System (AWARE). The ICS control functions are separated into independent subsystems. Like the IPS, the criteria for separation is based on functional independence. A variation of the two-out-of-four configuration is associated with the ICS Signal Selector.

SOFTWARE STRUCTURE

Integrated Protection System Software Structure

One of the main objectives of modern software engineering discipline is to develop a design methodology which lends itself to the production of reliable software. Proven, reliable tools are an important part of this because they support a high-level approach to the software design. Even though no single design method and no single tool is perfect, to the extent that a design tool reliably automates some of the work involved in proceeding from requirements to implementation, it frees the designer to use a more comprehensive overall design strategy. It also tends to reduce the incidence of human error if a given step in the design process can be reliably automated. In particular, the overall software structure should support making the application software (the software that will change from subsystem to subsystem or from system to system) as simple as possible. This type of approach is sometimes embodied in a Problem-Oriented Language. Making the application software simple will make the support software more complex. However, this software does not change with the application, and the overall design testing and verification effort will be less.

One of the important elements in a high-level design approach is the use of a high-level language compiler which can take structured source code and convert it into efficient machine language code. Without the efficiency provided by the high-level language, concentration would be forced more on the low-level implementation details and less on the higher level design considerations. Principles of data hiding and loose coupling of modules to improve execution times might have to be sacrificed. A low-level approach is felt to be far more detrimental to the goal of producing error-free software.

There is a tension in the design and implementation of software between the high-level view of the software design and the constraints of real-world implementation. Westinghouse has tried to concentrate as much as possible on the high-level view of the software design, applying principles which are known to lend themselves to the production of reliable software. The software is designed to be modular and reusable. The modules are loosely coupled. Details of computer system interface requirements are embedded in the reusable support modules so that application code can be simplified. Data are hidden within the modules which produce them and are supplied to other modules via data passing procedures. Procedure structures are kept simple to the extent feasible. Readability of code is emphasized over efficiency. The use of interrupts is avoided; events are detected and responded to by polling rather than by interruption. Where concurrent processing is necessary, it is supplied by multiple processors rather than by a multi-tasking operating system. Most of these principles, which are intended to enhance the reliability of the software, also have the effect of producing code which is less efficient than that which could be produced by concentrating attention upon the low level implementation details. Some attention to efficiency is necessary, and Westinghouse has sacrificed design simplicity to efficiency in a few time critical places but has attempted to give priority to higher level design considerations wherever possible.

However, the software design approach is well defined and tends not to produce code which uses the more esoteric constructs. Considerations of "real-time" operation are not significant since interrupts are not used, little use is made of global variables, and contention control is provided for shared memory access. Furthermore, the very deterministic, non-interrupt driven nature of the software enhances the verification testing process. It is important that the code must be designed to be verifiable, and the software design approach has been oriented towards that goal. It should be noted that the verification process includes, in addition to examining the source code, performing extensive testing on the actual compiler-generated object code of each procedure.

In addition to the deterministic nature of the software design, the nature of the protection functions themselves is reasonably deterministic with input ranges that are limited. This enhances the capability of performing comprehensive software validation testing, which can provide a significant additional level of confidence.

Applicability of Other C&I Systems

Whatever the system, the production of error-free software is a universal goal throughout the entire distributed digital C&I system. The motivation goes beyond plant safety. The IPS software design approach that is oriented to producing error-free software is a software approach that is the most effective with respect to quality, cost, and schedule in the long term.

The IPS common functions are used in all systems of the C&I architecture that are composed of microcomputer subsystems with architectures similar to the IPS subsystems.

EMBEDDED SELF-DIAGNOSTICS AND FAIL-SAFE DESIGN PRINCIPLES

Integrated Protection System Self Diagnostics

The IPS incorporates two levels of on-line testing. The first level consists of continuous self checking which verifies that circuits are performing correctly and automatically adjusts the input calibration. The second level of testing is initiated by the operator but proceeds automatically after initiation. This test checks the conversion accuracy of the analog to digital converters on the input cards, checks the accuracy of all trip levels, checks the response time of the dynamic algorithms and the overall system response time, injects a large number of combinations of trip and no-trip inputs to confirm the correct operation of the protective logic functions, and produces a permanent record of the test and its results on a printer on the test console.

The always on-going first level of testing is performed with the IPS in its normal state of operation; that is, no trips or bypasses are required or applied. During the second level of testing, the dedicated microprocessor which performs the testing applies bypasses to the logical outputs from the train to avoid spurious alarms being generated and to prevent possible spurious trips in the event of a fault or disturbance occurring in another train.

Automatic logic functions are incorporated into each train of the IPS to monitor the bypasses applied in all trains. These functions automatically adjust the trip logic to ensure that the whole system is always able to accept a single failure without failing to trip when required. If so many bypasses are applied that this can no longer be achieved, reactor trip is automatically initiated. Sufficient interlocks and alarms are incorporated to prevent the operator from putting the system into such a state inadvertently.

Many techniques have been developed to deal with the various issues inherent in the fault-tolerant design of critical real-time systems. Central to these techniques is a defense-in-depth philosophy, in which different layers of the design address both different and overlapping fault detection and recovery issues. The addition of microprocessor-based technology offers a new opportunity to extend the defense-in-depth philosophy for critical real-time systems, particularly in the nuclear industry.

Fail-safe design principles are traditionally applied by designing circuits such that, to the extent possible, all the plausible failure modes of the components would lead passively to predictable safe states. A microprocessor is driven by a clock signal, and its operation is inherently dynamic. The function of a microprocessor-based system is defined by programming which, in the case of the IPS, is embedded in EPROMs (Programmable Read Only

Memory). This programming contains algorithms that define the safety functions of the system. It may also contain algorithms that test the operation of the microprocessor and the hardware elements that support its operation as a protection system. Fail-safe design principles can be combined with the inherent characteristics of microprocessors and applied to the protection system design implementation. This approach can be viewed as equivalent to the traditional UK/CEGB fail-safe design approaches for safety systems.

The IPS design includes continuously executing hardware diagnostics. The purpose of these diagnostics is to detect and identify random failures of the hardware elements that comprise the IPS safety circuits. Upon detection of a hardware failure in the safety circuits by the diagnostics, the IPS outputs will be set to a preferred state. The basis for the diagnostics is derived from with the plant risk assessment, which requires the protection system to attain certain reliability and availability goals for the various safety functions. The required scope and effectiveness of the continuously executing hardware diagnostics must be at least that which is assumed in the reliability assessment for the IPS equipment. A secondary goal is to identify the occurrence of a fault so that it may be repaired and to provide information concerning the nature of the fault so as to facilitate the repair process.

It is desirable that the effectiveness of the diagnostics exceed the minimum requirement stated above. However, since the embedded diagnostics run while the system is performing its safety functions, it is also desirable that they be kept as simple as possible. An attempt to detect every possible fault would increase system complexity. It would also increase the time needed to detect any given fault, as well as increase the response time of the system. Excessive complexity in the diagnostics would also detract from the goal of designing the software in a way that minimizes the chance of programming error and that maximizes the effectiveness of the verification and validation process.

The following criteria are balanced against each other in the design of the embedded diagnostics.

a) The diagnostics should concentrate on detecting the more probable types of faults. Engineering judgment and experience are used to identify the more likely types of faults which may occur.

b) The diagnostic software should be kept as simple as possible and should not conflict with the application of good software engineering principles. Where a type of fault can be detected with a very simple test, it is not critical to show that the fault is likely, in order to justify the inclusion of the test. Where a type of fault can be detected only with great difficulty or complexity, a test for the fault should be included only if the fault is likely enough that it could impact the minimum reliability requirements of the IPS.

c) Faults should be detected as quickly as possible.

d) Execution of the diagnostics should not delay the execution of the safety functions in a way that conflicts with the system timing requirements.

Diagnostics can be grouped into two broad categories: tests of the CPU and its resources, and tests of peripheral resources. The first category attempts to detect faults that could impact the ability of the microprocessor to correctly execute its programs. This includes faults in the memories (RAM and PROM), the CPU, the processor clock, timers used for program timing, and the arithmetic coprocessor. When a fault of this nature is detected, the microprocessor halts as quickly and directly as possible after taking some prescribed means of reporting the fault. The system design includes means of detecting the halting of any microprocessor that is necessary for safety functions and placing the IPS outputs in the preferred safe state. The design includes automatic restart capability, but its use is limited.

The second category of diagnostics attempts to detect faults that do not impair the ability of the microprocessor to execute correctly, but may affect the integrity of one or more safety function calculations. These include faults in the hardware devices with which the microprocessor has interfaces, both microprocessor-based and non-microprocessor-based devices. Examples include analog inputs and contact inputs (sensors, signal conditioners, and peripheral signal processors), inter-processor shared memory communications, inter-subsystem serial communications, the Dynamic Trip Bus, and ESF actuation outputs. The microprocessor that detects faults of this category continues to execute and will take such action as necessary to force all affected safety outputs to the preferred safe state.

When any fault is detected, the system generates an external alarm indication so that the fault may be repaired. It is also be a goal of the design to provide sufficient diagnostic information that the location of a fault may be easily identified to the level of a replaceable component.

Applicability to Other C&I Systems

The meaning of fail-safe is most appropriate when referring to a protection system such as the IPS. This does not mean that embedded self-diagnostics are less important in systems that are not protection systems. However, in other systems the primary role of the embedded self-diagnostics is to detect and control failures. The details of how failures are controlled depends on the detailed system design and plant function of the particular system. The systems in the distributed digital C&I architecture that are a one-out-of-two configuration based on the detection and control of failures (that is, configurations with an active control elements and an active standby elements) rely on the embedded self-diagnostics for the required failure detection.

DATA MANAGEMENT

Integrated Protection System Data Management

The IPS is a distributed microprocessor-based system with a requirement for communication of data among many of the microcomputer elements. In distributed microprocessor-based C&I systems, the inter- and intra-subsystem communication requirements are defined by the overall system architecture. The IPS protocol addresses the intra-subsystem communications.

Specifically, the protocol allows for multiple processors to exchange information through a shared-memory interface. The primary goal is to provide a reliable means for information to be exchanged between central application processor boards (masters) and dedicated function processor boards (slaves) in a single computer chassis. The resultant Multiprocessor Shared-Memory Information Exchange protocol, a standard master-slave shared-memory interface suitable for use in nuclear safety systems, is designed to pass unidirectional buffers of information between the processors while providing a minimum, deterministic cycle time for this data exchange. This is achieved by providing multiple buffers for each unique block of information passed between the two processors.

This interface protocol is optimized for the IPS real-time critical communications requirements. By distributing the processing requirements of a time-critical function across multiple processors, the tasks to be performed by each component processor are reduced. Furthermore, the processing tasks of most subsystems within a system can be functionally viewed as a unique application function and a set of common functions such as I/O handling and pre-processing, external communication processing, and diagnostics. By off-loading the dedicated common functions onto individual "slave" processors, two distinct advantages are gained. First, the hardware and software for the processors performing the common system tasks may be of a standard, configurable design. Secondly, the processing burden of the subsystem application processor, or "master" processor, is substantially reduced, both in volume and execution time. However, the use of multiple processors to implement a single subsystem creates the additional communications burden of communications between the processors within the subsystem.

The communications burden is not only associated with the performance of the system, but also with the configuration or setup of the system, and the optimum solution requires tradeoffs. That is, improvements in the configurability are usually at the expense of the performance.

In order to address subsystem configuration requirements, the IPS common function software is table driven. In particular, the data communicated between subsystems is defined by tables associated with the communications common function software. The tables are generated by a data base manager after the configuration data is entered into the data base. This approach provides the applications engineer with an interface for configuring the subsystem that is equivalent to the use of a high level Problem-Oriented Language for the application software.

Applicability to Other C&I Systems

The data management concepts can be applied to other systems that comprise the distributed digital C&I architecture. If the system uses the same common functions software, then the same data base manager can be used. As stated previously, the Integrated Control System (ICS), Plant Process Data System (PPDS), the Alarm System (AWARE), and some of the special monitoring systems such as the Flux Mapping System (FMS) use the same common functions software.

For inter-system communications, the data management problem becomes more complex. In the Westinghouse C&I architecture, the inter-system communications take place mostly through the Monitor Bus. This bus is associated with real-time data acquisition restricting control function communications to the inter-subsystem communications.

In general, two types of data transfers are required in a real-time data acquisition system. For example, process data must be transferred frequently at exact time intervals, while file transfers are likely to be transferred infrequently and upon demand. The data highway architecture separates these periodic and aperiodic data transfers onto two separate data highways so that their operations will not interfere with each other. That is, there is a distinct separation of periodic and aperiodic data transfer functions onto two separate dual data highways whose protocols are appropriate to the function. The protocols selected for each data highway are oriented to support the nature of the data transfer of that highway. Both data highway protocols are based on industry standards, which is necessary for an open system approach. The configuration uses proven hardware and software elements. The implementation will support high performance requirements.

Since an open system approach is required at this level of the C&I architecture, the selection of the data highways is an application-specific design decision. Highway protocols based on industry standards are a necessary condition for an open system architecture, which is the design intent. However, it should be recognized that open systems that support the complete seven layers of the ISO communications architecture may not always be appropriate and may require significant additional development by the industry. At this time, Westinghouse is analyzing a periodic highway that is a MAP protocol compatible with IEEE 802.4 token bus and ISO 8073. The protocol under analysis for the aperiodic highway is an ETHERNET protocol compatible with IEEE 802.3 CSMA/CD and the ISO standard.

Using the IPS data base manager, which is designed to configure the IPS common functions software, is not directly applicable to this portion of the C&I architecture. Although the concept of a data base manager in lieu of manual configuration is even more appropriate to this portion of the C&I architecture. In fact, Westinghouse believes that a data base manager to coordinate the communication associated with the Monitor Bus is critical to the configuration and maintenance of the distributed digital C&I system.

SUMMARY

It is now practical to apply distributed digital processing technology to all the nuclear power station's controls. Westinghouse has had significant experience with distributed digital processing C&I systems for commercial nuclear power stations. In particular, the Westinghouse Integrated Protection System (IPS) embodies many of the technologies required for complete distributed digital processing technology. Principles and elements of the IPS architecture contain several different types of redundancies, and these elements and approaches are applicable to other C&I systems. A software design process and structure that produces error-free software has almost universal application if the boundary conditions can be met. Traditionally, in protection systems for commercial nuclear applications, a complete off-line functional test of the system was performed. Now, embedded self-diagnostics can provide a continuous test of the system to speed fault identification and repair. These embedded diagnostics are an additional layer of defense which was never before possible. The various elements of the distributed system are connected on a Monitor Bus to communicate real-time data acquisition data. The Monitor Bus consists of periodic and aperiodic data highways based on industry standards to support an open systems approach.

ACKNOWLEDGMENTS

Some of the concepts described in this paper have been taken from internal Westinghouse documents authored by William D. Ghrist III and John W. Pepper.

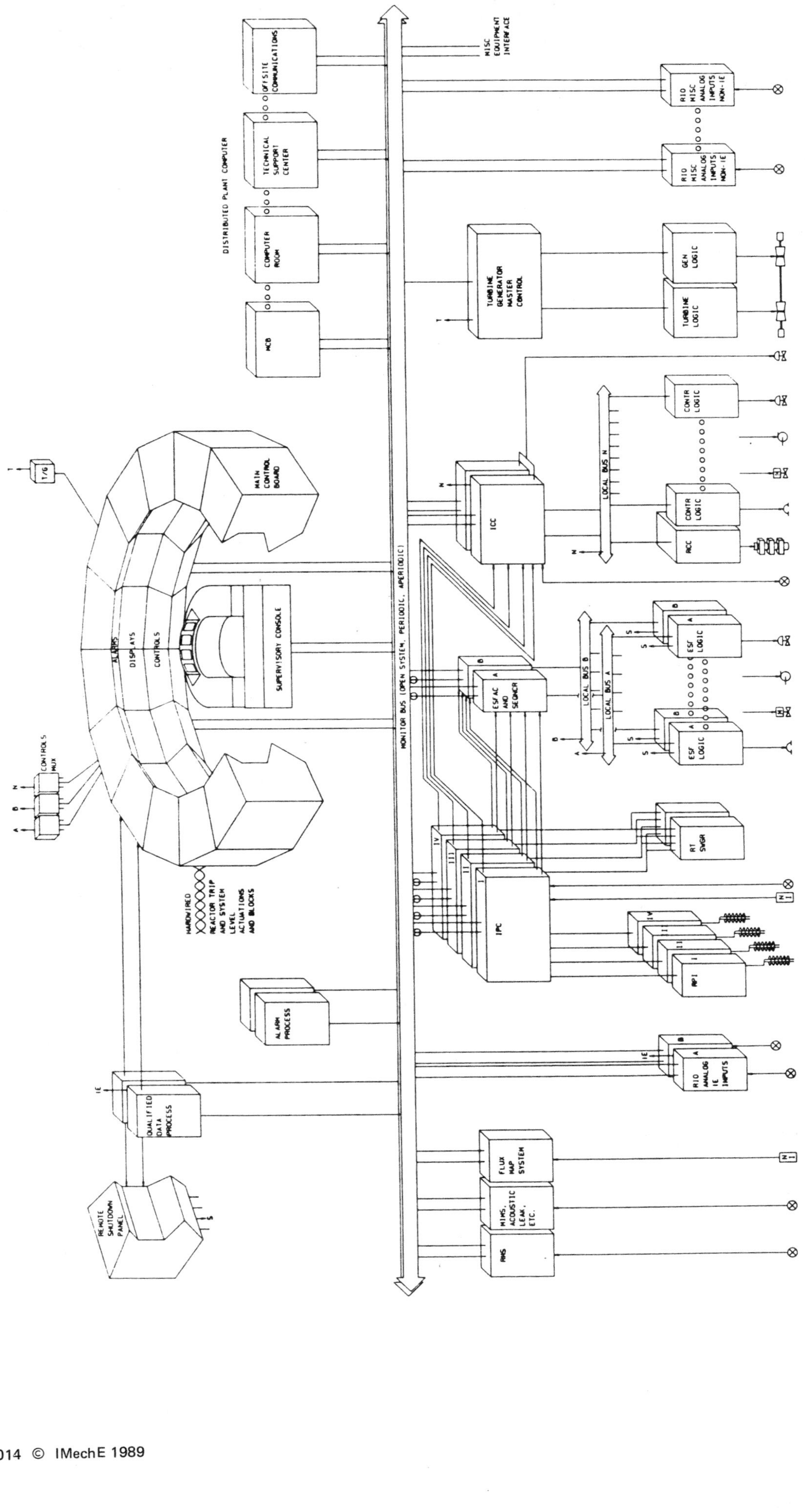

Fig 1   Instrumentation and control architecture

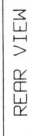

REAR VIEW

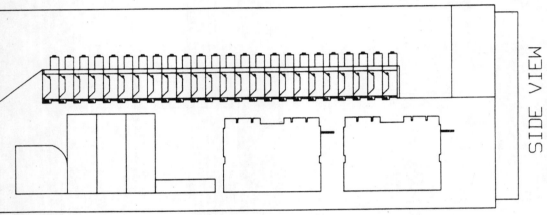

SIDE VIEW

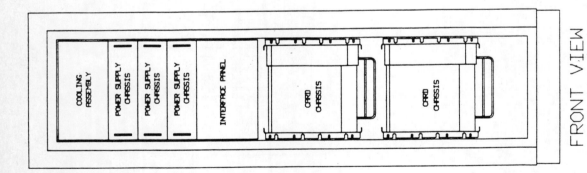

FRONT VIEW

COOLING ASSEMBLY

POWER SUPPLY CHASSIS

POWER SUPPLY CHASSIS

POWER SUPPLY CHASSIS

INTERFACE PANEL

CARD CHASSIS

CARD CHASSIS

Fig 2   Typical bay configuration for a PPS cabinet

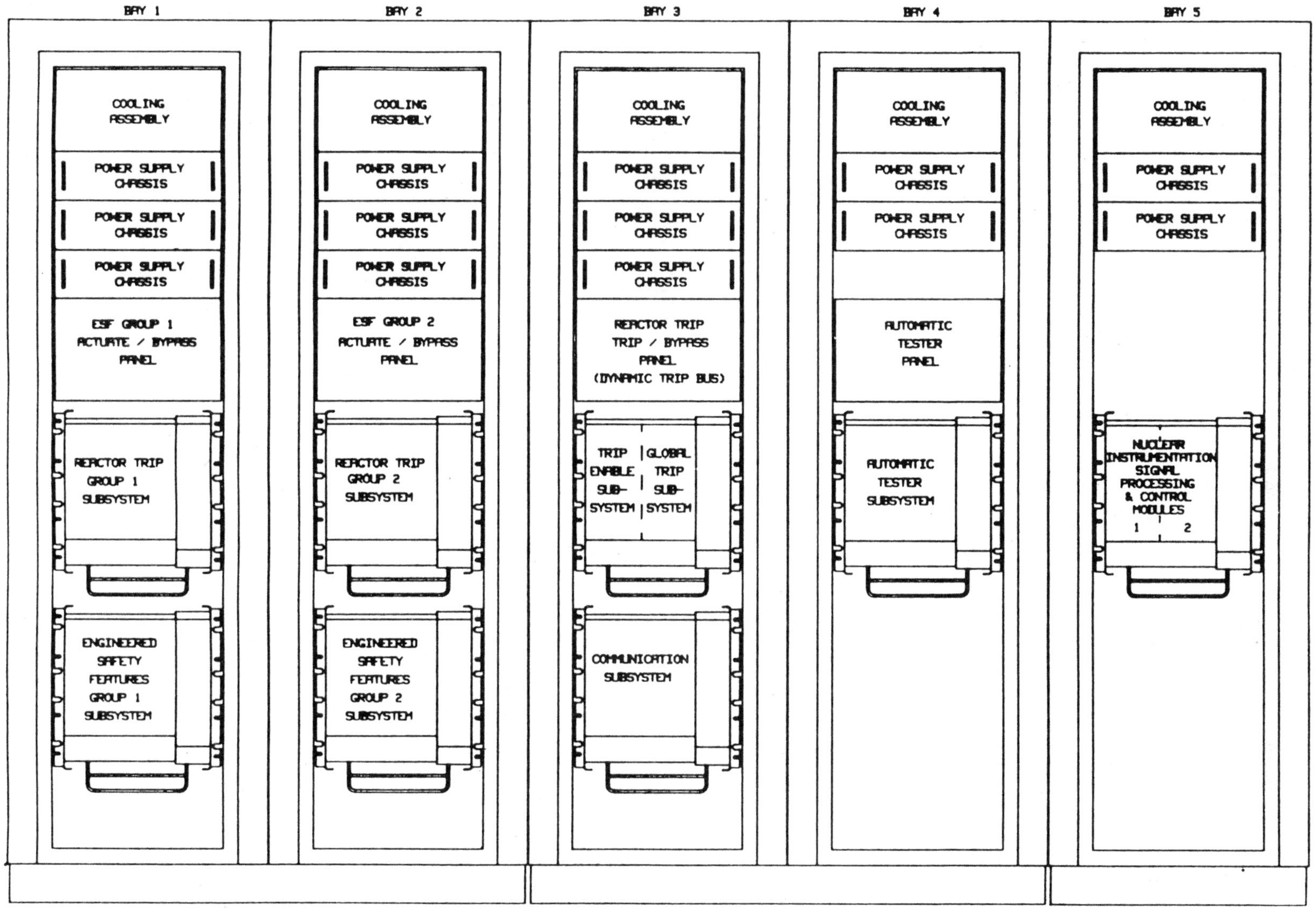

Fig 3   Integrated protection cabinet front layout

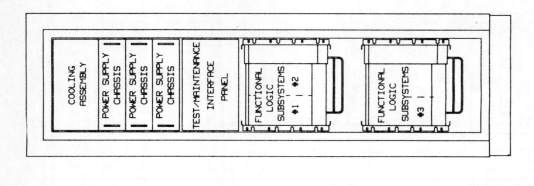

Fig 5   ESF interface cabinet front view

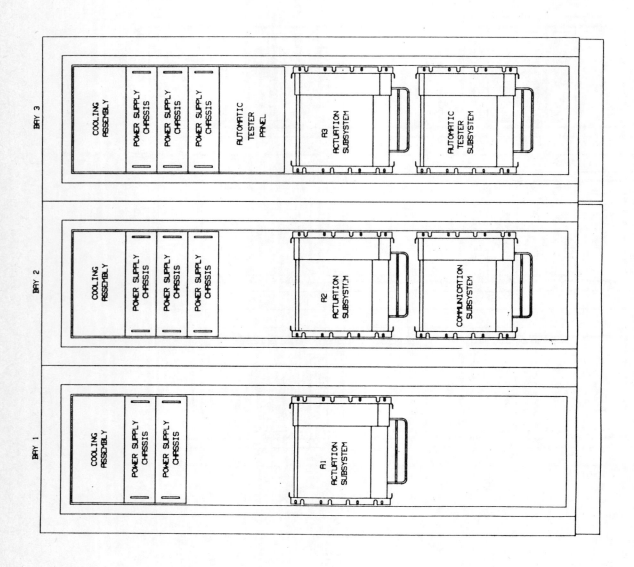

Fig 4   Engineered safety features actuation cabinet front layout

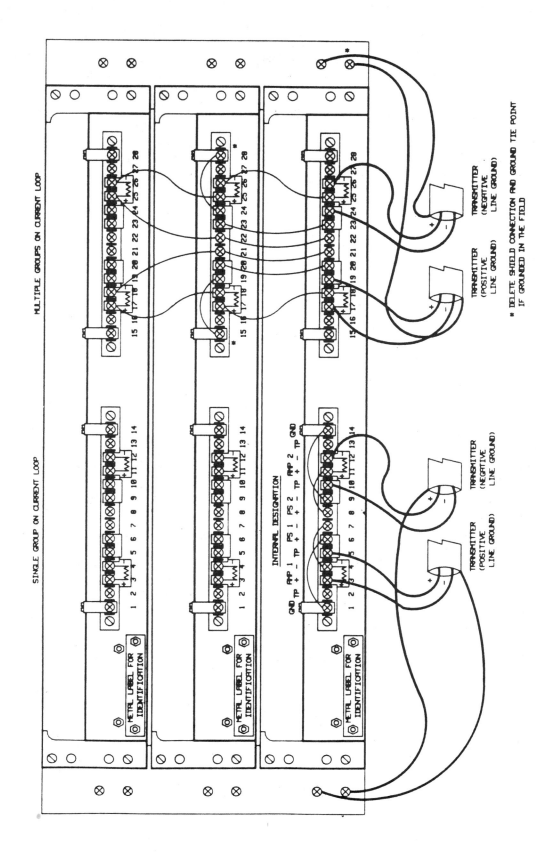

Fig 6   Typical current loop termination

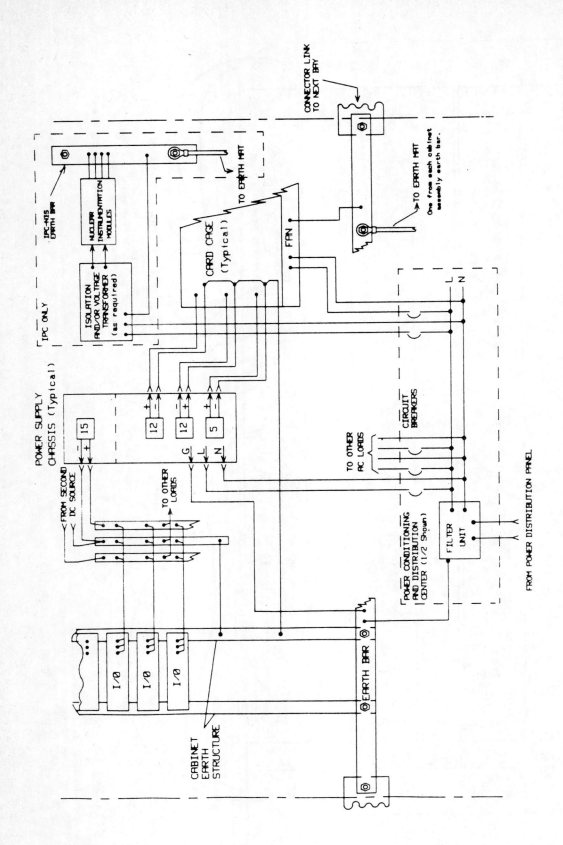

Fig 7   Typical power distribution/earthing details

C388/038

The life cycle benefits of an integrated system approach to control and instrumentation

J C HIGGS, BSc, CEng, FIEE
GEC Power Instrumentation and Control Limited, Leicester

SYNOPSIS

The data acquisition, control and monitoring system for the Sizewell B PWR is based on an integrated system product known as P20, which has been jointly developed by CGEE ALSTHOM and Electricité de France. The product uses an hierarchy of Local Area Networks supporting distributed plant interfaces, processing and man-machine interfaces. High integrity and availability are obtained through multiple redundancy and self-checking techniques. Object Oriented Design techniques are used to analyse and implement the C & I requirements. The paper describes the product, the application and the benefits which result from this product and design approach.

CONTENTS

1. C & I REQUIREMENTS FOR SIZEWELL B

2. SIZEWELL B INTEGRATED SYSTEM CONTRACT

3. UNDERLYING PRINCIPLES OF THE INTEGRATED SYSTEM APPROACH

4. P20 INTEGRATED CONTROL AND MONITORING SYSTEM

5. SIZEWELL B APPLICATION

6. DESIGN METHODOLOGY

7. LIFECYCLE BENEFITS OF THE INTEGRATED SYSTEM

8. CONCLUSION

1. C & I REQUIREMENTS FOR SIZEWELL B

Sizewell B power station is based on the standard SNUPPS design (Standard Nuclear Unit for Power Plant Systems). However, in order to licence the operation of a PWR in the UK, there have been various changes made to the design of the plant and to the way in which information will be presented to the operators. These changes particularly influence the design of the plant Control and Instrumentation (C & I), and the man/machine interfaces.

In particular, the control and monitoring systems on Sizewell B are required to have a very high level of availability since station operation is dependent upon the full operation of the majority of the systems. Many of the control and monitoring functions have duties related to safety, and the systems which carry out these functions must therefore have clearly determined failure modes to permit fail-safe system design. For this type of application, the product development, the application design and the manufacturing implementation are all subject to review by the Nuclear Licensing Authority from a safety point of view.

Another safety requirement is that the system should be segregated into up to eight groups and up to three safety categories, with associated electrical, fire and data interaction isolation between these groupings. All equipment related to safety must be designed for a high level of seismic withstand.

The extra safety requirements on Sizewell B call for a considerable increase in equipment compared with that of the original SNUPPS design. However, the space and HVAC (Heating Ventilation and Air Conditioning) services are constrained to be generally as in the original SNUPPS design. This demands an equipment range having a high packing density, low power consumption and the flexibility to multiplex large numbers of signals between the plant areas and the control and instrument room complexes.

The safety considerations in a nuclear power station also require an additional control room, the Auxiliary Shutdown Room (ASR), to control safe shutdown if the main control room cannot be used due to smoke or for other reasons. Remote display, logging and analysis of very large amounts of the control and monitoring data is required in the Technical Support Centre (TSC) located away from the main control building.

Most aspects of the plant mechanical, electrical and civil design are proven SNUPPS designs, and there is every intention and expectation that these aspects of the power station will be completed on, or before the scheduled completion date. The main control and monitoring system requirements are much altered from SNUPPS. Achieving short design, manufacturing and setting to work timescales into this area is critical within the power station programme.

One of the major causes of delay in the design and setting to work of many power station control and monitoring systems has been the difficulties experienced in successfully interlinking several different sub-systems often supplied by different contractors. To lessen this problem on Sizewell B, the CEGB has required that the main control and monitoring system shall be a fully integrated design obtained from one supplier.

This control and monitoring system contract is termed the Integrated System for Centralised Operation (ISCO).

2. SIZEWELL B INTEGRATED SYSTEM CONTRACT SCOPE

The Integrated System for Centralised Operation (ISCO) comprises the distributed plant interface input/output equipment; the distributed processing nodes for all analogue and logic processing; the data communication networks which feed the various databases; the operator display stations; and the logging and alarm processing printers and displays. All the control panels and desks for the Main Control Room and the Auxiliary Shutdown Room, and the computer equipment for the Technical Support Centre is included in the ISCO scope along with the independant Local Alarm and Alarm Fascia systems.

The functions implemented in the ISCO include the main closed loop Station Automatic Control Systems (SACS) plus a variety of other control loops. It includes the main plant systems' interlocking and sequencing, monitoring of all essential analogue and status information in the station, and the processing and presentation of this information on display units, printers, picture copiers and magnetic storage media.

The processed information is provided for operators, maintenance staff and off-line analysis teams, and is presented as animated mimic displays, bar graphs, trend graphs, tabular displays, alarm lists, and an historical data storage and retrieval record.

Analogue and status controls and indications are provided through discrete devices on the control rooms

panels. Such devices include discrepancy switches, raise/lower pushbuttons, meters and indicators. The majority of these are multiplexed through the ISCO, however, all the station electrical system controls are directly cabled. In addition, an overview panel provides sufficient independently derived information and alarms to permit assessment of conditions and to enable the operators to initiate and monitor safe shutdown should a major failure occur in the multiplexing system.

In addition to the main data display systems, there is a safety category 1 Safety Instrumentation Display System (SIDS) which provides an independent, redundant, high integrity route for displaying information critical to the safe shutdown of the reactor.

3. UNDERLYING PRINCIPLES OF THE INTEGRATED SYSTEM APPROACH

The basic principles of the ISCO approach are that the plant sensor data should be captured by the processing and data communications network as early in the signal conditioning process as possible, and as geographically close to the sensor as possible. The processing of this signal in terms of conditioning and its use for real time control should be carried out at the lowest point in the system heirarchy at which the necessary signals and processing are available. The control output signals should likewise be contained in the network up to the point of the most direct and simple interface with the controlled plant device.

Where the signals acquired or generated within the system are required for multiple purposes, this should be achieved by access to simple communication highways, not by extending hardwired current loops and relay buffered signals around the station.

In particular, the data display and logging part of the system should be a natural upward extension of the data acquisition and control processing networks. It should not be considered as a separate system.

The integrated system is designed from the outset for complete compatibility between the data structures, information rates and communications protocols utilised in the various interconnected sections of the system.

Perhaps less obviously, but of even greater significance in the integrated approach, is the methodology and application definition process by which the total functional content of the integrated system is specified. This methodology is based on analysis of the way in which the plant operates, and leads to a logical breakdown of the control and monitoring functions to reflect the plant operating structure. The methodology follows an object oriented design analysis of the plant processes. Through this analysis, self-contained processing groupings are identified for logically associated items of plant and mechanical/fluid processes and their associated signals. All control and monitoring aspects of such a plant process grouping and its signals are considered together in a unified and standardised manner. This aspect of the design is considered in more detail in the section on Design Methodology.

4. P20 INTEGRATED CONTROL AND MONITORING SYSTEM PRODUCT

The integrated system product used for the control and monitoring ISCO on Sizewell B is the P20 system. The P20 product has been developed by CGEE ALSTHOM and EdF (Electricité de France) and its first implementation is on the Chooz B 1400 MW PWR power station being constructed by EdF, currently due on commercial load in 1991.

The P20 system product is being further extended by CGEE ALSTHOM and GEC Power Instrumentation and Control Limited for its application to Sizewell B.

The P20 product is based on the use of proprietary LAN (Local Area Network) communication technology. It employs dual channel redundancy and extensive self-checking techniques in order to obtain the high availability and integrity figures required for the nuclear control application.

The basic product has a two level hierarchical structure which accommodates the different communication and processing strategies associated with the control functions at one level, and the monitoring and display facilities at a higher level. Further hierarchical levels can be used where appropriate within the application.

Referring to Figure 1 - Basic P20 Product Structure, the data acquisition and autonomous control level is shown in the lower section of the diagram and is titled the Controbloc Level. The data display and logging part of the system is the Centralog level, and is shown at the top of the diagram.

4.1 Controbloc Level

The data acquisition and control level is implemented with several dual redundant communication LANs known as Controbus. The Controbus communication LAN and the various Controbloc subscribers associated with one LAN are collectively termed a Cluster. Within a Cluster the Controbus LAN is controlled at the Cluster Head by the Cluster Controller subscriber. The Cluster Head also contains the analogue and logic processing subscribers, which service the cluster processing requirements, and the gateway which allows information to be passed up to the Centralog man/machine interface level.

In the case of Sizewell B the information passed through this gateway only passes from the Controbloc level to the Centralog level. However, the product can accept setpoint and control information sent from the man/machine interface level down to the Controbloc level where this is required within a station operating strategy.

The Controbus LAN can extend for up to 2.5 kilometres and allows the various plant interface subscribers to be located at convenient geographical locations within the plant, thereby minimising plant cabling and utilising available local instrument room space.

Plant Input/Output:- The plant interface subscribers are designed to accept signals from normal plant sensing devices, and feed output signals to plant actuators and switchgear cabinets for the control of electrical drives. The plant interface circuit cards accept analogue inputs in the form of 4-20mA signals, direct thermocouple signals, or resistance bridge signals. Status (contact) inputs are sensed using either simple or complementary contact detection. Proportional control actuators are driven using 4-20mA signals, and power drivers are available for interfacing with electrical switchgear cabinets or driving indicating lamps.

Plant Interface Standards:- An important principle in the application design philosophy of the P20 system is that of using standard hardware/function groupings comprising, for example, the sensing devices, the interface devices, the processing functions and the output devices. This principle is described later under the Design Methodology section, but an aspect of this philosophy which impacts on the plant interface circuit cards is that a standard interface card may contain a group of inputs and outputs designed to interface to a specific piece of equipment. For example, the standard switchgear interface card provides three status output drives and eight contact status feedback inputs. This allows a standard interface cable, with standard terminations to be connected with a one to one correspondence between a standard interface card and the standard design of electrical contactor switchgear terminations.

Field Bus Interface:- Another type of subscriber on the Controbus LAN is a proprietary field bus interface. This field bus can itself support plant interface subscribers or intelligent devices such as the auto/manual control plaques used as the man/machine interface for the station automatic control systems. This field bus, known as Locabus, may be extended for up to 150 metres, and provides electrical isolation of its subscribers from the Controbus.

Data Link Isolation:- Where, for safety reasons, high levels of isolation are required, or because of electrically noisy environments, optical fibre links can be used to couple sections of a cluster together or as an interface to alien systems.

High Integrity Display System:- In the particular nuclear application of Sizewell B, the Controbus also supports a high integrity display driver subscriber which provides the independent displays of safety related parameters - the Safety Instrumentation Display System (SIDS).

High Availability and High Integrity:- The Controbloc level is designed for application in situations where very high availability and integrity are required. In order to achieve this, extensive use is made of dual redundancy and fail-safe self checking and credibility checking of all equipment and signals within the Controbloc level. This necessitates the use of proprietary hardware which has been specially designed from the outset to provide these facilities. All processing and data communication within the Controbloc level is carried out in a fully deterministic manner, in which all the processing and communication activities within the system operate in a pre-ordained, predictable order and time structure. These principles are further expanded later in this section. The P20 Controbloc level equipment is being qualified for operation in the seismic and environmental conditions of all potential nuclear sites in the U.K. and in France. It can therefore be used for applications requiring the use of Class 1E equipment, as defined by the IEEE.

4.2 Centralog Level

The Centralog level system is also based upon the use of a dual redundant LAN structure. This LAN, known as the Contronet, can be extended for a distance of up to 1.5 kilometres. Like the Controbus LAN, the Contronet supports a variety of subscriber equipments, which may be geographically distributed as required by the application.

The Centralog LAN carries one main (dual redundant) database known as the data Server. The Data Server also controls the communication on the Contronet. Typically, the Contronet will interface with several Controbloc clusters through the gateway subscribers referred to previously. The data obtained from the supporting clusters is rationalised and processed within the Data Server, and appropriate subsets of this data are supplied to Video Server subscribers also located on the Contronet. These Video Servers each support two high resolution colour graphic displays with keyboard and trackerball interface, and permit the presentation of data to the operator in the form of mimic diagrams, bar graphs, trend graphs, tables, and alarm displays.

Appropriate levels of redundancy are employed at the Centralog level to provide the availability levels demanded by the application. In comparison with general industrial systems, the Centralog is a high integrity system utilising extensive self-check techniques, however, it is not fully deterministic, and uses general industrial standard computer hardware. It is not suitable for operation in a seismic event. The Sizewell B application requires this equipment to be used for functions significant to safety, which include the monitoring of all station alarm conditions, and the Category 1 plant and services on the station. It is therefore classified in the U.K. as Category 2, and its construction, QA and standard is appropriate to this level.

4.3 P20 System Functions

The functions carried out at the Controbloc level include:-

- the acquisition of plant operating information in both analogue and status form

- the conditioning of these input signals

- the use of the signals for analogue closed loop

control, plant equipment sequencing and safety interlocking

- the derivation of alarm levels and information messages

- the execution of certain on-line specialist calculations

- the output of control signals to the plant actuators and motor control switchgear

- the upward transmission of information to the Centralog level for display, logging, and long term archiving purposes.

At the Controbloc level, all data transfers within the communication structure, and all processing activities, are carried out on a regular basis in a pre-determined sequence. The processing delays and data latency between inputs and outputs, and between inputs and the gateway to the Centralog level, are all of a determined value and are not susceptible to failure or abnormal operation during periods of high transient activity resulting from station operational disturbance. Time tagging of plant status changes is carried out at the Controbloc level, and the time tagged status is made available through the gateway to the Centralog level.

The Contronet LAN potentially has to carry all the data available from the supporting clusters. Since this can total a very large information flow, the communication protocols employed at the Centralog level in the Contronet are status change reporting (updating the database only when there has been a change of status), phased scanning (setting up different update rates for different groups of signal data), and the establishment of temporary update paths for specific data items, for example, those variables required by the specific mimics on display at a particular point in time.

4.4 High Integrity Design Techniques at Controbloc Level

In order to understand the need for specific proprietary hardware at the Controbloc level, it is necessary to examine the particular design provisions which have to be made in the product in order to provide the high availability and high integrity required at the Controbloc level.

The integrity requirement (the need to ensure that the equipment never produces a dangerous command or misleading indication) is satisfied within each channel independently. Each channel has sufficient self-checking, credibility checking and internal redundancy cross checking built into it to ensure that a malfunction within that channel is either flagged to the external monitoring systems, or is such that external monitoring systems can locate the malfunction in that channel. Provisions are made within the channel such that equipment failures, or invalid data, results in reversion of the output to a safe state and appropriate labelling of monitored data as suspect or invalid.

The use of two channels enhances the integrity aspects of the system, but is primarily necessary in order to provide the high availability capability. Comparisons carried out between the two channels supplement the internal self-checks in ascertaining that a faulty condition exists, and when necessary, can be used to promote automatic testing of the equipment to determine which channel is faulty, and thereafter, direct control to the remaining healthy channel. The availability enhancement resulting from the dual redundant architecture stems from the ability of the equipment to operate safely on either channel.

In order to achieve the self-checking described above, the following provisions are made in the product hardware design:-

- Plant interface channels self-check back on themselves by transient injection of test signals.

- Where possible, credibility and consistency checks are carried out on back contacts and signal range.

- Where possible, external plant cable continuity is monitored.

- Comparison of signals from the two redundant channels is made at every signal processing and signal interfacing point.

- Where appropriate, comparison is made between repeat transmissions of data on highways.

- System monitoring subscribers exercise the system and provide automatic directive diagnostics.

A design consideration which is important in the context of high integrity and high availability is the principle of limiting the effects of an equipment failure, whether this failure has occurred internally or externally. This is achieved by designing galvanic isolation barriers at frequent intervals throughout the system, and limiting the potential spread of data corruption by means of dual access memory interfaces and uni-directional data links.

The galvanic isolation is provided at the following positions:-

- on each input and output plant interface channel

- at every interface between the subscribers and the Controbus

- at the interface between the Controbloc Cluster and the Centralog LAN

This galvanic isolation is generally at 1500 volts ac, and more than satisfies the CEGB equipment isolation requirements.

The dual access memory interfaces are located within the plant I/O subscribers, and at the interfaces between the Controbloc Clusters and the Centralog LAN.

Optical link isolation is provided for links to the ISCO from the Primary Protection Systems (PPS), and also at various strategic positions along the Controbloc Cluster Controbus and Centralog Contronet LAN.

These optical isolation barriers provide the necessary electrical isolation where a connection may be needed between equipment in different fire segregation groupings, or between equipment at Category 1 and Category 2 or 3. They provide limitation to the extent of system degradation which can be caused by fire in a particular area of the plant in which part of the P20 system may be located or through which the communication LANs may pass. This can be seen more clearly on Figure 2 which shows the way in which the P20 product is applied to Sizewell B.

4.5 P20 System Hardware

Both the Controbloc and Centralog levels are based on the use of Local Area Networks. The Controbus and Contronet LANs use a low-loss coaxial cable of the type used in the Ethernet standard. The coaxial LAN cable, comprising a central conductor and an outer coaxial return braid is illustrated in Figure 3. The LAN cable is about 1 centimetre in diameter, is unarmoured and is generally run in a trunking or on a separate tray within the power station cable routes. The Controbus LAN carries serial signal data at the rate of 2.5 Mbits per second. The Contronet LAN operates at 10 Mbits per second.

Connections are made to the LAN coaxial cable using special insulation displacement connectors which penetrate the sides of the cable and make connection to the central core and to the outer coaxial return conductor. The connector makes a gas tight seal to the coaxial cable, and is housed in a robust termination box along with the transformer coupled 1500 volts ac isolation barrier and local buffer electronics.

The termination box is normally located in the cable races, and parallel signal lines connect from the termination box through the floor or ceiling (as appropriate) to the equipment cubicle located in the Instrument Room. This arrangement ensures that a fire in the Instrument Room will not jeopardise the integrity of the Controbus or Contronet cable. Where modifications are required, the insulation displacement connector may be removed from the coaxial cable, and the penetration of the LAN cable can be plugged.

For each Controbloc cluster there is a dual cubicle cluster head of proprietary standard hardware construction. All the other Controbloc level subscribers are housed in proprietary standard plant interface cubicles as illustrated in Figure 4.

The standard plant interface cubicles are normally supplied to site at a fairly early stage in the contract before full definition of the C & I functions have been completed. These cubicles are shipped with their power supplies, card files and backplanes, but without the communications, processing and plant interface cards.

The plant cabling is terminated directly onto special sockets mounted on the card file backplanes. These sockets accept small single pole plugs, crimped onto each plant cable core. The plant cable core termination is generally completed before the circuit cards are installed, and before hardware and functional tests are carried out on the equipment. The design of the input/output circuit cards is such that hardware testing of the correct operation of the circuit cards, and of the rest of the cluster hardware can be carried out with the plant cabling connected.

This facility of being able to install and cable the plant interface cubicles at an early stage of the contract has obvious benefits in terms of station build cost and timescale.

The Controbloc equipment is required to withstand the environmental and seismic qualification requirements for safety category 1 equipment in line with the British PWR all-sites seismic spectra.

The Controbloc level of the P20 system is supplied from dual 48 volt dc sources.

The high availability and high integrity requirements described earlier in this section lead to considerable complexity in the circuitry in providing both the multiple redundancy and the extensive testing and self-checking circuitry. These requirements have to be reconciled with a need to maintain high packing densities and low power dissipation. The majority of the circuitry is implemented on multi-layer circuit boards with surface mount components on both sides of the boards. This construction, and robotic assembly techniques, coupled with extensive circuit board level burn-in and testing, results in a high reliability of the basic circuit elements.

The extensive communication structure and the comprehensive self-check and system testing facilities, in addition to the basic cluster functions of analogue and logical control, demand extensive processing capabilities on the cluster. Powerful processing capability is installed both in the various plant interface subscribers and in the cluster head service units. Extensive use is made of transputers and programmable logic arrays.

The Centralog portion of the P20 system is configured from industry standard VME computing hardware. The VME standard is derived from an original Motorola Company packaging and computer internal bus standard, known as Versa Module. This has now been internationally recognised in a repackaged form based on the European DIN standard module sizes, thus leading to the acronym VME - Versa Module European.

The VME modules all interconnect using the VME bus protocol and are mainly based on the Motorola 16/32 bit processors in the 68000 series. These modules can be grouped in a standard 19" VME sub-rack to form substantial computing systems.

The VME modules are produced by many different manufacturers, including Motorola. The various types of modules include:- processors; memories; VDU drivers; printer drivers; storage peripheral interfaces; and communications interfaces, including those necessary for communication to the Contronet LAN.

The various Centralog subscribers comprise sub-racks of standard VME modules, housed in standard cubicles.

5. SIZEWELL B APPLICATION

In applying the P20 system product to Sizewell B, various project specific requirements have been taken into account:-

- the safety critical plant is divided into four main separation groups in which all monitoring and control equipment must be completely segregated and isolated between these separation groups.

- all data in the power station system arises from equipment of various safety categories. These are, from highest category to lowest: category 1, category 2 and category 3.

- altogether eight separation groups are employed in order to accommodate the 4-way split of the category 1 equipment and the segregation of category 1 and non-category 1 equipment data.

- main and auxiliary shutdown control rooms are provided on Sizewell B and the application design must avoid common mode fire or equipment faults which could disable both control rooms.

- in addition to information displays in the two station control rooms, there is a requirement for large quantities of information transfer to the separated Technical Support Centre.

- the quantity of data handled is high. The acquisition level is expected to monitor 22 000 plant status signals and 4000 plant analogue variables. Some signals are used only at Controbloc level, but including the derived or calculated signals, the traffic upwards to the Centralog level is approximately 14 000 status signals and 4000 analogue variables.

The diagram shown in Figure 2 - General Sizewell B ISCO Architecture gives an indication of the way in which the P20 system product is applied on the Sizewell B project. The diagram shows the principles of the architecture but is not representative of the total system scope.

In the main control room there is a single, dual redundant Centralog LAN, known as the supervisory LAN, which drives the displays on the supervisor's desk and the operator's desk. This supervisory LAN is fed from three lower level Centralog LANs associated with each of the following three main plant sections:-

- Reactor and Engineered Safety Features Actuation System (ESFAS)

- Turbines and Steam & Feed

- Electrical and General Services.

In addition to feeding the supervisory LAN, the plant section LANs drive area specific displays mounted on the control panels located around the sides of the main control room. These panels contain tiled mimic panels upon which are mounted the discrete controls and indicators required for the operation of the power station.

The Controbloc Clusters which carry out the data acquisition and autonomous control, feed data through to the plant section Centralog LANs. The Cluster allocation is as follows:-

Within each separation group there is a cluster allocated to the Safety Instrumentation Display System function (SIDS). These four clusters are interconnected via optical links, and receive safety related data by unidirectional optical fibre links from the Primary Protection System. The SIDS clusters display their information on seismically qualified display screens located in the main control room panels. The SIDS Clusters also pass data through into the Reactor section Centralog display system.

Four further reactor clusters, allocated one to each separation group, carry out the data acquisition and autonomous control for the reactor section plant. Each of these clusters feeds data through to the reactor section Centralog LAN.

In a similar manner, the Turbine Centralog LAN and the Electrical and General Services Plant Centralog LAN are each fed from their own set of four Controbloc clusters allocated across the four main separation groups.

In additional to the sixteen main clusters, there is a dual redundant common data bus which makes available essential information to each of the individual clusters. Galvanic and data corruption isolation is maintained between this common data bus system and each of the individual clusters.

The operator control interface with the plant is effected through the main control room control panels, using switches, pushbuttons and auto/manual control stations. All essential control indications are fed back to the operator using discrete indicator devices. These control panel devices are coupled via multiplexing cubicles to the various Controbloc clusters.

The various Station Automation Control System (SACS) loops are assigned to four different clusters, both to take account of the appropriate plant associations, and to ensure that no single failure can adversely affect the total automatic control function.

All sixteen clusters operate in the safety category 1 areas, however, several of the clusters have optical fibre isolated extensions into lower category areas. Provision is made in the design process to ensure that data acquired from category 2 and 3 devices does not mix with, or could in any way contaminate, functions being implemented using category 1 data.

Several of the clusters are also extended at the category 1 level through optically isolated links into the Auxiliary Shutdown Room (ASR). The ASR cluster extension supports the multiplexed connections to the discrete control and indicating devices located on the ASR control panel. These controls and indications are primarily associated with the safe shutdown of the reactor and the operation of the ESFAS plant.

There is also an optically isolated extension of the MCR supervisory Centralog LAN into the ASR for the purpose of feeding the ASR display screens.

The Technical Support Centre (TSC) has a single, dual redundant Centralog LAN supporting its displays and the mainframe computers which draw data from the Centralog system for the purposes of off-line calculations. The TSC LAN is fed with data along optically isolated datalinks from each of the three plant area LANs and from the MCR supervisory level LAN.

The TSC has access to all the monitored data in the Centralog system, and uses this data for logging, analysis and engineering back-up activities. The TSC facilities do not permit any control command to be sent back to the plant, and activities in the TSC cannot affect the operation of the station control and monitoring systems.

6. DESIGN METHODOLOGY

As mentioned earlier, the design aim in an integrated system is to capture the C & I sensor source data as early in the processing train as possible. This early data capture is not only aimed at reducing the cabling and signal conditioning costs, but is also intended to allow the full processing of the C & I data to be accomplished under the control of the integrated system.

With the majority of the C & I data and functions in a common type of hardware and software environment, it is possible to establish standard methods of signal conditioning, signal processing, signal interfacing with the plant, and signal presentation on the data display systems.

The design aims associated with the establishment of these standard methods is to:-

- make the standard cover as many aspects of the signal handling as possible

- apply the standard as widely as possible

- have as few different standards as possible.

In practice, these three design objectives are to some extent conflicting, and a trade-off is inevitably made between them.

The degree to which effective standard methods can be established and adopted, depends upon the three factors of:-

- how well the standard methods are designed

- how early in the overall power station design cycle the standards are established and promulgated

- the degree to which the standards can be authoratively impressed upon the various plant system designers specifying C & I functions.

The use of standard methods in establishing clearly associated groups of functions or processing, is allied to object oriented design techniques. In the context of object oriented design, a group of standard functions, such as signal conditioning, processing and data display which are associated together, is termed a Standard Model. When the Standard Model is applied, data which is specific to that instance is entered into the Standard Model, thereby creating an Object.

An example of a Standard Model might be a Discrepancy Control function. In such a Standard Model, all the following aspects are defined and standardised:-

- the discrepancy switch itself.

- the discrepancy switch contact arrangement.

- the cable between the discrepancy switch and the input/output circuit card, including the plugs and the core identifications.

- the interface card with the correct mix of input/output channels.

- the discrepancy logic implemented in the integrated control system.

- any indication on the data display system of discrepancy switch position or status.

When this Standard Model is called up for use, the specific data relating to the instance of its use will be added to the Standard Model. In this case, the specific data is likely to be the switch circuit identifier; the plant equipment references; and display identifiers such as on/off or open/close. Once this specific data has been added, this discrepancy circuit Standard Model becomes a specific device discrepancy circuit Object.

Other typical Standard Models include:-

- standards for switch drive logic and connections

- low level analogue input signal connections, conditioning and processing

- high level analogue input signal connection, conditioning and processing

- incremental valve control

- modulating valve control

- pump control

- duty/standby logic

- group alarm generation

- sequence logic elements

An important facet of the use of standards in this design process is that the method by which all variable information is presented at the data display level is also standardised. The display of variables may be in the form of numbers, bar charts, graphs or icons which can be animated in shape, colour or flashing. The particular ways in which a variable may be displayed at the Centralog level is designated at the time the Standard Model is specified as a particular Object.

The use of repeated standards has several advantages in terms of accuracy, comprehensibility, hardware cost reduction and simplification of design. However, an outstanding advantage is that the use of CAE (Computer Aided Engineering) techniques becomes possible, which in turn results in a reduction in the application engineering design costs.

A very important element of the P20 system product is therefore the advanced graphical CAE tool known as Controcad, which is used to collect the application C & I design and convert it to a form which can be directly loaded into the Controbloc and Centralog target systems. The Standard Models are represented as logic and control diagrams and are held in graphical form as a library within the Controcad tool. The design methodology using Controcad is illustrated in Figure 5.

Using the graphics manipulation facilities, typical of a modern Computer Aided Drafting scheme, the Standard Models can be called up, characterised with data to become specific Objects, and then grouped together and interconnected to provide the required C & I function. The resulting C & I scheme can be plotted out by the Controcad in order to provide the C & I engineer with a hard copy statement of the C & I scheme captured in the Controcad. This hard copy record is then used for verification purposes. In parallel with this hard copy plot, the Controcad tool interprets the interconnection logic described on the graphical representation, and provides the floppy discs for loading the configuration data into the standard hardware of the Controbloc and Centralog systems.

The Centralog VDU mimic diagrams form part of the C & I application data which is entered using the Controcad tool, and in particular, the association between specific animated variables and the particular mimic diagrams upon which the variables are displayed, is established in the Controcad tool. The automation of the coupling between input data and the mimic formats is a major timesaving and accuracy advance on earlier data display system design methods.

One of the major technology advances which has made possible the machine interpretation of schematic graphical diagrams into a logical mathematical statement of the functions depicted by those diagrams, is the development and use of object oriented programming languages. Such languages are employed in the system software of the Controcad tool.

Another aspect of the highly structured approach which is being adopted for application engineering the integrated system, is the object oriented design decomposition of the whole Control and Instrumentation function of the power station. Using this approach, the power station plant systems are progressively broken down into logically grouped operational systems. The smallest coherent grouping of plant and its associated control is termed an Operative Unit.

The application C & I tasks are divided up along the lines of the Operative Units, and the document systems, application software load files, check procedures and change control procedures are all based on division by Operative Unit. The first level of commissioning of the plant is also carried out by

Operative Unit. Within Controcad, the work areas are divided into Operative Units within which, the C & I design is constructed in terms of objects, interconnections and Centralog display formats.

This highly structured approach to the design process requires co-ordination of the basic C & I design of the power station by all plant contractors from a very early stage in the overall station design. Ideally, the establishment of station-wide standards for use in the Standard Models should be established before any of the individual plant C & I is defined. On Sizewell B, joint working between the PMT and the contractors has allowed many of these design principles to be employed even though timescale limitations have prevented a universal application of the methodology.

7. LIFECYCLE BENEFITS OF THE ISCO APPROACH

7.1 Specific Benefits for Sizewell B

In chapter 1 of this paper the Sizewell B control and monitoring system requirements were outlined. In the body of the paper, an integrated system product has been described, along with the way in which it is being applied on Sizewell B and the methodology which is used to capture the Control and Instrumentation application data. In the following paragraphs, the way in which the product is used to satisfy the Sizewell B requirements is considered, along with general benefits for any large C & I installation.

The high availability and high integrity requirements specific to the Sizewell B nuclear station are satisfied by the dual redundant self-checking aspects of the product architecture, backed up by the quality control of both the manufacture of the hardware and the configuration of the application data.

The requirement of a nuclear power station to have fully auditable records is greatly helped by the use of the Controcad Computer Aided Engineering tool which holds the input Control and Instrumentation data, and which incorporates the necessary change control procedures.

The strategic positioning of high voltage galvanic isolation barriers and the availability of optical fibre isolating links, enables the product to handle the complex requirements for multiple segregation between separation groups and safety categories, and also to provide safeguard against major system degradation as a result of fire in any particular area.

The communication flexibilities of the system, and the way in which the product supports several geographically separated databases, helps the system designer who is faced with providing full data display facilities in two separate and isolated Control Rooms and also in the Technical Support Centre.

The particular requirements of Sizewell B for high packing density and low power dissipation are greatly assisted by the fact that the product is based on the most modern techniques in circuit board design and component packaging. The facility to distribute much of the equipment on a wide geographical basis also gives flexibility to the power station layout designer in finding sufficient space to house the C & I equipment.

7.2 General Benefits of the Integrated Systems Approach

Various of the principles employed in the integrated system product and its design methods, assist in reducing cost and timescale, and in improving accuracy and project control throughout the complete power station lifecycle. These benefits are evident throughout the stages of design, manufacture, installation, cabling, setting to work, functional testing, and commissioning. The benefits also extend to operation and maintenance, and should yield advantage at the time of power station mid-life C & I upgrade or refit. The benefits result from the following factors:

Geographical Distribution:- The facility of being able to locate the various parts of the system at the most convenient locations offers major cost savings in cabling. Where full advantage is taken of the P20 system, the control cabling length can reduce to 40 percent of that required for conventional C & I systems.

The location flexibility also helps to provide better plant setting to work facilities and can allow a greater degree of parallel working during commissioning. This is of value in shortening the station commissioning period.

Functional Standardisation:- The use of Standard Models, particularly where these models embrace a fairly large group of functions, can result in very considerable application engineering cost and timescale reductions through low cost repetition in the Controcad engineering design tool. The application of this standardisation can also greatly reduce the specification and application engineering error rates since the standard models are likely to be understood in detail by both the plant system designer and the Control and Instrumentation engineer. The existence of such standards also assists the engineering interfacing between different Contractors, and between the Contractors and the main design authority.

The reduction in training time, the lower level of mistakes made, and the greater ability to communicate between teams and disciplines, which results from the employment of standards, facilitates the setting to work and commissioning. The operator's task is made easier through an understanding of the standard models used in the control functions, and the maintenance task is likewise also simplified.

The use of standard models has a bearing on the accuracy of the design verification process and upon the safe running of the plant by the operator. The safety of the design is improved because of the simplification of the processes of design capture, design coherency checking, production of design information for validation purposes, production of design and test documentation, the control of modifications and the accumulation of lifecycle records. Operational safety is improved as a result of providing the operator with a consistent presentation format and control implementation strategy.

The maintenance of a complete statement of the Control and Instrumentation function of the integrated system within a CAE tool, combined with the fact that the application runs in standard hardware and calls up standard software functions, means that a totally definitive statement of the C & I functions is maintained throughout the life of the station. This is clearly of great advantage when maintaining, modifying, extending or even replacing the system.

Hardware Standardisation:- There are three major advantages which result from the standardisation of the hardware and the associated standard software in the integrated system. The first of these advantages is that with a standard design of plant input/output interface cubicle and the standard cluster head cubicle design, it is possible to order and manufacture these cubicles at an early stage of the programme. The cubicles can then be installed at site, and cable drawing and termination can be carried out in advance of completion of the C & I application design and testing. This gives much greater flexibility to the scheduling of station installation and cabling.

The second advantage of standardising the hardware design is that a set of standard hardware setting to work tests can be devised at a product level, and using these test programs, the installed and cabled system can be progressively and fully hardware tested in advance of the C & I functional application files being available for loading into the system. Furthermore, subsets of the standard hardware can be mounted in the design offices, and tests on the C & I application functions can be conducted on this equipment with confidence that these tests are representative of the performance which will be repeated in the site installation. The ability to confidently test the application function in an office based environment has obvious advantages in terms of cost and timescale, and promotes more accurate working and proper control of changes.

The third advantage of standard hardware and its associated software, is that all the main system interfaces are designed from the outset as part of the product. This reduces one of the biggest problems which has arisen in commissioning power stations in the past: this is the difficulty of interfacing large and complex systems of different types from different suppliers, and ensuring, not only that the systems are able to operate together under normal operating conditions, but also that they continue to operate under the conditions of plant abnormalities and equipment failures, and furthermore, that a workable mechanism exists for ensuring that changes in one system are properly accommodated in the other system.

Interfaces with Other Contracts:- To be fully cost effective, an integrated system should carry out the majority of the control and monitoring functions on the total power station. Using the integrated system in this way requires some reconsideration of the conventional contractual responsibility boundaries, puts extra obligations on the C & I integrated system supplier, and puts extra requirements on the product. Committing all of the power station control and monitoring to one generic system type, and obliging plant system suppliers to utilise this control and monitoring system and yet retain responsibility for the correct operation of their plant, requires that the control and monitoring system should be highly reliable. The extensive provisions made in the the P20 product design to achieve a high level of availability and system integrity satisfy these requirements.

A requirement which departs, in some cases, from conventional practice, is that the various plant system suppliers should provide specifications of their control and monitoring requirements to the integrated system supplier, rather than place separate contracts for stand-alone control and monitoring systems for their particular plant areas. Handling the specification of these requirements, and ensuring that contractual responsibilities are still properly maintained, is greatly assisted by the establishment of the Standard Models defining groups of monitoring and control functions. Although this contractual interface has to be handled carefully, the result, in avoiding equipment interfacing problems, and providing a more coherent control strategy, greatly outweighs any contractual complication.

8. CONCLUSION

In conclusion, the adoption of an integrated systems approach, encourages the C & I design to be addressed right at the start of the power station design programme. Cost effective use of the ISCO requires the station designers to establish standards and work out the main C & I design strategies at an early stage. Having accepted these disciplines, the benefits of this early design work and the intrinsic advantages of the integrated system, confer benefits in cost, timescale, design accuracy, simplification of contractual boundaries, and compatibility of system interfaces. The approach also gives benefits in terms of ease of commissioning the main plant, and subsequently in operating and maintaining the power station.

The adoption of an integrated system approach on Sizewell B is a necessary and technologically appropriate decision. It is expected that this approach to power station Control and Instrumentation is likely to become predominant internationally in the next decade.

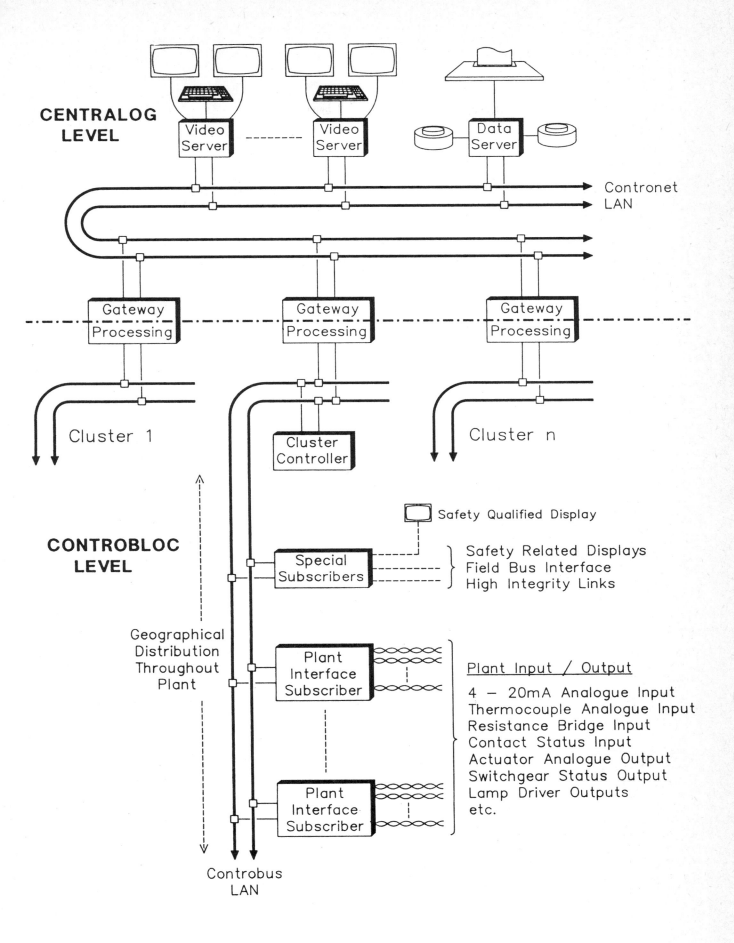

CENTRALOG LEVEL

Video Server

Video Server

Data Server

Contronet LAN

Gateway Processing

Gateway Processing

Gateway Processing

Cluster 1

Cluster Controller

Cluster n

CONTROBLOC LEVEL

Safety Qualified Display

Special Subscribers

Safety Related Displays
Field Bus Interface
High Integrity Links

Geographical Distribution Throughout Plant

Plant Interface Subscriber

Plant Input / Output

4 — 20mA Analogue Input
Thermocouple Analogue Input
Resistance Bridge Input
Contact Status Input
Actuator Analogue Output
Switchgear Status Output
Lamp Driver Outputs
etc.

Plant Interface Subscriber

Controbus LAN

Fig 1   Basic P20 product structure

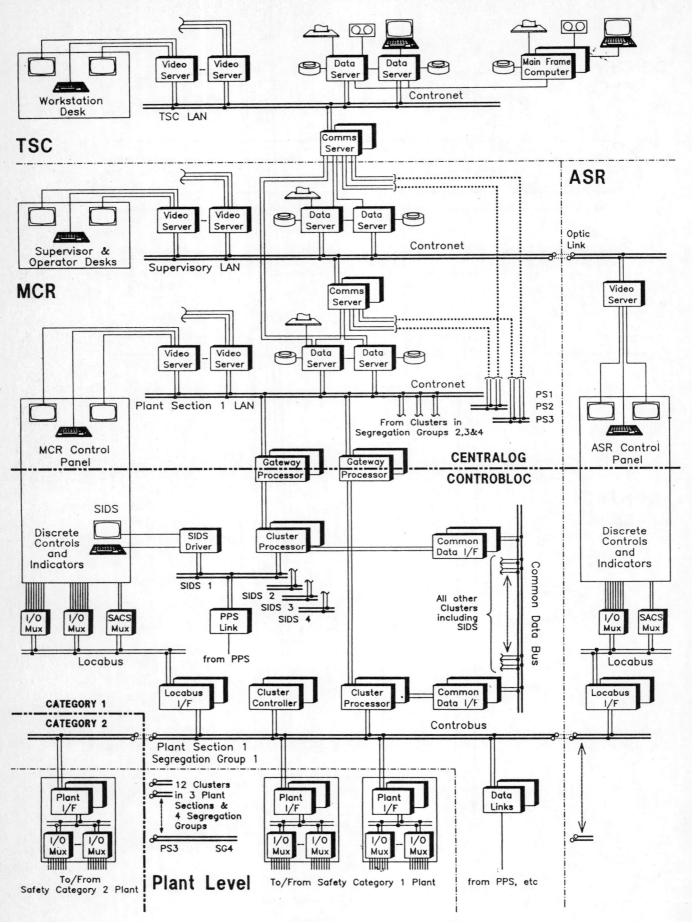

Fig 2   General Sizewell 'B' ISCO architecture

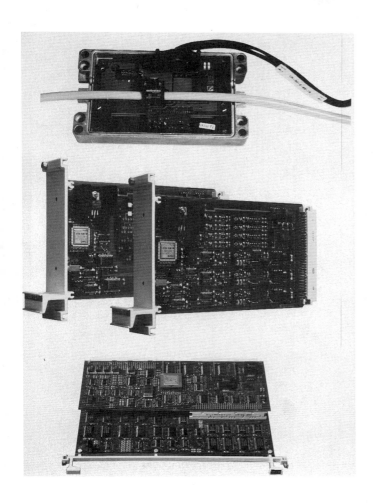

Fig 3   P20 Controbus connector, plant input/output
          interface and processing circuit cards

Fig 4   P20 plant interface cubicle

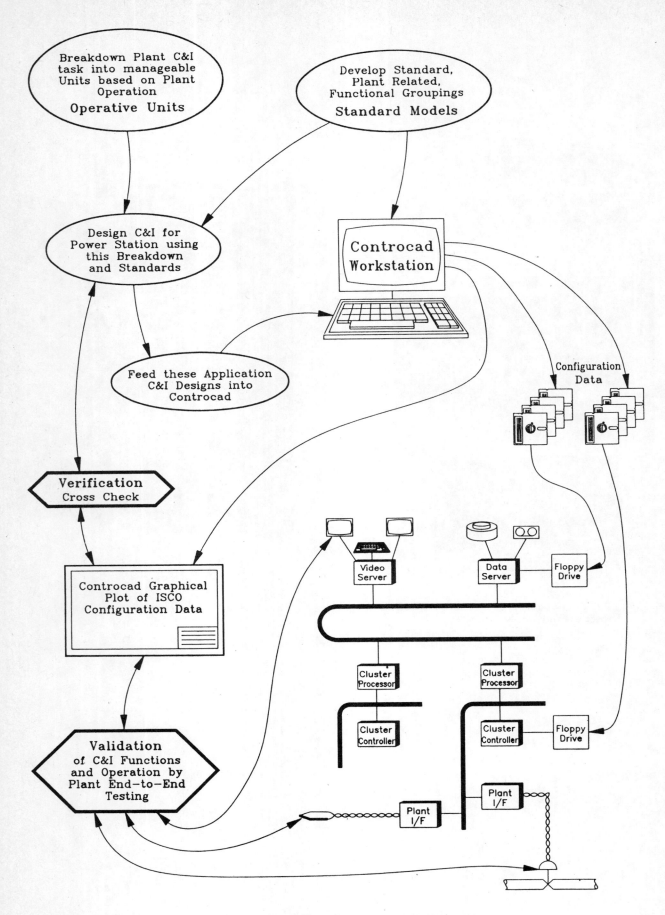

Fig 5   Design methodology using Controcad

Inspection of the Sizewell 'B' PWR

P JOHNSON, BSc
PWR Project Group, National Power Division of CEGB, Knutsford, Cheshire

SYNOPSIS   The inspections of Sizewell 'B' are described together with arrangements for the validation of inspections.   Problems of integrating inspection and validation arrangements into the Project are discussed.

1   INTRODUCTION

All items of power plant are subjected to extensive non-destructive examination (NDE) as a means of quality control and to ensure that safe and economic operation of the plant will be achieved in service.   In nuclear power stations certain components are designated as being 'incredibility of failure' (IOF) items and for these on Sizewell 'B' special inspection measures have been introduced.   A requirement of the licence for Sizewell 'B' was that the safety case for IOF components had to include a programme of repeat ultrasonic inspections, additional to those normally carried out by the component supplier.   In addition, the ultrasonic inspections had to be subject to independent validation in order to demonstrate that they were capable of detecting defects at a size which provided an adequate margin when compared with the defect sizes determined by the fracture analysis.

These requirements have had a substantial impact on the manufacture of the IOF components for Sizewell 'B'.   The arrangements made to implement the required ultrasonic inspections will be described and in particular the problems of integrating additional inspections, and validation of inspections, into an ongoing project will be discussed.

2   EXTENT OF INSPECTION AND VALIDATION

Different arrangements were put in place in recognition of the differences between the various components and the role that ultrasonic inspection plays in their safety cases.   These arrangements fall into three basic categories:

(a)   Reactor pressure vessel (RPV).

(b)   Other ferritic components.

(c)   Austenitic components.

These are described in turn below.

2.1   Reactor Pressure Vessel

2.1.1   Forgings

The forgings which make up the RPV are inspected by the supplier using manual ultrasonic inspection.   A second inspection is then carried out using an automated system.   Both inspections are subject to independent validation carried out by the Inspection Validation Centre (IVC) operated by the UKAEA.   The IVC was established in response to the needs of the Sizewell 'B' project and provides validation of ultrasonic procedures and operators.

2.1.2   Welds

The welds are subjected to manual inspection, using both pulse-echo and tandem techniques, by the supplier both pre-stress relief and post final stress relief.   At the pre-stress relief stage the nozzle-shell welds are also inspected using an automated system.   The nozzle-shell welds have historically had the highest incidence of defects and also pose problems for the manual inspection due to their geometry.   This automated inspection is, therefore, aimed at providing additional demonstration of the integrity of these welds prior to the final stress relief of the RPV. After stress relief the supplier inspects all the welds a second time and the RPV is then hydrotested.   Following the hydrotest all the welds are inspected again using the automated shop inspection system.   To provide even further assurance that the RPV could not possibly enter service containing any defects of concern another inspection is carried out using the mast manipulator utilised for the in-service inspection (ISI) of the RPV.   All the inspections in this extensive programme are subject to independent validation at the IVC.

2.2 Other Ferritic Components

Forgings which make up the steam generators and pressuriser are of relatively simple geometry. Redundant inspection of these forgings is performed by two ultrasonic inspections using procedures and operators which have been independently validated.

Welds in the steam generator have been reduced or located in areas of simple geometry wherever practicable. For all welds the fabricator will carry out manual ultrasonic inspection at two stages -the first after welding, the second following final stress relief. In addition the CEGB has arranged for further inspections to be carried out on their behalf using techniques similar to those of the fabricator (to achieve redundancy) supplemented by other methods as appropriate to achieve diversity. All of these inspections will be subject to independent validation.

The detailed arrangements for validation of these inspections are different to the RPV. In this case the validation of procedures and operators is carried out separately.

The validation of the ultrasonic procedures is carried out by the IVC utilising a representative operator selected from the inspection teams who will ultimately carry out the inspections. Once the procedure has been satisfactorily tested Lloyds Register (the independent inspection agency for Sizewell 'B') will carry out a practical test of each operator's ability to apply the validated procedure and maintain a register of approved personnel.

2.3 Austenitic Components

Providing they have been subjected to an adequate degree of mechanical working the ultrasonic inspection of austenitic forgings and plate does not provide any significant problems. Such items can, therefore, be dealt with as for ferritic forgings.

For in-process inspection of the austenitic cast materials, such as the reactor coolant pump casing and welds in the primary pipework, the effectiveness of ultrasonic inspection will be limited compared to ferritic materials and will be very dependent on the metallurgical condition of the component in question. The problems of ultrasonic inspection of cast austenitics have always been recognised by the CEGB and the contribution of such inspection to the safety case is much reduced for these materials. The detectable defect sizes will depend on the variations in macrostructure and geometry in the area being inspected. It was recognised that it was not possible to predict in advance the capabilities of these inspections and there was, therefore, no basis on which validation requirements could be established.

It was, therefore, agreed that the CEGB would validate the ultrasonic inspection by carrying out a research programme which would optimise, and establish the capability of, the procedure to be applied. This research programme will take account of all relevant aspects such as the macrostructure and geometry. The ultrasonic operators will then be validated in their ability to apply the optimised procedures.

3   THE NEED FOR VALIDATION

The effectiveness of ultrasonic inspection can vary dramatically depending on the details of the techniques applied, the design of the component being inspected and the quality of the personnel used to carry out the inspections. These factors have long been recognised by the CEGB both in the construction of new plant and in the inspections carried out on operational plant. The specifications produced for Sizewell 'B' reflected this concern about the quality of NDE and introduced significant improvements compared with US practice on PWR's. However, at the time of the Sizewell 'B' Public Inquiry views on the capability of ultrasonic inspection were strongly influenced by a round robin exercise, known as PISC, which had been carried out to assess current procedures for the inspection of PWR reactor pressure vessels. The exercise demonstrated that US procedures designed in line with the ASME Code were not capable of achieving the 'virtual certainty of detecting a 25 mm defect' required by the CEGB's safety case for the RPV.

The reasons for this become clear when the effect of defect orientation on the detectability of planar defects by ultrasonics is considered. The CEGB NDT Applications Centre has done considerable work on the justification of ultrasonic inspections, and particularly in quantifying the effect of defect orientation on detectability. For any particular probe type and recording threshold it is possible to determine the angle between the beam axis and the defect plane at which a defect will no longer be detectable. By combining the results for a number of probes a picture can be produced illustrating the capability of an inspection procedure. Figure 1 shows a comparison of inspection procedures devised in line with a number of different pressure vessel codes. It is apparent that the ASME procedure with a recording level of 50% DAC, used for many years as the basis of in-service inspections on PWR RPV's, has an extremely limited capability. Even modified ASME procedures utilising 20% DAC as a recording level have a limited capability. The main defects of interest with regard to structural integrity, planar defects oriented normal to the surface, are only detectable if they are at, or very close to the surface. By comparison procedures employed for Sizewell 'B' utilise a wider range of probe angles and a recording level of 10% DAC. The capability of these procedures is significantly better and in particular is capable of detecting the defects of greatest significance.

The relationship between fracture analysis and inspection is one of the major elements of the safety case for large, heavy walled pressure vessels such as those in the PWR primary circuit. This, together with the inherent poor design of the ultrasonic procedures in common use in PWR inspections, and concerns about the effectiveness with which they were being implemented, are major reasons why validation of inspections became a requirement of Sizewell 'B'.

4 NEW CONSIDERATIONS INTRODUCED BY VALIDATION

The basic concept of validating ultrasonic inspections is quite simple. In essence a test piece is manufactured containing known defects and this is inspected using the equipment, procedures and personnel to be used in the actual inspections. The implementation of this seemingly simple principle has, however, proved to be very costly and time consuming and has required the solution of a number of unique problems.

One particular area in which a new approach had to be developed was in answering the question 'what defects should be introduced into the validation test pieces'. Historically component manufacturers have developed a good understanding of the types of problems which can occur in their particular products and this experience has guided the approach to the inspections carried out. This rather adhoc situation is perfectly adequate in the normal situation where quality control is the main objective. However, in establishing an IOF safety case a more systematic approach was called for. It was important to provide the validation centre and the inspection agents with a clear definition of the type of defects of interest.

The starting point is the results of the fracture analysis which provides information on the throughwall extent of defects of interest. This is, however, of relatively little use in relation to the capability of the ultrasonic inspection. Far more important are details of:

(a)   Defect orientation.

(b)   Defect roughness.

(c)   Defect location (surface or embedded).

A metallurgical review and analysis of forging and welding defects has been carried out to determine the characteristics of the relevant defects. This review has looked at the frequencies of occurrence, orientations, morphologies and size distributions of defects and has critically re-examined common assumptions implicit in normal NDT practice.

These reviews have looked at the potential mechanisms for defect formation and the evidence available on the frequency of occurrence and characteristics of such defects. The result is a judgement of the relative probabilities of defect occurrence within different ranges of tilt and skew orientation, for both large fitness-for-purpose defects and smaller acceptance size defects.

When inspections have to be validated the derivation of such precise defect descriptions is an essential part of the process both from the view of designing an acceptable inspection procedure and manufacturing a test specimen containing relevant defects.

5 IMPACT ON THE PROJECT

5.1 Existing Inspections

The majority of ultrasonic inspections carried out on Sizewell 'B' are also carried out on other PWR's. The CEGB recognised the need to improve inspection techniques prior to the requirement for validation of inspections being introduced in order to bring them into line with normal practice in the Electricity Supply Industry (ESI). The need to validate inspections has not, however, resulted in major changes to the intended approach to the ultrasonic inspections and the techniques have been found to be capable of satisfactorily meeting the required validation targets.

The main impact on the ultrasonic procedures has been on the level of detail which it has been necessary to include rather than on the basic techniques employed.

The validation of the ultrasonic procedure is only meaningful if that procedure is then applied during the component inspections in the same manner as during validation. This is largely ensured by independent witnessing of the inspections. In addition it proved necessary to incorporate in the procedures checklists for the recording of relevant information on calibration, scanning and details of any recordable indications. Whilst producing an improved record of the work it did substantially increase the complexity of the procedures.

Another consequence of validation is the need to anticipate every possible aspect of the inspection. When a defect is found in a component it tends to be dealt with in a way which is determined by its particular characteristics. The exact method of sizing a defect is, within certain general guidelines, left to the skill and experience of the operator. This approach is incompatible with the formal validation of a procedure during which a range of defects of various types will be encountered. Each of these defects has to be dealt with in a manner which is both pre-defined and will be consistently followed by any appropriately trained operator. This situation, where solutions had to be available in advance for a range of problems not normally encountered during inspections, has been one of the major practical problems in carrying out validations.

5.2   New Inspections

One of the novel features of the RPV inspection programme is the extent to which automated ultrasonic inspections have been utilised. This approach was followed in the expectation that it would prove (a) higher reliability of inspection and in particular guaranteed coverage of components (b) reduced inspection durations compared with manual inspections.

In practice for this application the benefits of an automated inspection have proved to be limited and far outweighed by the disadvantages. The procedures required to control an automated inspection are far more extensive and detailed than for the equivalent manual inspection, since every step in the inspection has to be very precisely defined. Very exact knowledge of the component geometry is required to ensure proper coverage is obtained and this information has to be available early on in the manufacturing process in order to allow sufficient time for the necessary documentation to be produced. One of the advantages of manual inspections is its flexibility and the ability to cope with minor deviations from the intended shape of components. Manual inspections are able to cope with late changes, for example due to repairs, which would cause major disruption to the preparations for an automated inspection and subsequent delays to the start of the inspection.

Far from being quicker than manual inspections the automated systems have taken significantly longer to complete inspections, even on defect free components. There are also no simple means of speeding up such inspections, whereas for a manual inspection the number of operators can be readily increased in response to overall programme pressures.

Despite these problems there are applications where automated inspections are necessary to obtain the required quality of inspection. Such an example is the nozzle-to-shell welds in the RPV. The detection of transverse defects in these welds requires the use of techniques which cannot be applied manually, due to the need for probes of specified and varying skew. The number of such applications is, however, very limited.

In a number of areas ultrasonic inspections have had to be devised and applied to components which have previously never been subjected to such inspection. The principle example is the reactor coolant pump casing.

The normal method of inspecting large stainless steel castings of this type is by radiography. In the view of the CEGB this is the appropriate inspection method for this product form, however, to allay concerns regarding near-surface planar defects an ultrasonic inspection was required. In view of the absence of any previous experience in applying ultrasonic inspection to this material a significant programme of work was necessary, initially to establish the feasibility of such an inspection, and then to quantify the standard of inspection which could be achieved.

5.3   Programme

The requirement for diverse, redundant and validated inspections has had a substantial effect on the manufacturing programmes for the IOF components. These fall into two main categories:

(a)   At the start of the Sizewell 'B' project there was no organisation in existence which could provide the facilities required to validate ultrasonic inspections of PWR components. It was, therefore, necessary to establish such an organisation and put in hand the manufacture of suitable test pieces. In addition, there was very little experience available on the automated inspection of RPV components on this scale and to such stringent requirements. The establishment of the necessary expertise in both these areas was a significant problem in relation to the target project programme.

(b)   The time required for repeat inspections represents periods during the manufacture where the supplier has to hand over the component to an inspection agent. This represents substantial disruption and extension to the manufacturing programme.

For a RPV from the making of the first weld to delivery to site takes approximately 5 years. For the Sizewell 'B' RPV the repeat inspections utilising automated systems represent a total of 46 weeks. The validated inspections by the supplier involve a similar period of time. The complete programme of validated inspections represents, therefore, approximately 40% of the manufacturing time.

It is not so easy to readily quantify the impact on other components and whilst it is not as severe as for the RPV it is without doubt substantial.

6.   CONCLUSIONS/EXPERIENCE TO DATE

A large number of inspections and validations have now been completed for Sizewell 'B' and there are a number of lessons which can be learned from the experience to date which it is hoped may be useful in optimising the inspection programme for the follow on PWR stations.

(a)   The effort expended on validation need to be kept in proportion with the effort expended on the actual inspections. For the automated shop inspections of the RPV validation of the inspections takes almost as long as the inspections themselves.

(b)   The validation process is easier to manage where procedure and operator validations are separated.

(c)   Automated manufacturing inspections should only be employed where they are essential. The penalties in terms of cost, programme and long preparation times outweigh the benefits for most applications. There are, however, cases like the RPV nozzle-to-shell welds where it would be extremely difficult to devise an adequate manual inspection procedure.

(d)   Inspection targets and arrangements for implementing the inspections need to be put in place very early on in a project. It is also essential to get the inspection targets right since modifications are likely to lead to substantial disruption and delays.

There are two particularly positive aspects of the extensive inspection and inspection validation requirements applied to Sizewell 'B'. Firstly, the repeat inspections carried out have not detected any significant defects not detected by the components suppliers inspections and that overall, despite these stringent requirements the repair/rejection rate has been very low. Secondly, the validation work has confirmed that the basic approach utilised by the CEGB to the design of its inspections has been well founded and able to meet the needs of the PWR safety case.

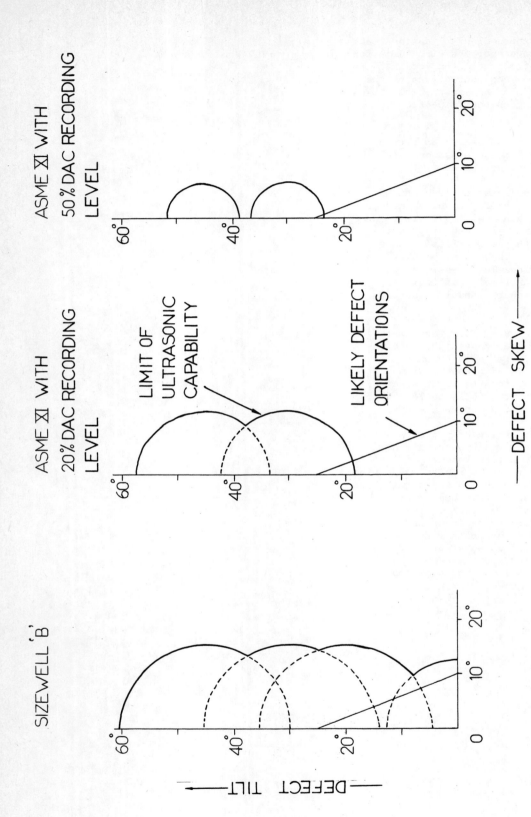

Fig 1   Detection of smooth embedded flaws in RPV weld

C388/042

Sizewell 'B' PWR reactor pressure vessel pre-service and in-service inspection requirement

A C ASHTON, BSc, CPhys, MInstP, **P D KELSEY**, IEng, MInstNDT and **G C SHAND**, AMIEE
Rolls-Royce and Associates Limited, Derby

SYNOPSIS This paper describes the in-service inspections required and the examination methods proposed for the Sizewell 'B' reactor pressure vessel. Outline details are provided of the work undertaken by Rolls-Royce and Associates Limited, the in-service inspection contractor to the CEGB. This includes meeting the inspection requirement and providing equipment for use during the second inspection following the manufacturing hydrostatic test and the site pre-service inspection. The equipment described will be subsequently used during in-service inspections at the site.

1 INTRODUCTION

The safety case for the Sizewell 'B' PWR was examined at a Public Enquiry which finished hearing evidence in March 1985. Non-destructive examination is an important aspect of demonstrating the safety case of the reactor pressure vessel and primary circuit.

So far as inspection is concerned, the CEGB placed great emphasis on ensuring that the parts of the primary circuit whose failure must be shown to be 'incredible' are free of defects that could jeopardize their integrity at the start of plant life. However, comprehensive in-service inspection will also be carried out to ensure that unanticipated defects are not arising during plant life.

In carrying out the in-service inspections it is essential to be able to draw upon, and make comparison with, the inspection results obtained during the manufacturing process. For defects that are to be detected by the in-service inspection system, defect descriptions such as 'smooth planar', as well as defect positions and orientations within the material, form a subset of the defect descriptions specified for the manufacturing inspections thus allowing less complex probe array systems to be used for the in-service inspections. The techniques proposed by Rolls-Royce and Associates Limited utilize a broad beam pulse echo ultrasonic inspection in order to cover a large volume of material and thus increase the chance of specular reflection from any defects which may exist within the metal. If defects are detected then a high resolution technique such as 'time-of-flight' diffraction would be used to size accurately the defects.

The use of contact probes which physically follow the surface contour of the component under examination enhance the accuracy of the inspection. Consequently, variations between the as manufactured outline and the theoretical profile are kept to a minimum. The use of contact probes also reduces the need for complex software necessary to ensure geometric conformity between the theoretical component outline and the scan path of the probe array.

Although the prime inspection technique is automated ultrasonics, other inspection methods such as magnetic particle, dye penetrant and eddy current techniques are used for the detection of surface breaking defects. In addition alternating current potential drop is used as a supplementary technique for sizing surface breaking defects in certain components. Extensive use is also made of remote visual inspection techniques for examining key areas of the reactor vessel.

2 INSPECTION REQUIREMENTS AND EQUIPMENT DESCRIPTIONS

2.1 Reactor Vessel

The reactor vessel is manufactured from ferritic steel with an austenitic cladding. The inspections to be carried out on the reactor vessel will be performed using a design of manipulator based upon a well proven concept devised by ABB-TRC of Sweden, which is shown schematically in Fig 1. The manipulator consists of a rail ring which attaches to the flange of the vessel once the reactor closure head and internals have been removed. A limited examination can be carried out with the lower internal structure in the vessel. A rotating frame locates off this ring which in turn carries a transverse trolley holding a vertical telescopic mast. This general design concept offers the following advantages:

(a) High positional accuracy and reproducibility since radial mast movements allow for scanning devices to be brought into close proximity with the areas under examination.

(b) It is rigid yet lightweight in construction compared with most manipulators of the 'central mast' concept. This makes for ease of assembly, disassembly and transportation.

(c) The general design and choice of materials and surface treatment make for ease of decontamination.

2.1.1 Main Circumferential Welds

The main circumferential welds will be inspected using contact probe full immersion techniques off the inner surface of the reactor vessel. In effect, there are four main circumferential welds requiring inspection, all basically needing the same probe angles and orientations. The only significant change is the requirement for skewed probes for examination of the transition ring to bottom dome weld.

The inspection is required to have a proven capability to detect, locate and size smooth or rough planar defects near the vessel inner and outer surface whose size in the ferritic material is greater than or equal to 25mm through-wall extent by 50mm length, and whose ligament to the clad ferritic interface, at the inner surface, is less than 5mm.

The ultrasonic probes are attached to a sprung suspension arm with the probe holder allowing the probes to follow the scanning surface with the right contact pressure. The cardanic suspended probe holder mounted at the end of the arm allows the probes to follow a wide range of scan path deviations. Schematic representations of the scanning devices are shown in Fig 2 and Fig 3.

The probe array will include the following probe types:

(a) 70 degree twin crystal probes designed to operate to a depth of 30mm below the cladding and pointing in both directions perpendicular to the weld and both directions parallel to the weld.

(b) 41 degree, single crystal shear wave probes pointing in both directions perpendicular to the weld.

(c) 49 degree, single crystal shear wave probes pointing in both directions parallel to the weld and both directions perpendicular to the weld.

(e) 53 degree shear wave and 63 degree shear wave probes pointing in both directions perpendicular to the weld.

(f) 70 degree, single crystal compression wave probes pointing in both directions parallel to the weld.

(g) a single 0 degree compression wave probe.

In addition to the above detailed probes, a number of supplementary probes are also included in the probe array:

(a) 45 degree, 1.5 MHz, tandem probes. These probes will be used to detect service induced defects near the outer surface of the vessel.

(b) 0 degree, 3 MHz probes mounted in perspex stand-off shoes which allow refracted angle of 45 or 60 degree compression beams in the component in a 'V' path configuration, i.e. 'time-of-flight' technique.

The probes described above will be scanned on the cylindrical and hemispherical internal surfaces of the vessel.

2.1.2 Bottom Dome Inspection

The requirement to carry out ultrasonic inspection of the bottom dome of the reactor vessel is a unique feature of the Sizewell B reactor vessel examination. The inspection is required to have a proven capability to detect, locate and size planar defects that are equal to or greater than 10mm by 10mm in the bottom dome parent material, and that lie within 10 degrees of a radial-axial plane with respect to the instrumentation tube, or tilted so as to be within 10 degrees of the normal to the surface of the bottom dome, or tilted at any angle in between.

The main manipulator will be equipped with a supplementary manipulator especially designed for the task. The manipulator will be equipped with two sets of probes diametrically opposed, each set consisting of:

(a) a single 65 degree/61 degree tandem, compression wave probe,

(b) a single 61 degree/45 degree tandem, compression wave probe,

(c) a pair of 70 degree twin crystal compression wave probe.

The probes will be scanned on the bottom dome inner surface, the device locating off one of the bottom dome penetrations. The tandem probes will be mounted side by side on a carrier which can be positioned at different radial distances from the instrumentation tube and scanned tangentially, with the beams directed towards the penetration. A pair of the twin 70 degree probes will be mounted at right angles to the tandem probes, one on each side, with the beams directed along the axis of the tangential scan. An identical probe and carrier arrangement will exist on each side of the instrumentation tube so that full coverage will be achieved by rotating the mechanism through only 180 degrees.

2.1.3 Nozzle Inspection

The areas to be inspected and the defects to be detected can be summarized as follows.

The nozzle to shell welds are to be inspected together with the parent material to a distance 50mm either side of the weld centre-line. Highly reliable location and sizing is required for potential service-induced defects, near the vessel inner surface, whose size is greater than or equal to 25mm through-wall extent by 50mm length and whose ligament to the clad-ferritic interface is less than 5mm. Similarly, near the vessel outer surface, highly reliable location and sizing of defects whose size is greater than or equal to 25mm through-wall extent by 50mm length is also required. The nozzle to shell weld inspection devices are shown in Fig 4 and Fig 5 for the outlet and inlet nozzles respectively.

In addition the inspection is to have a proven capability to detect, locate, and size defects whose size is greater than or equal to 10mm through-wall extent by 25mm length in the near surface and outer surfaces zones.

The nozzle inner surfaces, extending from the nozzle to safe-end weld to the edge of the inspection zone for the nozzle to shell weld, and to a depth of 30 mm, are also to be inspected using ultrasonics. Highly reliable detection and sizing is required for defects whose size is greater than or equal to 30mm length by 15mm through-wall extent. The inspection technique must also have a proven capability to detect defects of 25mm length by 10mm through-wall extent. The scanning device for inspecting the nozzle inner surfaces of inlet nozzles is shown schematically in Fig 5, and for outlet nozzles in Fig 6.

(i) Outlet Nozzles

The main manipulator will be equipped with a supplementary manipulator especially designed for the task. The probe array will consist of the following probes:

(a) eight 70 degree twin crystal compression wave probes inspecting to a depth 30mm below the cladding and pointing in both directions perpendicular to the weld and both directions parallel to the weld and focussed at two different ranges in the inspection zone. The probes will be scanned on the vessel inner surface in a circumferential direction relative to the nozzle axis.

(b) a single 10 degree single crystal compression wave probe inspecting the full volume of the weld from the vessel inner surface.

(c) a single 0 degree twin crystal compression wave probe inspecting the near surface volume from the vessel inner surface.

(d) a single 49 degree single crystal shear wave probe scanned on the nozzle bore, parallel to the nozzle axis, searching for defects in the near surface volume.

(e) a single 41 degree single crystal shear wave probe scanned on the nozzle bore, parallel to the nozzle axis, searching for defects in the inner region volume.

(f) a single 0 degree twin crystal compression wave probe inspecting the inner and outer region volumes from the bore of the nozzle.

(g) a single 15 degree single crystal compression wave probe inspecting the entire volume from the bore of the nozzle.

The probes described in (a) to (g) above will be included in an array scanning on the vessel inner surface. The primary scanning direction will be circumferential to the nozzle axis and the facility for incremental movement in a nozzle radial direction will be provided.

The probes described in (d) to (g) above will be mounted in a linear array around the nozzle bore. The primary scanning direction will be in the nozzle circumferential direction and the facility for incremental movement along the nozzle axis will be provided.

In addition to the probes described above, the following probes will also be deployed:

(a) a single 0 degree single crystal compression wave probe used for positioning and centralizing the nozzle manipulator relative to the nozzle axis.

(ii) Inlet Nozzle Inspections
The areas to be inspected and defects to be detected are essentially as per the outlet nozzles described above.

The main manipulator will be equipped with a supplementary manipulator specifically designed for the task. The probe array will consist of the following probes:

(a) eight 70 degree twin crystal, one 10 degree single crystal, and one 0 degree twin crystal compression wave probes as described above for the outlet nozzles.

(b) a single 56 degree single crystal shear wave probe inspecting the near surface zone from the 53 degree conical region of the nozzle bore.

(c) a single 49 degree single crystal shear wave probe scanned on the nozzle bore parallel to the nozzle axis searching for defects in the near surface zone.

(d) a single 6 degree single crystal compression wave probe inspecting the centre and far surface volumes from the bore of the nozzle.

(e) a single 30 degree single crystal compression wave probe inspecting the entire weld volume from the bore of the nozzle.

In addition probes of different angles will be skewed along nozzle axis to ensure optimum detection of defects in the 45, 135, 225 and 315 degree azimuthal positions.

A particularly difficult development was that associated with the detection and sizing of transverse defects in the nozzle to shell welds. The primary technique employed is two probe 'time-of-flight' with the probes positioned on either the vessel inner surface or nozzle bore such that the beams intersect the outer wall with a convergence angle of 40 degrees in the circumferential direction. The probes are mounted in a purpose built manipulator which attaches to the TRC main mast manipulator and has the facility for primary scanning in the nozzle circumferential direction with secondary scanning in the direction radial to the nozzle axis.

Coverage includes the outer blend radius region up to 50mm from the outer vessel wall of the nozzle to shell weld together with the parent material up to a distance of 50mm either side of the weld centre line.

2.1.4 Safe-end Weld Inspection
There are eight nozzle to safe-end welds and eight safe-end to pipe welds requiring examination using automated ultrasonics from the inner surface of the nozzle. It is recognized that inspection of this austenitic weld region is complicated by the difficulty associated with penetrating the weld metal with ultra-sound.

Nonetheless, the inspection must have a capability to detect planar defects of 10mm through-wall extent by 20mm length, or larger, which either break the inner surface or have a ligament of less than 10mm to the inner surface, or, lie parallel to and within 5mm of the buttering to nozzle fusion face.

The welds will be inspected with ultrasonic probes mounted off the same inspection device as is used for the inspection of the nozzle inner surfaces, shown schematically in Fig 5. The probes will locate off the nozzle inner bore and be scanned to a point 200mm either side of the weld centre line, with the primary scan in the circumferential direction and the secondary scan in the axial direction with respect to the nozzle axis.

The probe array will consist of the following probes providing the following beam angles:

(a) 45 degree, single crystal shear wave probe, inspecting in both directions axially and both directions circumferentially searching for defects in the mid-wall and far-wall regions.

(b) 70 degree, twin crystal compression wave probe, inspecting in both directions axially and both directions circumferentially. The crystal configurations will be optimised to detect near surface defects.

(c) 70 degree, twin crystal compression wave probes, inspecting in both directions axially and both directions circumferentially. the crystals for this probe will be stacked one behind the other and the probe performance optimised to detect defects in the mid-wall and the far-wall regions.

(d) 45 degree, single crystal compression wave probe, inspecting in both directions axially and both directions circumferentially, utilizing the 'self-tandem' technique to detect through-wall planar defects in the mid-wall and far-wall regions. It is recognized that the detection capability becomes less effective as the shear wave path length increases.

(e) 30 degree, twin crystal compression wave probe, inspecting in both directions circumferentially to the nozzle axis searching for defects in the far-wall region.

In order to minimize the number of probes it is intended that only one of each beam angle and scanning direction be used. To obtain the opposite hand scanning direction the whole probe pan of probes will be rotated through 180 degrees on an axis normal to the nozzle radius and the remaining scans completed.

2.1.5 Threads in the Vessel Flange

There are 54 threaded stud holes, equi-spaced, around the vessel flange and the inspection will be carried out with the studs removed. The inspection technique is designed to locate and size radial and circumferential planar defects

emanating from the threads, of a size 5mm radial by 10mm circumferential or larger.

To achieve this, ultrasonic scanning of the inspection volume is performed by means of a rotating unit which allows a range of 364 degrees about the threaded hole, with a second motor allowing for radial movement. With this unit a single ultrasonic probe is sprung loaded onto the vessel flange surface. The manipulator is required to position the inspection probe without fouling the sealing plug in the stud hole, or the three guide studs used not only to assist in relocating the closure head but also the reactor vessel inspection manipulator.

Any defects detected by the rotational scan of the probe around the threaded hole will be sized in depth using either 'time-of-flight' or Synthetic Aperture Focusing Technique (SAFT). Both of these techniques require the probe to be scanned radially outward from the stud hole.

The probe types deployed will be optimised following experimental trials, but will be either 0 degree or 5 degree single crystal compression wave probes.

2.2 Closure Head

2.2.1 Closure head to flange weld

Inspection of the closure head to flange weld is required using automated ultrasonic techniques, preferably deployed from the outside surface of the closure head. The defect detection criteria is as specified for the main circumferential welds within the reactor vessel. In addition however, magnetic particle inspection of defects breaking the outer surface is also required.

A total of three ultrasonic probe arrays are required in order to carry out the necessary inspection of the closure head to flange weld. The probes selected are required to interrogate the weld in both the axial and circumferential directions for defects which are generally planar in nature.

The probe array will consist of the following probes scanned on the closure head outside surface, perpendicular to the weld centre-line:

(a) two 41 degree single crystal probes, two 57 degree single crystal probes, and two 70 degree twin crystal probes.

(b) one 45 degree tandem probe.
    An identical array will be scanned parallel to the weld centre line. In addition a single 45 degree probe will be utilised for 'time-of-flight' sizing when necessary.

The manipulator comprises a circumferential drive module which is mounted on a track of approximately 5500mm diameter, made up of seven individual sections. Attached to this module is a second axial drive module which in turn moves a probe carriage along a pair of side support arms at specified speeds. Stability is improved by the use of a pair of outriggers equipped with magnetic wheels attached to the side support arms.

2.2.2 Control Rod Drive Mechanism (CRDM) Housing Welds

All peripheral CRDM housing welds are to be inspected using manual dye penetrant testing when the closure head is removed and positioned on the storage stand. The inspection is designed to be able to detect all surface breaking defects of any orientation.

All defects with a surface length equal to or greater than 6mm will be further examined to determine their through-wall size. The examination method to be deployed utilizes the alternating current potential drop (a.c.p.d) technique. The a.c. potential drop is measured by a pair of spaced, sprung electrical contacts in contact with the surface of the CRDM housing.

2.3 Stud and Nut Inspection

2.3.1 Stud Inspection

There are 54 studs, each made of ferritic steel, to be inspected. Prior to inspection they will be removed from the vessel, cleaned and stored dry. The outer surface of each stud extending from the upper limit for the threads for the nut to the lower limit for the threads to engage in the shell flange is to be examined using surface examination methods. In addition ultrasonic examination is required over a similar distance to a radial depth of 30mm.

The inspection is to have a proven capability to detect, locate and size smooth planar defects originating either at the threads or at the outer surface of the plain shank, of a size 10mm radial by 20mm circumferential or larger.

The stud inspection manipulator is based upon the 'Magnaflux' magnetic particle bench unit, constructed of 3mm steel framework enclosed in steel panels. A stainless steel tank is fitted into the framework to catch the magnetic ink or ultrasonic couplant. Fixed to one end of the framework is a headstock mechanism incorporating a lathe chuck. A track way consisting of two mild steel bars attaches to the top of the framework and extends over the full length of the bench, parallel to the axis of rotation of the chuck.

During ultrasonic examination the stud is held in the chuck at the nut thread end, with the opposite end supported on a nylon roller steady rest. The nylon support is adjustable along the length of the stud allowing free access for inspection along the stud.

In addition to the above techniques it is also proposed to use alternating current potential drop (acpd) techniques to measure through-wall extent of surface breaking defects. This technique is not designed for prime defect detection.

2.3.2 Nut Inspection

There are 54 ferritic steel nuts, each requiring surface examination of their external surfaces.

The nuts will be removed and stored dry prior to the inspection.

Nut examination is carried out using the same inspection rig as used for stud inspection. Nylon rollers mounted of the steel track are used to support the nut during examination. The threaded inner surface and the plain external surfaces of each nut will be examined using a.c. manual yoke and jig assisted encircling coil magnetic particle inspection, applying the field in two mutually perpendicular directions.

In addition to the magnetic particle examination described above, eddy current examination of the outer surfaces of the nut is also carried out. In order to facilitate this eddy current examination of the outer surfaces, the nut is held from within the bore by means of internal chuck jaws. During eddy current examination of the bore the nut is supported in the chuck using external chuck jaws. Each nut will be examined using a helical path surface scanning eddy current inspection technique.

2.4 Vessel Interior Visual Examinations

In addition to the ultrasonic and surface examinations described above, there is also a requirement to carry out remote visual examinations on a number of areas associated with the reactor vessel and closure head assembly.

The areas requiring examination can be summarized as:

(1) Vessel interior attachments - including the surfaces of the core support pads, their attachment welds and the adjacent cladding to a distance of 25mm from the attachment weld.

(2) The surfaces of the attachment welds to all of the instrument penetrations in the lower head together with the adjacent cladding and instrument tube, to be viewed from inside the reactor pressure vessel.

(3) The surfaces of the partial penetration welds which attach the head adaptor tubes to the vessel closure head together with the adjacent cladding, to be viewed from inside the closure head whilst the head is in its storage position.

(4) The nozzle bores, inlet and outlet, up to the pipe to safe-end weld.

(5) The vessel and closure head interior surfaces, to the maximum extent possible.

(6) The closure head flange sealing face.

In addition visual examination will also be carried out to the maximum extent possible on the vessel internal structures when placed in the refuelling cavity.

In order to meet the above inspection requirement, six separate cameras are to be provided for attachment to either the main vessel manipulator or supplementary manipulators, or the stand-alone closure head manipulator. In addition, specialist lighting systems are to be installed, especially designed to facilitate inspection underwater, and for ease of decontamination when used dry under the closure head.

Over and above the cameras supplied to carry out the detailed visual examinations, there will be three surveillance cameras, used particularly for observing the performance and operation of the ultrasonic inspection devices.

The visual inspection equipment is designed to meet the visual inspection requirements laid down in Reference (1). In addition it is possible to locate and size any defects detected. Details of the inspection system are provided in section 3.3 of this paper.

3 DATA ACQUISITION INTERPRETATION AND CONTROL SYSTEMS

From the above inspection descriptions it is apparent that a considerable amount of data acquisition and interpretation equipment is required. As pointed out some of the inspections employ manual techniques utilizing standard inspection systems. In this paper, only those parts of the inspection system which are unique to the Sizewell 'B' reactor vessel inspection will be described.

3.1 Ultrasonic Data Acquisition and Analysis System

3.1.1 Overview
The data acquisition and evaluation equipment is centred around the use of two well established inspection devices, namely, the Micropulse multichannel flaw detector as produced by Rolls-Royce Mateval and the ZIPSCAN time of flight defect sizing system supplied by Sonomatic. The two systems complement each other to provide an efficient inspection system with good defect sizing capability.

For most inspection areas the Micropulse is used for location of indications and sizing. It acquires data continuously, firing up to 48 separate tests at each inspection point. The analysis and evaluation software presents the data in a form which can be easily assessed by the operator. The Micropulse units are controlled via an IEEE-488 interface, by a Hewlett Packard HP9000 computer system.

Zipscan is used as a confirmatory technique for the location and sizing of defects in difficult areas - such as transverse defects in the nozzle to shell weld and for through wall sizing. Its high performance, in terms of its ability to resolve very weak diffracted signals, makes it invaluable in these situations.

3.1.2 Micropulse

Two Micropulse inspection systems are used, which enables two inspections to be performed concurrently. The Micropulse is a fully programmable multi-channel flaw detection system which records the amplitude and time-base of up to eight indications within the gate. It can be configured to fire up to 240 tests each having its own ultrasonic parameters such as transmitter and receiver probe number, gain, gate and reporting threshold etc.

3.1.3 Hewlett-Packard Computer System

The computer system is based on the Hewlett-Packard series 9000 range. It uses three computers which share mass storage devices via a central Shared Resources Management (SRM) system. Two model 350's are dedicated to acquiring data from the two Micropulses, which is passed via the SRM to a model 520 for analysis and evaluation.

3.1.4 The Hewlett-Packard Inspection Suite

The inspection software is all menu driven, the operator being presented with a list of options. The system checks that any necessary previous operations have been carried out by the operator before allowing the inspection to continue. The inspections are based upon a series of tables which completely define the inspections from calibration through inspection and data acquisition and on to data analysis and data evaluation. Only in the latter stages does the operator have a choice of actions.

The inspection suite can be split into the following functions:

(a) The Calibration Function - where the probes are calibrated prior to and after an inspection.

(b) The Data Acquisition Function - where the probes are scanned over the area to be examined in a pre-defined manner and fired at appropriate intervals. This function also includes a facility to automatically or on demand, perform a verification of the probes and equipment on verification blocks attached to the manipulator.

(c) The Data Analysis Function - where the positional information recorded during scanning is converted to vessel co-ordinates appropriate to the item being inspected.

(d) The Data Evaluation Function - where the analysed data is plotted showing three orthogonal views of an area on which the engineering outlines of the component being inspected are given. The Evaluation Function can also implement a data processing technique known as 'SIFT'. In the SIFT process, indications are correlated with their neighbours by dividing the inspection volumes into cells and comparing the sum of the weighted amplitudes of indications within the cell against a threshold. If the threshold is exceeded then the cell is said to be significant.

(e) The next stage of the process is to link adjacent significant cells together in three dimensions to form 'boxes', and to link together boxes from different test descriptions to form 'crates'. Each box is labelled and the data interpretation engineer then decides the nature of the defect from the plots.

3.1.5 Zipscan

Zipscan digitises, averages, displays and records the whole of the gated section of the RF wave form. This is different to the Micropulse where only data above a preset threshold is recorded. As a result, Zipscan allows for defect sizing almost independently of signal amplitude, consequently coupling quality, material attenuation and defect orientation are much less critical than when using conventional flaw detectors. To enhance the signal to noise ratio, Zipscan can average the received signal up to 256 times which has the effect of reducing random noise. This allows up to 120 dB of gain to be used, a figure which would completely saturate a conventional flaw detector.

Zipscan has a built-in DEC LSI 11/73 computer. The programs are written in FORTRAN with the routines which actually drive the Zipscan hardware being written in assembler language.

3.1.6 The Zipscan Inspection Suite

The Zipscan software suite is also menu driven and again is based on a set of inspection tables which completely define the inspection. Calibration and data acquisition are performed in a similar manner however the data processing is performed differently.

The options available for data processing include:

(a) SAFT - where the image is improved by removing the hyperbolic tails caused by beam spread of the transducer, producing an image equivalent to that collected with a parallel beam of half the transducer diameter.

(b) Time to depth linearization - which converts the B or D scan data image, which has a horizontal scale of distance and a vertical scale of time, into an image which has a vertical scale linear in depth. This allows depth measurements to be made directly from the display.

(c) Picture manipulation - where data is retrieved for further analysis, the picture enhanced using non-linear video transforms, text and calibration grids overlaid on A or B scans, and where measurements can be taken directly from the display screen using cursors controlled by the joystick.

3.2 The Manipulator Control System

The manipulator control systems (MCS) have been especially developed and designed for the Sizewell B reactor vessel inspection system. Two are used and they are capable of driving one of up to eight axes of movement consisting of a dc motor/tacho combination with absolute positional information being provided by resolvers. These devices work on a transformer principle and are rugged and resistant to electrical noise and radiation. Resolvers are not affected by momentary or long term loss of power and they therefore provide the security of positional information which is essential for safety reasons.

The systems continually monitor the resolvers and act as a 'watchdog' for the manipulator position. They will not allow any manipulator axis to move outside a predetermined area even if instructed to do so. Again this is necessary to remove any possibility of damaging the manipulator or vessel.

The MCS is driven remotely during an inspection by an HP computer or by Zipscan, but can be driven manually when it is off the vessel to change supplementary manipulators. The system incorporates a built in VDU to provide status and warning information.

3.3 The RVI System

The Remote Visual Inspection system (RVI) has been designed specifically for the Sizewell B inspections and it provides the following features:

(a) It provides surveillance of the probes on the surfaces of the vessel and confirms that they are correctly seated. The operator can adjust the focus and light intensity and certain inspections have extra degrees of control, such as a zoom camera and a pan and tilt unit.

(b) It performs an automated RVI of pre-defined areas, where the cameras are scanned in a pre-defined path with the pictures together with positional and sound-track information being recorded on a video recorder.

(c) The system has facilities to add identification labels and manipulator positional information to the pictures from the camera, and a facility to make 'hard copies' at full camera resolution.

(d) It provides an 'on-screen' defect sizing capability where the extent of a defect can be measured by positioning cursors at the extremities of the defect. The system then computes and displays the distance between the two cursors.

The RVI system incorporates a series of full communication systems from the remote shelter back to the inspection area.

4 TRAINING

It is a requirement that all organizations involved in the inspection of the Sizewell 'B' reactor vessel are formally approved and registered in accordance with the requirements of CEGB Standard 989904. This Standard outlines the training, certification and work experience requirements necessary to qualify for CEGB approval.

To meet this requirement, Rolls-Royce and Associates (RRA) has put in place an extensive training programme. This training programme constitutes 12 RRA developed training modules and examinations interfaced with UK certification schemes, and complements well the qualification and training requirements already used and established by RRA.

The exact training requirements are determined by the ultimate job function of the personnel involved but can be broadly described as follows:

(a) Automated Ultrasonic Personnel - will undergo a series of training modules which will cover both technical and practical instruction. Personnel will, as appropriate, receive technical instruction on the Sizewell 'B' automated ultrasonic system. In addition a series of practical work modules will be provided for those people who do not satisfy the work experience requirement. Finally, all personnel will be involved at the equipment post commissioning stage when hands-on practical experience will be gained using the full Sizewell 'B' ultrasonic inspection system.

(b) Surface Examination Personnel - will not be required to undergo detailed internal training as the personnel chosen will be recruited from established experienced engineers. They will however be involved in practical training at the full system commissioning stage.

(c) RVI Personnel - will undergo in-house training. Practical experience will be gained via in-house training using the RRA RVI equipment supplemented by site work experience where possible. Familiarisation with the full Sizewell 'B' inspection system will be provided at the commissioning stage.

In addition to the inspection personnel training outlined above, system support engineers and mechanical engineers and fitters will also undergo training in order to more fully understand the inspection tasks being undertaken.

RRA have an established Personnel Development Function (PDF), which controls all further education and technical training both inside and outside the Company. All in-house NDT training for the Sizewell contract will be controlled by the PDF, however, most of the courses and all of the practical training will be given by experienced senior NDT personnel. Performance will be assessed by internally set examinations and practical tests.

5 VALIDATION

The CEGB has set up an Inspection Validation Centre (IVC) at the UKAEA Risley Laboratories to provide assessment and certification of inspection procedures, equipment and personnel.

For the reactor vessel inspections described above only those associated with ultrasonic examination of the vessel main circumferential welds, the nozzle to shell welds, the nozzle inner surfaces, the closure head dome to flange weld and the closure studs will be subject to independent validation by the IVC.

The validation process falls into three stages:

(1) Assessment of procedures and equipment

(2) Practical demonstration of capabilities of procedures, equipment and personnel

(3) Validation of personnel

The practical demonstration involves the application of the inspections to test assemblies which are representative of the geometry of the Sizewell 'B' reactor vessel and which contain defects.

In addition, it is also necessary to provide a written technical justification of each of the inspection procedures relevant to the components itemized above. This technical justification is required to give a reasoned case explaining why the procedures adopted will have a high reliability for the detection of defects and why they will be able to locate and size the defects to the required tolerance.

The role of inspection personnel falls broadly into two categories; those where the work is carried out in strict accordance with a step-by-step procedure and those where the exercise of judgement is required.

In the first category, Validation will involve the assessment of the training and approval scheme and the performance of those applying the procedure during validation. Assuming that there is satisfactory performance by personnel applying the procedures during the practical trials, personnel subsequently trained in the same manner will be considered acceptable, i.e. the training and approval scheme is validated rather than the personnel involved.

In the second category, Validation will involve the assessment of the training and approval scheme and also the assessment of the individual undertaking the inspection role.

6 CONCLUSIONS

Rolls-Royce and Associates are confident that they can carry out the necessary inspections to a very high standard, using optimised techniques which give very high levels of defect detection reliability. Repeatability is guaranteed by a commitment to the use of automated inspection techniques wherever possible. Accuracy of sizing is ensured by the use of high sensitivity, state-of-the-art techniques, which are necessary to give precise details of the through-wall extent of a defect which may compromise the structural integrity of the pressure boundary.

For Sizewell the CEGB has adopted a policy of diverse inspections, i.e. ones carried out with a range of probe configurations and angles at high sensitivity, so that defects are often detected more than once. In addition, inspections are repeated independently, during manufacture and before the reactor enters service, with the aim of eliminating the overlooking or incorrect sizing of defects by any one inspection.

To give added confidence the CEGB has also undertaken to require the inspection contractor

to undergo independent validation to assess the proposed inspection techniques, equipment and personnel.

It is worth remembering at this stage that the Inspectors report at the Public Enquiry recognized and highlighted the fact that repeated and careful ultrasonic inspection is of outstanding importance and that the proposal to use two independent inspection organizations, for the in-process and in-service inspections, to provide assurance that ultrasonic inspections

are adequate is an invaluable reinforcement to the integrity case.

At the time of writing this paper RRA has completed its work in defining the inspection methods to be deployed and the design of the inspection manipulators and data acquisition systems required. Manufacture of the manipulators and electronic systems is well advanced as is training of personnel. It is intended that RRA will undergo Validation at the IVC during the latter part of 1989 and early 1990.

REFERENCES

(1) Boiler and Pressure Vessel Code, Section XI, Division 1. (ASME)

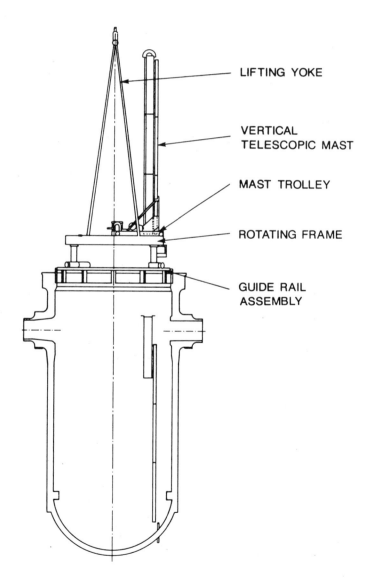

Fig 1   Schematic of main mast manipulator

LIFTING YOKE

VERTICAL
TELESCOPIC MAST

MAST TROLLEY

ROTATING FRAME

GUIDE RAIL
ASSEMBLY

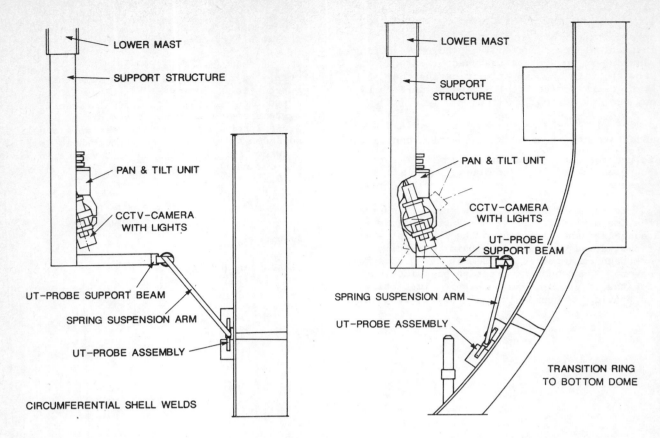

Fig 2   Shell weld inspection device (side view)

Fig 3   Shell weld inspection device (side view)

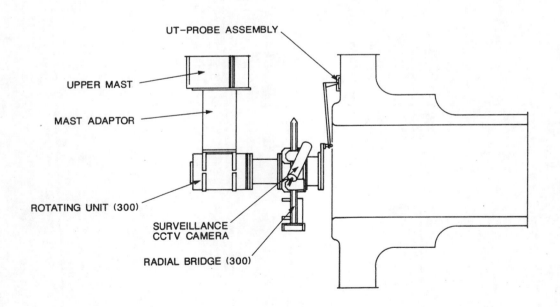

Fig 4   Nozzle to shell weld inspection device

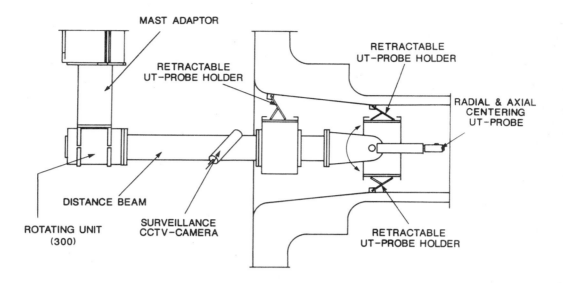

Fig 5   Inspection device for nozzle to vessel, pipe to safe-end and
           nozzle to safe-end welds and the nozzle inner surfaces

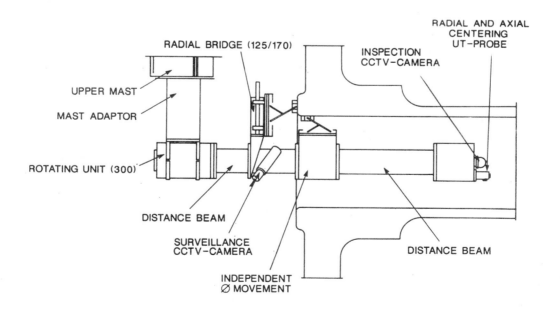

Fig 6   Nozzle inner radius scanning device

C388/047

Validation of inspections for Sizewell 'B'

G J LLOYD, PhD
United Kingdom Atomic Energy Authority, Risley, Warrington, Cheshire

SYNOPSIS As part of its inspection strategy for the Sizewell 'B' PWR station the CEGB has decided the ultrasonic inspection procedures will be subject to validation to give independent confirmation of their adequacy. Much of this work is being carried out at the Inspection Validation Centre, established at the NRL Risley Laboratory of the UKAEA.

This paper describes the historical background of the setting-up of the Centre, its method of operation, the reactor system components it is concerned with and the operational experience to date. Possible future directions for the Centre are also described.

1   INTRODUCTION

The structural integrity of key components of the pressure circuit of a pressurised water reactor (PWR) is ensured by special provisions taken during design and construction. These are such that the probability of failure of these key components is so low that failure may be regarded as "incredible". The Reactor Pressure Vessel (RPV) and other components of the Sizewell B PWR are thus collectively known as "incredibility of failure" (IOF) components.

To ensure that the probability of failure is acceptably low, it is essential that the components do not enter service containing flaws which could jeopardise their integrity. To ensure integrity, special care is taken in the design of the components, in the selection of their manufacturers and during manufacture. However, to check that the required standards have been achieved, intensive inspection is carried out. The inspection programme not only addresses quality but also supports the safety case for the components. The requirements of the inspection programme are designed to give a high assurance that the inspection will detect and correctly reject flaws which might lead to failure. However in order to provide further assurance the programme also contains redundant and diverse elements and is subject to validation. The large scale application of these facets of the inspection programme is unique to the British PWR.

Although the inspection programme utilises well-proven non-destructive (NDT) techniques eg radiography, ultrasonic methods potentially enable the inspection requirements to be fully covered. Redundancy of ultrasonic inspection is introduced in order to provide assurance that the total inspection programme is adequate to avoid random failures of flaw detection. This is achieved by the repeat application of the same ultrasonic procedure by different teams of inspectors. A diverse ultrasonic inspection is one which goes beyond basic good practice and incorporates additional features aimed at achieving the detection of any particular flaw by several means. Such additional features would be extra beam angles or scanning from other surfaces. As described above IOF components are subjected to a comprehensive programme of non-destructive examinations including ultrasonic (UT), radiography (RT), magnetic particle (MT) and penetrant testing (PT). The capabilities and limitations of the traditional NDT methods are well understood and it is not felt necessary to independently validate the PT, MT and RT techniques. The ultrasonic inspection, however will be subject to independent validation. For the RPV this was recommended by the second Marshall study group (1) and confirmed by the Sizewell B Public Inquiry (2).

2   THE VALIDATION CENTRE

The majority of the inspection validation work for Sizewell B PWR will be carried out by the Inspection Validation Centre (IVC), which is staffed by UKAEA personnel. Its work for the pressure vessel is closely monitored and guided by a Management Advisory Committee, chaired by Sir Alan Cottrell, and with members recognised as acknowledged experts in the fields of fracture mechanics and non-destructive testing. An important function of this committee is to ensure the independence of the IVC in carrying out its validation activities.

A special feature of the IVC's facilities is a large test hall (Fig 1), designed to accommodate test assemblies to be used in the validations and to enable teams to inspect these under realistic conditions. It contains a pit (Fig 2) which enables test assemblies to be submerged in water during inspection and which provides adequate head room to enable the mast of any likely in-service inspection system to be lifted by the overhead travelling crane. The 50 tonne capacity of the crane enables the test assemblies to be moved around the test hall. The building also contains laboratories and offices, mainly for use by the IVC's validation staff, but also to provide facilities for visiting inspection teams during their stay for validation. The aim of validation is to provide independent confirmation that the ultrasonic inspections are capable of achieving the purpose for which they are intended. Although the aims for the RPV and other components of the pressure circuit whose failure is regarded as incredible are the same, different specifications have been placed on the IVC by CEGB for these latter validations and they are discussed separately below. Where inspection procedures are very similar they are grouped together to reduce the number of validations.

3   REACTOR PRESSURE VESSEL VALIDATIONS

A schematic view of the pressure vessel is shown in Fig 3 and the ultrasonic inspections of the RPV requiring validation are summarised in Table 1 reflecting the philosophy of redundancy and diversity. Inspections are carried out at several stages during production by the manufacturer manually and by an independent inspection agent using automated equipment. The complete vessel is also inspected after hydro test at the manufacturers' works, before operation after installation at site and at intervals during its life using remotely controlled automated inspection equipment.

The IVC is required to validate the inspection procedures, the equipment and the operators. Following a successful validation, the IVC provide CEGB with certificates and statements on the effectiveness of the ultrasonic inspections. This written evidence is in two different forms. Firstly, IVC provide certification that the inspection procedures, equipment and operators are capable, with high reliability, of detecting, locating and sizing within specified tolerances, flaws substantially smaller than those which CEGB consider are of structural concern. Secondly, statements are provided on the capability of the inspection procedures to detect, locate and size flaws (i) which are smaller and (ii) which are unlikely to occur in practice. The smaller flaws are those just above manufacturing acceptance size and the unlikely flaws are of fitness for purpose size but with larger misorientation to the weld direction than those for which certification of the inspections are required.

The fitness for purpose (FFP) flaw sizes defined in Table 2 are significantly smaller than sizes regarded by CEGB to be of structural concern.

The manufacturing acceptance sizes which are given in Table 3 depend on the depth of the flaw in the material.

4   MANUFACTURE OF TEST ASSEMBLIES FOR VALIDATION

Several methods of flaw insertion in the IVC test assemblies are used. Figure 4 illustrates one method whereby a flaw within a cuboid is machined into a 'bobbin' and welded into a 'matrix strip' before being set into the final assembly. The flaw is definitively sized in the cuboid form using ultrasonic and radiographic methods and the weld material thoroughly checked for unintended flaws both in the intermediate matrix strip and the final weld.

Typical examples of IVC test assemblies, showing a flange to nozzle course section and outlet nozzle and also a section of the upper dome closure head of the vessel, are shown in Fig 5.

5   THE PROCESS OF VALIDATION

The validation process starts with the preparation by the CEGB of technical justification documents for the procedures and equipment to be validated. These contain reasoned arguments for their selection, and present theoretical and experimental evidence to justify their adequacy. With this background the IVC review the written procedures for completeness and clarity. Of particular concern is the elimination of ambiguity and the inclusion of comprehensive checklists. The training and certification status of individual operators is audited and the equipment is verified as representative. Only then can the practical stage of validation begin. Each operator is allocated a section of one or more test assemblies simulating the component for which validation is required. The operator is required to complete all the scans specified for this section. The results of the detection stage are compared to the known flaw population in the test assembly. The scans which have detected each flaw and the recorded amplitude are compared with theoretical predictions to minimise chance results. All stages of the inspection are subject to close scrutiny to ensure that calibration and scanning do not depart from the written procedures. For certification the operator must have detected all the major fitness for purpose flaws of types deemed credible in the component. Systematic failure on other less likely types of flaw might justify withholding certification. Procedure certification requires all the major credible flaws in all test sections to be satisfactorily detected. Statement regarding the procedures performance on other flaws are provided to CEGB.

Success in the detection stage permits progress to location and sizing. The operator is required to group and analyse indications recorded during detection. Working strictly to the written procedures, he reports the flaw location with respect to a specified datum and the flaw extent. The permitted errors differ dependant on flaw location, being smaller for near surface flaws than for those buried in the section thickness. The most critical are the extent of the flaw in the through thickness direction and the ligament between flaw and surface. Typical tolerances for these being 5mm. Again for certification all major credible flaws have to be correctly located and sized.

6   OTHER INCREDIBILITY OF FAILURE COMPONENTS

The IVC have also been asked to validate inspection procedures to be used on the steam generators, the pressuriser, the reactor coolant pumps and some of the reactor internals as shown in Fig 6. A list of such procedures is given in Table 4.

For these validations, the IVC is required to assess the capability of the inspection procedures including demonstration that a typical operator is capable of applying them satisfactorily. Statements on the findings of the IVC are to be issued to CEGB subsequent to each validation.

7   OPERATIONAL EXPERIENCE TO DATE

The validation work performed to date (Figs 1 and 7) has had a major impact on the ultrasonic inspections for the Sizewell B RPV and other IOF components. As a result some improvements have been made to the intended inspection procedures which make a positive contribution to the overall programme designed to ensure the structural integrity of the plant.

For the RPV inspection programme interim and final validation work has shown that inspection procedures can be written in an unambiguous manner which are capable of being followed by the approved operators, and which are able, by application of suitable quality control, to be applied during the actual inspections in an identical manner to that demonstrated during validation. Checklists are used during validation to enable IVC to ensure that the operators follow the inspection procedure. A validation certificate is not issued if the procedure is not followed, even if the flaws are correctly identified. Experience during practical validation has shown that operators are in general able to detect and locate flaws reliably, but some operators have failed to size flaws within the specified tolerances. Practical validation work has involved manual inspections for welds, forgings and underclad cracking and automated inspection for welds and forgings.

For the other IOF components inspection programme validation has consisted of theoretical assessment work which has been completed on procedures that will be used to inspect the steam generator and pressuriser shell forgings, the steam generator tubesheet forgings and the pressuriser upper and lower head forgings. Preliminary practical work using these procedures has indicated to IVC that the procedures have the capability to detect and size within tolerance all the types of volumetric flaws that are available to be examined and that are within the validation requirement. Theoretical and practical work is being carried out on procedures that will be used on the steam generator circumferential butt welds, the steam generator secondary

nozzle forgings and the steam generator channel and upper head forgings.

The validation work is supported by an engineering programme to manufacture test pieces containing implanted flaws. For ferritic components flaws can be satisfactorily implanted using welding techniques. However some IOF components are fabricated from austenitic material which is unsuited to flaw implantation by welding. This is due to the large grain growth at the flaw implant boundary which makes the flaw too easy to detect by ultrasonic techniques. An alternative method of flaw implantation based on Hot Isostatic Pressure (HIP) bonding has had to be developed to allow flaw implantation into austenitic material. This method has allowed the manufacture of an Inconel test piece containing closely controlled flaws and this test piece will be used in the validation of the ultrasonic procedure to be applied to the steam generator divider plate which is fabricated from Inconel.

8   POSSIBLE FUTURE DIRECTIONS

As described earlier the first work for the IVC has been on the PWR nuclear reactor system but it is already clear that the facilities and staff skills are equally applicable to any industrial technology where high reliability inspection is required. Thus, for example, the IVC has begun work on inspection validation for some UK oil industry interests and has provided services on high-reliability inspection to heavy fabricators and nuclear concerns overseas.

This trend is expected to continue with the IVC developing to become a major applied technology centre in the field of NDT.

REFERENCES

(1)   United Kingdom Atomic Energy Authority. An assessment of the Integrity of PWR Vessels. A report by a study group under the Chairmanship of Dr W Marshall. UKAEA Report HMSO (1982).

(2)   Sizewell B Power Station Public Inquiry Structural Integrity of the Primary Circuit. PWR/LPA/P4(Add 2).

(3)   Validating the inspection of PWR pressure vessels. D K Cartwright. Atom 367. May 1987.

TABLE 1

INSPECTION VALIDATION CENTRE
Ultrasonic Inspections of the Sizewell 'B' Reactor Pressure Vessel
Requiring Validation

COMPONENT	TYPE AND EXTENT OF INSPECTION
A MATERIAL PROCUREMENT STAGE	
1 All vessel forgings	i,iv
B FABRICATION STAGE - WELDS (UNCLAD)	
2 Nozzle shell course to vessel flange weld	i
3 Inlet Nozzle/shell welds	i,iv
4 Outlet Nozzle/shell welds	i
5 Transition ring/bottom head weld	i
6 Closure head flange/dome weld	i
7 Core shell course/transition ring weld	i
8 Nozzle shell course/core shell course weld	i
9 Inspection for underclad cracking	ii,v
10 Inspection of bars for studs, washers and nuts	iii
C POST STRESS RELIEF INSPECTION OF FULL PENETRATION BUTT WELDS (CLAD)	
11 Closure head/flange dome weld	i
12 Vessel flange/nozzle course weld	i
13 Nozzle shell course/core shell course weld	i
14 Core shell course/transition ring weld	i
15 Transition ring bottom head weld	i
16 Inlet nozzle/shell welds	i
17 Outlet nozzle/shell welds	i

TABLE 1 (CONTINUED)

COMPONENT	TYPE AND EXTENT OF INSPECTION
D POST-HYDRO INSPECTION STAGE FULL PENETRATION WELDS (CLAD)	
Items 11 - 17 above	Automated inspections from both inside and outside the vessel
18 Items 12-17 above plus	Remote automated inspection from inside nozzle inner radius only using in-service inspection equipment
19 Item 11 above	Automated inspection from outside only using in-service equipment
20 Inspection studs and nuts	Using in-service inspection equipment
E PRE-SERVICE INSPECTION	
21 Repeat inspection of items 18	Remote automated inspection inside only using in-service inspection equipment
22 Repeat inspection of item 19	Automated inspection from outside only using in-service inspection equipment
23 Repeat inspection of item 21	Using in-service inspection equipment
24 In-service inspections repeats of items 22, 23 and 24.	

Key: i   Manual inspection from both sides
      ii Manual inspection from inside only (sample areas)
      iii Manual
      iv Automated inspection from both sides
      v   Automated inspections from inside only (sample areas)

TABLE 2

Fitness-for-purpose Flaw Sizes For RPV Work

FLAW POSITION	Bore and Inner Radii of Reactor coolant Nozzle Forgings (mm)	All other regions of Forgings and all welds (mm)
Near Surface Flaw	15	25
Embedded Flaw	25	25

A near-surface flaw is one for which the ligament between the flaw and the surface does not exceed the lesser of

(a) the defect through-wall extent

(b) 30 mm

TABLE 3

Maximum Manufacturing Flaw Acceptable Sizes For RPV Work

DEPTH FROM FERRITIC SURFACE (MM)	MAXIMUM-THROUGH-THICKNESS DEPTH (MM)
0 - 5	3
5 - 25	5
25 - 75	8
>75	12

TABLE 4

INSPECTION VALIDATION CENTRE
Sizewell 'B' IOF Plant Inspections Requiring Validation

1. STEAM GENERATOR

a) MANUFACTURING INSPECTIONS

```
FORGINGS                 10)
CIRC WELDS                6)
NOZZLE/SHELL WELDS        6)  MANUAL
DIVIDER PLATES           1)
```

b) IN-SERVICE INSPECTIONS

```
CIRC WELDS               5)
NOZZLE/SHELL WELDS       1) AUTO
NOZZLE INNER RADII
```

2. PRESSURISER

a) MANUFACTURING INSPECTIONS

```
FORGINGS                 4) MANUAL
CIRC WELDS               4)
```

b) IN-SERVICE INSPECTIONS

```
CIRC WELDS               2) AUTO
NOZZLE INNER RADII       3)
```

3. REACTOR COOLANT PUMP

a) MANUFACTURING INSPECTIONS

```
FLYWHEEL PLATE           1  MANUAL
```

b) IN-SERVICE INSPECTIONS

```
FLYWHEELS                1  MANUAL
```

4. REACTOR INTERNALS

a) MANUFACTURING INSPECTIONS

```
FORGINGS                 2) MANUAL
PLATES                   1)
```

```
                         ──
                         49
                         ══
```

Fig 1   View inside main test hall

Fig 2   The pit facility

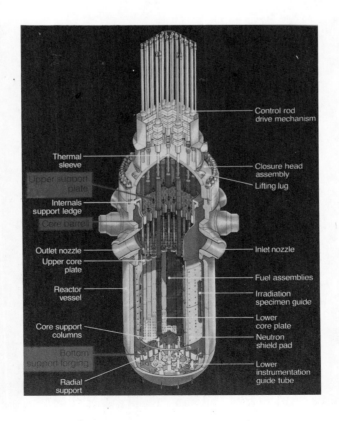

Fig 3   Cut-away schematic of the reactor pressure vessel

Method of flaw insertion

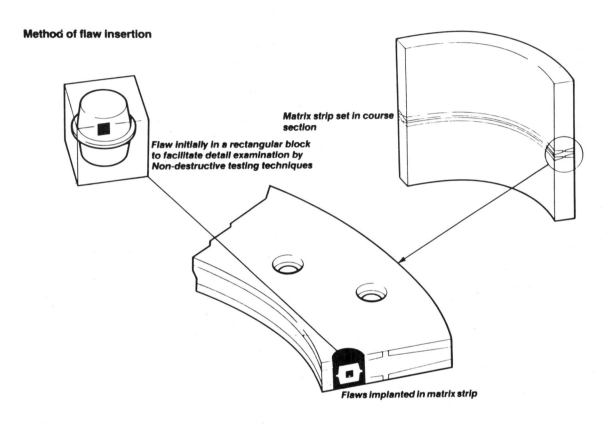

Flaw initially in a rectangular block
to facilitate detail examination by
Non-destructive testing techniques

Matrix strip set in course
section

Flaws implanted in matrix strip

Fig 4   Method of inserting flaws in full-scale test assemblies

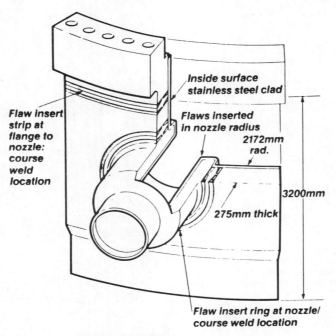

Inside surface
stainless steel clad

Flaw insert
strip at
flange to
nozzle:
course
weld
location

Flaws inserted
in nozzle radius

2172mm
rad.

3200mm

275mm thick

Flaw insert ring at nozzle/
course weld location

**Test assembly No. 24 flange/nozzle course and
outlet nozzle Weight 28 tonnes**

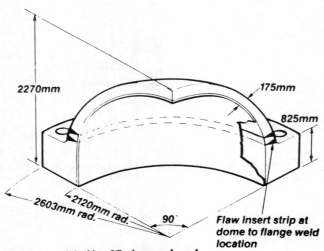

2270mm

175mm

825mm

2603mm

2120mm rad.

90°

Flaw insert strip at
dome to flange weld
location

**Test assembly No. 27 closure head
Weight 20.3 tonnes**

Fig 5   Typical IVC test assemblies

C388/047

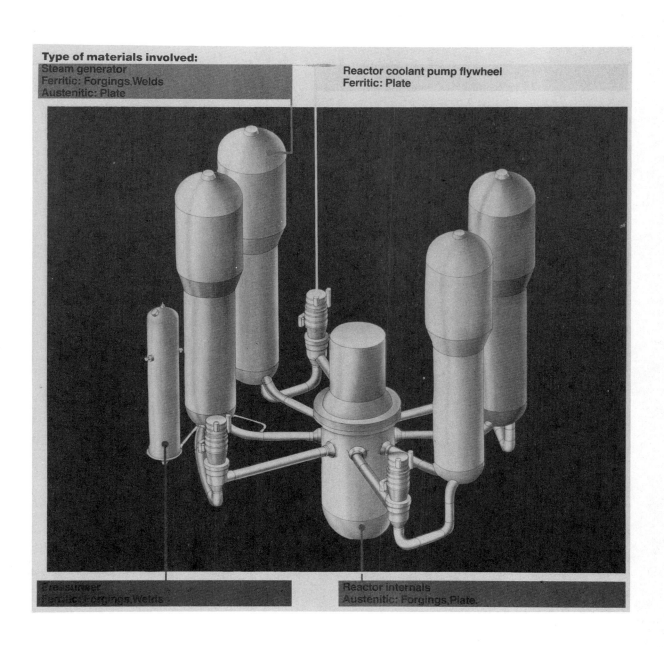

Type of materials involved:

Steam generator
Ferritic: Forgings, Welds
Austenitic: Plate

Reactor coolant pump flywheel
Ferritic: Plate

Pressuriser
Ferritic: Forgings, Welds

Reactor internals
Austenitic: Forgings, Plate.

Fig 6   General view of 'incredibility of failure' items

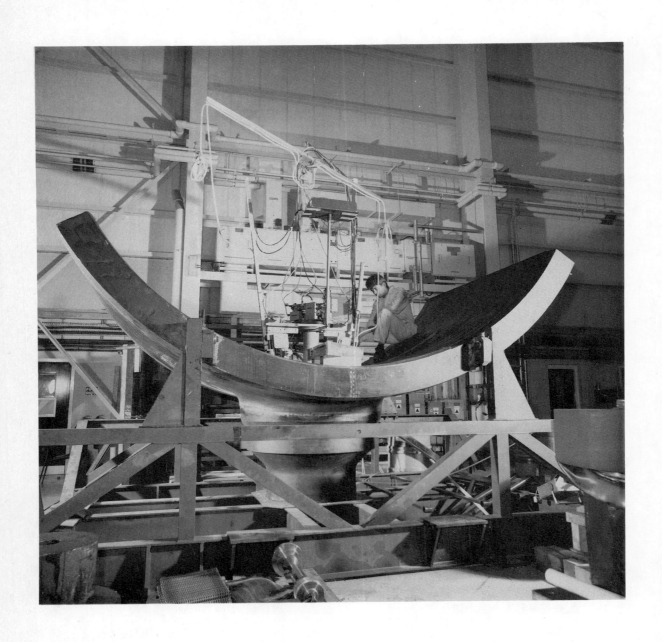

Fig 7   Automated inspection validation in progress

C388/023

Sizewell 'B' steam generator design builds upon the Westinghouse Model F to meet United Kingdom safety case

R L SYLVESTER, BSME, MBA, PE
Westinghouse Electric Corporation, Pensacola, Florida, USA
J P FOGARTY, BE, CEng, MInstE
Babcock Energy Limited, Crawley, West Sussex
J L THOMSON, BSc, MInstNDT
Babcock Energy Limited, Renfrew

SYNOPSIS The Model F steam generator is the result of an intensive on-going Westinghouse program aimed at improving the efficiency and reliability of steam generators. Design of the four steam generators for the Sizewell 'B' pressurized water reactor (PWR) is that of the latest Westinghouse Model F, with specific features aimed at the United Kingdom safety case and the requirements for inspectability of the pressure boundary. The background to the nondestructive examination requirements for Sizewell 'B' and the impact of these requirements on the steam generator pressure boundary design are discussed.

1 INTRODUCTION

The Westinghouse Model F Steam Generator was developed in the mid-1970's to address the evolving needs of the power industry, while incorporating plant experience gained from steam generators in operation since 1960 (1). The emphasis of the initial Model F was on the development of design features to address the issues of the then current operating plants. These issues were primarily those dealing with performance and the reliability of internal steam generator components. The features that address the most significant of these issues are highlighted in this paper, and are the basis for the initial Model F steam generator design.

The first Model F steam generators were placed in service in 1983. Currently there are a total of 39 Model F steam generators operating at 12 plants in both the United States and overseas. In addition, 17 replacement units (models 44F and 51F) with Model F features are in operation at six power plants. The data obtained from these initial units have shown that the enhanced design features initiated with the Model F have successfully addressed the issues arising from the pre-Model F steam generators.

Since the initial Model F design, ongoing development programs within Westinghouse and the nuclear industry, supported by the latest plant data, have led to further enhancements. These enhancements are aimed at providing additional margins and increased reliability. The most significant of the advanced Model F features are those dealing with the choice of tubing material and upgrade of the anti-vibration bar (AVB) design. Coupled with the initial design features, they constitute the current Model F design. The latest Model F design enhancements have been incorporated into the eight replacement units produced by Westinghouse in 1988, as well as in the design of the steam generators for the Sizewell B power station.

In addition to the features that characterize the typical Model F, and address performance and internal component reliability, several design choices can be and have been initiated at the option of the individual customer. These features, dealing with the pressure boundary, include the use of materials with added margin against brittle fracture, the reduction in the number of weld seams by use of forgings, and design enhancements to provide greater access for production and in-service nondestructive examination (NDE). For the Sizewell B project, design details in these areas have been developed consistent with the U.K. Safety Case, and the specific requirements for NDE and fracture mechanics analysis required by the CEGB.

2 MODEL F DESIGN

2.1 Principle Of Operation

The Westinghouse Model F is a vertical U-tube heat exchanger, which uses high temperature pressurized water on the primary side as a heat source, and produces dry saturated steam on the secondary side. (See Figures 1 & 2). The primary water, which is heated in the reactor vessel, enters the steam generator at the channel head inlet nozzle at a temperature of 326°C (619°F) and is maintained at a pressure of 155.1 bars (2250 psia) to prevent boiling. The water flows through the U-tube, where heat transfer takes place, and exits from the opposite side of the divided channel head.

The primary and secondary sides are separated by a thick forged plate called a tubesheet. The U-tubes are held firmly in the tubesheet, and are supported laterally along their length by tube support plates. In the U-bend area, support is provided by anti-vibration bars.

On the secondary side, feedwater enters through a feedring and is directed downward by inverted J-tubes. The feedwater, mixed with recirculated water from the moisture separators, flows down the annulus between the tube bundle wrapper, and the lower shell and enters the tube bundle just above the tubesheet. A flow distribution baffle enhances horizontal sweeping velocities across the top of the tubesheet, thereby minimizing a lower flow zone at the centre. The steam-water mixture rises through the tube bundle where heat is transferred from the primary to secondary fluid.

The steam-water mixture that leaves the tube bundle passes through a primary centrifugal moisture separator, and then through a secondary moisture separator, to produce dry saturated steam at a pressure of 68.95 bar (1000 psia) with a moisture content of less than 0.25 percent by weight. Steam exits through a nozzle in the upper head. The steam nozzle incorporates an integral flow limiter that restricts flow during a postulated steamline break. Water that is separated from the steam is mixed with the entering feedwater and recirculated through the steam generator.

Steam generator design issues in the early 1970's, based on operating plant feedback, were those primarily dealing with corrosion of internal parts. Historically, corrosion in steam generators has taken one or more of the following forms: stress corrosion cracking (SCC) and the related condition of intergranular attack (IGA), occurring on the tubing outer surfaces in areas of concentrations of contaminants; stress corrosion cracking detected on the tube inner surfaces; thinning or wastage (a general dissolution of the tube wall resulting from high concentrations of certain contaminants); and denting, a local constriction of tubes resulting from accumulation of the by-products of carbon steel support plate corrosion. In almost all occurrences of secondary side tube degradation, the major contributing factor has been the presence of contaminants in the steam generator. With the knowledge that complete elimination of contamination may not always be achievable, Westinghouse selected for the Model F, design features and materials which provide added margins against corrosion and related conditions.

Field data also indicated some units were subject to conditions leading to excess moisture carryover, tube vibration, and water hammer in the feedwater delivery system. In each case, the Model F steam generator has addressed these issues, both in the initial design as well as continued enhancements and upgrades. The key developments to the Model F are discussed below.

2.2 Quatrefoil Tube Support Plates

Early steam generators employed carbon steel plates with round holes to provide lateral support for the tube bundle. Some of these units experienced a phenomenon at the tube-tube support interface called denting. Denting, a local constriction of the tubes, is believed to result from the acid chloride corrosion of carbon steel support plates. To provide additional margin, based on an understanding of the denting process, the Model F utilizes tube support plates fabricated from Type 405 stainless steel (405 SS). Testing of 405 SS in laboratory programs, conducted under realistic secondary side conditions, has shown this material to be much more resistant to the denting phenomenon than carbon steel. The qualification program completed prior to the utilization of 405 SS tube support plates also demonstrated the suitability of this material with respect to other properties, such as strength and machinability. For additional margin, the tube support plates in the Model F employ a broached quatrefoil hole rather than a drilled cylindrical hole. Four-lobed flow areas in the plate surround each tube, providing advantages in resistance to chemical concentration. The tube contact area is minimized, and flow along the tube surface is increased. This reduces the potential for dryout and subsequent impurity concentration. High structural load carrying capability is retained in this tube support design.

2.3 Thermally Treated Tubing (TT)

The initial Model F steam generator employed Alloy 600 tubing, as did earlier models. However, the Model F tubing is thermally treated to produce a semi-continuous grain boundary precipitate, and to reduce residual stresses produced during tube fabrication. This treatment is accomplished by heating the tubing in a vacuum at 760°C (1325°F) for 10 hours. The thermal treatment enhances the SCC resistance of the material while allowing it to retain the general corrosion resistance of mill annealed Alloy 600. In addition, to reduce the high residual stress in the U-bend due to the tube bending process, the small radius tubes near the tube bundle center are stress relieved after bending.

In order to arrive at the choice of material for Model F tubes, Westinghouse conducted a comprehensive qualification program before thermally treated Alloy 600 was introduced in 1977. Steam generators utilizing thermally treated Alloy 600 tubing with stress relieved U-Bend have been in operation for over nine years. The data collected from laboratory and field programs continues to indicate that thermally treated Alloy 600 is an appropriate material for use in steam generator tubing. However, as a part of the ongoing Westinghouse program to increase the reliability of the steam generators, evaluations of tubing materials have continued. Comprehensive comparative evaluation of Alloy 690 thermally treated tubing versus Alloy 600 thermally treated tubing and other candidate alloys have been conducted over the past 10 years. The results of these studies, coupled with design and manufacturing assessments, have been reviewed systematically and in depth. Based on these evaluations, Westinghouse has arrived at an enhanced tubing material and now recommends the use of Alloy 690 TT. This recommendation represents a change from the initial selection of Alloy 600, and reflects the superior performance consistently demonstrated in corrosion testing and other evaluations, in both primary and secondary side conditions. Alloy 690 TT heat transfer tubing has been proposed and accepted for the Sizewell 'B' steam generator, and has also been used in the last eight replacement steam generators delivered by Westinghouse to two U.S. utilities in 1988.

2.4 Flow Distribution Baffle

Corrosion of steam generator tubing is usually found in areas with high concentrations of impurities. The concentration process can result from certain local conditions and geometries. One area where concentration can occur is sludge deposits. Sludge deposits form when particles, brought into the steam generator in the feedwater, settle in areas of low fluid velocity. The region directly above the tubesheet, where the secondary flow changes direction from cross flow to axial flow, has been observed to be a location of sludge deposition. The flow distribution baffle in the Model F controls the upward fluid flow near the outside of the tube bundle, creating a higher velocity flow along the tubesheet and retarding deposition of sludge. This sweeping flow minimizes the number of tubes exposed to low velocity and establish the low velocity flow area at the centre of the tube bundle. The placement of the blowdown extraction in this area facilitates removal of sludge. Flow bypass through the central tube lane is restricted by tube lane blocking devices.

2.5 Full Depth Hydraulic Expansion

Crevices or narrow gaps are also areas where contaminant concentration can occur. Crevices are subject to dryout, or liquid deficiency, when located in conjunction with a heat transfer surface, and promotes contaminant concentrations. The tubes in a steam generator extend through the tubesheet and are welded to its primary side. The tubes are expanded to eliminate the crevice between the tube O.D. and the I.D. of the tubesheet holes. This full depth expansion process minimizes a potential concentration zone in the tubesheet. Dimensional control of the crevice is made possible by machining of both primary and secondary sides of the tubesheet to close tolerances, followed by detailed surveys to establish the as-built tubesheet thickness. The full depth tube expansion is accomplished hydraulically in the fabrication of the Model F. The process uses high pressure water to expand the tube and

minimizes the residual stress in the expanded-to-unexpanded transition zone, thereby providing margin against stress corrosion cracking.

2.6 Anti-vibration Bars

The initial Model F units utilized three sets of chromized Inconel anti-vibration bars to support the tubes in the U-bend region, and to minimize flow induced vibration and potential tube wear. Tube-to-AVB gaps were controlled through assembly methods and procedures in the same manner as was done in the pre-Model F units. However, the Model F employs an additional AVB set over that used for earlier steam generators of similar size. Plant feedback from some operating Model F's indicated potential for tube wear in the U-bend region. This wear has been attributed to large tube/AVB gaps, caused by the AVB assembly process, and a build up of dimensional tolerances in tube diameters and in the thickness of the AVB's. A program was initiated to address the U-bend wear by an upgrade to the Model F U-bend/AVB assembly. The primary emphasis of the Model F AVB assembly enhancement was aimed at the reduction and control of the tube/AVB gap, which was considered to provide the greatest margin against tube vibration and the initiation of tube wear. As an added benefit, and to provide margin against wear in the event of tube vibration, a change in the AVB material was implemented.

The tube to AVB gap for the latest Model F design is minimized and controlled by improvements in two areas:

o Tube and AVB tolerances

o Assembly techniques and procedures

Data from early units indicated that tube diameters varied greatly in the U-bend region, due to tube bending tolerance variation from small bends to large bend tubes. Working closely with tubing manufacturers, Westinghouse has been able to procure tubes with diameter variations in the U-bend of 0.13 mm (0.005 inches) or less. Similarly dimensional controls have been introduced in the fabrication of the AVB's themselves. Early units had thickness variations of up to 0.18 mm (0.007 inches) with no specific control of bar flatness and twist. Development work into the AVB problem has indicated that bar tolerance also plays a major part in gap control. As a result, the current design controls AVB thickness to within $\pm$ 0.03 mm (0.001 inches) and bar twist to within 0.13 mm (0.005 inches) along the entire bar length, when measured from a flat plane.

Along with the change to the component parts, significant improvements in control of the AVB installation process have been implemented. The revised procedures utilize specific bundle orientation, tube spacers, fixtures and specified welding sequences to control the effect of gravity and weld shrinkage on AVB/tube gap. The result is a mean tube-to-AVB gap, for the entire bundle, one third to one fourth of that experienced in early Model F units. Dimensional inspections and surveys throughout the installation process document and confirm that design criteria are met.

The analysis and testing performed as part of the overall AVB development (2) indicate that the enhanced Model F AVB design, with the gaps that have been achieved in replacement units, will perform satisfactorily for the plant design life. However, to provide additional margin the material of the AVB's has also been changed from chromized Inconel to type 405 stainless steel. The selection of 405 SS was based on data available on 405 SS as a wear couple with Alloy 600 and 690 TT tubing, obtained from the tube support plate development program, and from the related AVB modification development program for operating steam generators.

3 SIZEWELL 'B' MODIFICATIONS TO MODEL F

The design of the four steam generators for the Sizewell 'B' PWR incorporates all of the above Westinghouse developments to the Model F unit, with certain detailed design changes to the pressure boundary to address the UK safety case and inspection requirements. The most significant of the additional requirements for the UK unit can be summarized as:-

o   The use of forgings throughout the steam generator pressure boundary.

o   A change in the ferritic material specifications for the primary and secondary pressure boundaries.

o   The specification of minimum elevated temperature fracture toughness properties for the pressure boundary materials.

o   The introduction of an auxiliary feed water nozzle.

o   The use of safe-ends on the channel head nozzles.

o   The requirement for ultrasonic inspection during manufacture.

3.1 Use Of Forgings

The Sizewell B steam generator utilizes ring forgings, as opposed to plate fabrication, for the upper and lower shell strakes and for the transition cone between the upper and lower shells. In addition the primary head is manufactured as a one piece forging with integrally forged nozzles and manway access

reinforcements; and the secondary head is manufactured as a one piece forging with an integrally forged steam outlet nozzle. The use of forgings offers several advantages:

(a)   The more highly stressed longitudinal seam welds in the shell strakes and cone, and the meridional seam weld in the secondary head are eliminated. This has the additional benefit of significantly reducing the extent of the pressure boundary welds.

(b)   Similarly, the length of welds requiring in-service inspection is reduced, bringing important cost and radiation dose savings over the life of the plant. For the channel head this is particularly beneficial by minimizing the in-service inspection requirement in a potentially difficult area in terms of radiation level.

(c)   The use of forgings reduces the problems of mismatch and ovality associated with circumferential welding of shell strakes manufactured from rolled plate. This is particularly important in view of the stringent surface form tolerance requirements for NDE. To facilitate further the achievement of the required form tolerance, forgings are being manufactured with surplus material on section thickness at weld locations, to provide an allowance for dressing to a 'flat and flush' finish on completion of welding.

(d)   A forging with upstands on both ends, rather than welded plate construction for the transition cone, has the advantage that the weld seams to the upper and lower shells can be removed from the cone to cylinder geometric discontinuity. In this way, ultrasonic examination of the welds can be applied without the limitations that would be associated with the geometric discontinuity.

3.2 Ferritic Material Specification Changes

In order to maximise assurance against fast fracture, liquidation cracking and reheat cracking, the steam generator forging material for the pressure boundary components is in accordance with the requirements of the ASME code material specification for SA 508 Class 3. The adoption of this material as against SA 533 Grade A Class 2 and other grades of SA 508 materials previously utilized is in line with the recommendations of the UKAEA study group report (3).

The available data base for SA 508 Class 3 forgings is now considerable, and much greater than that for other classes of this material. The data base also demonstrates satisfactory fracture toughness properties of the materials for the required duties.

Liquidation and reheat cracking are fabrication defects which can occur in the heat affected zones associated with structural welding and weld overlay cladding operations.

Liquidation cracking occurs during the welding thermal cycle prior to any post weld heat treatment, and the probability of it's occurrence is considered to be reduced by lowering the levels of carbon and increasing the manganese/sulphur ratios. (see Table 1).

The lower carbon levels and higher manganese/sulphur ratio of the SA 508 Class 3 forgings make this material less susceptible to liquidation cracking than Class 2.

Reheat cracking occurs most frequently during post weld heat treatment when the relaxation strains exceed the ductility of the material. The probability of occurrence is considered to be reduced by reducing the levels of chromium and molybdenum.

The lower levels of chromium and molybdemum in the proposed material make it less susceptable to reheat cracking than the other grades.

In addition the maximum level of residual elements is subject to tight control through the Sizewell 'B' forging specification placed on material suppliers. This assists significantly in reducing the probability of both liquidation and reheat cracking.

For the U.K. steam generator however, the allowable stress levels are lower by approximately 15% for the selected materials than those normally used by Westinghouse. In consequence, the primary and secondary ferritic pressure boundary requires redesigning to allow for the lower allowable stress levels, as discussed in section 4 of this paper.

3.3 Elevated Temperature Fracture Toughness Specification

The UK Specification for the steam generator requires a minimum value of the upper shelf fracture toughness of the pressure boundary materials of 165 MPa√m. Although there is a reasonable availability of data for the proposed forging material, the data available on weld consumables is less extensive. A weld consumable selection and validation programme was carried out early in the contract.

The programme consisted of three phases. The first being a market survey of all the available data and a selection of the best potential consumables. The second phase consisted of sorting trials on the selected best potential consumables, culminating in the selection of the overall best submerged arc and manual metal arc welding consumable. The final stage required the full validation of the consumable for production use.

The validation programme, completed in 1985, concluded that for the Sizewell 'B' contract, the Babcock 35B wire with the Oerlikon OP41TT flux is the best combination for submerged arc welding, whilst Soudometal Comet J66 ELH electrodes is the preferred option for manual metal arc welding. Both materials have demonstrated toughnesses in the order of 220 MPa√m at 300°C using the ASTM E813 method of calculation.

3.4 Auxiliary Feedwater Nozzle

An auxiliary feedwater nozzle is provided for low feed flows from the motor driven auxiliary feed pumps. This is to overcome problems which have been experienced on the main feed water nozzles in the past, due to cracking believed to be caused by thermal stratification and temperature oscillations at very low or intermittent feed flows.

3.5 Safe-ends On The Channel Head Nozzles

A site weld is required between the steam generator channel head nozzles and the primary loop pipework. The elbow on the primary loop pipework to which the steam generator is welded is of cast austenitic material, while the channel head is of ferritic material with stainless steel cladding. The U.K. specification requires a wrought austenitic stainless steel safe-end, manufactured in SA 182 Type 316LN, to be welded with an inconel weld to the channel head primary coolant nozzles. The wrought safe end replaces the weld build-up safe end, historically used on the Westinghouse steam generators. The wrought safe-end offers the advantages of:

(a) improved access for ultrasonic inspection (both safe end to nozzle and nozzle to pipework welds)

(b) improved ultrasonic inspection as the wrought safe-end is much more transparent to ultrasound than the cast elbow material

(c) constant thickness across the weld geometry

3.6 Ultrasonic Inspection

The UK specification requires volumetric examination of all pressure boundary material and welds by ultrasonic examination, in addition to the radiography requirements of the ASME code. The Sizewell B Public Inquiry has been involved in considering all aspects of the CEGB's case for a PWR, including the issue of plant safety. In their evidence, the CEGB has demonstrated that the failure of major components within the pressure circuit, including the steam generator shells, is an extremely unlikely event. The CEGB's safety case, detailed in their Proof of Evidence, and in the Sizewell B pre-construction safety report, is that the structural integrity is assured by the combination of adequate well proven design to recognised codes, and the appropriate selection of materials and fabrication methods, with quality assurance being used to verify compliance with the specification. NDE in conjunction with extensive analytical fracture mechanics is regarded as a further important element in the safety case, since it can provide a high degree of confidence that the pressure boundary is free from potentially serious defects.

For NDE to provide this added degree of assurance, the techniques used must be capable of reliable application. Evidence on the effectiveness and reliability of the NDE method was presented to the public inquiry by Whittle (4), in the CEGB's Proof of Evidence. Ultrasonic examination is identified by Whittle as the principal NDE method for confirming freedom from serious defects.

Among the main factors that the CEGB considers important in enabling reliable inspection to be achieved are:

(a) adequacy of design and specification of procedures, for example:

-high sensitivity ultrasonic examination (10% ASME DAC reporting levels)

-adequate range of ultrasonic beam angles, generally 0, 45, 60 and 70 degree beams, with the tandem technique as an additional requirement for the reactor pressure vessel

(b) design to facilitate NDE by careful consideration being given to:

-component geometry

-weld placement

-access designed to permit full coverage both of welds and highly stressed areas

(c) satisfactory surface finish by dressing welds on both inner and outer surfaces with waviness and roughness controlled to achieve full volumetric inspection of weld and forgings.

The CEGB's commitment to a high reliability of NDE has been translated into a set of requirements for Sizewell B, that are substantially more stringent than those generally applied to PWR steam generator inspection during manufacture (e.g. ASME III and V). A more detailed discussion on the incorporation of these requirements in the Sizewell B steam generator can be found in reference 5.

4.0 DESIGN SOLUTION TO UK MODIFICATIONS

As a result of the changes to the pressure boundary material specifications to SA 508 Class 3 with its lower allowable stress limits, a complete ASME III class 1 code design validation is being performed on the primary and secondary pressure boundaries of the steam generator. This design validation process also takes account of the modified thermal transient loadings on the vessel as a result of the Sizewell B specific mode of operation, caused by an auxiliary feedwater nozzle. In addition, the design process has ensured that the pressure boundary welds are located, such that they can be subjected to a satisfactory ultrasonic examination, both in manufacture and service.

The required increase in thickness of the secondary shell by approximately 21mm, has been catered for on the outside of the steam generator. The difficulties arise in relation to the increased thickness of the tubesheet (approximately 90mm), the increased thickness of the channel head, and the requirement for safe ends on the primary nozzles. This could have the effect of raising the steam generator in relation to the reactor pressure vessel compared with that of the Westinghouse standard model F design. The degree to which this occurs has to be severely limited for two important reasons. Firstly, the relative height of the steam generator to the reactor pressure vessel has to be closely controlled, or it would upset the overall hydrodynamic performance of the primary circuit. Secondly, if not limited, the height relationship would upset all steam generator interfaces with the civil engineering structures and pipework, which would cause a significant amount of re-engineering.

Several arrangements of primary nozzle configuration were considered in the design process, and extensive use of the Babcock in-house preprocessors for mesh generation, and post-processor for ASME III stress assessment allowed a rapid turnaround of results. The stress analysis itself is being performed on the finite element package FINEL, which has been fully validated, quality assured, and approved for the design and validation of components for Sizewell B, such as the steam generators. A typical finite element model used in this work is shown in Figure 3. The final design configuration of the primary nozzle (Figure 4), is a compromise between the arrangement of the safe-end for ultrasonic inspection, while adequately meeting the channel head stress requirements, but also maintaining the minimum increase in height of the steam generator relative to the reactor pressure vessel.

4.0 DESIGN SOLUTION TO UK MODIFICATIONS

As a result of the changes to the pressure boundary material specifications to SA 508 Class 3 with its lower allowable stress limits, a complete ASME III class 1 code design validation is being performed on the primary and secondary pressure boundaries of the steam generator. This design validation process also takes account of the modified thermal transient loadings on the vessel as a result of the Sizewell B specific mode of operation, caused by an auxiliary feedwater nozzle. In addition, the design process has ensured that the pressure boundary welds are located, such that they can be subjected to a satisfactory ultrasonic examination, both in manufacture and service.

The required increase in thickness of the secondary shell by approximately 21mm, has been catered for on the outside of the steam generator. The difficulties arise in relation to the increased thickness of the tubesheet (approximately 90mm), the increased thickness of the channel head, and the requirement for safe ends on the primary nozzles. This could have the effect of raising the steam generator in relation to the reactor pressure vessel compared with that of the Westinghouse standard model F design. The degree to which this occurs has to be severely limited for two important reasons. Firstly, the relative height of the steam generator to the reactor pressure vessel has to be closely controlled, or it would upset the overall hydrodynamic performance of the primary circuit. Secondly, if not limited, the height relationship would upset all steam generator interfaces with the civil engineering structures and pipework, which would cause a significant amount of re-engineering.

Several arrangements of primary nozzle configuration were considered in the design process, and extensive use of the Babcock in-house preprocessors for mesh generation, and post-processor for ASME III stress assessment allowed a rapid turnaround of results. The stress analysis itself is being performed on the finite element package FINEL, which has been fully validated, quality assured, and approved for the design and validation of components for Sizewell B, such as the steam generators. A typical finite element model used in this work is shown in Figure 3. The final design configuration of the primary nozzle (Figure 4), is a compromise between the arrangement of the safe-end for ultrasonic inspection, while adequately meeting the channel head stress requirements, but also maintaining the minimum increase in height of the steam generator relative to the reactor pressure vessel.

5.0 CONCLUSIONS

The Model F steam generators for the Sizewell 'B' power station represents the current state-of-the-art in Westinghouse steam generators. Its design has benefited from the ongoing development of the Model F, which has drawn significantly from the operating experience accumulated by pre-Model F designs and by earlier Model F units. Specific detailed design enhancements in the materials, contour, and inspection of the pressure boundary have been emphasized in the Sizewell 'B' Model F to address the U.K. Safety Case requirements. These enhancements, as well as the changes in tubing material and AVB design, have responded to the needs of the CEGB and are a product of a combined Westinghouse Nuclear Components Division and Babcock Energy Ltd. design and manufacturing effort.

REFERENCES

(1) Wilson, R.M., and Roarty, J.D., "Westinghouse Aims to Improve Reliability with its Model F Design", Nuclear Engineering International, October 1985.

(2) Langford, P.J., "Design, Assembly and Inspection of Advanced U-Bend / Anti-vibration Bar Configurations for PWR Steam Generator". 1988 International Symposium on Flow-Induced Vibration and Noise, presented at the Winter Annual Meeting of ASME.

(3) Marshall, W., "An assessment of the integrity of PWR pressure vessels - second report by a study group". UKAEA, London, March, 1982

(4) Whittle, M.J., "CEGB Proof of Evidence to Sizewell 'B' power station, Public Inquiry P13, non destructive testing". Central Electricity Board, London, Nov. 1982.

(5) Thomson, J.L., and Fogarty, J.P., " The design of pressurised water reactor steam generators with reference to the requirements for non-destructive examination". Nuclear Engineer, 1986, 25, No. 6, Dec., page 377-384.

Table 1 Product analysis and tensile requirements for Pressure boundary materials

Element	Westinghouse Material SA 508 Class 2A % Composition	Sizewell 'B' Material SA 508 Class 3 % Composition
Carbon	0.27 max.	0.20 max.(1)
Manganese	0.5 to 1.0	1.14 to 1.56
Phosphorus	0.025 max.	0.012 max. (1)
Sulphur	0.025 max.	0.010 max. (1)
Silicon	0.15 to 0.40	0.15 to 0.32
Molybdenum	0.55 to 0.70	0.41 to 0.64
Nickel	0.50 to 1.00	0.60 to 0.83
Chromium	0.25 to 0.45	0.15 max. (1)
Vanadium	0.05 max.	0.015 max.
Tensile Strength (MPa)	620 to 795	550 to 725
Yield Strength (MPa)	450	345
Elongation in 50mm Min. %	16	18

Note (1) These are tighter requirements than ASME imposed for Sizewell 'B'

(2) In addition the following restrictions have been imposed on trace elements for Sizewell 'B':

> Antimony 0.010 max.
> Arsenic 0.020 max.
> Tin   0.015 max.

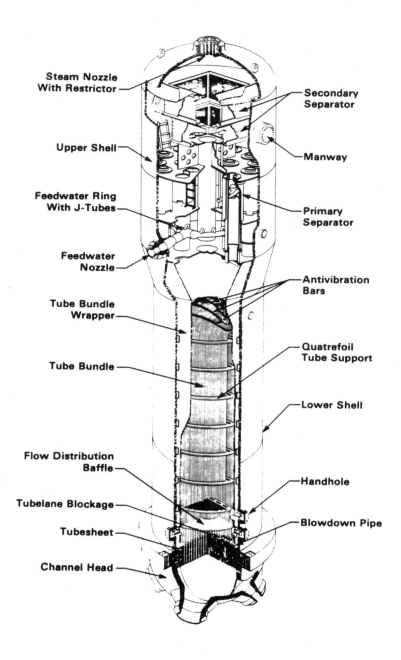

Steam Nozzle
With Restrictor

Secondary
Separator

Upper Shell

Manway

Feedwater Ring
With J-Tubes

Primary
Separator

Feedwater
Nozzle

Antivibration
Bars

Tube Bundle
Wrapper

Quatrefoil
Tube Support

Tube Bundle

Lower Shell

Flow Distribution
Baffle

Handhole

Tubelane Blockage

Blowdown Pipe

Tubesheet

Channel Head

Fig 1   Westinghouse Model F steam generator

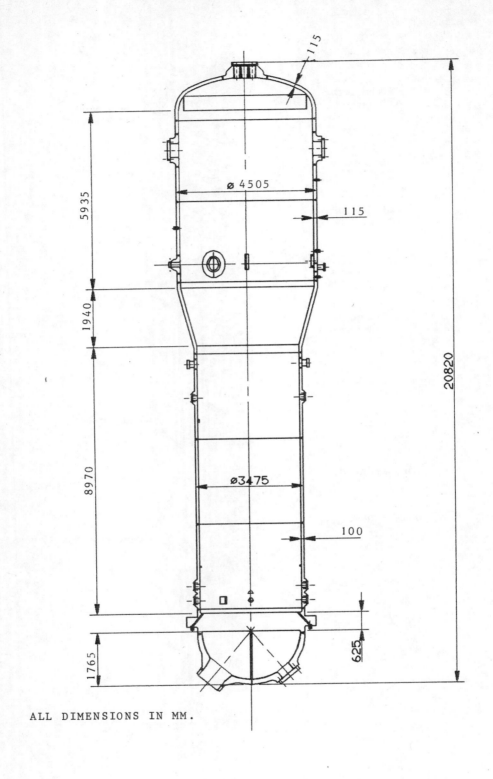

ALL DIMENSIONS IN MM.

Fig 2   Overall dimensions of Sizewell 'B' steam generator

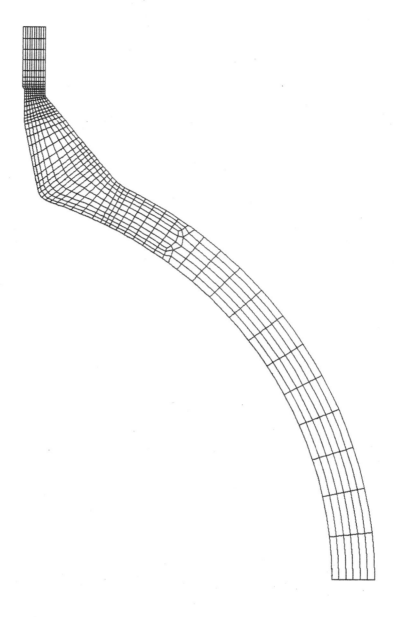

Fig 3   Finite element model of primary coolant nozzle

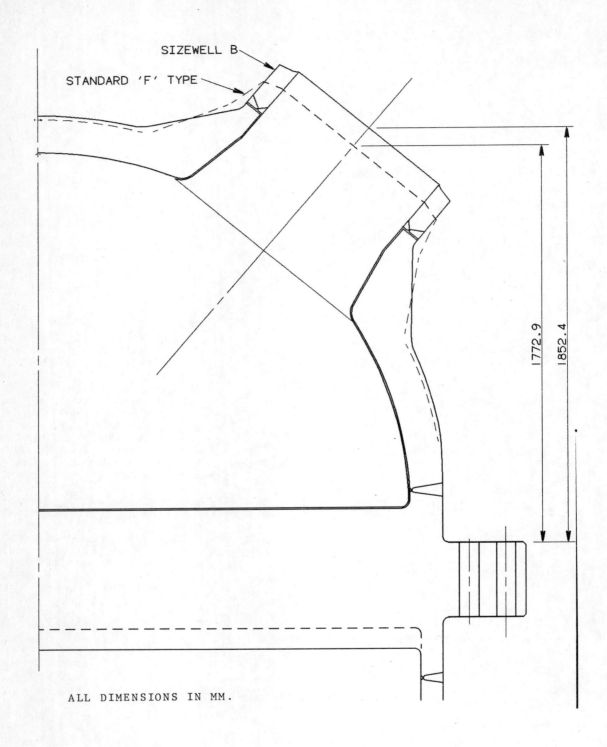

SIZEWELL B

STANDARD 'F' TYPE

1772.9

1852.4

ALL DIMENSIONS IN MM.

Fig 4   Comparison of Sizewell 'B' and Model F type primary nozzles

C388/007

Test facility for pressurized water reactor coolant pumps

I S PATERSON, BSc, CEng, FIMechE, FIMarE, MemASME and **G C MULHOLLAND**, CEng, MIMechE
Weir Pumps Limited, Glasgow

SYNOPSIS The Sizewell 'B' reactor is cooled by water which is pressurised and pumped through four closed primary circuits, each of which includes a steam generator and a pump. A test facility is described which enables comprehensive testing of these reactor coolant pumps, under safely controlled site conditions of temperature and pressure, and pump full load.

The pump primary circuit is first defined, then the extensive auxiliary circuits required for heat rejection; system pressurising; and water supply and quality control. The micro-processor based test control and data acquisition system adopted to enable operation of the test from the control room is also outlined.

1 INTRODUCTION

The Nuclear Steam Supply System (NSSS) for Sizewell 'B' power station is based on the Westinghouse four-loop layout of pressurised water reactor (PWR) comprising essentially a central reactor vessel and four primary loops, each with steam generator and associated coolant pump, as shown in Figure 1. A useful summary of major plant technical data and design features is given in reference (1).

The reactor coolant pumps are vertical, single-stage, mixed-flow design with bottom suction and radial discharge configuration. The hydraulic assembly of impeller and diffuser is fitted in a basically spherical casing designed to accept the 155 bar a suction pressure and 293°C suction temperature demanded under normal system operation. Features of particular relevance to the safe operation and reliability of those pumps are:

- thermal barrier and integral heat exchanger to limit heat flow to pump bearing and seal

- three element, controlled leakage shaft seal system

- motor flywheel for extended coast-down to assist in transfer from forced to natural circulation in event of power failure

- water quality control.

Fundamental to Central Electricity Generating Board (CEGB) philosophy on the introduction of pressurised water reactor stations are enhanced safety and reliability and expeditious construction and commissioning. Scrutiny of the reactor coolant pumps with these aspects foremost shows the basic design to be well proved as a component of the NSSS. However, pump hydraulic performance is derived from model tests and the requirements for the Sizewell pumps differ from previous units, thus entailing modifications to the impeller/diffuser design, while mechanical performance of the unit, comprising Westinghouse pump and UK licensee motor, has yet to be proved. These considerations identified a need for full load testing. The decision to design and construct a reactor coolant pump test facility to satisfy this need before the pumps are installed in the reactor containment building at site is further justified by the extension to test capabilities offered thereby: the ability to establish and monitor the performance of component features peculiar to these pumps under normal and abnormal operation; the availability of replicated site geometry local to the pump to try out maintenance techniques and permit operator training in a nuclear-free environment; the scope for pump and component evaluation relative to future PWR development.

This paper outlines the design and construction of the test facility.

2 TEST REQUIREMENTS

Discussions with the pump manufacturer and the C.E.G.B. established spectra of testing requirements for the reactor coolant pump and auxiliary servicing requirements from the test facility.

Comprehensive pump proving takes the form of an endurance run at full speed, power, and flow, under reactor system operating conditions of pressure and temperature and embracing hydraulic performance, mechanical performance, normal and critical abnormal operation, and identified fault situations. Pre- and post- test safety and data checks are mandatory. A typical proving test is outlined in Table 1.

The basic function of the facility is to provide a primary test circuit designed to receive the pump and permit precise determination of head, flow, power and speed, throughout the pump flow range at temperature and pressure. This entails provision of extensive auxiliary systems to deal with heat rejection of motor input power, pump and motor component cooling, pressurising and pressure control of primary circuit, and water supply, quality control, and make-up. Control, alarm annunciation, emergency back-up and data logging equipment must be tailored to the operational philosophy adopted for the facility.

3 TEST FACILITY CONCEPT

An overall impression of the test facility designed to meet these requirements is given in Figure 2.

The primary circuit comprises a pump casing to receive the reactor coolant pump; discharge pipework including an ultrasonic flowmeter; a low noise control valve; and suction pipework which reproduces the reactor system bends immediately upstream of the pump.

The heat generated from the motor input is rejected to a battery of four equal-surfaced, coiled-tube type heat exchangers, using the pressure drop across the main control valve to circulate a proportion of primary circuit water. Effective control of temperature under the different loads and circuit operating conditions is accomplished by varying the number of heat exchangers in service.

The heat removed by these and other auxiliary heat exchangers is ultimately discharged to atmosphere by way of an air circulated, packed cooling tower, with controlled make-up based on an acceptable maximum concentration factor for total dissolved solids.

Table 1   Typical proving test for reactor coolant pumps

Stage	Test	Acceptance Criteria	Appx Duration (h)
Pre-test	Motor insulation	Specified min resistance)	
	no load run	Vib limits)	
	thrust brg	End play data)	30
	Thermal barrier p.d.	Press drop v flow data)	
	Confidence hydro	No leakages)	
	Seal static	Leakage limits)	
Cold start-up	Start-up	Seal leakage, vib limits)	1
	In situ balance check	Vib limits)	
	Establish reactor system temp and press	Specified temp ramps press v temp limits	10
Endurance run (reactor system temp & press)	Normal operation	Operational limits Acceptance limits on seal leakage, vibration & brg temps	20*))))
	Hydraulic performance	Contractual guarantees	10)
	Seal leakage/inj temps	Seal leakage limits	35) 100
	Loss of injection	Seal leakage & temp limits	15)
	Loss of thermal barrier flow	Seal temp limits	5))
	Loss of power	Seal leakage & temp limits	1)
	Normal operation		14)
Cool-down	Reduce temp and press	Specified temp ramps press v temp limits	10
	In situ balance	Vib limits	1

* minimum continuous operation

Primary circuit pressurising and pump high pressure seal injection are both effected by reciprocating pumps with a common standby unit. By-pass flow control valves around the pumps are regulated by feed-line flow meters to maintain a constant inflow to the primary circuit, while the set pressure is maintained by operation of two pressure let-down valves fitted in series between the primary circuit and main storage tank. This let-down flow passes through a heat exchanger, where the temperature is reduced automatically to a value acceptable to water quality control equipment.

Water supply is governed by the stringent water quality requirements, in particular chloride and oxygen levels, demanded for the primary and other directly connected circuits. Relatively soft water is brought in by tanker from a local loch supply to a holding tank, where it is demineralised and heated before forwarding through a deaerator to fill the test pipework and tanks. The filling operation is preceded by a vacuum and nitrogen purge cycle to ensure that the low oxygen content of the water is preserved.

Cooling water for the secondary side of the heat exchangers is sourced from the local towns water which requires extensive chemical treatment.

Components of the pump and motor under test also require cooling water services which are provided, using demineralised water from the main storage tank, by an auxiliary circuit comprising tank, pumps and heat exchangers. A high level gravity tank provides sealing water to the low pressure end of the shaft seal.

Control and instrumentation falls into three categories, namely:

- pump hydraulic performance measurements,
- pump and motor mechanical performance monitoring,
- test facility monitoring and control,

Pressures, temperatures, motor input kW and speed present no problems, conventional instrumentation being used in accordance with reference (2).

For this high pressure, high temperature, high velocity, closed test circuit an ultrasonic flowmeter consisting of two sets of four chordal paths, installed in planes at right angles, is selected. Flow is measured by precise determination of the difference in transit time of pulses projected across the pipe with components in the direction of flow and against.

Pump and motor vibration are monitored using contacting and non contacting transducers and a real time analyser and

filtering system is available for diagnostic and in situ balancing purposes.

All critical parameters in the facility are monitored and logged through the test. Data can be called up on a visual display unit (v.d.u.) in the control room, and alarm signals are displayed on the v.d.u. when parameters exceed set values. Short term fast logging and display is also available for analysis of transient tests or fault conditions. Computing facilities can accommodate all applicable test calculations.

The test is basically under operator control by push buttons from the control room but system functions, such as holding set primary circuit temperature and pressure and ramping, are delegated to a programmable controller with fail-safe transfer to operator control or automatic shut-down as applicable. Control is aided by a basic panel mimic of the system, covering main operating components. This is augmented, using a second v.d.u., by paged-mimics of sub-systems which display values of critical parameters.

Emergency back-up is provided by equipment redundancy, an uninterruptible power supply to the computer and controller, a diesel generator set for maintenance of supplies essential to a safe shut-down and system design safety analyses.

While the test facility is designed primarily to test reactor coolant pumps for Sizewell 'B' and similar PWR stations additional capacity is built-in and space allowed for extension of equipment to cater for future development.

4   PRIMARY CIRCUIT DESIGN

Referring to Figure 2, the layout of the primary test circuit was dictated by adequate straight lengths of pipe upstream and downstream of the flowmeter, inclusion of a control valve to enable variation of system resistance, and simulation of the pipework configuration immediately upstream of the pump suction. In the optimised layout which resulted, flow from the pump passes through ten diameters of 699 mm bore straight pipe to the chordal path flowmeter then through a right angled flow control valve and back through a series of 787 mm bore bends and interconnecting pipework to the pump suction. The configuration from the third bend upstream of the pump is a true representation of site pipework geometry. The angular position of the suction pipe relative to the discharge pipe does not represent either of the two site options but, taking pump design into account, it is considered that this will not affect pump performance.

The cast stainless steel pump casing at the heart of the primary test circuit is the same design as, and replicates internal dimensions of, the casings for the reactor coolant pumps at site. Casing, pipework and other components were in this case validated for maximum operating conditions of 185 bar a and 305°C to cater for possible future variations in pump duty.

The forged pipework (which includes the chordal path flowmeter body) and the cast bends are also made in stainless steel while the control valve, forged in low alloy steel, has the water passages completely lined in stainless and is fitted with stainless steel trim. The primary circuit thus forms a closed, welded stainless steel test loop, designed, manufactured, and pressure tested to the appropriate sections of ASME Boiler and Pressure Vessel Code III Division I.

The flow control valve is of the low noise, perforated-cage and plug, design with slow stroking electrically operated actuator for ease of control. The design is based on a pump duty of 23 235 cubic metres per hour at 89.3 metres generated head and permitting testing out to at least 120 per cent duty flow. For possible future extension provision is made for fitting a by-pass round the valve to enable a maximum flow of 32 500 cubic metres per hour.

Overpressure protection is provided by a spring loaded relief valve and flash tank. Valve duty is based on a 'worst case' assessment of pressure injection flow, let-down valves failed closed and change in circuit inventory around maximum operating temperature.

The primary circuit is sufficiently rigid to be supported at two locations, namely pump casing and pipework adjacent to the control valve. The casing support structure is of pin-jointed design to carry vertical loads from pump unit, pipework, and water mass, and to accommodate radial thermal expansion of the casing while maintaining the vertical axis of the pump fixed in space. Three horizontal tie rods locate the pump and absorb horizontal loads from torque reaction, frictional resistance at the sliding support under the pipework and live loads from the pumped fluid. Where relative motion takes place in a high temperature environment, hardened steel spherical bearings with high temperature grease are used, elsewhere conventional grease lubricated bearings are employed.

The primary circuit pipework design was subjected to specific detail analyses. Pipework stresses were checked, using adverse tolerances to maximise stresses; forces and moments, caused by thermal expansion, weight, internal pressure and momentum, were established to evaluate pump and valve branch loadings; stresses at the interface between the stainless steel pipework and the low alloy steel valve body were checked by finite element analysis, using the Bersafe suite, and extended to cover maximum combined stress intensities. All analyses demonstrated acceptability of the basic design in terms of code requirements and suitable pump casing and valve branch loads.

Dynamic analysis disclosed a number of resonances in the pump support structure close to 25 hz and beam sections were increased accordingly. A rocking moment resonance at 10 hz demanded assurance of balancing standard before test and checking during test run-up.

The circuit is fully insulated to a maximum surface temperature of 50°C for personnel protection.

5 AUXILIARY CIRCUIT DESIGN

5.1 Heat rejection (refer Figure 3)

All of the sub systems require heat exchangers for the temperature control of the fluid being handled.

The magnitude of a heat exchanger thermal capacity is governed by

a) the amount of heat transfer surface in service
b) the heat transfer co-efficient
c) the log mean temperature difference (LMTD) of the fluids being handled.

The heat rejection section comprising heat exchangers 2, 3, 4 & 5 constitutes the main area of heat rejection.

The cooling water supply temperature to this section will be held constant at 27°C, and, as the primary circuit operating temperature increases, the LMTD or temperature driving force correspondingly increases and less heat exchange surface is necessary to transfer a given quantity of heat. In addition the amount of heat to be rejected decreases with increasing operating temperature through liquid density changes. Thus the heat exchanger surface required to transfer the hydraulic heat input from the reactor coolant pump at 300°C is appreciably less than that required at 100°C. The lower temperature, therefore, was used to establish the maximum heat rejection surface necessary. A review of the operating conditions indicated that four equal sized heat exchangers to make up this total surface provided the required flexibility to allow surface adjustment during operation. Whilst it may seem simple to keep the total available surface in operation at all times, this leads to unacceptably high cooling water outlet temperatures on the heat exchangers and the probabilty of scale formation.

Of the other heat exchangers in service only HX1, handling the pressure let-down flow, is subject to similar conditions of temperature and pressure. In this case, however, the heat load variation reduces with reducing temperature and it is possible to operate over the full temperature cycle without the need to adjust the surface in service.

The heat rejection system is designed to meet the following requirements:-

a) To remove hydraulically generated heat at all pump loads of from 20 to 120 per cent design flow, and, in addition, be suitable for maintaining the primary circuit in thermal equilibrium at all temps between the maximum of 305°C and lower operational limit of 121°C.

b) To allow system cool down to 177°C at a rate not exceeding 27.8^{o}C per 30 minute interval.

c) To restrict the temperature rise above 100°C to a rate of 55.5^{o}C per hour nominal with a maximum rate of 33.3^{o}C in any 30 minute period.

d) With pump stopped, to allow system to be cooled at a rate not greater than 27.8^{o}C per 30 minute interval from 177°C to around 121°C.

The heat exchangers are designed to handle the worst condition of temperature change and be suitable for easy extension to meet possible future uprated conditions.

Coiled-tube heat exchangers are chosen for this duty and the main factors taken into consideration in the selection of this type were:-

Absence of dead spaces and baffles.
Higher heat transfer coefficients possible.
100 per cent counter flow design.
Easy to clean and inspect shell side by removing casing.
Minimum number of joints reducing possibility of leakage.
Spring like coil absorbs thermal expansion.

The heat exchanger bodies are constructed of carbon steel and the secondary cooling water is treated to avoid corrosion of the steel. Primary water being cooled flows through the inside of the tubing. The secondary cooling water may contain a maximum of 25 parts per million (ppm) of chlorides but concentration, through cooling tower evaporation, can increase this level to over 50 ppm. At this concentration, and with aerated water temperatures greater than 70°C, the possibility of stress corrosion cracking of austenitic stainless steel is significant. For this reason duplex stainless steel has been selected for the tubing of heat exchangers 1 to 5. These heat exchangers are mounted on a platformed structure above the ground level and HX1, 7, 9 and 10 are also

accessible from this level. The location of the heat exchangers provides space to accommodate the large expansion movements and the units are arranged to allow the casing to be removed for inspection, or cleaning the shell side of the coils. Material of a similar specification to that for the main circuit is used for the primary water supply and return piping to the heat rejection exchangers.

The component cooling water circuit is designed to remove the motor generated heat and that from the pump thermal barrier exchanger. This amounts to about 860 kW and the water flowrate in this circuit is 135 cubic metres per hour. A plate type heat exchanger HX6 is provided to remove the heat load from motor bearings and motor ventilating air coolers. Two separate pumping systems are provided in the component cooling circuit. One set of two 100 per cent capacity pumps provides the reactor coolant pump driving motor cooling requirements. The thermal barrier circuit is handled by another set of two 100 per cent capacity pumps. Plate heat exchanger No 8 controls the thermal barrier cooling water supply temperature within the range 26.7^o to 41.1^{o}C.

A forced draught cooling tower of standard manufacture is provided for secondary cooling. The tower is designed to handle a normal flowrate of 450m^3/hour of water at up to 49.5^{o}C and reduce the temperature to 27°C when the ambient wet bulb temperature is 17.22^{o}C. Thus the heat rejection capability is 11.75MW and for most of the year a lower outlet temperature from the tower is possible. A common sump of 16m^3 capacity is located below the tower.

Water distribution is by way of a trough and gutter distribution system over a double layer of vertically fluted vacuum formed pvc plate packing. This packing, which is suitable for temperatures up to 60°C, is assembled into holding frames then arranged in an interlocking fashion within the tower in a manner to give high rigidity. Mist from the tower top is minimised by a single pass pvc high efficiency drift eliminator.

The tower is equipped with two thermostatically controlled forced draught direct driven fans which incorporate silencers to minimise noise emission. Four anti-frost heaters each 4kW are provided in the sump and the support frame cladding panels and sump are manufactured from galvanised and painted carbon steel. For a constant air flow rate the outlet temperature of the circulating water passing through the cooling tower varies according to the ambient air wet bulb temperature. To maintain a constant cooling water supply temperature to the heat exchangers hot water is automatically diverted around the tower through the flow control by pass valve provided for this purpose. The number of fans in operation is dependent on ambient conditions and heat loads. Piping on the secondary cooling side is of duplex stainless steel local to the heat exchangers and in areas of high temperature. Piping material of abs plastic is provided for the remainder of this system.

Whilst the design intent is to provide cooling water at a constant temperature of $27^{o}C$, there are occasions when a proportion of lower temperature water is required for the component cooling water and No 1 seal heat exchangers. To meet this requirement the tower sump is sectioned such that one area is segregated from the mixing hot by-pass flow stream. This water can be drawn preferentially by one cooling water pump and supplied to the system as and when necessary.

5.2 Pressurising and let-down
(refer Figure 4)

Primary circuit pressure level is maintained at the desired value by a 'feed and bleed' system. A supply of cooling water is also required by the No 1 seal. These systems are served by three horizontal triplex reciprocating pumps each driven by an electric motor through a single reduction gear box. The duties of these pumps are as follows:-

a) Pressurising Pump: This pump is provided to maintain the desired operating pressure within the primary circuit by constantly injecting a nominal flow of 1.27 l/s grade 'A' water into the system. This flowrate is monitored by a flowmeter in the supply line which regulates the amount of spill-back through the pump by-pass flow control valves.

b) No 1 seal injection pump: A similar but smaller pump is provided for the No. 1 seal injection duty. This pump injects up to 0.63 l/s of grade 'A' water through heat exchangers HX9 and 10 into the No. 1 seal area, flow again being held constant through by-pass valves.

c) Standby pressurising/seal injection pump: Identical in size to the pressurising pump, in the event of either the pressuring or No 1 seal unit failing the standby automatically comes into operation and takes over the duty of the failed pump.

To minimise the possiblity of suction vibration problems, pulsation dampeners of the inert gas filled bladder type are installed in the suction line to each pump. To meet the requirements of permissible ripple on the static pressure in the primary circuit, large volume pulsation dampeners are fitted on the discharge line of each pump.

The water in the No 1 seal requires to be controllable over a temperature range of $26.7^{o}C$ to $65.6^{o}C$ and, because the temperature of grade 'A' supply water to the reciprocating pumps is maintained at $35^{o}C$, then means of heating and cooling the seal injection water must be provided. HX10, cooled by water from the main cooling water system is located in the injection line to allow operation at temperatures below $35^{o}C$. Following HX10, the seal injection flow is directed through the shell of HX9 where it can be heated by hot primary water flowing through the tubes. Once an injection temperature is selected, the facility programmable controller logic selects and controls the appropriate heat exchanger to meet the temperature requirement.

Bleed control is maintained by a pressure let-down system which discharges to the main storage tank through two valves arranged in series to share the large pressure breakdown. Heat exchanger HX1 reduces the temperature of this flow to $35^{o}C$ immediately upstream of these valves. This is to prevent downstream flashing and damage to the demineralising resin. After pressure reduction the flow is first screened to 25 micron in one of two cartridge filters before being divided to allow a fixed flow to be polished in the mixed-bed ion exchange plant. The balance of this flow goes directly to the main storage tank.

5.3 Water supply and quality control
(refer Figure 5)

The total water supply requirements of the facility are divided into four categories as follows:

(a) Primary water designated as grade 'B' having minimum resistivity of 250 kohm-cm, maximum chloride of 1 ppm, maximum fluoride of 0.15 ppm and a pH of 5.8 to 8.0.
(b) Fill and make up water for the primary circuit designated as grade 'A' water. The fluoride ion and pH limits are as for the primary water but the resistivity requires to be 500 kohm-cm minimum and the maximum chloride ion 0.15 ppm. The water is filtered to better than 5 micron nominal particle size before introduction into the test circuit.
(c) Component cooling water for the pump and motor is similar to that of the primary water but filtration is to better than 40 micron particle size.
(d) The circulating water used in the secondary sides of the heat exchangers is treated to ensure compatability with the operational characteristics and materials of the system.

The test facility site receives domestic water from two sources. Jellyholm treatment works provides the bulk of the supply and this is supplemented by a proportion of Loch Turret water which is of better quality. Assessment of analyses of the two water sources resulted in the decision to tanker-in water from the nearest solely Loch Turret supply point for 'primary' and associated circuits, but use the normal towns mains supply for secondary cooling purposes.

The maximum chloride ion permitted in the primary water is 1 ppm and, to avoid stress corrosion cracking of the austenitic stainless steel, it is necessary to remove the oxygen in the circulating water to a level less than 1 ppm when operating at a temperature of 260 to 300°C. Since the Loch Turret water can contain oxygen in levels up to 14 ppm, depending upon temperature, both demineralisation and deaeration are necessary before the fill water can be introduced into the primary circuit.

Both the primary and component cooling water circuits require to be continuously polished to prevent build up of impurities.

The secondary water supply, with approximately 250 ppm of hardness as $CaCO_3$, requires to be chemically treated before it can be circulated through the heat exchangers, where temperatures up to 100/120°C are possible. An additive programme to prevent scale, corrosion and biological growth is provided. During operation this water passes through an atmospheric cooling tower where evaporation, and loss to the system through windage, takes place. The design is based on a feed make up rate to limit the concentration of the salts in the circulating water to a value of about 2.

Four storage tanks are provided in the facility in addition to the reservoirs at the base of the cooling tower and deaerator.

The Loch Turret storage tank, constructed in glass reinforced composite, receives the total water requirement of the system (40 cubic metres) and is provided with an immersion heater. The immersion heater raises the water temperature to around 35°C before introduction into the deaerator.

The main storage tank acts as the reservoir for the seal injection & pressurising primary water supplies. The tank is suitable for vacuum conditions and is constructed in carbon-steel, protected on the inside by glass flake reinforced polyester. Under normal conditions the tank operates with a small positive pressure provided by an inert gas blanketing system. The tank is capable of accepting the total circuit contents on drain down.

The component cooling water tank is an atmospheric horizontal cylindrical tank with a gross capacity of 6 cubic metres. It is constructed in glass reinforced composite and is supported on an extension of the main heat removal system platform

staging. The tank is located within a closed loop, but any losses from the system can be made up via the deaerator extraction pumps through a float level controlled valve on the tank.

Located in the roof structure of the test shop No 3 seal water supply tank provides the necessary static head (approx 2 bar a) at the reactor coolant pump seal faces. The atmospheric tank is of glass reinforced polyester composite. Top up is automatic through the float operated inlet valve on the tank.

The Loch Turret water reception system comprises storage tank, circulating pump, demineralisation package and 10 micron cartridge filter. The time to heat 40 tonnes of water to 35°C depends upon the supply temperature which can be as low as 3°C during the winter and reach 15°C in mid summer. Demineralising and polishing the primary circuit water is accomplished by a battery of six mixed-bed deionising cartridges. These are arranged in three parallel groups of two cartridges in series. This arrangement allows optimum use of the cartridge capacity whilst maintaining production of high purity water. An installed exchange capacity of double the expected level is provided and the water quality is constantly monitored and displayed. An audio-visual alarm is activated should the final water quality fall below the desired level.

Once the Loch Turret water is demineralised and heated it is deaerated to reduce oxygen down to low levels before introduction into the primary circuit. Oxygen reduction is by a single stage, polypropylene packed, vacuum deaerator. The vessel is of carbon steel cylindrical construction with support skirt. The internal surfaces of the shell are protected by glass flake lining, and the spray pipe and packing support are of stainless steel construction. The deaerator is designed to provide water with an oxygen level of 0.02 ppm with an inlet water temperature of 35°C. At this temperature the operating pressure is 5.6 kPa.

Air evacuation is by a liquid ring vacuum pump provided with an atmospheric air operated vacuum augmentor. This latter unit compresses the extracted gases by a pressure factor of about two, but with the motivating air, increases the gas flow to the liquid ring pump. Overall this has the beneficial effect of restricting cavitation in the internal passages of the vacuum pump. Two units are provided to allow 100 per cent standby.

To ensure that the oxygen level in the deaerated water is not significantly raised on filling the system air must first be removed. One or two air evacuation units can be used for this purpose. After air removal, the system is filled with nitrogen to provide a small positive pressure before the introduction of the deaerated, demineralised grade 'A' water.

Duplicate pumps, one working, one standby, transfer the treated water from the main storage tank to the deaerator. Another pair of pumps withdraw treated and degassed water from the deaerator and pump it into the supply header feeding the pressurising and injection pumps. These two pairs of pumps are rated at about one third greater than the combined maximum demand of the pressurising and injection systems. The excess flow is directed back to the sealed main storage tank via duplicate 25 micron cartridge filters.

Make-up and fill water for the component cooling and No. 3 seal supply tanks is taken from the discharge of the Loch Turret supply pump at start up and thereafter from the discharge of the deaerator extraction pumps.

From biological considerations treatment of the local towns water is to dose with an oxidising biocide to provide a free bromine level of 1 to 2 ppm. This provides control of planktonic organisms without the safety and corrosion risks associated with chlorination. In addition a non oxidising biocide is used periodically (once or twice per test) to disperse biofilm and kill sessile organisms. A constant feed rate has been chosen for operation, and blowdown is controlled by the water level in the tower sump. This mode of control results in a variable salt concentration of the cooling water in the circuit as the basic water composition and cooling tower evaporation losses are not constant.

Referring to Figure 3, the scale/ corrosion control additive is dosed prior to the feed introduction into the tower sump. In addition, feed water pH correction by the addition of acid is also carried out to maintain a system pH of around 7.2.

There are ten heat exchangers served by the circulating water system requiring a maximum demand of about 450m³/h. Three cooling water pumps (one - standby) discharge into a common header. Two supply lines are connected to this header; one supply line provides the water requirements of the main heat rejection circuit and the other line supplies the remaining heat exchangers. A flowmeter and associated control valve in each of the supply lines regulate the flowrates such that the return temperature to the cooling tower is maintained at around 40°C.

6 TEST CONTROL AND DATA ACQUISITION

6.1 Instrumentation

Test facility instrumentation, categorised by function is summarised in Table 2. Two items in the pump hydraulic performance measurement merit further discussion.

Pump generated head (90m) is low relative to the system pressure (155 bar) and so demands careful attention in order to achieve the required accuracy. The differential pressure transmitter selected to measure the head increase across the pump is the twin isolating diaphragm type, with central sensing diaphragm and capacitor plates giving a capacitance change proportional to change in pressure differential. The instrument is capable of the required accuracy under system pressures but requires calibration. In order to effect calibration under operating conditions a gas operated differential deadweight tester is used. An equalising valve between twin piston assemblies allows these to be accurately balanced at working pressures sourced from a gas bottle. By closing the equalising valve the high pressure piston can then be balanced by adding deadweights appropriate to the differential required, in the usual way. The tester is certificated to National Measurement Accreditation Service (NAMAS) requirements.

Pump flows are high, primary circuit velocities are high and losses in the circuit must be kept to a minimum to permit circulation of flows up to at least 120 per cent of duty flow. To meet these conditions with the desired accuracy, and without the need for periodic calibration against known flows, an ultrasonic, chordal path type flowmeter was selected to measure reactor coolant pump flowrate. The meter operates on the principle that the flow path velocity of sound pulses travelling between two points is dependent on the length of the path between the points, the travel time, and the velocity of sound in the fluid, as outlined in Figure 6. The necessary dimensional measurement of the flowmeter body, and the electronic time measurement, processing and subsequent computations are all controllable to a predetermined reliability and limit of uncertainty during manufacture.

The effect of upstream flow conditions is less easily quantified. The meter manufacturer has established the straight lengths of pipework upstream of the flowmeter, relative to various pipework bends and fittings, which result in an overall error budget of better than + 0.5 per cent when established integration techniques are applied to mean chordal-plane-velocities. Since a direct non-compliance comparison with pump discharge branch conditions is not possible a straight pipe length twice the manufacturer's recommendation for the nearest equivalent is adopted. Again in the interests of minimising uncertainties the four chordal path array is fitted thus taking account of velocity profile in the measurement and enabling profile analysis when installed. Two sets of chordal paths are arranged at right angles on the same centre, and at 45^0 to the pipe axis, giving the facility of flow confirmation and averaging, the latter automatically countering any residual swirl effects, since these affect the opposed planes by an equal and opposite amount.

As further overall assurance before installing the meter in the test facility, the flowmeter body, probe arrays, and associated electronics were calibrated up to 31 per cent of pump design flow at a NAMAS approved U.K. flow laboratory. This flow corresponds to a Reynolds Number of 3.8 million, above which calibration is expected to remain constant.

With this type of meter, temperature and pressure corrections are calculable and can be fed into the computational procedure.

6.2 Test control and data acquisition

Testing is conducted from the control room which accommodates a control panel, control desk and associated printer and computer equipment.

The control panel accepts all signal cables from the plant via junction boxes in the test area or the interface terminals of the motor control centre. It houses all signal conditioning instruments, back-up indication and display, mimic alarm annunciators, vibration monitoring equipment, and a programmable controller (p.c.).

The indicators show all critical control parameters and, in conjunction with the mimic, permit manual operation of the facility or emergency shut down in event of p.c. failure. Two annunciator arrays are included, one to accept signals direct from the plant, the other through the controller from analogue signals which have exceeded preset alarm values. Pump and motor vibration and speed signals are

Table 2   Instrumentation summary

Item measured		Instrument type	Calibration (uncertainty %*:cal/facility)
(a) pump hydraulic performance			
head generated across pump		diff press tranducer	dual deadweight (+.05/+.25)
power input to motor		watt transducer	lab std watt meter (∓.1 /∓.5)
flow		ultrasonic meter	NAMAS laboratory (∓.25/∓1.0)
shaft speed)		digital pulse counter	lab std freq - (∓.01/∓.05)
supply frequency)			period meter
suction temperature		resistance temp detector	Smithbridge (+.5°C/+.5)
suction pressure		pressure transducer	deadweight (∓.03/+∓.25)
(b) pump mechanical performance			
motor stator)	temp	r.t.d.	transfer std (+.5°C/+1.0)
brg)	flow	pelton or vortex	volumetric (∓.5 /+∓1.0)
motor frame vibration		velocity sensor	transfer std accr (∓5.0/∓10.0)
pump seals)	temp	r.t.d. (or vap-in-steel)	transfer std (∓.5°C/+1.0)
thermal barrier)	press	pressure transducer	deadweight (∓.03/+∓1.0)
	flow	pelton or variable area	volumetric (∓.5 /+∓ 1.0)
pump casing & shaft vib		vel sensor : displ probe	tr std accr:micr (∓ 5 /∓10)
(c) facility operation			
key equipt & services)	temp	r.t.d. (or vap-in-steel)	transfer std (+.5°C/+1.0)
heat exch, filters)	press	pressure transducer	deadweight (∓.03/+∓1.0)
seal inj,press & let down)	flow	orifice or pelton	volumetric (∓.5 /∓1.0)
water quality treatment,)		conductivity meter	std solution (∓- /∓10)
seal & prim circ inj)		pH meter	std buffers (- /∓ 2)

* 95 per cent confidence level

connected directly to panel mounted monitors. Vibration is analysed either by vector filter from amplitude and phase signals, or by a tracking filter comprising a narrow band pass filter, centred on fundamental frequency of rotation, which removes harmonics and indication jitter and gives output in form of 'x' and 'y' components of vibration relative to the phase marker pulse. Either of these outputs can be recorded on a multi-pen recorder. Vibration signals are also fed directly to a real time analyser with desk-top computer which, from time-domain samples, calculates frequency-domain amplitudes using Fast Fourier Transform conversion. Overall levels, in 'root mean square' units, and predominant peaks are logged and available for trend analysis on the computer.

The programmable controller complete with analogue, digital and serial interfaces is located in the control panel. The p.c. monitors all analogue signals and converts the 4 to 20 mA signals to engineering units with 0.18 per cent full-scale-reading accuracy. Values are compared with programmed alarm set points and alarm indicated if appropriate. Selected parameters are made available by the p.c. for logging every two minutes throughout a test. For example during a one hundred hour run under system conditions the following parameters are typical:

> Motor volts, amps, power and frequency; bearing and stator temperatures.
> Seal injection and leak off flow, temperature, and pressure; pump bearing and seal housing temperature.
> Pump and motor cooling water services flows, and temperature differentials.
> Pump and motor vibration amplitude and phase.
> Primary circuit (pump) flowrate, suction temperature, pressure, and head generated.

In addition the p.c. also permits up to ten signals to be recorded at two second intervals for fifteen minutes in order to examine trends during transients or simulated fault conditions.

The p.c. is capable of processing and analysis of pump performance, including comparison against acceptance criteria from direct application of contractual tolerances, through test code 'error ellipse' techniques, reference (2), to recently proposed statistical evaluations, reference (3).

Automatic control sequencing and interlocking can also be programmed as desired. Pump start-up, system temperature and pressure ramps, logic sequencing to control primary circuit set pressure and temperature during test, performance guarantee point test routines, and pump shut down are obvious contenders.

When 'auto' mode is selected and enabled on the control panel the control desk becomes active. The control desk is normally used by the operator throughout a test. It contains a control mimic, two v.d.u., operator keypad and selected controls and indicators. Only those systems which are controlled remotely are shown on the mimic, with push buttons incorporated for pumps and valves and indication that flow has been established in main circuits.

The system diagram is also available on one v.d.u., both this and the main mimic being colour coded to identify sub-systems. These can be called up on the v.d.u. using a touch sensitive screen facility which also enables allocation of control loop set-points, displayed on the paged mimics in bar chart form. The other v.d.u. is principally for logging and display with the option to record on one of the printers. All analogue signals, performance guarantee data, alarms and short range signal histories are available for display.

The operator keypad permits control of the logging v.d.u. and both printers, provides back-up to failure of the v.d.u. touch-screen facility and initiates programmed routines.

An uninterruptible power supply is provided for the data logger system and most of the instrument loops. It also supplies the emergency shut down system covering for two possible failure modes of the programmable controller: firstly, a fault in the memory, or a programme corruption, which causes the 'watchdog' relay to trip and switch all control loops onto the manual back-up controllers, secondly failure of the current output module resulting in loss of control and error between desired and actual values in affected loops, detection of which causes switching of these channels to manual back-up control.

In the event of failure of the electrical supply the emergency diesel generator cuts in and supplies power for all essential services in the test facility to ensure a safe run-down of the reactor coolant pump.

7 CONCLUSION

The test facility described is designed to test the reactor coolant pumps for Sizewell 'B' and subsequent power stations at full power, flow, and speed, under reactor system conditions of temperature and pressure. Additional capacity has been designed-in to cater for pump and system development as indicated in Table 3.

The facility is also ideally suited to operator training and equipment or procedures development.

At the time of writing this paper the design phase has been completed. Civil work on site is complete, procurement and delivery to site of all major equipment is accomplished, and fabrication of the primary circuit is almost finished. The project is on target for testing of the first reactor coolant pump for Sizewell to commence in November 1990.

ACKNOWLEDGEMENT

The authors wish to thank the Directors of Weir Pumps Limited for permission to publish this paper.

REFERENCES

(1) Anon 'A technical outline of Sizewell 'B', the British pressurised water reactor' C.E.G.B. Publication G.1310, Aug 1988.

(2) Anon 'Acceptance tests for centrifugal, mixed-flow and axial pumps' BS 5316, Part 2, 1977 (ISO 3555 : 1977)

(3) E Grist & R P Hentschke 'Verification of centrifugal pump performance guarantees by acceptance tests - an alternative method' I.Mech.E.Sem. 'The performance testing of Hydraulic Machinery' London, March 1989, S.695.

Table 3   Facility capability

	Present		Future	Notes
	Normal	Maximum		
Flowrate M^3/hr	23235	28800	32500	Provision for additional by-pass around control valve
Static Pressure bar g	171		184	All pressure components are capable of 184 bar g
Generated Head	90 (typical)		No restrictions within the 184 bar g maximum pressure and control valve p.d. limit	
Temperature, max. operating °C	300		305	
min operating °C	121		121	
Power absorbed at 121°C, kW	6850		10000	Electrical supply and control gear suitable for 10500 kW
Power rejected at	6850		10000	Space allowed for additional auxiliary equipment

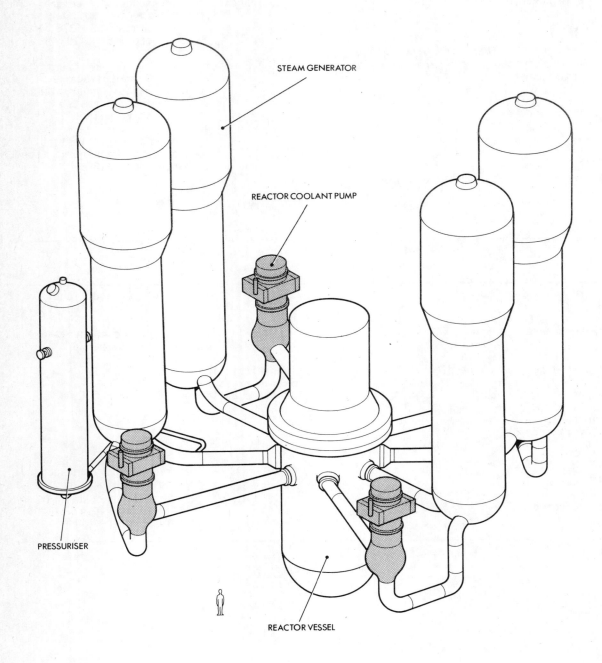

STEAM GENERATOR

REACTOR COOLANT PUMP

PRESSURISER

REACTOR VESSEL

Fig 1   Reactor system

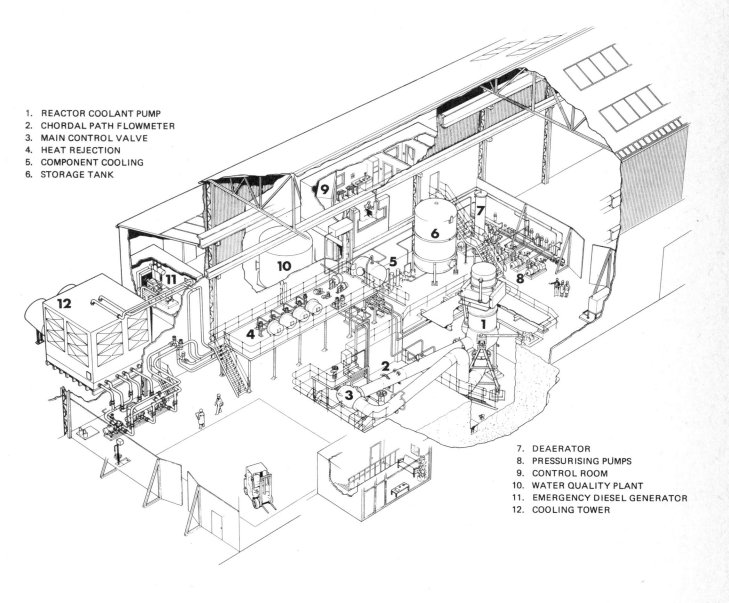

1. REACTOR COOLANT PUMP
2. CHORDAL PATH FLOWMETER
3. MAIN CONTROL VALVE
4. HEAT REJECTION
5. COMPONENT COOLING
6. STORAGE TANK

7. DEAERATOR
8. PRESSURISING PUMPS
9. CONTROL ROOM
10. WATER QUALITY PLANT
11. EMERGENCY DIESEL GENERATOR
12. COOLING TOWER

Fig 2   Test facility layout

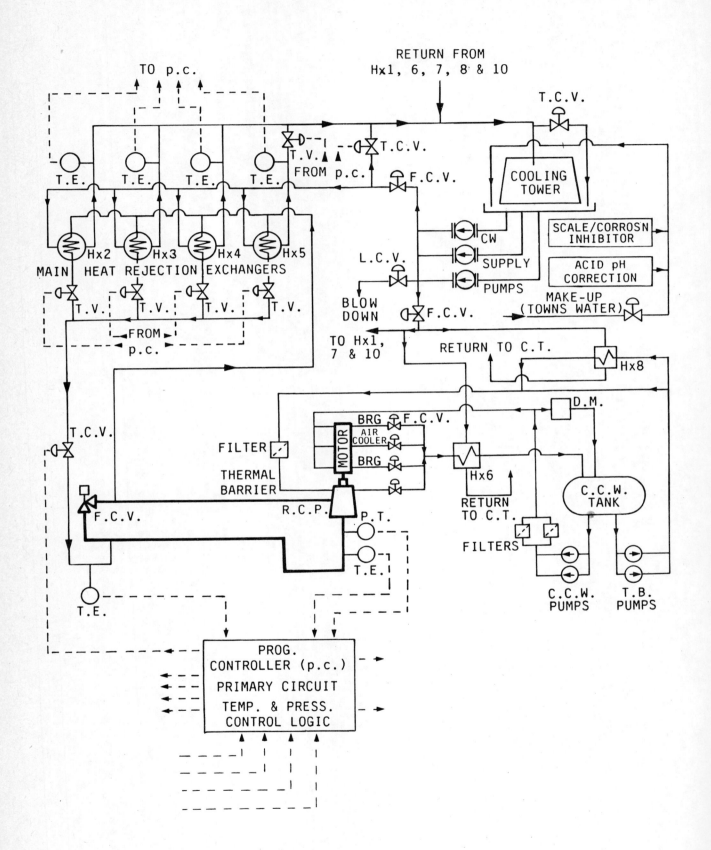

Fig 3   Heat rejection subsystem

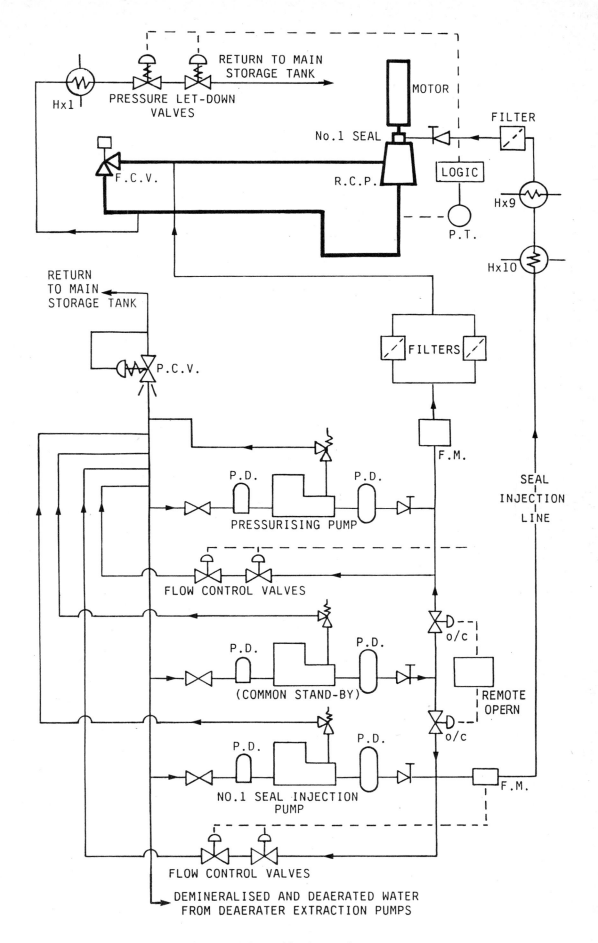

Fig 4   Pressurizing and let-down subsystem

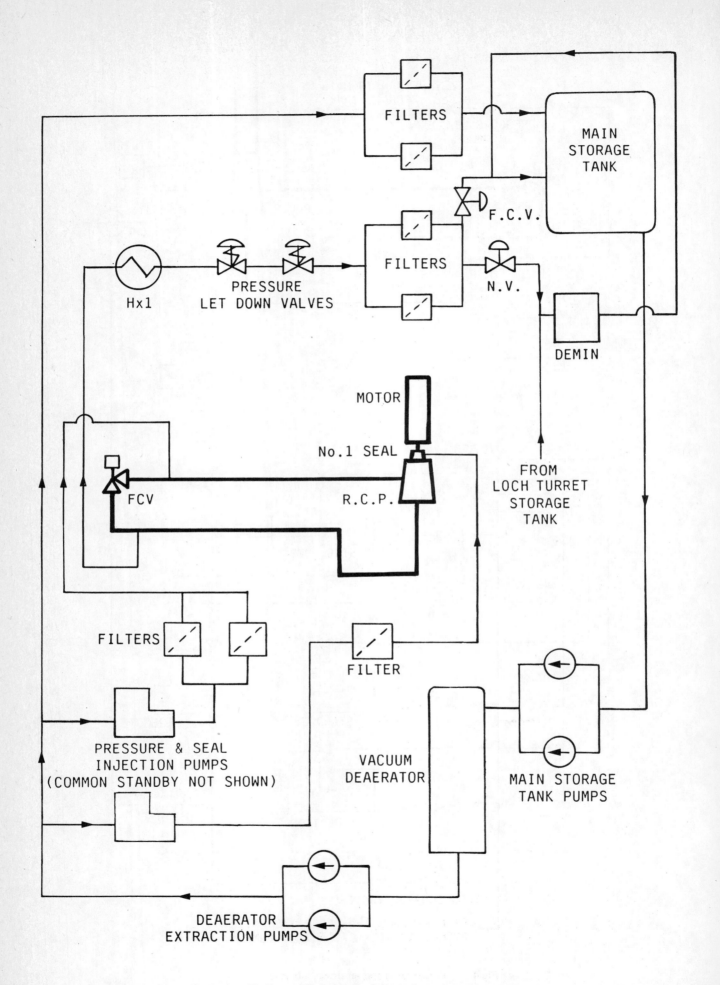

Fig 5   Water supply and quality subsystem

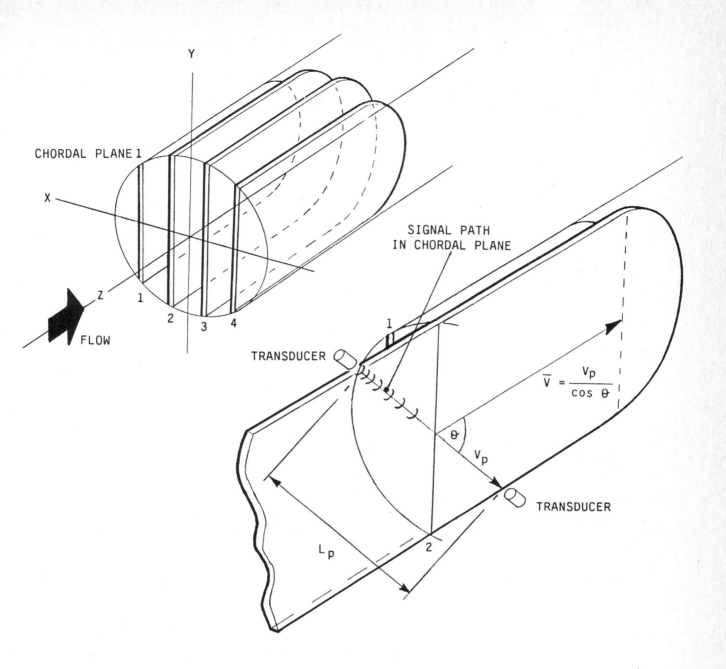

CHORDAL PLANE 1

X

Y

Z

FLOW

1 2 3 4

SIGNAL PATH
IN CHORDAL PLANE

TRANSDUCER

$$\overline{V} = \frac{V_p}{\cos \theta}$$

θ

V_p

TRANSDUCER

L_p

$$\text{TRANSIT TIME WITH FLOW} = t_w = \frac{L_p}{C+V_p}$$

$$\text{TRANSIT TIME AGAINST FLOW} = t_a = \frac{L_p}{C-V_p}$$

$$\text{HENCE,} \quad \overline{V} = \frac{V_p}{\cos \theta} = \frac{L_p (t_a - t_w)}{2(t_a)(t_w) \cos \theta}$$

C = SPEED OF SOUND IN FLUID

V_p = VELOCITY ALONG PATH

V = MEAN AXIAL VELOCITY IN PLANE

ULTRASONIC INTEGRATION IN Y-DIRECTION FOR $\overline{V}$

GAUSSIAN NUMERICAL QUADRATURE INTEGRATION OF $\overline{V}$ IN
X-DIRECTION FOR TOTAL FLOW

Fig 6   Chordal path flowmeter principle

C388/024

Primary system pipework for Sizewell 'B'

H STIGTER and **J HAENTJENS**
Westinghouse Energy Systems International, Brussels, Belgium

The paper on primary system pipework for Sizewell B deals with 2 important aspects in the design of piping : Analysis (Part 1) and Layout (Part 2).

Part 1 of the paper addresses : Structural Evaluation of Primary Piping and Part 2 addresses - Primary System Pipe Work Layout Aspects.

1 STRUCTURAL EVALUATION OF PRIMARY PIPING

1.1 Introduction

The reactor coolant piping of the Sizewell B Nuclear Power Plant has been the subject of a very detailed structural and mechanical evaluation to ensure that the public health and safety are protected.

The detailed evaluation compares the results obtained from the piping analysis with acceptance criteria as set forth in the ASME Boiler and Pressure Vessel Code, Section III, Nuclear Power Plant Components, Winter 1982 edition (hereafter referred to as the Code) for the conditions stated in the Design Specification.

Normal operation and safe shutdown of a nuclear plant depend upon the design adequacy and structural integrity of the reactor coolant loop/supports system. To demonstrate this design adequacy and structural integrity, analyses were performed for loading under normal conditions, seismic disturbances, and postulated loss-of-coolant accident conditions. The results were compared with the allowable stress limits of the Code in accordance with the design specification.

Typical Data of the Westinghouse closed cycle PWR for Sizewell B

The Westinghouse PWR built for the Sizewell B Power Plant consists of four reactor coolant loops (figure 1). Each reactor coolant loop comprises one reactor coolant pump (RCP) and one steam generator (SG). The reactor coolant pumps are Westinghouse vertical, single-stage, mixed flow pumps of the shaft-seal type. The steam generators are Westinghouse vertical U-tube units.

In the Westinghouse pressurized water reactor system (PWR), the primary system is designed for a pressure of 17.1 MPa and a temperature of 343°Celcius.

Total weight of four closed reactor coolant loops is 3250 tons. Below typical weights and dimensional data are given for the Sizewell B PWR including fluid and insulation weight.

Component weights:

RPV weight = 783 tons,
Hotleg pipe weight = 14.0 tons/loop

SG weight = 463 tons,
Crossover leg pipe weight = 22.8 tons/loop

RCP weight = 106 tons,
Coldleg pipe weight = 11.8 tons/loop

Typical length of hotleg pipe between RPV and SG nozzles is 4766 mm with nominal OD of 907 mm and wall thickness of 83 mm. Length of coldleg pipe between RCP and RPV nozzles is 6072 mm with a typical nominal OD of 859 mm and wall thickness of 78 mm.

Length of crossover leg pipe is 5907 mm with a typical nominal OD of 967 mm and wall thickness of 88 mm. Material for reactor coolant loop piping is SA376 type 304LN for straight pipe and SA351CF8 for cast elbows.

1.2 Design loadings and evaluation criteria for primary piping

The design loadings result from thermal expansion, pressure, weight, operating shutdown earthquake (OSE), safe shutdown earthquake (SSE), loss of coolant accident (LOCA) and plant operational thermal and pressure transients. OSE/SSE are CEGB requirements/definitions.

Seismic loads

Seismic motion of the earth is a random process. Since the piping is supported by components that are attached to the containment building, it rarely experiences the actual seismic motion at ground elevation. A band of frequencies are associated with the ground earthquake motion but the building itself acts as a filter to this environment. It will effectively transmit only those frequencies corresponding to its own natural modes of vibration. As such for the seismic analysis of Sizewell B primary piping a 4 loop model was used including pressurizer and attached to a building model.

A time history dynamic analysis was made for Sizewell B to obtain the total response loading for OSE and SSE for the primary piping. The total response loading obtained from the seismic analysis consists of two parts : the inertia response loading of the piping system, and the differential anchor movements loading.

To calculate the resultant moment (M_i) used in equations 9, 10, 11 and 13 of the Code (see Table 1), the seismic loads must be known. The design specification stipulates the plant operating conditions (full load) during which the specified earthquake is assumed to occur. Two sets of seismic moments are required to perform a Code analysis. The first set includes only the moments resulting from inertia effects; these moments are used in the resultant moment (M_i) value for equations 9 and 13. The second set includes the moments resulting from inertia effects plus the moments resulting from seismic anchor motion; they are used in equations 10 and 11.

Loss of coolant accident loads (LOCA loads)

Blowdown loads are developed in the broken and unbroken reactor coolant loops as a result of transient flow and pressure fluctuations following a postulated pipe break in one of the reactor coolant loops occuring at full power. Structural consideration of the dynamic effects of a pipe break requires the postulation of a number of break locations for an adequately detailed analysis.

The locations and types of breaks for the Sizewell B primary coolant loop comply with industry criteria and with Regulatory Guide 1.46, and thus provide a basis for the safety requirements of Sizewell B with Code-designed Westinghouse components. The break locations selected are those that have the largest probability of occurring on the basis of fatigue and stress analyses for normal, upset, and test transients. These postulated break locations are independent of the seismicity of the plant site. Both longitudinal and guillotine breaks have been considered at each location; the break type and orientation chosen at a given location are those most likely to occur from consideration of the detailed stress field there.

The following criteria determine the characteristics of the postulated pipe rupture.

In each leg of the main reactor coolant loop piping system, a minimum of three postulated rupture locations are selected in the following manner:

- Breaks are postulated at the terminal points and at all locations in a run or branch in which the cumulative usage factor exceeds 0.2 for normal and upset operating conditions, or in which the range of primary-plus-secondary stress intensity for normal and upset operating conditions exceeds 80 percent of the intensity allowed by the Code on an elastic basis (2.4 S_m). In the event that a location between the terminal points cannot be chosen in this manner, a third location is chosen on a reasonable basis, considering such factors as points of maximum stress intensity and/or cumulative usage factor.

- For the purpose of LOCA analysis, the two severed portions of the pipe for postulated guillotine failure are conservatively assumed to separate instantaneously, so that the break opening on either side of the severance is equal to the cross-sectional flow area of the pipe. Postulated longitudinal rupture is conservatively assumed to have an area of

opening equal to the cross-sectional flow area of the pipe.

- A break opening time of one millisecond to full flow area is conservatively assumed.

By applying the above criteria to the results of the stress and fatigue analysis, pipe break locations and orientations are postulated for the main RCL piping system. Broken loop and unbroken loop time-history dynamic analyses are performed for these break cases.

Hydraulic models are used to generate time-dependent hydraulic forcing functions used in the analysis of the reactor coolant loop for each break case. For Sizewell B hydraulic forcing functions were generated by CEGB. Also reactor pressure vessel time history motion from detailed reactor pressure vessel dynamic analysis is used in the LOCA analysis of the primary piping. Further inputs are break release forces at the location where the break occurs and jet impingement forces.

Operating and transient loads

In addition to meeting the requirements for design temperature, design pressure, and design mechanical loads, the Code requires satisfaction of certain requirements relative to operating conditions. The Code states that each condition to which the component may be subjected is to be categorized in accordance with the definitions presented in the design specification in such detail as to provide a complete basis for design, construction, and inspection in accordance with these rules.

Transient loads:

To provide the necessary high degree of integrity for the Sizewell B RCS, the transient conditions selected and specified by CEGB for fatigue evaluation are based on conservative estimates of the magnitude and anticipated frequency of occurrence of the temperature and pressure transients which results from various plant operation conditions. The design specification gives fluid system pressure, temperature, and flow transients. The transients selected are representative of operating conditions which may occur during plant operation, and which are severe enough or occur frequently enough, that they may have some significance to component cyclic behavior. For purposes of component evaluation, the number of transient occurrences is based on a plant life of 40 years. All standard Westinghouse transients were reviewed and a number of these transients were modified by CEGB for Sizewell B.

Normal conditions:

A normal condition is defined as any condition in the course of system startup, operation in the design power range, hot standby, and system shutdown other than upset, emergency, faulted, or testing conditions.

Several new normal transients have been defined by CEGB for Sizewell B such as:

Grid Frequency Regulation Transients
Loss of Generation Incidents

Feedwater Heaters out of service
On-load Turbine Stop Valve Testing

Upset conditions:

An upset condition is any deviation from normal conditions anticipated to occur often enough that the design should be able to withstand the conditions without operational impairment. The upset conditions include those transients which result from any single operator error or control malfunction, transients caused by a fault in a system component requiring its isolation from the system, and transients due to loss of load or loss of power.

Two new transients have been defined by CEGB for Sizewell B such as:

Inadvertent RCS System Overcharging
Inadvertent Borating System Actuation

In addition operating shutdown earthquake (OSE) loading is an upset condition.

Faulted conditions:

Faulted conditions are defined as those combinations of conditions associated with extremely low probability - postulated events which might impair the integrity and operability of the nuclear energy system to the extent that considerations of public health and safety are involved. Such events are required to comply with whatever safety criteria are specified by the responsible safety authorities. Typical faulted conditions are pipe rupture and safe shutdown earthquake (SSE) loadings.

1.3 Criteria

In general, the criteria for the structural evaluation of the reactor coolant loop piping are based upon two types of general loading conditions : for self-limiting loads, and non-self-limiting loads. A non-self-limiting load is an applied load. The code provides separate protection criteria for each of these general loading conditions. These criteria protect against membrane or catastrophic failure such as Eq 9 as indicated in Table 1 and fatigue or leak-type failure such as Eq 10 through 14 of Table 1. In applying the criteria one must consider the various types of loadings applied to the system.

1.4 Modeling considerations of primary piping models

General

The complexity of the reactor coolant loop/supports system requires the use of a large mainframe computer (Cray 1S) to obtain the displacements, forces, and stresses in the piping and support members. An accurate and adequate mathematical representation of the system is required to obtain these results. The modeling considerations depend upon the degree of accuracy desired and the manner in which the results will subsequently be interpreted and evaluated. The integrated reactor coolant loop/supports system model is the basic system model used by Westinghouse to compute loadings on components, component supports, and piping. The system model includes the stiffness and mass characteristics of the reactor coolant loop piping and components (that is, the reactor pressure vessel, steam generator, and reactor coolant pump) and the stiffness of supports and auxiliary line piping which affect the system. The deflection solution of the entire system is obtained for the various loading cases from which the internal member forces and piping stresses are calculated.

Dynamic Analysis:

The model used in the static analysis is modified for use in the dynamic analyses by including the mass characteristics of the piping and equipment. The lumping of the distributed mass of a segment (or elbow) is accomplished by locating the total mass at the midpoint of the segment. The effect of equipment motion (that is steam generator and RC pump motion) on the reactor coolant loop/supports system has to be included by modeling the mass and the stiffness characteristics of the equipment in the overall system model. For loss of coolant accident analysis two masses (each containing six degrees of freedom and located on each side of the break) are included in the mathematical model.

1.5 Conclusion

The structural evaluation of the primary piping of Sizewell B has been described at some length in this paper. Separate protection criteria in the code for each of the general loading conditions in Table 1 protects against membrane or catastrophic failure such as Equation 9 and fatigue or leak type failure such as Equation 10 to 14 of Table 1. As such the reactor coolant loop piping of the Sizewell B Nuclear Power Plant is subject of a very detailed structural and mechanical evaluation, will maintain its structural integrity and meet the safety related design requirements under all specified conditions.

2 PRIMARY SYSTEM PIPEWORK LAYOUT ASPECTS

From the very beginning, the CEGB was concerned by the In-Service Inspection (ISI) Requirements and the man-rem exposure reduction requirements during operation and maintenance shutdowns. These goals were defined by rules and guide lines in CEGB specifications. Specifically, the ISI aspects were analyzed with a view of using robots. To allow for this, geometric rules were set up and additional rules included to record ultrasonic results.

For these 2 aspects, ISI geometry and ISI results, the basic rules and their major consequences are outlined as follows.

2.1 ISI results

Ultrasonic results are better for a forged component than for cast component and therefore, a forged-to-forged connection was ideal, a forged-to-cast connection acceptable and a cast-to-cast connection forbidden.

Consequently, a forged component had to be inserted between two cast components.

Keeping in mind that all the components such as elbows could not be forged, at the design

Table 1   Loading combinations and stress evaluation for primary piping

PRIMARY STRESS EVALUATION

$$\text{Equation 9 (Design)} = B1\frac{PDo}{2T} + B2\frac{Do}{2I}Mi \leq 1.5\,Sm$$

Condition/Agreement	Loading Combinations	Stress limits for Code Subarticle NB-3650 method of analysis
Design	Design Pressure Weight	Equation 9 of Code (See NB-3652)
Fatigue (Normal/Upset/Test)	Normal Transients Upset transients Test transients Weight + OSE	Equations 10,11,12,13 & 14 of Code (See NB-3653.2)
Upset	Upset Pressure Weight OSE	Equation 9 of Code with min. (1.8 Sm*,1.5 Sy*) substituted for 1.5 Sm, PO$_{max}$. 1.1 Pa*
Emergency	Emergency transient Pressure Weight	Equation 9 of Code with min. (2.25 Sm, 1.8 Sy) substituted for 1.5 Sm, PO$_{max}$. 1.5 Pa*
Faulted	Faulted transient Pressure Weight	Equation 9 of NB-3650 with min. (3.0 Sm, 2.4 Sy) substituted for 1.5 Sm, PO$_{max}$. 2.0 Pa*
	Operating pressure Weight + SSE	Equation 9 of NB-3650 with min. (3.0 Sm, 2.4 Sy) substituted for 1.5 Sm
	Faulted transient Pressure associated with pipe rupture Weight + SSE + pipe rupture	Equation 9 of NB-3650 with min. (3.0 Sm, 2.4 Sy) substituted for 1.5 Sm PO$_{max}$. 2.0 Pa*

* NOTE: Pa = calculated maximum internal pressure as defined in NB-3641.1.
Sm = allowable design stress intensity value of pipe material at temperature
Sy = yield strength value of pipe material at average fluid temperature of the transient under consideration

time, by means of a qualified forging process, some components had still to be castings.

The concerned areas where an intermediate forged piece was necessary, are: the Steam Generator nozzles forged safe ends, and the Reactor Coolant Pump inlet nozzle, where a forged spool piece was inserted between the 90° elbow and the inlet nozzle.

It is to be noted that the forged extrusion process was recommended for the pipes by CEGB.

2.2   ISI geometry

Circumferential welds

The weld preparations for ISI should meet the following requirements:

- the material thickness on both sides of the weld shall be the same,

- the outside and inside surfaces shall be smooth and parallel to the pipe axis for distance called DIM B (see table 2) for outside surfaces and DIM A for inside surfaces. The values of DIM B and DIM A depend on the component (equipment nozzle, pipe, fitting)

Table 2

Dimension (Minimum)	Wrought Components	Cast Components
A	T + 25 mm	25 mm
B	2T + 50 mm	1.5 T

Notes:

1. 'T' is wall thickness adjacent to weld
2. 'E' is equivalent to nominal pipe wall thickness

and its nature (forged or cast). This had a major effect on the design of the cast elbow and impacted basically all the dimensions.

These 2 major rules induced a "Controlled chain reaction" in the primary loop layout modification.

In the standard design, the pipe OD was less than the equipment nozzle OD and the thickness difference was taken care of by a tapered transition weld.

For the Reactor Coolant Pump, the nozzle OD could not be changed and consequently the pipe OD had to be increased. This had 3 major consequences:

- the pipe was heavier and could not be extruded in one piece anymore and thus an intermediate circumferential weld was required in the cold leg.

- the ASME criteria for nozzle strength versus pipe strength became more delicate and consequently the safe end materials had to be changed or modified.

- the pipe OD at each end was different and thus a pipe OD transition location was foreseen. Of course this location had not to interfere with ISI surfaces already defined.

The pipe section dimensions had also to be redefined because the extrusion process implied specific tolerances and some allowance had to be made for radial weld shrinkage, in order to obtain good ISI surfaces after weld grinding.

Babcock Power Limited Renfrew has the capability to perform circumferential shop welds by means of a narrow gap welding machine. This fact helped to get the surface width (DIM B left) + weld width + (Dim B right) shorter than that for manual welding.

Nozzle weld to main pipe

In this case manual ISI scanning will be performed and reserved for nozzles of 4 inch and above.

The most difficult one was the 45° Safety Injection System (SIS) nozzle. On the US Wolf Creek plant (reference plant for Sizewell B) 45° SIS nozzle, no ISI "flat" surface was foreseen and the cold leg pipe section was thus modified. A 3-D CAD model was generated to define a modified 45° nozzle with a 1 inch "flat" surface next to the saddle weld edge, which represents the shortest saddle perimeter for those constraints.

Despite the fact that the major equipment locations and layout working points were fixed before the detail design was completed the ISI requirements of CEGB were satisfactory met.

CONCLUSION

To obtain good ultrasonic results in the main loop piping the forged to forged or forged to cast connection was successfully used.

Weld preparations were optimized to obtain smooth and parallel surfaces. The length of smooth surfaces satisfactorily met CEGB ISI requirements.

A special 45 deg. SIS nozzle was successfully designed for ISI and incorporated in the main loop layout.

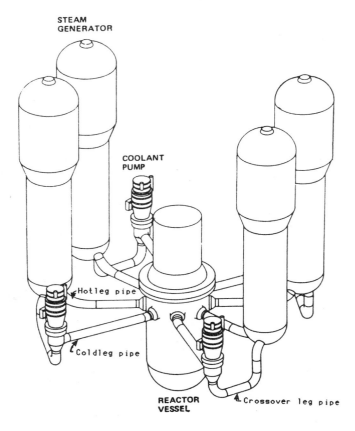

Fig 1   The four Westinghouse reactor coolant loops for Sizewell 'B'

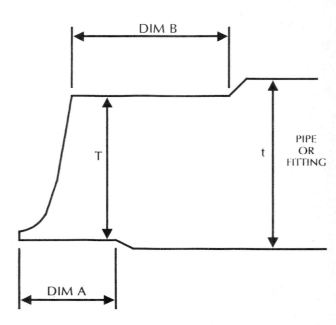

Fig 2

C388/027

Development of improved methods for seismic design and pipebreak protection

G D T CARMICHAEL, BSc, PhD, CEng, MIMechE
Berkeley Nuclear Laboratories, CEGB, Berkeley, Gloucestershire
P T GEORGE, CPhys, MInstP
PWR Project Group, National Power Division of CEGB, Knutsford, Cheshire

SYNOPSIS   This paper describes development work being carried out by the CEGB and its contractors aimed at simplification and improvements to the aseismic and pipebreak protection design methods to be used on future UK PWR plant.

It has been recognised that progress in agreeing changes with the UK licensing authorities would be affected by the close alignment of the Sizewell 'B' design to the American SNUPPS plant and particularly the use of ASME and ANSI design codes and application of USNRC design guidelines.

Accordingly the aseismic strategy is centred on an exchange of research by BNL and NNC into the non-linear response of pipework with a complementary programme of work underway by EPRI. To assess the validity of NUREG 1061 leak-before-break methodology the CEGB has initiated a pilot study.

1   INTRODUCTION

Over the past 10 to 15 years, there has been progressive worldwide recognition that the design approach and licensing rules used for nuclear power plants to protect them against low probability earthquakes and postulated loss of coolant accidents are extremely conservative. The result has been a dramatic increase in the cost of providing related equipment such as seismic snubbers and pipewhip restraints. This in turn has led to difficulties in layout and installation of this equipment, restricted access for in-service inspection and maintenance, with associated increase in radiation dose to plant operators.

In response to these problems, research and development programmes have been established in the UK, France, Germany, Italy, Japan and USA. An evaluation of the overseas programmes shows there are marked differences in the achievements to date reflecting, in part, the level of investment, the ability to co-ordinate national activities and the attitude of the various licensing authorities. Major changes to the licensing approach have taken place in Germany with the introduction of 'Basissicherheit' (Basis Safety Concept) which allows the possibility of catastrophic failure of piping to be excluded from the design provided the applicant demonstrates high quality manufacture, inspection and quality control.

In the USA, a Piping Review Committee was commissioned in 1983 to examine the position with respect to pipebreak protection and seismic design. Their recommendations, presented in NUREG 1061 (1) have led to a progressive revision of General Design Criterion No.4 of 10 CFR 50 Appendix A permitting use of leak-before-break (LBB) analysis to replace the need to provide protection against pipe rupture for a wide range of high energy pipework systems. Also, based on NUREG 1061, extensive programmes of experimental and analytical work have been commissioned by EPRI to develop improved seismic design rules for incorporation into the ASME code. This work has been monitored by the WRC/PVRC arrangements with broad international support.

Research and development work on these topics has been underway in the UK for some time by the CEGB and its associates in support of the gas cooled and fast reactor systems. However, the decision to adopt a PWR design for Sizewell 'B' has required a re-evaluation of development strategy taking into account the close alignment of the Sizewell 'B' design to the American SNUPPS plant and particularly the use of ASME and ANSI design codes and relevant USNRC standards for the British PWR.

Against this background, in the autumn of 1987, the CEGB PWR Project Management Team (PMT) approved work to start on two development programmes aimed at achieving specific improvements to the pipework design of future British PWRs and ultimately, the elimination of seismic snubbers and pipewhip restraints. The first programme was aimed at development of simplified non-linear methods for seismic piping design centred on an exchange with EPRI. The second programme was required to establish whether the LBB methodology outlined in NUREG 1061 was applicable and could be validated against UK design practice. Both programmes were formulated to take maximum advantage of recent overseas developments and international programmes so as to provide the largest possible database for validation purposes.

This paper outlines the seismic and LBB programmes and discusses their likely impact on plant design. Higher priority is being given to the LBB programme since this could provide the basis for early removal of pipewhip restraints. Already based on current changes to the USNRC rulemaking, the PMT has advised the Nuclear Installations Inspectorate (NII) that the requirement to provide restraints to protect against Arbitrary Intermediate Break will be removed from the design criteria for Sizewell 'B'. The seismic programme is longer term but nevertheless will provide valuable information on the design margins available for replication of pipework systems on different UK sites.

The paper concludes by reflecting that on future stations, assuming an acceptable LBB safety case can be made, the potential benefits to be obtained by widespread application of LBB may have to be balanced against the effect on seismic snubber reduction. This arises because the piping for the British PWR need only satisfy the design criteria for the Safe Shutdown Earthquake (SSE) whereas the equivalent American plant has to meet both the Operating Basis Earthquake (OBE) and the SSE design requirements. Meeting the design limits for the OBE provides the more severe design constraint, and consequently, on this basis, the pipework for the American plant would require a larger number of seismic restraints than the corresponding British station. In turn the piping in the British PWR may be more highly stressed than the counterpart lines in the equivalent American plant when the design is constrained solely by the need to meet piping stress criteria.

2 ASEISMIC PIPING DESIGN DEVELOPMENT STRATEGY

2.1 Sizewell 'B' Piping Design Approach

The safety related pipework for Sizewell 'B' meets the requirements of the ASME Boiler and Pressure Vessel Code, classes 1, 2 and 3 or ANSI/ASME B31.1 as appropriate together with the corresponding USNRC guidelines. The pipework contract has been placed with a Joint Venture BPA-JV (comprising Babcock Power, PED and Aiton) and the design is achieved through use of the Computer Aided Engineering and Management System (CAEMS) incorporating the support and snubber/restraint optimisation programme HANGIT. Improved co-ordination with other PMT engineering departments and their contractors, particularly civil and cabling, is obtained by utilising accurate 1/20 scale models.

The effects of earthquakes are taken into account by designing the Sizewell 'B' station against the SSE at a horizontal free field peak ground acceleration of 0.25g. This compares with the aseismic design for SNUPPS which is governed by the OBE set at half the SSE. The Sizewell 'B' SSE of 0.25g is consistent with an exceedance probability of 10^{-4} per annum and the response spectra and synthetic time histories used for design purposes are appropriate to the Sizewell site. In considering other potential UK sites, an 'All-sites' response spectra of 0.25g pga has been derived based on earthquake records obtained on a range of soft medium and hard sites appropriate to UK conditions. However, for piping design purposes site specific spectra will be used.

The arguments and consequences of this difference in design philosophy (SSE cf OBE) are examined in Appendix 1, where it is shown that for identical SSE, the minimum seismic piping design margin available for UK PWRs is x 2.35 the seismic design margin available for SNUPPS designs. Put another way, coupling the OBE to half the SSE with the seismic margins permitted by the ASME Piping Code for OBE loadings effectively means US plant, with the overall objective to safely withstand an SSE with a peak ground acceleration of 0.25g, would actually be designed against an SSE of

$$2.35 \times 0.25g = 0.59g$$

This flaw in the US aseismic piping design methodology was identified in NUREG 1061 and should be corrected by proposals recently submitted to the ASME for removal of OBE from 'Equation 9' of the ASME III code.

It is believed that the UK design approach taken into account with SSE/OBE differences outlined above will lead to Sizewell 'B' piping systems requiring significantly fewer snubbers than the estimated 1043 in the reference SNUPPS plant at Callaway. The assumption that the number of snubbers required is simply related to the peak ground acceleration suggests that rather less than 500 snubbers should be required at Sizewell 'B'. This is a simplistic approach, which ignores other factors such as seismic input specification, effects of site soil properties and different functional requirements but does provide some guidance and leads to a key conclusion as far as the development strategy is concerned; namely that Sizewell 'B' piping systems will be unique and therefore foreign experience must not be drawn on too intensively as it may very well be totally inappropriate.

The possible use of advanced design methods for Sizewell 'B' were considered, including the use of increased damping levels, pseudo-elastic techniques (i.e. energy absorbers and seismic stops) and empirical routing methods for small bore pipework systems. However, it was recognised that all of these developments would have required substantial confirmatory testwork on representative Sizewell 'B' systems and would not in general be compatible with Project timescales. The Project nevertheless strongly supported the proposed R&D approach to pipework analyses with the ultimate goal of demonstrating that aseismically designed pipework does not require seismic restraints.

It follows that successful development programmes to eliminate seismic restraints would produce more flexible piping systems with higher dynamic responses. In these circumstances revised design criteria would need to be considered involving pipe-displacement, valve accelerations and equipment/nozzle loads.

2.2 Experience with US piping design

There was a marked increase in the number of snubbers utilised at BWR and PWR facilities in the US during the period 1967-1975. If the only implication of this increase had been increased capital expenditure, then it is unlikely that US piping system designers would have become too concerned. However, the snubbers exhibited 'field problems' which led to the need to reduce the interval between inspections. It was believed that if the number of snubbers in plants were not reduced and the reliability increased, this could lead to

increased radiation exposure of personnel, and a very real possibility of extended plant outages as statistical test sample sizes were increased due to test failure. Thus the spur to minimise the number of snubbers would not seem to be the need to minimise the US PWR snubber capital costs ($> £10^6$), nor even, at the design stage, to save on maintenance costs ($> £10^7$), but to ensure plants do not remain shut down due to snubber failure.

The escalating requirements for the testing of snubbers due to snubber failures emphasised the need to minimise the number of dynamic restraints while maximising snubber reliability. A two pronged approach was adopted in the US, one approach aimed to increase snubber reliability, while the other aimed to reduce the number of snubbers and seismic restraints actually required. In this paper the latter aspect is considered i.e. the 'Equation 9' design constraints.

Publication of NUREG 1061 V2 (1), has been accompanied by a significant shift in the regulatory climate in the US, with a corresponding renewal of investment in research aimed at snubber reduction. The outstanding US initiative is the EPRI Research Project RP 1543-15, 'Piping and Fitting Dynamic Reliability', which started in 1985. This initiative, which meets the needs identified by the PVRC Task Group on Dynamic Allowables, seeks primarily to develop an improved, realistic and defensible set of design rules which can be adopted by the ASME Boiler and Pressure Vessel Code for treatment of dynamic plus static piping loads. It is anticipated that by drawing on the conservatisms incorporated in piping design methodology to derive new rules, the benefits will include snubber reduction combined with improved system safety and reliability.

2.3 CEGB Research Activities

Following experience with the aseismic design of the Heysham II piping systems in the late 1970's, two research programmes were started at the CEGB Berkeley Nuclear Laboratories (BNL) to develop an understanding of the design margins. One programme concerns the analysis of nozzles and branch connections subjected to seismic loading while the other programme involves dynamic testing of straight pipes and attached components.

To support the BNL programme of experimental work, PMT placed a contract with the National Nuclear Corporation (NNC) in 1986 for theoretical analyses of some of the BNL tests. The NNC work aims to derive a practical design route to assess piping systems against seismic loading which will enable the excessive conservatisms incorporated in current design practices to be safely removed.

2.4 The EPRI–CEGB technical exchange agreement on 'Seismic Testing and Analysis'

Because of the complementary nature of the EPRI 'Piping and Fittings Dynamic Reliability' Project to the BNL dynamic testing programme and the NNC theoretical analyses, the CEGB initiated an exchange with EPRI on 'Seismic Testing and Analysis' under the terms of an existing CEGB–EPRI Agreement. It is believed that by this means the UK is better placed to influence and recommend possible ways of revising the ASME Code. This approach acknowledges the limit on UK resources which could have been deployed to solve this problem in isolation, the difficulties inherent in a unilateral approach and, most important, final acceptance by the NII.

The first two provisions of the EPRI/CEGB collaboration call for the exchange of test results and analyses of US (ANCO) and UK (BNL) component tests. This will provide a platform for the main theoretical programme which is concerned with application of non-linear analysis to more complex systems.

The EPRI 'Piping and Fitting Dynamic Reliability' Project and the NNC/PMT Contracts are concerned with evaluating the current provisions and implications of the ASME Piping Codes, and identifying, developing and deriving practical alternative rules and analysis procedures. While it is too soon as yet to be certain which particular approach proves most successful, it is possible to identify the solutions in general terms as either:-

(i) retaining the present conservative linear elastic dynamic analysis approach but combined with either recast or completely new ASME evaluation procedures

or:-

(ii) develop completely new dynamic analysis and response evaluation techniques for seismic loadings taking into account inelastic energy absorption.

A provision of the EPRI/CEGB Exchange Agreement commits the CEGB to commission a piping system test to complement the EPRI system tests being carried out by ETEC. Following discussions with KfK (Kernforschungszentrum) an agreement was reached with the German Federal Ministry of Research and Technology (BMFT) which resulted in the UK piping system tests being carried out at the HDR facility (Heissdampfreaktor). The tests formed part of an international collaborative programme of seismic pipework testing entitled SHAM and were all completed by the middle of 1988. The principal objectives of the CEGB tests were to demonstrate the seismic margins in the current piping design process and to provide a comparison between the effects of Sizewell 'B' and "All-sites" seismic input. Measurements were made to establish system response at high input levels for comparison with conventional ASME III linear elastic analysis and to provide a data base for comparison with non-linear analysis, aiding validation.

A comprehensive programme of theoretical and comparative assessments is now being developed to support the HDR test series, although it has already been concluded that the principal objectives of the test programme have been fully met.

3. PIPEBREAK PROTECTION DEVELOPMENT STRATEGY

3.1 Sizewell 'B' design approach

The safety design approach used for Sizewell 'B' is based closely on the USNRC requirement as set down in General Design Criteria No.4 (GDC-4) of the Federal Regulations 10CFR50 Appendix A which requires that structures, systems and components important to safety must be protected against the dynamic effects of pipewhip and fluid discharge. The selection of postulated pipebreak locations is also based on USNRC Standard Review Plan 3.6.2 which specifies break locations at terminal ends and various intermediate locations where stress or fatigue exceed specified limits based on ASME allowables. The requirement for Arbitrary Intermediate Break locations has now been removed from GDC-4 and the NII have been advised accordingly.

Initial estimates suggested that based on the USNRC guidelines approximately 400 pipe whip restraints would be required for systems located inside the primary containment at Sizewell 'B'. The effect of this large number of restraints on the layout and civil design was appreciable and accordingly a review was carried out to identify those restraints which could be eliminated by consideration of pipewhip motion and potential impact with safety classified equipment. Based on this review and elimination of arbitrary breaks, the likely number of restraints has now been reduced to less than 100, the majority of which are associated with the main steam, main feed and reactor coolant loops.

It should be noted that for Sizewell 'B' a significant proportion of the cost of pipewhip restraints has already been committed and that cost benefit of removal would be modest. However for future plant significant capital cost reductions could be achieved together with additional operational savings for reduced inspections, maintenance and associated reduction in man-rem burden.

3.2 NUREG 1061 LBB methodology

The LBB methodology contained in NUREG 1061 V3 (1) involves detailed engineering analysis including fatigue crack growth evaluation to establish whether pipe rupture mitigation hardware such as whip restraints and jet impingement barriers could be removed. The high energy pipelines selected for LBB application are assessed with respect to their freedom from problems related to corrosion, erosion, water hammer and excessive fatigue.

Having selected a pipeline, the locations of highest stresses must be identified coincident with minimum material properties. At these locations a throughwall crack of a size sufficient to assure detection by leakage using the plant installed leakage equipment with margins is postulated. Given that the station limiting detectable leak rate for unidentified leakage has been determined, application of NUREG 1061 methodology involves 3 key stages:

(i)   leak rate calculations for the cracked pipe under normal operating loads – margin x 10 i.e. the leak rate through the postulated crack must be x 10 greater than the lowest detection limit.

(ii) crack stability evaluation for normal plus SSE loads – margin x 2 between leakage crack and critical crack size.

(iii) stability check for excessively high loads – margin x $\sqrt{2}$ (normal plus SSE loads).

More recent work (2) has contended that the margins adopted may vary from place to place (i.e. inside, outside containment), reflecting leakage detection capability, and thus have not been firmly established at 10, 2 and $\sqrt{2}$.

In the above analyses the SSE loads are treated as static.

3.3 Application of NUREG 1061 LBB methodologies in the USA

LBB applications for BWR and LWR pipework following the guidelines contained in NUREG 1061 (1) have been presented by General Electric (3), Babcock and Wilcox (4), Combustion Engineering (5), Westinghouse (6), and Robert L Cloud Associates (7). Aspects considered include limitations, priority in applying the LBB concept to lines attached to the main primary reactor coolant piping, cost benefit aspects, and LBB implementation with snubber optimisation.

Robert L Cloud Associates used the LBB methodology of NUREG 1061 in applications for certain piping systems inside containment at Beaver Valley 2 (8) and in two further example analyses (7). A presentation was made to the ARCS in March 1987. Beaver Valley experience had indicated that less than 0.5 gpm unidentified leakage would be detected and identified in a timely manner (8). In the two further example analyses (7) it was argued that the long term PWR detectable leakage inside the containment for many operating plant ranges from 0.33 to 0.5 gpm, although it was recognised that for some plants a more conservative detectable size leak would be 1 gpm. Thus in both the Beaver Valley 2 and the two further example analyses a margin of x 10 for detectable leakage resulted in a leak rate of 5 gpm for calculating the leakage size crack.

Crack leakage predictions were performed using the EPRI Pipe Crack Evaluation Programme PICEP (9). PICEP is a code which calculates the crack opening area, the flow rate through the cracks in pipes and the critical crack length by combining a fracture mechanics model with a two phase model. Flow rate calculations are based on normal operating loads, i.e. pressure, dead weight and thermal expansion, at the location in the system with the highest stress combined with minimum material properties under (normal plus SSE) loadings.

It is essential to predict conservative values for the leakage size cracks, and to this end mean values of the materials properties are used and the individual normal operating load cases are combined algebraically. The results are in the form of a curve of flow rate versus crack length. The 'leakage detectable crack size' is determined from this curve by intersecting the flow rate value equal to the detectable flow rate with margin, in this case 5 gpm.

The variation in 5 gpm leakage crack size for the successful LBB application at Beaver Valley 2 (8), and the two further PWR examples considered by Robert L Cloud Associates (7), is presented in Figure 1. It is seen that the 5 gpm crack size ranges from approximately 75mm to 225mm.

3.4 Implementation of NUREG 1061 LBB methodology to UK PWR

If UK and US piping seismic stresses were to be identical, implementation of the LBB methodology contained in NUREG 1061 V3 (1) in the UK would require the following:-

(a) A review of NUREG 1061 V3 requirements.

(b) An assessment of whether the methodology/provisions are tenable in the UK design and safety context.

(c) Identification of areas requiring further supporting research and development.

However, aseismic design of SNUPPS is governed by the OBE, set at half the SSE, whereas aseismic design for the UK PWR is governed by the SSE. The arguments and consequences of this difference in design philosophy have been examined in section 2.1 and Appendix 1. Essentially it has been established that for all classes of piping systems (ASME Class 1, 2 and 3, and ASME/ANSI B31.1), the probable maximum UK PWR piping SSE stresses will be significantly larger than the probable maximum SNUPPS SSE piping allowable stresses, e.g. for Class 1 piping designed to Level D service limits the probable maximum allowable UK PWR SSE pipe stress is around 2.4 times the material design stress, (see equation (4) Appendix 1). This compares with the probable maximum SNUPPS SSE piping allowable stress of around 1.0 times the design stress.

Moreover, as the research and development into aseismic piping design described in section 2 succeeds in securing revisions to the appropriate ASME Code provisions, with fewer seismic restraints required to aseismically qualify piping systems, this will be associated with increases in the permissable level of SSE piping allowable stress.

The implications of UK PWR piping SSE stresses and higher seismic loadings on LBB arguments are explored in Appendix 2 which presents results from basic R6 (10) analyses of a notional pressurised straight pipe subjected to bending moments. These analyses were felt necessary to establish an understanding of the R6 analysis technique in the context of the NUREG 1061 V3 methodology.

The crucial result is the variation in the magnitude of the critical defect size with bending stress, illustrated in Figure 5. It has been assumed that in designing UK PWR piping in order to minimise the number of snubbers needed to qualify the systems aseismically, CAEMS will 'drive' the piping as near as possible to the probable maximum SSE stress level. For UK conditions this is around 1.6 x yield stress: for US conditions the maximum SSE stress is around 0.67 x yield stress due to the OBE design requirement discussed above. It can be seen from Figure 5 that the smallest UK critical circumferential semi-crack length (corresponding to the equivalent leakage crack length) is about 25mm compared with the corresponding US defect greater than 125mm.

In these circumstances it has been decided that an off-line pilot study is required to establish whether the LBB methodology outlined in NUREG 1061 V3 (1) can be validated against UK design practices. Auxiliary pipework inside the primary containment building has been chosen in the first instance for the pilot study. While adopting this approach the PMT have recognised the substantial potential benefits of LBB application to the main loop pipework, but consider this area subject to the outcome of other on-going licensing issues relating to LOCA-seismic load combinations and inspection.

The pilot study will attempt to achieve the NUREG 1061 V3 (1) LBB margins since it is believed any relaxation would require detailed substantiation. In addition it is necessary to demonstrate that the piping systems under consideration in the pilot study are not susceptable to fracture from stress-corrosion, erosion, water hammer or excessive fatigue.

3.5 UK research and development supporting the LBB pilot study

In addition to the pilot study a programme of supporting research and development has been established in the UK to complement the International Piping Integrity Research Group (IPIRG) activities which have been supported by the CEGB since they joined in 1986. IPIRG was established with the objective of developing the technology to justify plant life extension and simplification in nuclear plant piping design criteria, initially focussed on fracture mechanics assessments. Work started in March 1986 and is scheduled for completion in 1990.

The CEGB is giving highest priority to research aimed at increasing the accuracy of predicting leakage through postulated cracks in the pipe wall and improving in-plant leakage detection and measurement capability. These requirements dominate all others because as explained in the previous section, the predicted critical throughwall crack sizes may already be considerably smaller for the UK design than for the equivalent US plant and successful applications of LBB by US utilities (8) does not, by itself, provide sufficient justification and further methodology development may be required.

High priority is also being given to the quantification of margins, not just the margins associated with the NUREG 1061 V3 (1) LBB methodology, but the margins thought to be available in the CEGB R6 crack assessment procedures (10) which will be used for the pilot study. It is felt from above that justification may be required for claiming substantial increases in predicted critical crack lengths.

Another consequence of the assumed higher seismically induced stresses for UK piping under SSE loadings is the relative importance of axial and circumferential defects as discussed in Appendix 2. Based on lowly stressed US pipework, the LBB methodology contained in NUREG 1061 addresses primarily circumferential cracks. It can be shown, however, that ratchetting occurs when a pressurised tube sustains a bending stress, σ_b such that:-

$$\sigma_b > \left(\sigma_y - \frac{PR}{2t}\right)$$

where σ_y is the yield stress

P is the internal pressure

R is the mean radius

t is the tube thickness

The essentials of the argument are presented in Appendix 3. Experiments have confirmed that incremental hoop strains are accumulated under dynamic loading (11) and in the absence of strain hardening failure would occur, Figure 7. Strain hardening effects are believed likely to limit the ratchetting phenomenon observed in both UK and US laboratory experiments and thus strain hardening is a very important material property. It is accepted that a comprehensive technical position needs to be established in order to discount axially aligned postulated defects.

To a very great extent at the present time it is being assumed in the UK that IPIRG achievements will satisfy the need to establish:-

(i) Developed and validated methodologies for evaluating the effects of dynamic loading on pipes contained defects, to include treatment of both inertial stresses and displacement controlled stresses.

(ii) Materials properties data base for parent pipes and associated welds.

It has been established that for ASME Class 1 systems the maximum UK PWR piping SSE allowable stress is approximately 2.4 times the maximum SNUPPS SSE allowable stress (Appendix 1). In these circumstances it is reasonable to suppose that at the present time the testing programme agreed within the IPIRG framework may not reflect completely the requirements identified in this paper and that further work may be needed to support implementation of LBB arguments to UK PWR piping systems.

4. OPTIMISATION OF RESTRAINT PROVISIONS FOR FUTURE PWR STATIONS

Because UK PWR piping systems will be unique for the reasons outlined in section 2, an assessment of the Sizewell 'B' piping systems is being carried out to identify the location, number and design requirements for seismic and pipewhip restraints, to aid the establishment of priorities and regions of greatest potential saving.

In addition to overseas experience the lessons drawn from the seismic snubber reduction programme on AGR pipework also need to be taken into account (25). Re- analysis of the Torness main steam pipework using current analytical techniques and realistic building response spectra has demonstrated that all 70 seismic snubbers can be removed without exceeding either the ASME Level D allowable stresses or acceptable loads and moments on remaining supports and equipment. Moreover it has been recognised that scope exists for significant reductions in the number of snubbers employed on all other seismically qualified pipework systems at Torness (25).

Using this information, cost effective programmes to eliminate seismic and pipewhip restraints for future PWRs can then be considered by the Project in the context of potentially more onerous site conditions as follows:-

(A) through reviewing existing piping design constraints, either by

(a) more detailed elastic analysis i.e. ASME Section III NB 3200

(b) non-linear analysis i.e. ASME Section III Appendix F

(c) use of simplified non-linear methods, developed by NNC. This approach would involve submissions to the NII on a case by case basis.

(B) through reviewing existing equipment design constraints by considering the potential benefit to be derived by more detailed analysis of the ability of equipment (nozzles, pumps, tanks etc) to accommodate seismic loads

(C) through adopting any revised piping seismic design requirements secured through the EPRI/CEGB Collaborative Research Programme i.e. 'equation (9)' type revisions to the ASME code taking into account inelastic energy absorption

(D) through application of NUREG 1061 LBB methodology

Successful programmes to eliminate seismic restraints produce more flexible piping systems with higher dynamic responses. In these circumstances additional new potential design criteria have to be considered involving

(i) Pipe displacement – minimum piping system separation criteria have been developed which may be violated by more flexible systems

(ii) Valve acceleration – active valve design inertia accelerations are typically in the range 2-4g. In more flexible systems valve accelerations may increase by between 2 to 3 times current values

(iii) Equipment/nozzle loads – revised piping system seismic design requirements may increase the loads to be sustained by sensitive equipment

The above work may give rise to the need for a number of 'UK specific' R&D programmes to validate the design proposals but it should be possible to draw on US experience to an extent.

Successful aseismic and LBB developments will permit the progressive elimination of seismic and pipewhip restraints. However, these achievements may not be fully realised together because the potentially high seismic stresses associated with the elimination of seismic restraints may not permit the complete application of LBB.

General Electric (3) considered the role of seismic stresses in LBB applications to NUREG 1061 V3 criteria (1). It was recognised that for piping systems where snubber optimisation would precede the LBB application it is desirable for a piping analyst to know how high the seismic stresses can be such that the LBB criteria on critical flaw and stability margin can be satisfied. In other words, if the piping analyst has a prior knowledge of the acceptable SSE level from LBB considerations, then the snubber optimisation process can be performed in such a way that LBB application at a later date is not foreclosed for that pipe system.

5. CONCLUSIONS

5.1 A significant reduction in snubbers and seismic supports is likely on UK PWRs compared with comparable USA stations due to the use of the CAEMS/HANGIT support optimisation approach and different UK and US seismic design criteria.

5.2 Any further reduction of seismic restraints on future stations will require changes to the ASME code allowables to recognise inelastic energy absorbing processes and more sophisticated equipment/nozzle loading evaluation procedures.

5.3 A collaborative programme of research and development into seismic response of pipework has been established with EPRI. This should provide a sound base for improvements to seismic design on future PWR stations meeting ASME requirements.

5.4 Widespread application of NUREG 1061 LBB methodology to UK piping systems may require substantial improvements to both fracture and leakage assessment methods together with corresponding improvement to leakage prediction and detection capability.

5.5 It is concluded that the CEGB has a comprehensive programme of design and development work underway, which should provide a sound base for improvements to pipework design on future PWR stations.

ACKNOWLEDGEMENT

This paper is published by permission of the Central Electricity Generating Board.

REFERENCES

1. USNRC Report of the USNRC Piping Review Committee USNRC NUREG 1061 Volumes 1 to 5, 1984, 1985.

2. Chexal, V K, Norris, D M and Server, W L, 'Leak Before Break. An Integrated Approach for High Energy Piping', Post SMiRT Seminar on Extreme Loading, Paris, August 1987.

3. General Electric, 'Application of the Leak Before Break Approach to BWR Piping' EPRI NP-4991, December 1986.

4. Babcock and Wilcox, 'Application of Leak Before Break Approach to PWR Piping Designed by Babcock and Wilcox', EPRI NP-4972, January 1987.

5. Combustion Engineering, 'Application of the Leak Before Break Analysis to PWR Piping Designed by Combustion Engineering' EPRI NP-5010, February 1987.

6. Westinghouse, 'Application of the Leak Before Break Approach to Westinghouse PWR Piping', EPRI NP-4971, December 1986.

7. Robert L Cloud Associates, 'Applying Leak Before Break to High Energy Piping', NSAC 114, November 1987.

8. NUS, 'Status of the US Utility Application of 10 CFR 50 Modification to General Design Criterion 4 and the Reduction in Snubber Usage in Piping Systems', Report No. 4991, Revision 2, to CEGB, July 30th 1987.

9. PICEP 'Pipe Crack Evaluation Program', EPRI NP 3596 SR, August 1984.

10. Milne, I, Ainsworth, R A, Dowling, A R and Stewart, A T, 'Assessment of the Integrity of Structures Containing Defects', CEGB Report R/H/R6 - Revision 3, 1986.

11. Beaney, E M, 'Plasticity in Resonant Pipework Vibration', Paper presented at the Second Conference on 'Pipework Engineering and Operation', Inst. Mech. Engineers, 21-22 February 1989.

12. Applied Nucleonics, 'Seismic Design of Nuclear Power Plants -An Assessment', EPRI 273, June 1975.

13. Miller, A G, 'Review of Limit Loads of Structures Containing Defects', CEGB Report TPRD/B/0093/N82 (Revision 2), Third Edition, 1987.

14. Miller, A G, 'Review of Test Results for Ductile Failure Pressure of Cracked Spherical and Cylindrical Pressure Vessels', CEGB Report TPRD/B/0489/N84, 1984.

15. Ranta-Mannus, A K and Achenbach, J D, Nuclear Engineering and Design, 60, 339, 1980.

16. Eiber, R J, Maxey, W A, Duffy, A R and Atterburg, J J, BMI 1908, 1971.

17. Kastner, W, Roehrich, E, Schmitt, W and Steinbuch, R, Int. J Pressure Vessels and Piping V9, p.197-219.

18. Ainsworth, R A, Chell, G G and Milne, I, CEGB Report TPRD/B/0480/N84, 1984.

19. Delale, F and Erdogan, F, Q. App. Maths 37, 239, 1983.

20. Sanders, J L, ASME J. Applied Mechanics, 50, 221, 1983.

21. Folias, E S, 'On the Fracture of Nuclear Reactor Tubes', SMiRT 3, Paper C4/5, London.

22. Rooke, D P and Cartwright, D J, 'Compendium of Stress Intensity Factors', HMSO, 1974.

23. Carmichael G D T, 'Assessment of Ratchetting', Contribution to 'TPRD Views on Seismic Matters', Edited by J Bethell, 1985.

24. Edmunds, H G and Beer F J, 'Notes on Incremental Collapse in Pressure Vessels', J. Mech. Eng. Sci. 3, 3, p187-199, 1961.

25. Kennedy, P A and Harkin, N J, 'Seismic Snubber Reduction on AGR Pipework', Paper Presented at the Second Conference on 'Pipework Engineering and Operation', Inst. Mech. Engrs., 21-22 February 1989.

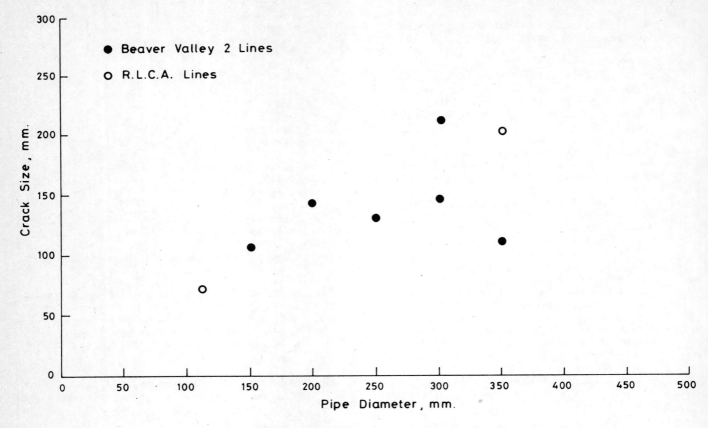

Fig 1   Variation in the 5 gpm crack size with pipe diameter at Beaver
Valley 2 and lines analysed by R L Cloud Associates (7)

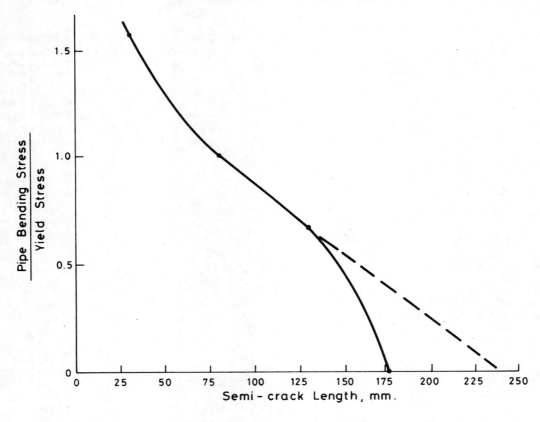

Fig 2   Variation in semi-crack length with sustained bending stress for
penetrating circumferential defects — notional pressurizer surge line

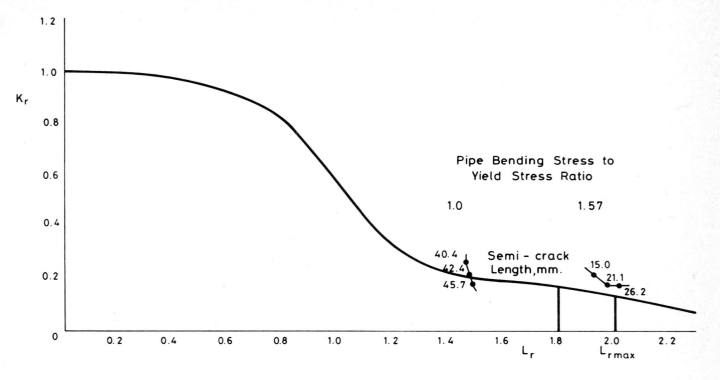

Fig 3 The general failure assessment diagram (option 1) penetrating circumferential defects R6 category 3 stability analyses

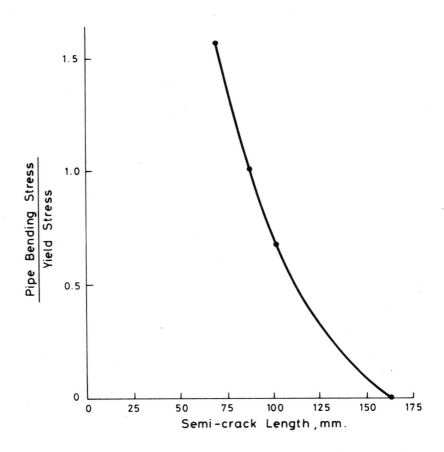

Fig 4 Variation in semi-crack length with sustained bending stress for penetrating axial defects — notional pressurizer surge line

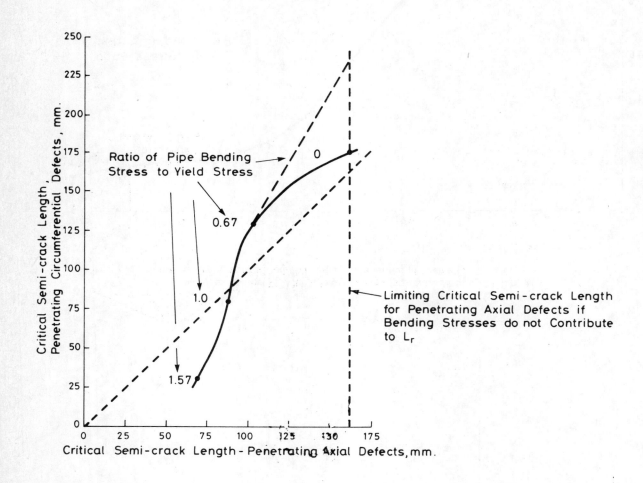

Fig 5   Variation in critical semi-crack length for both penetrating axial
and circumferential defects with sustained bending stress — notional
pressurizer surge line

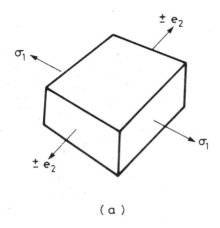

(a)

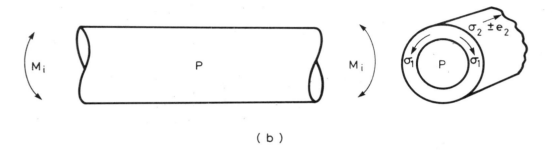

(b)

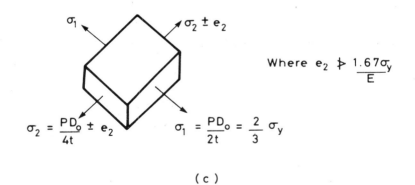

Where $e_2 \not> \dfrac{1.67\sigma_y}{E}$

$$\sigma_2 = \frac{PD_o}{4t} \pm e_2 \qquad \sigma_1 = \frac{PD_o}{2t} = \frac{2}{3}\sigma_y$$

(c)

Fig 6   Incremental collapse of pressure vessels
       (a)   Case considered by Edmunds and Beer (24)
       (b)   Pressurized pipe subjected to in-plane seismic load
       (c)   Top segment of pressurized tube meeting ASME code
               Section III Class 1 provisions

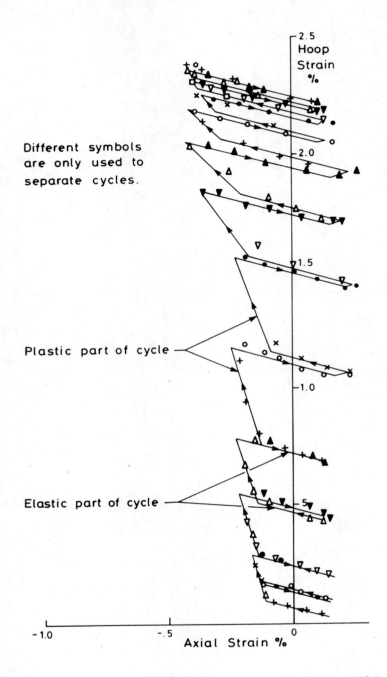

Different symbols
are only used to
separate cycles.

Plastic part of cycle

Elastic part of cycle

Fig 7   Hoop and axial strains on the top of the pipe in test 7 [after
         Beaney (11)]

APPENDIX 1

ASEISMIC DESIGN OF PIPING SYSTEMS TO MEET SNUPPS AND U.K. PWR CRITERIA

1. INTRODUCTION

Aseismic design of piping systems for both SNUPPS and U.K. PWR is governed by the ASME Boiler and Pressure Vessel Code Section III, Division 1, subsections NB (Class 1), NC (Class 2) and ND (Class 3), and ASME/ANSI B31.1.

In all instances in this Appendix, the analysis procedures assume elastic behaviour and response spectra to U.S. NRC Regulatory Guide 1.60.

Consider initially the design of a straight tube to satisfy both SNUPPS and U.K. PWR aseismic requirements.

2. CLASS 1, ASME SECTION III NB 3600

2.1 Governing Equation

Aseismic design is governed by the equation:-

$$\frac{B_1 P D_o}{2t} + \frac{B_2 D_o M_i}{2I} \leq x_k S_m \qquad (1)$$

Where B_1 B_2 are primary stress indices for the specific product under construction

P is design pressure

D_o outside diameter of pipe

t nominal wall thickness of product

I moment of inertia

M_i resultant moment loading due to loads caused by weight; earthquake, considering only one half the range of the earthquake

S_m allowable design stress intensity

x_k constant, dependent on Service Limits

2.2 SNUPPS

SNUPPS was designed to the 1974 version of the ASME Code. It can be shown that meeting the OBE requirement is more demanding than meeting the SSE requirement when the OBE is set at half the SSE (12). Thus in equation (1), for OBE Service Limits, $x_k = 1.5$, and provided the tube is remote from welds or other discontinuities,

$$B_1 = 0.5 \qquad B_2 = 1.0$$

In a straight tube,

$$\frac{PD_o}{2t} = S_m$$

Thus equation (1) can be re-written as

$$0.5 S_m + \frac{D_o M_i}{2I} \leq 1.5 S_m \qquad (2)$$

In a well designed PWR piping system the stress due to self weight $\leq 0.1 S_m$, which can be compared with the maximum system stress indicated in the ANSI/ASME B31.1 support spacing table.

Thus account can be taken of weight affects, and equation (2) can be re-written as:-

Allowable Piping OBE stresses $\leq 0.9 S_m$ (3)

2.3 UK PWR

UK PWR will be designed to the 1983 version of the ASME code, up to and including the Winter 1983 Addenda for the BPA Contracts, and the service level corresponding to the loadings indicated in the SNUPPS evaluation is an SSE meeting the Level D service limits. For Level D, $x_k = 3.0$.

Thus taking account of the pressure stress, self weight effect, as above

Allowable Piping SSE stresses $\leq 2.4 S_m$ (4)

2.4 SNUPPS cf UK PWR

To contrast SNUPPS with UK PWR piping seismic allowables, account must be taken of damping as specified in the appropriate NRC Regulatory Guides, 1.60 and 1.61. Using the effective damping amplification factors appropriate to OBE and SSE in accordance with these guides, the ratio of the ground level input motions is give by:-

$$\frac{\text{SNUPPS OBE}}{\text{UK PWR SSE}} = \frac{0.9 S_m}{2.4 S_m} \times \frac{(3.13)}{(4.25)} \frac{\text{SSE (Building 5\%)}}{\text{OBE (Building 2\%)}} \times$$

$$\frac{(4.25)}{(5.52)} \frac{\text{SSE (Piping 2\%)}}{\text{OBE (Piping 1\%)}}$$

i.e. $\dfrac{\text{SNUPPS OBE}}{\text{UK PWR SSE}} = 0.213$ (5)

Taking SNUPPS OBE = 0.5 SSE, then

$$\frac{\text{SNUPPS SSE PIPING ALLOWABLE STRESSES}}{\text{UK PWR SSE PIPING ALLOWABLE STRESSES}} = 0.426$$

i.e.

| UK PWR SSE PIPING ALLOWABLE STRESSES (CLASS 1) | = 2.35 x | SNUPPS SSE PIPING ALLOWABLE STRESSES (CLASS 1) | (6) |

Thus the seismic stresses in UK PWR (Class 1) straight tubes can be 2.35 times the seismic stresses in SNUPPS (Class 1) straight tubes while both stations sustain an earthquake with the same peak free field ground acceleration.

3. CLASS 2, ASME SECTION III NC 3600
   CLASS 3, ASME SECTION III ND 3600

Similar arguments to the above established that the seismic stresses in UK PWR Class 2 and 3 straight tubes can be 3.55 times the seismic stresses in SNUPPS Classes 2 and 3 straight tubes while both stations sustain an earthquake with the same peak free field ground acceleration.

4. ASME/ANSI B31.1

Very similar analyses to the above can be conducted for ASME/ANSI B31.1 straight tubing, when it can be shown that the seismic stresses in the UK PWR tubes can be 2.65 times the seismic stresses in the SNUPPS ASME/ANSI B31.1 straight tubes while both stations sustain an earthquake with the same peak free field ground acceleration.

5. COMPONENTS

Identical analyses to the above can be carried out to indicate the margins for components such as elbows, branches etc. These analyses suggested margins on Class 1 components of 5.29 on elbows, 7.94 on branches.

APPENDIX 2

R6 LEAK-BEFORE-BREAK APPLICATION

1. INTRODUCTION

This Appendix presents results obtained by the authors from basic R6 (10) analyses of a notional pressurised straight pipe subjected to bending moments. The objective of the analyses was to help establish an understanding of the R&D required to support Leak Before Break (LBB) arguments for UK PWR stations, in the context of the methodology presented in USNRC 1061 V3 (1).

Axial and circumferential through wall defects were considered. As essentially qualitative rather than quantitative insights were sought, the approximations introduced by using thin shell solutions were accepted. In all the analyses, constant internal pressure was assumed and dynamic stresses were treated as static stresses. Critical defect lengths were calculated for three values of bending stress, x 0.67, x 1.0 and x 1.57 a nominal yield stress, through R6 Category 1 Option 1 analyses. Category 3 analyses were used to study the stability of cracks, assumed to be identifiable through installed leakage detection systems, subjected to load x $\sqrt{2}$ greater than (normal + SSE).

The analyses considered a straight pipe in a notional pressuriser surge line with an external diameter of 381mm. Parameters essential to the R6 analysis were taken to be reasonably representative of 316 stainless steel.

2. BASIS OF ANALYSIS

2.1 Penetrating Circumferential Defects

The critical defect length for a penetrating circumferential defect in a pressurised pipe under internal pressure in the absence of bending was derived from the evaluation presented by Miller (13). Miller (14) compared the solutions proposed by Ranta-Maunus and Achenbach (15), Eiber et al (16) and Kastner et al (17) with experimental results, and concluded that the expression given by Kastner et al (17) gave the best agreement.

The solution routine adopted for penetrating circumferential defects in pressurised pipes subjected to bending followed Ainsworth, Chell and Milne (18), based in turn on the work of Ranta-Maunus and Achenbach (15), Delale and Erdogen (19) and Sanders (20).

2.2 Penetrating Axial Defects

The collapse pressure for penetrating axial defects was obtained from the revised Folias (21) expression quoted by Miller (13).

It was assumed that axial defects had no effect on the limit moment.

Stress intensity factors for penetrating axial defects were obtained from Rooke and Cartwright (22).

3. PENETRATING CIRCUMFERENTIAL DEFECTS

3.1 Critical Defect Lengths

It was assumed that the ratio of axial pressure stress to yield stress was 0.25. The approach outlined at section 2.1 was followed and critical semi-crack lengths derived, Figure 2.

3.2 Stable Detectable Flaws

Stability analyses under loads $\sqrt{2}$ x (normal plus SSE) were conducted for bending stress to yield stress ratios of 1.0 and 1.57. It was assumed in these calculations that the leakage detection equipment detected defects with the appropriate margin on leakage i.e. 10 and the appropriate margin on flaw size i.e. 2, i.e. semi-crack lengths of 40.4mm and 15.0mm respectively. A category 3 R6 approach was used (10) to assess the behaviour of these leakage size cracks. The results of the stability analyses are presented in Figure 3.

With a bending stress to yield stress ratio of 1.0 stability was demonstrated: the final assessment point is below the R6 failure assessment line. Thus a double ended pipe break would not occur. However, with a bending stress to yield stress ratio of 1.57, Figure 3, stability was not demonstrated, all three assessment points lie above the failure assessment line. Further the final point lies beyond the cut-off for the material at L_r max = 2.0, Figure 3.

4. PENETRATING AXIAL DEFECTS

The approach outlined at section 2.2 was followed to derive the approximate critical defect lengths illustrated in Figure 4.

These critical axial defect lengths were established through R6 Category 1 Option 1 analyses with the bending stress contribution to L_r incorporated by simply adding both pressure and moment contributions to L_r. The correct contribution of bending stresses to L_r in the presence of axial defects is not immediately apparent. It is certainly normal to assume that axial defects have no effect on the limit moment, possibly conservative to include the moment contribution with the pressure component. However, a case can be developed to ignore the effect of bending stresses when determining critical axial defect lengths provided

$$\sigma_b \leq (\sigma_y - \frac{PR}{2t})$$

The basis of this inequality can be derived from Appendix 3.

When bending stresses can be ignored then the critical crack length is 327.6mm

5. SUMMARY

The variation in critical semi-crack length for both penetrating axial and circumferential defects, as determined in the previous two sections, is illustrated in Figure 5. Irrespective of whether axial or circumferential defects are limiting, it is apparent that bending stresses play a crucial role in determining critical defect lengths. With no bending stresses acting, the critical defect length is approximately 350mm, yet when the bending stress is around 1.6 x yield, the critical defect length is less than 63 mm.

ACKNOWLEDGEMENT

The authors wish to thank Bob Ainsworth and Martin Crossley of CEGB Research Division (BNL) for their help in the preparation of the analyses.

APPENDIX 3

ASSESSMENT OF RATCHETTING

This Appendix summarises the argument presented previously (23).

Aseismic design of piping to Section III, Division 1, Sub-section NB of the ASME Boiler and Pressure Vessel Code is governed by the equation:-

$$\frac{B_1 P D_o}{2t} + \frac{B_2 D_o M_i}{2I} \leq 3 S_m \qquad (1)$$

Where B_1 B_2 are primary stress indices for the specific product under consideration

P is design pressure

D_o outside diameter of pipe

t nominal wall thickness of product

I moment of inertia

M_i resultant moment loading due to loads caused by weight, earthquake, considering only one half the range of the earthquake

It is usual to assume that $S_m = 2/3\,\sigma_y$, where σ_y is the yield stress.

Consider a straight pipe, remote from welds or other discontinuities. For this situation $B_1 = 0.5$, $B_2 = 1.0$.

Now we know that in a straight pipe that:-

$$\frac{P\,D_o}{2t} = S_m$$

Thus we can re-write equation (1) as:-

$$\frac{\sigma_y}{3} + \frac{D_o\,M_i}{2I} \leq 2\sigma_y$$

For the purpose of this assessment, let us assume that the self weight stress is zero. Then half the stress due to the earthquake must be limited to $1.67\,\sigma_y$.

Now Edmunds and Beer (24) have considered the incremental collapse of pressure vessels. A particular case, conjugate strain cycles superimposed on constant direct stress, is illustrated in Figure 6(a).

Edmunds and Beer (24) showed that the total increment of irrecoverable yield in a complete cycle is given by:-

$$\overline{\varepsilon}_1 = \frac{3\sigma_1}{(2\sigma_y - \sigma_1)} \left[2e_2 - \frac{(2\sigma_y - \sigma_1)}{E} \right] \quad (2)$$

where E is Young's modulus

It can be shown that a follow up stress, (σ_2, say), in the conjugate direction, has no effect on the magnitude of the net strain/cycle.

Now when a pressurised pipe is subject to an in-plane seismic load, we have the situation illustrated in Figure 6(b).

Thus the top segment of the tube can be considered as shown in Figure 6(c).

The increment of strain/cycle can be computed from equation (2). Discounting σ_2, taking $\sigma_1 = 2/3\,\sigma_y$, $e_2 = \frac{1.67\,\sigma_y}{E}$,

and using typical values for σ_y, E, of $210\ N/mm^2$ and $210 \times 10^3\ N/mm^2$, respectively,

then $\overline{\varepsilon}_1 = 0.3\%/\text{cycle}$.

If failure occurs when $\overline{\varepsilon}_1 = 24\%$, then, in the absence of strain hardening, the tube will fail after 80 cycles.

C388/018

Safety and relief valve testing

S BRYANT, BSc, CEng, MINucE, **P T GEORGE**, CPhys, MInstP and
D R AIREY, MSc, PhD, CEng, MIMechE, MIEE
National Power — Nuclear, Marchwood Engineering Laboratories, CEGB, Marchwood, Southampton

SYNOPSIS Two major programmes of safety relief valve testing have been established in support of system design and the selection of valves for Sizewell 'B'. The CEGB has constructed the BRAVO facility at its Marchwood Engineering Laboratory to reproduce PWR pressuriser fluid conditions for the full scale testing of pressuriser relief system valves. Current tests on BRAVO, on a full size tandem pair of pressuriser pilot operated safety relief valves, will be followed by the full flow testing of a pressuriser safety valve. Tests at secondary circuit conditions have been carried out at the Siemens Kraftwerk Union Test Facilities, W. Germany, where candidate MSSV's have been tested at full scale blowdown conditions.

1   INTRODUCTION

The CEGB has considered it prudent to support the introduction of PWR Technology into the UK by investing in development and testing programmes with the objective of demonstrating the operability, integrity and reliability of specified plant and components considered to be significant in relation to plant maintenance and outage.

The significance attached by the CEGB to valve operability in PWR systems is reflected in several testing programmes aimed at ensuring both the quality of design and manufacture of valves to be supplied to Sizewell 'B', and meeting commitments in the safety case for pre-service and in-service testing.

The subject of this paper is the testing of safety and relief valves for the UK PWR programme.

2   SIZEWELL 'B' SAFETY RELIEF VALVES

There are nearly three hundred safety relief valves on Sizewell 'B', the large majority being conventional spring loaded safety valves affording over-pressure protection to liquid, vapour or gas circuits in auxiliary systems similar to those providing services in any conventional plant.

However, a small number of safety and relief valves on Sizewell perform a key role in the over pressure protection of the nuclear plant and those which are important to nuclear safety are procured to Section III of the ASME Boiler and Pressure Vessel Code and subjected to an extensive programme of testing by the valve suppliers to meet CEGB Specifications.

To complement this production testing, the CEGB has established several programmes of testing to investigate the operating characteristics of valves used in key applications, with the principal aims of providing data for fault transient analysis and the development of in-service testing procedures.

The test programmes discussed in this paper are concerned with two valve applications on the Sizewell pressuriser relief system providing over pressure protection to the primary circuit, and a third application on the main steam system protecting the secondary circuit.

The paper includes a discussion of some of the findings of the secondary circuit valve test programme: the programmes associated with primary circuit valves are at an early stage and the paper is necessarily confined to a discussion of their objectives.

3 PRIMARY CIRCUIT SAFETY RELIEF VALVES

3.1 Pressuriser Relief System Description

The fluid pressure in the primary circuit of a PWR is controlled under normal operation by the pressuriser. Electric heating of saturated water, or spray cooling of saturated steam within the pressuriser vessel increases, or decreases, the primary circuit pressure. Pressure surges beyond the control capability of the spray are mitigated by the Pressuriser Relief System (PRS). The Sizewell 'B' PRS comprises three tandem pairs of pilot operated safety relief valves (POSRV), developed for use on Electricité de France (EDF) PWR's, and two conventional spring loaded safety valves.

Each tandem pair of POSRV's comprises a relief valve and a downstream isolating valve, both of which are pilot operated valves which operate hydraulically in response to the fluid pressure in the pressuriser or, at pressures below 165 bar, their nominal hydraulic set pressure, by means of electric solenoid actuators. The tandem POSRV's downstream isolating valve is open under normal operating conditions and is set to close as system pressure decreases below a certain value, thus providing each relief line with enhanced reclosure reliability. The POSRV's constitute the first line of protection in the pressuriser relief system and are designed to cater for steam relief and for all water discharge requirements including overpressure protection at cold shutdown.

The second line of protection in the PRS comprises two conventional spring loaded safety valves, which have a higher set pressure than the POSRV's and provide diversity of pressure relief and additional relief capacity for infrequent fault sequences.

3.2 General Testing Requirements

The Sizewell 'B' pressuriser relief system was designed in the light of a post Three Mile Island review of PRS performance requirements and differs from that of the reference design embodied in the US SNUPPS plants.

Confirmation of the adequacy of the modified system is required and, while extensive testing has been carried out on both valve designs intended for use on the Sizewell PRS, it was necessary to make provision for additional tests to confirm the ability of the valves to meet requirements unique to the UK PWR.

In anticipation of this need, the CEGB has constructed a high flow rate test facility at its Marchwood Engineering Laboratory (MEL), specifically for the full scale testing of valves for the pressuriser relief system of a PWR. Called BRAVO - Blowdown Rig for the Assessment of Valve Operability - the facility has the unique capability to reproduce primary circuit water chemistry as well as full system pressure, temperature and the maximum mass flow rates associated with each PRS valve. The facility is also capable of carrying out full flow tests on other primary circuit valves and high energy flow interruption tests on valves required to close in the event of a primary circuit pipe break have already been carried out on the BRAVO facility.

Test Programmes have now been defined to demonstrate the ability of the Sizewell pressuriser relief system valves to perform the range of functions required of them by the Sizewell 'B' safety case. There follows a description of the salient features of each programme.

3.3 Pressuriser POSRV

3.3.1 Testing Requirements

The POSRV was selected for Sizewell 'B' on the basis of an extensive programme of development and testing carried out by EDF. This programme addressed the duty the valve is required to perform on the pressuriser relief system of EDF PWR's on which it is now installed. However, as a result of differing licensing requirements, the claims made for the valve in the Sizewell safety case differ from those made for EDF plants in certain respects. As a result, some aspects of the Sizewell 'B' duty of the valve have not been investigated by EDF.

A programme has therefore been established in which full scale testing of a tandem pair of POSRV's will be carried out on the MEL BRAVO facility under a range of conditions representing the following aspects of the anticipated Sizewell 'B' duty of the valve, not covered by the EDF test work:

a) Low Pressure Performance

The over pressure protection of the Sizewell 'B' primary circuit at low temperature, i.e. during shutdowns, is provided by the Cold Over Pressure Mitigation System (COMS). This system ensures that the fluid pressure in the primary circuit does not exceed the limits imposed by the design code in respect of brittle fracture considerations.

The key component of this system is the POSRV which is commanded to open by a signal from the primary protection system according to a pre-specified relationship between set pressure and circuit temperature.

Previous EDF test work indicated that the operating time of the POSRV was inversely related to circuit pressure. The design of the COMS for Sizewell therefore requires precise information on the opening time of the POSRV for the range of pressures over which it might be required to provide over pressure protection. The need to maintain an intact circuit following the mitigation of an over pressure event demands information on the closure time of the valve also.

b)   Borated Water

The POSRV hydraulic pilot system is designed to operate on demineralised water to minimise the risk of the formation of boron crystals due to leakage through pilot valves and seals. However, to give assurance that the system will remain operable in the unlikely event of the inadvertent introduction of borated water, the tests in the BRAVO facility will be conducted with borated water in the pilot circuit.

c)   Loop Seal

To prevent the leakage of hydrogen across the valve sealing face, a condensate filled loop seal is fitted immediately upstream of each valve. Discharge of this water "slug" when the valve is operated gives rise to a mechanical loading on the outlet pipework which is taken into account in the pipework design.

Heating of the loop seal promotes flashing to steam when the valve opens and reduces the loading experienced by the discharge pipework, but allows the valve body and internals to reach higher temperatures during normal plant operation. The optimum temperature of the condensate in the loop seal is therefore being investigated in the BRAVO programme.

d)   In-service testing

The procedure developed for the in-service testing of the pressuriser POSRV by EdF will be assessed for use on Sizewell 'B'. The validity of the confirmation of the correct setting and general operability of the POSRV obtained from the test equipment will be confirmed by means of full flow testing on the BRAVO facility.

3.3.2 Interim Test Results

The tests completed to date have yielded data on the opening and closing times, lift characteristics and discharge mass flowrates of the tandem POSRV at system pressures between atmospheric pressure and 55 bar. Typical operating characteristics are shown in Fig1. The data has been used in the design of the Sizewell 'B' Cold Overpressure Mitigation System to define the valve set pressures necessary to maintain primary circuit pressure below the upper limit set by brittle fracture considerations and above the lower limits imposed to protect the reactor coolant pump seals, the geometric stability of which is maintained by circuit fluid pressure.

The tests have also given confidence in the cyclic operability of the valve: more than 100 operating cycles have been carried out with subcooled water or steam at pressures up to 55 bar. Subsequent leakage tests and visual inspection have shown that the valve has suffered negligible wear as a consequence of this duty. Furthermore, the pilot system has behaved faultlessly throughout.

3.4   Pressuriser Safety Valve

3.4.1 Testing Requirements

The Sizewell pressuriser safety valve is a conventional spring loaded safety valve, which has accumulated a large body of relevant operational experience, being used for this duty on the majority of PWR's in the USA.

Furthermore, the valve was included in a major programme of safety relief valve testing carried out under the auspices of the Electric Power Research Institute (EPRI) of the USA following the Three Mile Island incident (1).

The general conclusion of this programme was that, providing certain rules governing the design of inlet pipework geometry were followed, the valve exhibited stable behaviour during the discharge of steam. Some uncertainties remain however, and tests are to be carried out on the BRAVO facility on a full size pressuriser safety valve identical to the Sizewell valve. The following areas will be addressed:

a) Loop Seal Discharge

During the EPRI test programme some instability was observed during water discharge. It is, however, a basis of the design of the Sizewell PRS that the pressuriser safety valve is not required to discharge water during any design basis transient, all requirements for water discharge being catered for by the POSRV. The condensate filled loop seal does, however, involve a potential requirement for water slug discharge. Minor sealing face damage arising from loop seal discharge at the very low frequency of real demands on the pressuriser safety valve i.e once per reactor lifetime, is tolerable, but more frequent demands will result from in service testing, and the effect of the presence or otherwise of the loop seal on in service testing procedures will be investigated.

b) Valve Settings

The pressuriser safety valve is required to perform within certain limits on full lift pressure and re-seating pressure, in order to comply with the assumptions made in the Sizewell safety case. These limits are referred to as accumulation and blowdown – the difference between full lift or reclosure pressures respectively and the valve set pressure. Both values are normally expressed as a percentage of set pressure. A definition of set pressure in common use and that adopted for the test programme is: "The value of increasing inlet static pressure at which there is measurable displacement of the valve disc".

The EPRI test programme indicated that the required values of three percent accumulation and five percent blowdown could be achieved by the valve at certain settings of the valve control rings. Tests will be carried out in advance of production testing to confirm that the settings recommended by the valve supplier achieve Sizewell performance requirements.

c) In-service testing

As in the case of the POSRV, procedures are being developed for the in-service testing of the pressuriser safety valve. It is expected that these will be based on the use of an assist device for in-situ testing during hot shutdown of the plant. Confirmation of the validity of such methods and the optimisation of the test procedure will be addressed in the BRAVO programme of performance tests on the pressuriser safety valve.

4.0 SECONDARY CIRCUIT SAFETY VALVES

4.1 Main Steam System Description

The Sizewell 'B' Main Steam System comprises four main steam lines connecting the secondary side of the four steam generators to a common manifold feeding two steam turbines.

Each main steam line incorporates a power operated relief valve which is used to limit system pressure fluctuations during normal operation of the plant, a main steam isolation valve to interrupt the flow of steam from the steam generator, and five main steam safety valves (MSSV's), which provide the overpressure protection of the secondary circuit.

The MSSV's are conventional spring loaded safety valves similar to those used for steam relief on conventional boilers. The five MSSV's on each steam line have set pressures staggered between 82.7 bar and 85.4 bar to minimise unnecessary multiple MSSV operation in response to a pressure transient.

4.2 Main Steam Safety Valve Testing Requirements

The conventional nature of the MSSV and the fact that the valve is required only to relieve steam gives some confidence in the general operability of the valves. However two issues require attention.

a) Valve Settings

The test facilities necessary to carry out full flow tests on large steam safety valves are rarely available to valve suppliers on a production testing basis and, for safety reasons, full flow testing of MSSV's installed on a PWR steam line is unacceptable. Valves are therefore set by manufacturers to achieve specified values of blowdown and accumulation using a generic setting which may be derived from full flow testing of a single valve or from scale model testing.

Overseas operational experience has suggested that valve suppliers do not have sufficient information on the characteristics of large steam safety valves to enable them to define settings which achieve the values of accumulation and blowdown normally required. The CEGB therefore considered it prudent to confirm that candidate MSSV's could meet performance requirements before the supply contract was placed.

b) In-Service testing

The in-service testing of the MSSV must be carried out against the following constraints:

Insitu full flow testing is unacceptable because the quantity of steam necessary to achieve full discharge can only be produced with the reactor at full power. Testing under these conditions is prejudicial to nuclear safety. On the other hand, in view of the size and number of the MSSV's in the plant, offsite testing is impracticable.

The use of some form of assist device for insitu testing at reduced pressure provides a practical solution to these problems; it was considered necessary to confirm the validity of such methods.

4.3 MSSV Test Programme

4.3.1 Description

In order to address the above concerns the Main Steam Safety Valve Test Programme was commissioned. A full size MSSV from each of the potential Sizewell 'B' MSSV suppliers was tested at full system pressure and temperature on the Siemens Kraftwerk Union Large Valve Test Facility at Karlstein, West Germany, which is designed to reproduce PWR main steam system conditions for the full scale testing of large steam line valves.

One objective of the programme was to determine whether an empirical relationship could be established between valve performance and control ring settings by which the settings needed to meet Sizewell 'B' performance requirements could be predicted for the 20 Sizewell MSSV's, thereby obviating the need for full flow production testing.

It was envisaged that any such relationship would be influenced by spring stiffness and compression which would vary through the valve population. A means by which the relationship could be adjusted to take account of these variables was therefore required.

It was concluded that a parametric study capable of producing a fully quantitative model of valve behaviour would entail an impracticably large number of tests. The first phase of testing was therefore limited to a feasibility study, to assess whether the candidate valves would give sufficiently consistent and predictable performance to warrant the development of a more refined model.

To achieve this objective, a test matrix was developed, which included tests at three settings of each control ring. Two of the candidate valves had two control rings – a nozzle ring and a guide ring, (see Fig 3) one design had only a guide ring. For the two ring valves, one control ring was maintained at the reference (as supplied) setting while the other ring was moved through a range of settings defined by the supplier to achieve nominal blowdown values of 5, 8 and 10%. The tests were repeated with increased spring compression and with a spring of different spring rate. Other parameters varied in the programme were inlet pressure ramp rate and steam quality.

4.3.2 Test Results

There follows an overview of the principle findings of the test programme.

a)   General

Each of the candidate valves was subjected to about 30 tests at full pressure temperature and flow. In all cases the valves opened on demand and reseated, although the values of accummulation and blowdown specified by the ASME code were not always achieved.

During the sequence of full pressure tests, over twenty reduced pressure tests were carried out on each valve, using several commercially available assist devices which were shown to give an efficient and acceptably accurate measure of set pressure.

b)   Relationship between performance and settings.

Only one of the candidate valves, valve A, showed a pronounced trend in the relationship between performance and control ring settings. Full lift and reseating pressures plotted as a function of nozzle ring and guide ring settings for valve A are shown in figure 2 (Note: actual pressures are shown rather than accumulation and blowdown so that the effect of set pressure scatter is eliminated from the characteristic).

From fig 2A it can be seen that both full lift and reseating pressures increase as the nozzle ring is moved downwards i.e away from the valve disc. This trend would be expected since the increase in the area of the flow annulus between guide and nozzle rings causes a reduced exit pressure in the region and therefore a reduction in the fluid force acting on the disc. Conversely, the fluid forces tending to cause valve lift are increased by downward movement of the guide ring, producing a decrease in both full lift and reseating pressure (See Fig 2B).

The results did not show so pronounced a trend in the relationship between performance and settings for the other test valves.

The accumulation and blowdown specified for the test valves were three percent and five percent respectively. The results showed that control ring settings which produce low values of accumulation produce high values of blowdown and vice versa and, as a result, the range of setting combinations likely to achieve the specified values is small. The results also imply that the use of springs of marginally higher spring rate (and within normal tolerances) would further reduce this range. Given the additional uncertainty in the values which arises when scatter of results is taken into account, it was concluded that setting of the twenty Sizewell MSSV's to meet the performance requirements specified for the test valves could not be achieved, as originally intended, by means of a valve model.

In the light of the performance of the test valves, the main steam system requirements for blowdown and accumulation were reviewed and blowdown of eight percent for valves at the highest set pressures and accumulation up to six percent for the low set valves has been shown to be acceptable in terms of system requirements.

Further testing of a single contract valve is now expected to give sufficient confidence that all twenty valves can be set to meet revised performance requirements on the basis of a valve model.

SUMMARY

The programmes discussed above were established to provide early information on the safety/relief valves required for Sizewell 'B' in relation to operability and reliability over extended periods of operation, as an input to system design and the selection of components. The CEGB are also committed to providing the Nuclear Installations Inspectorate with assurance of the adequacy of the Sizewell Pressuriser Relief System and, more generally, to demonstrate the operability of key Sizewell safety and relief valves. While the programmes are not yet complete, results to date give a basis for confidence that this objective will be achieved and that Sizewell safety/relief valves will perform as required.

The pressuriser POSRV has already performed over 100 discharges under representative fluid conditions, with no detectable degradation in performance of the valve or pilot system.

The candidate MSSV's performed a total of over 150 operations. The information gained from the test programme has enabled a contract for supply of MSSV's for Sizewell to be placed in the knowledge that the valves could be set to achieve the required performance.

The programmes have already produced information about practical methods for the in service testing of Sizewell safety/relief valves and provided support for the proposals which must be submitted to the NII before such procedures can be implemented.

The programmes have promoted contact with the international community of PWR constructors and operators which has led to substantial benefit in the form of collaborative ventures and information exchange.

In conclusion therefore, the CEGB has recognised the importance of the operability of safety and relief valves on PWR plants and has entered into a substantial programme of testing in support of Sizewell 'B' and future PWR's. It is believed that the benefits of these programmes will include not only increased availability and reduced maintenance requirements, but also increased confidence in the safety of the plant.

REFERENCES

1. Singh A., Safety and Relief Valves in Light Water Reactors EPRI, NP-4306-SR Dec '85.

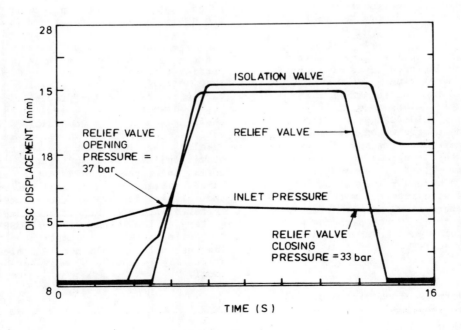

Fig 1   Typical low pressure operating characteristic for tandem pilot-operated safety relief valve

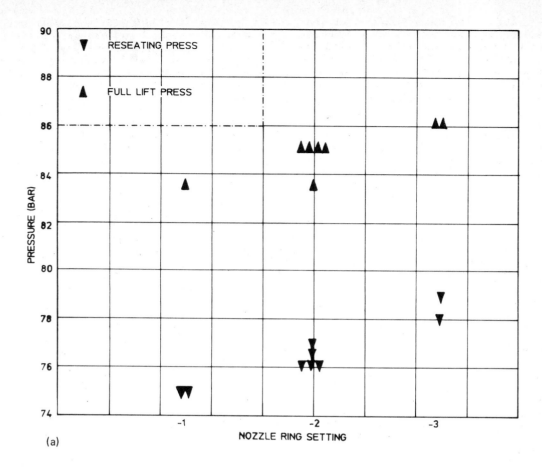

(a)

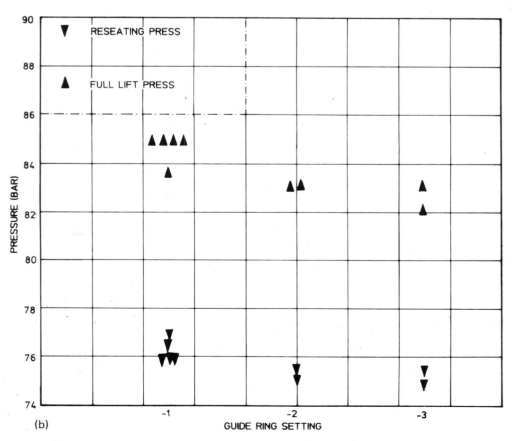

(b)

Fig 2   Valve A performance versus control ring settings (note; the numbering of control ring settings is illustrative only and does not indicate the actual settings used. A negative change of setting is towards the valve inlet)

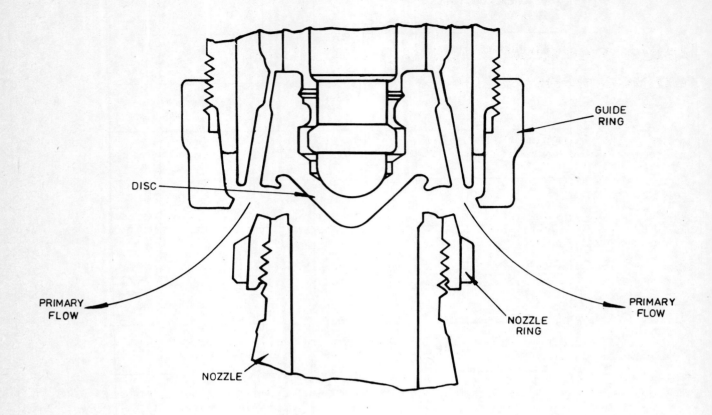

Fig 3   Illustration of typical main steam safety valve internals (two ring valve)

C388/008

Valve operability testing and stellite replacement

G P AIREY, BMet, PhD, S BRYANT, BSc, CEng, MINucE and D J W RICHARDS, BSc(Eng), ACGI
National Power—Nuclear, Marchwood Engineering Laboratories, Southampton

SYNOPSIS An extensive programme of isolation valve testing has been established at the CEGB's Marchwood Engineering Laboratories (MEL) with the objective of minimising the Sizewell 'B' valve maintenance burden and achieving optimum plant availability.

Tests are carried out in purpose built High Pressure and Low Pressure Loops in which valves are subjected to a simulated lifetime duty.

The test programme has 3 phases - candidate valve testing, contract valve testing and support of Stellite replacement activities.

Cobalt base (Stellite) hardfacings are considered one of the principal primary circuit cobalt sources and a programme is underway to qualify non-cobalt containing hardfacing alloys. ·

1 INTRODUCTION

There are of the order of 20000 valves in a pressurised water reactor (PWR) and it is essential that valve reliability be high to minimise plant outages. While the large majority of these valves have little or no nuclear safety significance, a high incidence of valve failure amongst almost 6000 stainless steel valves in systems containing radioactive fluid could make a major contribution to the plants' radiological burden through increased maintenance and associated man-rem exposure. Against this background, in 1980 the CEGB embarked on a large programme of isolation valve testing with the objectives of assessing the ability of candidate isolation valves to withstand a lifetime of cycling duty on Sizewell 'B' nuclear systems and, by providing an input to the selection of valves for Sizewell 'B', positively influencing valve reliability on the plant.

Activated cobalt in the primary circuit is the greatest contributor to the radiation exposure to operators and the CEGB have committed to reducing cobalt levels in the primary circuit. Cobalt base alloys (Stellite) are used for valve hardfacing applications and CEGB is undertaking a research and development programme to qualify non cobalt containing alloys for this application. Candidate alloys have been evaluated for weldability and wear, corrosion, erosion and cavitation resistance. It was recognised that valve reliability was not to be compromised by the use of cobalt free hardfacings and these materials are therefore to be qualified in valve tests in the MEL test facility.

This paper describes the results from the valve operability tests, Stellite replacement programme and the qualification of alternate alloys by the valve operability tests.

2 VALVE OPERABILITY TESTS

2.1 Test facilities

Facilities were constructed at CEGB's Marchwood Engineering Laboratories for the testing of stainless steel valves up to 75mm in diameter, thereby permitting the testing of over 90 per cent of the valves in Sizewell 'B' nuclear systems. The facilities comprised a High Pressure (HP) Test Loop, for the testing of primary circuit valves at a maximum pressure of 172 bar and a temperature of 343°C and a Low Pressure (LP) Test Loop for the testing of valves for chemical control, clean up and radwaste applications at pressures and temperatures up to 20 bar and 150°C respectively.

An important constituent of PWR primary circuit water chemistry is boric acid, precipitation of which, due for example to leakage, can impair valve performance, particularly when temperatures are high enough to result in the formation of the much harder boron oxide. It was therefore decided that the test loops should have the capability to reproduce PWR water chemistry conditions.

To allow test valves to be subjected to a variety of duties each test loop comprises 4 test valve positions in each of two legs (Figure 1). The test positions provide various combinations of blowdown and steady state fluid conditions depending on the computer control sequence selected.

2.2 Test specifications

The intent of the tests was to conservatively represent the duty which valves would be expected to experience on Sizewell 'B'. Each valve was therefore subjected to its 'design cyclic lifetime' of operations as defined by its technical specification. This amounted to 2000 cycles for motor and pneumatically operated valves and 4000 cycles for manually operated valves, a cycle comprising full stroke operation and return. A device was developed by MEL for the automatic actuation of manually operated valves in a manner representative of the actuation of a valve by hand.

The duty of PWR isolation valves principally comprises stroking i.e. opening and closing, in semi static fluid and for the majority of test cycles, the test valves were subjected to differential pressures up to a maximum of 3 bar. For the remainder of the test cycles the valves were required to open against significant differential pressures including blowdown to atmospheric pressure.

Leakage of fluid across the valve seat and also to atmosphere was monitored before, during and after the cycling tests and provided the major pass/fail criterion.

Also monitored during the test programmes were motor load, valve body temperatures and stem strain. Special tests were carried out to investigate reduced voltage operation and, for unidirectional valves, reverse pressure operation.

2.3 Test valve selection

It was realised at the outset of the programme that it would not be possible to test valves for all Sizewell 'B' applications and criteria were established for the selection of test valves for the programme. Priority was given to the testing of valves which would be present in large numbers in the plant, those which were safety related and those in systems containing radioactive fluids.

It was necessary to establish a commercially acceptable number of potential suppliers for all Sizewell valves and efforts were made to maximise the number of potential suppliers participating in the programme.

Since the first tests in 1982 approximately 190 valves of 85 different designs from 27 manufacturers have been tested. These have included motor, pneumatic and manually operated gate, globe, plug, ball and diaphragm valves as well as check valves ranging in pressure rating from 150lb to 2500lb and size from 20mm to 80mm.

2.4 Test results

The results of each valve test have been formally reported to the Sizewell 'B' Project Management Team and its principal contractors responsible for valve procurement and to the suppliers of the test valves who, in the event of shortcomings in their valve, have been invited to resubmit an appropriately modified valve for retesting. A total of 120 valves have been found to be acceptable after testing including approximately 30 valves which were resubmitted and found acceptable following retesting.

A number of recurrent problems have been highlighted by the test program: Seat leakage is the predominant failure mode of both gate and globe valves and, in general, increased as the tests progressed.

Excessive gland leakage is also a common problem on valves with packed glands. Improved gland performance was obtained by minimising the number of packing rings above the lantern ring thereby increasing the load transmitted to the bottom set of packing. The use of live loaded packed glands is being considered by the Project in the light of the improved performance obtained in the MEL tests with this type of gland design. (Live loading comprises a number of Belleville washers interposed between the gland bridge and packing thereby increasing the compressibility of the loaded gland). A drawback of live loading is the associated increase in stem friction load. It should be noted that boron was not found to play a significant part in the gland failures encountered in the test programme.

Consistent failures of packless metal diaphragms made this type of seal unacceptable, but metal bellows seals were generally satisfactory.

Stem galling, actuator lubrication and motor actuator adjustment problems were significant contributors to valve failures. Some cases of poor design and manufacture of internal guidance have resulted in galling and consequential gland and seat leakage. The principal causes of failure amongst soft seat valves was excessive seat leakage in ball valves and diaphragm rupture in elastomer diaphragm valves.

Of particular relevance to this paper however is the performance of sealing faces. The need for proven hardfacings has dictated a preference for cobalt base alloys (Stellite) on Sizewell 'B' valves and therefore its almost exclusive use on the valves tested. In general, the performance of Stellite has been good.

3 STELLITE REPLACEMENT PROGRAMME

3.1 Programme

The stellite replacement programme is proceeding in two phases. The initial phase of the programme, described in this section, established the weldability of the alternate alloys and evaluated their wear, erosion, corrosion and cavitation resistance. Based on the results of the first phase of the programme prime candidate alternate alloys are being qualified in the MEL valve operability test rig as described in Section 4.

The materials to be evaluated and the test conditions were selected based on a survey of overseas cobalt (Stellite) replacement programmes and a review of valve functions and operating conditions. Stellite replacement programmes in France, Germany, USA and Canada, covering boiling water reactors (BWR) and CANDU systems as well as PWRs, were taken into consideration.

Three iron based (Delcrome 910, Delcrome 90, Nitronic 60) and two nickel base (Colmonoy 5, Colmonoy 84) hardfacing alloys were selected for evaluation. In addition two wrought stainless steels (Type 17-4 PH, Type 440C) were evaluated since for flow control valves a hardfacing is not considered essential and these two materials are commonly utilised. The chemical composition of the seven alloys to be evaluated, together with Stellite 6 which was included as a reference material, are given in Table 1. The heat treatment and hardness of the wrought alloys are given in Table 2. The Stellite replacement programme is being undertaken at a number of laboratories within the UK. Weld deposition development is being carried out within CEGB (MEL) and at the Welding Institute. Wear, corrosion and erosion testing is being performed at CEGB, NNC and UKAEA laboratories while the cavitation tests were done under contract at Nottingham University.

3.2 Weld deposition

The hardfacing alloys were deposited by two techniques, mechanised tungsten inert gas (Mechatig) at the Welding Institute and plasma transferred arc (PTA) at MEL. It was not possible to obtain weld consumables for both deposition processes for all of the hardfacing alloys. The weld deposition programme was carried out in two parts. Initially working parameters were established and reproducability tests were carried out on all five alloys. In the second part of the programme variations in the quality of the weld deposit arising from variations in the welding parameters were assessed on selected alloys.

Working parameters were established with a Type 304L stainless steel substrate using two layers with the Mechatig process and one with PTA. Ten deposits were prepared for each alloy and were assessed for variability in deposit geometry, dilution, hardness, chemical composition, penetration, microstructure, machinability and residual stress using a centre hole rosette strain gauge technique. Representative values are given in Table 3 for all materials deposited. There were difficulties associated with the deposition of several of the alloys but with one exception these difficulties did not influence the selection of materials for qualification in the valve operability tests. A combination of poor weldability and inferior wear resistance eliminated Colmonoy 84 from consideration.

Weld factorial studies were performed on Delcrome 910 and Colmonoy 5 deposited by the TIG process and Colmonoy 5 deposited by PTA. Welding current, travel speed and rod feed speed are the parameters to be accurately controlled in the mechanised TIG process to ensure the quality of the deposits. Powder feed rate was the parameter which had the greatest impact on deposit quality in the PTA process.

3.3 Material evaluation

The wear, corrosion, erosion and cavitation resistance of the alternate alloys have been compared to Stellite 6 in test environments representative of the primary circuit either during normal operation or shutdown. Wear properties (material loss, friction coefficient, surface appearance) have been evaluated as a function of load, test duration and cyclic frequency. Delcrome 910 had the best wear resistance (Table 4) while Delcrome 90 and Colmonoy 5 also showed comparable wear performance to Stellite 6. Of the wrought alloys Type 440C had superior wear resistance to Type 17-4 PH.

Corrosion performance, including crevice and galvanic corrosion has been evaluated at the primary coolant operating temperature (300°C) and conditions representative of plant shutdown (60°C). At the higher test temperature all materials, which were exposed to lithiated (2.2 ppm lithium), borated (1200 ppm boron) water under a hydrogen overpressure (35cc/kg), had acceptable weight losses with weight loss increasing with coolant flow across the material surface (Figure 2). At the lower test temperature samples were exposed to oxygenated borated (2000 ppm boron) water and all materials had acceptable weight losses with the exception of Colmonoy 5. There was a high weight loss with Colmonoy 5 samples, associated with selected phase attack, and this was particularly prevalent in creviced samples.

To date, erosion tests have only been carried out at reactor operating temperatures at a flow rate of 40 msec^{-1} and all materials have shown acceptable release rates. It is apparent that the material loss is by a corrosion mechanism (Figure 2) and that there is no erosion taking place under these conditions. Further tests are planned at higher flow rates and under reactor shutdown conditions.

Cavitation tests, using a Lichtarowicz cell, have been restricted to four materials at 50°C. Stellite 6 and Delcrome 910 had comparable material losses and were superior to Colmonoy 5 and Type 17-4 PH.

4   VALVE OPERABILITY TESTS WITH STELLITE ALTERNATES

The second phase of the Stellite replacement programme consists of qualifying the prime alternate alloys in valve applications. Based on the results of the first phase of the programme two materials (Delcrome 910, Colmonoy 5) were selectd for further evaluation in the valve operability test rig. The material choice was substantiated by actual or anticipated operational experience with Delcrome 910 (Germany) and Colmonoy 5 (Canada, USA, Belgium). Valves which have previously undergone operability testing with Stellite 6 hardfacings are being refurbished with the alternate alloys and subjected to the same test procedure. The initial valve operability tests are being performed on pairs of 3" gate valves supplied by 4 manufacturers. Three pairs of valves will be refurbished with Delcrome 910 and one pair with Colmonoy 5, reflecting a preference for Delcrome 910.

To date one test has been completed on one pair of valves refurbished with Delcrome 910. These valves successfully completed the operability test and the seat disc performance, as measured by seat leakage (Figure 3), was comparable to that of the valve when it contained Stellite 6 hardfacings. The difference in seat leakage rates is not a consequence of the different hardfacing materials but is within the expected scatter. A preliminary tribological examination of the Delcrome 910 seats and discs indicates that they are in excellent condition and show less wear than the equivalent Stellite 6 seats and discs.

The operability tests on the three remaining pairs of 3" gate valves will be completed in the first half of 1989 and further tests will focus on 1" gate valves and 2" globe valves.

5   DISCUSSION

The isolation valve test programme has now been underway for some 6 years and its benefit to the Project to date can be assessed. During the life of the test programme, the Project has progressed from the evaluation of valve technical specifications produced by Bechtel and Westinghouse for the US SNUPPS plants on which the Sizewell 'B' design is based, through the production of Sizewell 'B' specifications by PMT and its principal contractors, PPP and BPA, to the placement of orders for Sizewell 'B' valves.

The test programme has resulted in departures from SNUPPS practice in the selection of valves for certain duties. For example, unsatisfactory test performance of packless metal diaphragm (PMD) valves, which are used on SNUPPS radioactive circuits where a hermetic seal to atmosphere is required, has resulted in the selection of bellows sealed valves for similar Sizewell applications. Similarly, poor performance of elastomer diaphragm valves on test has resulted in a preference for ball and plug valves for low pressure clean fluid applications.

Experience from the test programme of high seat leakage at low differential pressures has led to restrictions on the use of parallel slide gate valves on Sizewell 'B', particularly for Containment Isolation duties.

A number of requirements specified in the SNUPPS documents, such as those governing gland design have been revised in the light of testing experience and all valves of size 3 ins or greater designed to ASME III will now be fitted with live loaded glands.

Consideration is also being given to elimination of gland leak off connections with the exception of those on modulating control valves.

More generally, the CEGB has, through the programme, gained familiarity with valve designs for PWR duty and entered into a dialogue with potential UK suppliers who, in turn, have gained experience of the design and manufacture of valves for PWR duty.

The Project has encouraged valve suppliers to respond positively to failures of their valves on test by formally reporting the test results and inviting modifications for retesting. This has, on many occasions led to the availability of an improved product for Sizewell 'B'. On the other hand, valve operability problems not adequately addressed by the suppliers have been taken into account during the selection of suppliers for Sizewell 'B', through a policy of restricting tender lists, where possible, to suppliers whose valves have been successfully tested.

This policy has recently been extended to maximise the number of Sizewell 'B' valves proven by testing, and if a valve is ordered for Sizewell without having been tested in a similar form as a candidate valve, a valve from the production batch must be submitted for testing. It is a measure of the success of the candidate valve testing programme in covering the Sizewell valve population at the candidate testing stage that, as yet, only four valves have been put forward for this phase of the programme.

The Stellite replacement programme has progressed to such an extent that alternate alloys are now being qualified in the MEL valve operability test rig. The first phase of the test programme demonstrated that it was possible to deposit the alternate alloys using two techniques (PTA, mechanised TIG). Material evaluation tests have identified two prime alternate alloys (Delcrome 910, Colmonoy 5) for further qualification testing. It was recognised that is would not be possible to identify a single alloy which had equal or better properties that Stellite 6 for all applications. However both alloys had comparable properties to Stellite 6 for the majority of test conditions. It should also be noted that the properties of Stellite 6 are superior to those required for many applications.

It is considered essential to qualify any alternate alloy in valve operability tests since the test specimens were deposited and the deposits evaluated under conditions not necessarily completely representative of those in valves. This applies particularly to weld deposition procedures where the valve configurations are more complex than the simple laboratory deposits. The excellent performance of the valves hardfaced with Delcrome 910 has substantiated the conclusions drawn from the laboratory evaluations.

It is generally agreed that under normal operating conditions Stellite 6 valve hardfacings contribute only small amounts of cobalt to the primary coolant. However it has always been understood that only the complete elimination of Stellite will ensure against gross release of cobalt from component failures, poor maintenance activities and chemistry transients. It was accepted that complete elimination was impractical for Sizewell 'B' and the strategy was therefore to focus on those valves likely to release cobalt into the primary circuit because of their location in the circuit and mode of operation.

Flow control valves in the CVCS system have been identified as a prime candidate for Stellite replacement. This conclusion was based on the examination of valves removed from operating plants which had contributed significant amounts of cobalt to the primary circuit due to erosion. It is also known that wrought stainless steels rather than Stellite hardfacings were used in these valves in a majority of plants in the USA, as was the case in France. At an early stage PMT sought to eliminate Stellite from these valves. As a result Sizewell 'B' primary circuit flow control valves including valves, which as a result of their duty are likely to be the greatest contributor of cobalt in this category, will be manufactured with stainless steel seats and discs.

Hardfacings are generally considered necessary for isolation valves and therefore a qualified alternate alloy is needed before Stellite can be eliminated. The PMT strategy is that alternate hardfacing alloys will be qualified by undergoing valve operability tests in the MEL valve test facility. This programme is well advanced and the first valves have been tested. A further review of the technical specification may be possible by the end of 1989 to strengthen the procurement position to identify alternate alloys for future stations beyond Sizewell 'B'.

6.   CONCLUSIONS

(1)   A significant proportion of the isolation valves tested have successfully completed lifetime operability tests at the MEL valve test facility.

(2)   Improved valves will be supplied to Sizewell 'B' as a result of the correction by valve manufacturers of deficiencies identified in the valve test programme.

(3)   The Stellite replacement programme has identified two alternate alloys (Delcrome 910, Colmonoy 5) which are being qualified in the valve test facility.

Table 1 Nominal chemical composition of alloys evaluated

Alloy	Ni	Fe	Cr	C	Composition (wt %) Si	Mn	B	Co	N	W	Mo	Cu	Nb
Colmonoy 5	Bal	4.0	11.5	0.6	4.0	–	3.0	–	–	–	–	–	–
Colmonoy 84	Bal	2.0	24.0	1.1	2.0	–	1.2	–	–	10.0	–	–	–
Nitronic 60	8.0	Bal	17.0	<0.1	4.0	8.0	–	–	0.13	–	–	–	–
Delcrome 90	<2.0	Bal	27.0	2.75	<1.0	–	–	–	–	–	–	–	–
Delcrome 910	–	Bal	25.0	2.5	0.4	0.9	–	–	–	–	3	–	–
Stellite 6	1.5	1.5	29.0	1.1	1.25	<1	–	Bal	–	4.5	–	–	–
Type 17–4 PH	4.0	Bal	17.0	.05	–	–	–	–	–	–	–	3.2	.3
Type 440C	0.5	Bal	17.5	1.0	–	–	–	–	–	–	0.5	–	–

Table 2 Heat treatment and hardness of wrought stainless steels

Alloy	Heat Treatment	Hardness (VHN)
Type 17–4 PH (H900)	1038°C/30 min + 482°C/4hr	455
Type 17–4 PH (H1100)	1038°C/30 min + 593°C/4hr	380
Type 440C	1050°C/10 min + –80°C/2hr + 400°C/1hr	620

Table 3 Weld deposition characteristics

Alloy	Deposition	Hardness (VHN)	Dilution (%)	Bead (mm) Width	Depth	Residual Stress (N/mm^2)
Colmonoy 5	PTA	531	6.6	–	–	–500
Colmonoy 5*	PTA	524	6.6	24.9	4.3	–372
Colmonoy 84	PTA	385	9.0	24.9	4.8	–265
Delcrome 90	PTA	620	2.9	23.6	4.8	–238
Nitronic 60	PTA	217	6.5	23.8	4.3	–81
Stellite 6	PTA	434	4.0	24.4	4.4	–102
Colmonoy 5	TIG	450	13.1	24.1	4.8	–200
Delcrome 90	TIG	547	15.0	23.4	5.1	–268
Delcrome 910	TIG	498	–	22.2	4.4	–
Nitronic 60	TIG	216	11.1	22.7	5.6	+80
Stellite 6	TIG	449	8.2	23.7	4.8	–153

* With pre-heat at 300°C

Table 4 Merit order of materials based on various criteria in wear tests

	Ranking By Specific Wear Rate	Ranking By Friction Co-Efficient	Ranking By Damage	Weighted Overall Ranking
1	DEL 910	PTA STELL 6	DEL 910	DEL 910
2	MOD COL 5	TIG STELL 6	PTA DEL 90	PTA STELL 6
3	TIG COL 5	17-4PH 1100F	TYPE 440C	PTA COL5
4	PTA COL 5	17-4PH 1100 vs 900F	TIG DEL 90	TIG COL 5
5	PTA STELL 6	17-4PH 900 vs 1100F	PTA COL 5	MOD COL 5
6	PTA DEL 90	TIG COL 5	MOD COL 5	PTA DEL 90
7	17-4 PH vs PTA DEL 90	PTA COL 5	TIG COL 5	TIG STELL 6
8	TYPE 440C	MOD COL 5	PTA STELL 6	TIG DEL 90
9	TIG DEL 90	TIG NIT 60	TIG STELL 6	TYPE 440C
10	TIG STELL 6	17-4PH 900F	17-4 PH vs PTA DEL 90	17-4PH 900 vs 1100F
11	17-4PH 900 vs 1100F	TIG DEL 90	17-4PH 900F	17-4PH 1100F
12	17-4PH 900F	PTA COL 84	17-4PH 900 vs 1100F	17-4PH 1100 vs 900F
13	17-4PH 1100F	DEL 910	17-4PH 1100 vs 900F	17-4 PH vs PTA DEL 90
14	17-4PH 1100 vs 900F	PTA DEL 90	17-4PH 1100F	17-4PH 900F
15	TIG NIT 60	TYPE 440C	TIG NIT 60	TIG NIT 60
16	PTA COL 84	17-4 PH vs PTA DEL 90	PTA COL 84	PTA COL 84

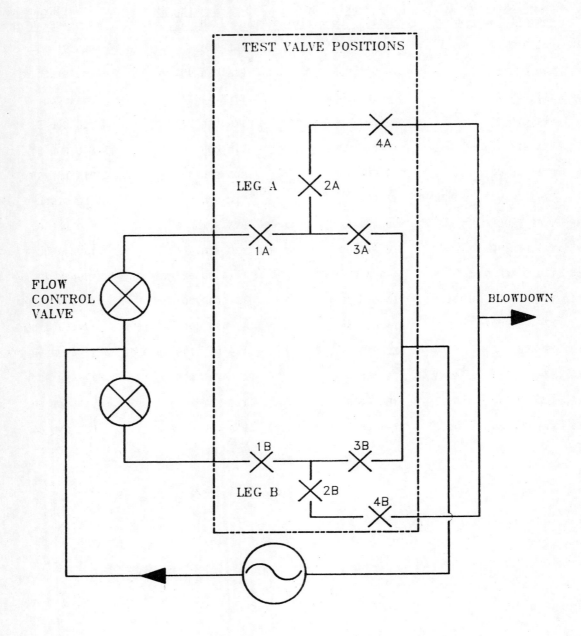

Fig 1   Rig circuit showing valve position identification, applicable to
both HP and LP loops

Corrosion/Erosion Performance
Alternative Hard-facing Materials

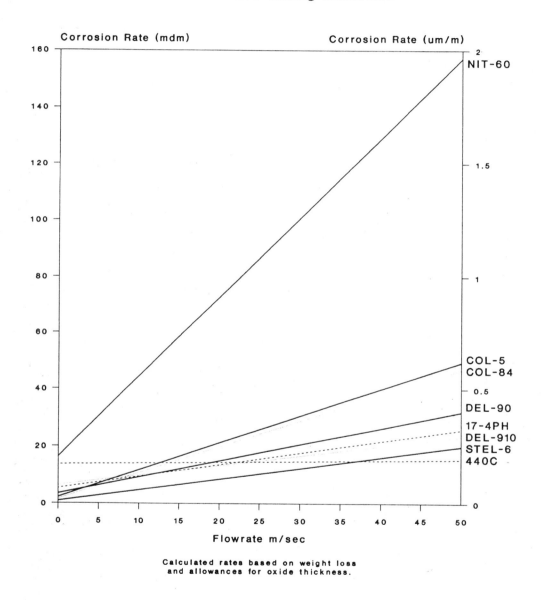

Fig 2   Corrosion rate as a function of coolant flowrate in elevated
temperature (300°C) corrosion tests

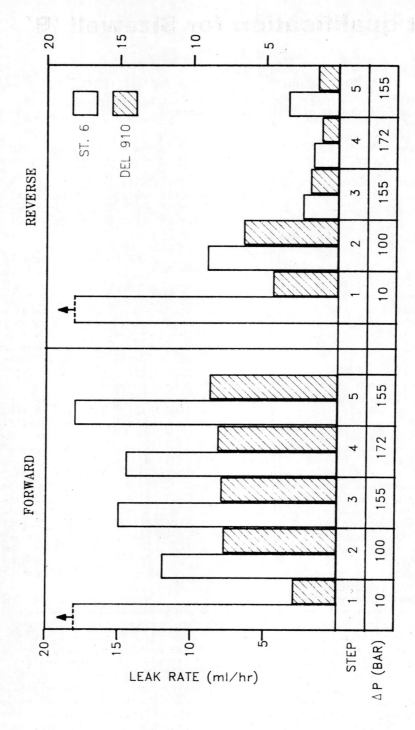

Fig 3   Seat leakage rates after operability testing for gate valves hardfaced
with Stellite 6 and Delcrome 910

Equipment qualification for Sizewell 'B'

A H FOX, BSc, CEng, MINucE
PWR Project Group, National Power Division of CEGB, Knutsford, Cheshire
J C CATLIN, BEngSc, PEng
Bechtel Limited, CEGB, Knutsford, Cheshire

SYNOPSIS   Qualification of safety classified equipment for the Sizewell 'B' PWR is required to demonstrate the adequacy of the equipment design to perform required safety functions over the range of potential design-basis event and fault conditions. The methodology to achieve this has been established and is being implemented through the equipment supply contracts.

1   INTRODUCTION

All safety classified equipment for the Sizewell 'B' PWR is required to undergo a formal process of equipment qualification (EQ) to satisfy the CEGB that it is capable of performing its specified safety function on demand and minimise the potential for common cause failures.

The potential for common cause failure of equipment arises principally from the stresses which can be imposed by seismic events and design basis faults. In particular, it is the combination of equipment ageing processes, followed by exposure to the extremes of vibration and environmental conditions during such events, which provides the most onerous challenge. It is thus necessary to demonstrate that the equipment safety functions can be realised at any time during the planned 40 years lifetime of the plant, and hence the equipment qualification programme for Sizewell 'B' is of fundamental importance in ensuring the safety of the station.

Work on developing the equipment qualification requirements for Sizewell 'B' commenced in the early 1980's and has progressed to the present time where the equipment qualification methodology is in place and testing and analysis is being carried out within many of the equipment supply contracts. This paper describes the level to which equipment qualification has been developed, is being implemented for Sizewell 'B' and the resources that have been made available to support this. It will be demonstrated that equipment qualification is now a well established discipline which is being carried out successfully for Sizewell 'B'.

2   STANDARDS AND PARAMETERS FOR QUALIFICATION

2.1   Standards

The methods which are being used to qualify safety classified equipment for Sizewell 'B' are similar to those developed for the US nuclear programme and embodied in standards published by the Institute of Electrical and Electronic Engineers (IEEE). The fundamental standards are:

IEEE Std 627 (1980) – 'Standard for Design Qualification of Safety Systems used in Nuclear Power Generating Stations'.

IEEE Std 323 (1983) – 'Qualifying Class 1E equipment for Nuclear Power Generating Stations'.

IEEE Std 344 (1975) – 'Recommended Practices for Seismic Qualification of Class 1E equipment for Nuclear Power Generating Stations'.

These standards are endorsed within the CEGB's general equipment qualification specifications (1,2) which, in addition, define specific UK requirements. Daughter standards for certain equipment items, such as IEEE Std 382 for valve actuators (3), IEEE 334 for motors (4) and IEEE Std 317 for electrical penetration assemblies (5), are also specified in the appropriate CEGB equipment specifications. Use of these and other standards, such as American National Standard ANSI B16.41 (6) for the qualification of active valve assemblies, is made wherever possible.

2.2 Qualification parameters

For safety classified equipment which is
subject to significant ageing it is necessary
to establish a qualified life. The qualified
life is defined as the period of time, prior to
the start of the design basis event or fault,
for which the specified performance can be
demonstrated for a specific set of service
conditions, and at the end of which the
equipment will function during the event or
fault. It is thus a prerequisite for equipment
qualification that environmental and seismic
boundary conditions are defined.

For each item of safety related equipment,
its location, the applicable environmental and
seismic hazard conditions, and the required
function must be specified. For Sizewell 'B'
plant areas, normal and abnormal environmental
conditions, such as temperature, pressure,
humidity, radiation etc, are available.
Bounding room-specific analyses have been
performed to determine the parameters for the
limiting design basis fault, during or
following which equipment located therein is
required to remain functional for a specified
period of time.

In general, the most onerous environmental
conditions apply within the reactor building
where a wide range of design basis faults, such
as Loss of Coolant Accidents (LOCA) or a Main
Steam Line Break (MSLB), have to be considered.
The approach adopted for the reactor building
has been to develop the qualification profiles
for temperature and pressure shown in Fig 1,
which conservatively envelop conditions during
and following any such fault. In addition,
integrated doses of 10^5 Gray for gamma and beta
radiation have been determined for the one year
post-fault period.

For external hazards, including seismic
events, it was determined that the hazard
severity for which qualification should be
demonstrated is that which has a probability of
exceedance of 10^{-4} per annum. The CEGB
intention however, to replicate Sizewell 'B'
and produce an 'all-site design', implied that
qualification would be to a somewhat greater
hazard severity. Thus, for equipment to be
seismically qualified by test, this is achieved
by basing qualification on the equivalent of a
0.4g horizontal peak ground acceleration
(pga). Qualification to this level therefore
precludes the need to requalify the equipment
for future stations. It should be noted that
the design level Safe Shutdown Earthquake
(SSE), consistent with a 10^{-4} probability of
exceedance, is 0.25g pga for Sizewell 'B'.
Although the Sizewell site is incapable of
transmitting earthquake motions significantly
in excess of 0.25g pga, testing to the
equivalent of 0.4g pga demonstrates a
significant margin in the ability of the
equipment to function under more severe but
less frequent seismic events at other sites.
The seismic response spectra for equipment
locations are provided by analysis of the
appropriate Sizewell building structures, based

on the design level 0.25g pga. Both the
'Sizewell specific' and 'all-sites' response
spectra are provided, with the latter being an
envelope of responses at hard, medium and soft
sites. The 'Sizewell specific' spectra are
applicable for equipment qualified by analysis
whilst the 'all-sites' spectra increased by
sixty per cent (equivalent to 0.4g pga) are
used for testing. Prior to testing at the SSE
level, equipment must be subjected to five
Operational Shutdown Earthquakes (OSE). The
OSE, at twenty percent of the SSE level,
accounts for fatigue effects and is the level
at which plant operation may continue. For
piping systems it is not practical to determine
response spectra at all equipment locations and
thus a required input motion (RIM) is specified
instead. This provides the input acceleration
to line-mounted equipment as a function of
frequency and is widely applied for valve
qualification.

For identical equipment that is located in
more than one area it is normal practice to
specify environmental and seismic parameters
which envelop those in all of the relevant
plant areas.

3   METHODS OF QUALIFICATION

Depending upon the required function of safety
classified equipment items, qualification for
either environmental or seismic hazards, or
both, is required. The methods by which this
can be achieved are:

(i)   type testing
(ii)   analysis
(iii) combination of the above

Operating experience could theoretically
be used as the basis for qualification, though
it would be necessary to prove that the
experience data envelops the most severe
conditions specified. Data of sufficient
quantity and quality, which includes ambient
temperatures and maintenance history, is
difficult to obtain. For this reason the CEGB
is not utilising operating experience as the
primary means for qualification of any
equipment, but only as supporting evidence to
supplement other methods of qualification.

3.1 Environmental qualification

Type testing is generally the preferred method
of environmental qualification, as it provides
the most realistic representation of the
postulated plant conditions. This method is
usually applied to complex equipment whose
characteristics cannot easily be modelled e.g.
electrical, control and instrumentation (C&I)
equipment. It is also used for equipment which
must be qualified to survive the most severe
environmental challenges found within the
reactor building. The drawback to type testing
is that it can be extremely time consuming and
is the most expensive method of achieving
qualification.

216

Qualification by analysis can be employed for equipment which can easily be modelled, by adherence to Section III of the ASME Boiler and Pressure Vessel Code for example, and thus is usually restricted to simple mechanical equipment. However, this method may be more difficult to justify than type testing, particularly where an electrical function must be demonstrated.

3.2 Seismic qualification

Safety classified equipment and non-safety classified equipment, the failure or deformation of which could potentially reduce or prevent the proper functioning of safety classified equipment, is subject to seismic qualification.

Analysis is the preferred method for qualification of equipment which can be easily modelled, for example mechanical equipment such as pumps, tanks and heat exchangers, and there is no limitation on the size of equipment which can be analysed.

Type testing, by means of a shaker table, is generally the most rigorous method for seismic qualification although remaining margins in equipment performance above the test level cannot be quantified. Testing is usually applied to complex equipment items which do not lend themselves to mathematical modelling. Very large equipment, such as a diesel generator engine, cannot be qualified by type testing, however, due to the physical limitations of available shaker tables. In such cases, testing and analysis may be used in combination, where low level vibration testing is often used to identify fundamental vibration modes and verify the analytical model. A combination of testing and analysis is also utilised where small but complex equipment such as control panel devices are fixed to larger, simple equipment. The equipment structure may be analysed and secondary response spectra developed for the control panel. The individual control and indication devices would then be qualified by shaker table tests using the secondary response spectra for their mounting locations.

3.3 Ageing considerations

The ability of equipment to perform its required safety function over a period of time may be degraded by the effects of operational (wear), environmental (irradiation, thermal) and system (vibration) processes. Thus, with the general objective of achieving a qualified life of 40 years for equipment, it is fundamental that the effects of ageing are addressed during qualification. Unless it can be otherwise justified, type testing requires that test samples are put into a condition, which simulates their expected end of qualified life state, prior to being exposed to the applicable seismic event or design basis fault conditions. To achieve this in a realistic time, accelerated age-conditioning techniques have to be applied. For example, electromechanical equipment may be operated at an accelerated cyclic rate to simulate mechanical wear and contact degradation. Arrhenius methodology is used for accelerating thermal ageing, following a detailed evaluation of the activation energies of the non-metallic materials of significance. A higher dose-rate of gamma irradiation, usually including the design basis fault dose, is applied to simulate long-term effects of radiation. Where there are known to be significant interactions, or synergisms, between the different forms of ageing, or methods used for ageing acceleration, these need to be addressed and accounted for in the qualification process.

In any test programme, attention is given to the sequence of tests performed with the requirement that the most severe sequence is used. Typically this may be,

> thermal ageing
> wear conditioning
> irradiation exposure
> seismic test
> harsh environment exposure test

with functional performance testing being carried out during and between each of these steps. It is thus apparent that a complete type test programme for seismic/environmental qualification, which can extend up to one year, requires careful coordination and a wide range of resources and facilities.

3.4 Previous qualification

It is often desirable to be able to use equipment which has been previously qualified for other nuclear power stations or purposes, since there can be substantial cost savings if new qualification testing is avoided. When previous qualification is employed, it must be demonstrated, nevertheless, that the qualification practices and levels meet the CEGB requirements, and any deviations in testing parameters must be justified. For example if the LOCA/MSLB test temperature had not exceeded the Sizewell 'B' profile, a thermal analysis may be used to show that the exposure of the equipment was nonetheless conservative. Traceability from the test specimens to the Sizewell 'B' equipment must also be provided. Any design or material changes that had occurred subsequent to the qualification testing must be fully documented and justified as not invalidating the qualification. In evaluating previous seismic tests, however, it is generally necessary only to establish that 'Sizewell specific' response spectra have been enveloped.

3.5 Mild environment qualification

Many items of plant, particularly switchgear and auxiliary systems, are located in environmental areas little different to those encountered in non-nuclear applications. In these mild environment areas, regarded as those in which the only design basis event of consequence is the safe shutdown earthquake, the equipment is not presented with any challenges due to increases in radiation, temperature, pressure, etc. For this reason the equipment can generally be qualified by relatively simple methods.

The most important aspect of mild environment qualification is to determine whether significant ageing mechanisms exist. If none are determined, it is not necessary to establish a qualified life for the equipment. Further, age-conditioning prior to any seismic testing is required only if there are significant ageing mechanisms which cannot easily be accounted for by a maintenance and surveillance programme. The methodology used to determine the approach is shown in Fig 2. The essential feature of mild environment qualification therefore is to establish a maintenance and surveillance programme, to take into account age related deterioration which could affect the ability of the equipment to perform its safety function. It may be necessary to implement regular calibration, component replacement, or refurbishment procedures to assure continued operation of the equipment up to the end of its design life and thereby effectively maintain it in the 'as new condition'.

For Sizewell 'B' a mild environment has been defined by CEGB as one in which environmental parameters do not exceed the following limits, or in which the design basis event environment is no more severe than the normal environment.

Temperature	40°C
Pressure	1.15 bar
Relative humidity	95%
Radiation	10 Gray

Where it can be demonstrated that conditions more severe than those above do not present a challenge to the equipment, then mild environment qualification may also be used. For instance, a device which operates continuously at a temperature of 50°C but is never exposed to a higher temperature can be considered to be in a mild environment. Similarly, equipment which is exposed to a radiation dose of say 1000 Gray, but for which evidence exists that its materials are not affected by such radiation levels, may be qualified using mild environment methods.

4 EQUIPMENT QUALIFICATION DEVELOPMENT PROGRAMME

In parallel with developing the requirements for qualification and to support the introduction of the PWR into the UK, the equipment qualification development programme was established by the CEGB with the principal objectives,

(i)   to establish UK testing facilities and expertise.
(ii)   to provide an understanding of qualification testing methodologies.
(iii)   to undertake preliminary and development testing of key equipment and materials.

4.1 UK test facilities

For type testing, facilities are required generally for:

(i)   Accelerated thermal ageing
(ii)   Irradiation testing, at gamma dose rates up to 5000 Gray/hour
(iii)   Seismic testing
(iv)   Harsh environment (LOCA/MSLB) tests.

Based upon surveys of the facilities available in the UK, it was readily determined there was an adequate number for thermal ageing, irradiation and seismic testing, but no suitable facilities existed for the new and special demands of harsh environment testing. To achieve and closely control a harsh environment test, for the conditions shown in Fig 1, demands unique facilities capable of providing superheated high temperature steam and operated by highly trained personnel. The CEGB has thus provided the three facilities considered necessary to meet the demands of the Sizewell 'B' programme. These facilities, employing sophisticated control and data logging features, are now fully established features at National Nuclear Corporation (NNC), Rolls Royce and Associates (RRA) and NEI International Research and Development (NEI-IRD), the HETF facility at the latter being shown in Fig 3. In general these UK test facilities have wider operating ranges than similar facilities in other countries.

To reduce the risk of test failures, ensure a high quality of work and minimise programme delays, the CEGB developed a strategy that only approved or recommended qualification test facilities and laboratories should be used by the various equipment suppliers. Given this, it was necessary to assess those facilities to be used. The exercise of approval considered the experience and technical capability of the organisation to conduct the type of testing required of it, together with a recognised quality assurance programme based upon British Standard 5882 (7). Through a process of technical questionnaires, demonstrated experience and quality audits, the following facilities/organisations have now been 'approved' by CEGB for EQ testing.

Thermal ageing
NNC, RRA, NEI-IRD - Wide range of oven sizes available.

Irradiation exposure
Isotron plc - Cobalt 60 gamma sources
UK Atomic Energy Authority - Gamma irradiation in spent fuel pond

Seismic testing

National Engineering Laboratory	) range of bi-axial
GEC Research Ltd	) and tri-axial
Imperial College/	) shaker tables
Principia Mechanica	– bi-axial shaker table

Harsh environment testing

NNC, LOKI facility – two chambers, each approx 1.7m^3

RRA, HETF-1 and 2 facilities) chambers

NEI-IRD, HETF-1) approx 4m^3

Additionally, within NNC, RRA and NEI-IRD, specialist equipment qualification teams have been established through CEGB development contracts, to provide the particular expertise necessary for EQ testing and thus enable the organisations to manage complete programmes on behalf of the CEGB or equipment contractors.

4.2 Equipment qualification methodology development

The qualification methods used for Sizewell 'B' are essentially those developed in the US, but nevertheless a general review of these was undertaken by CEGB and a number of technical uncertainties addressed. Harsh environment testing, particularly by NNC using the LOKI facility, identified the practical difficulties, dominant heat transfer processes and thermodynamic effects, which provided the opportunity to refine the specification for this testing. In particular, the spray chemistry composition and flowrate, and air requirements have been re-assessed and unambiguous test acceptance criteria established. Work has also been completed to review the effects of accelerated gamma irradiation exposure on non-metallic materials which are expected to be commonly used within safety classified equipment.

4.3 Development/evaluation testing

The earliest opportunity was taken to carry out an evaluation/development programme, particularly for harsh environment and seismic testing, using equipment provided by potential suppliers. In general, for this programme, ageing considerations (e.g. mechanical, vibration, thermal or irradiation) were omitted and formal qualification was not achieved. Nevertheless, the CEGB, equipment suppliers and the laboratories have all gained valuable experience since the pre-contract tests were carried out exercising, as far as possible, the procedures required for contract equipment testing. Feedback to the CEGB on potential problems with the testing specifications was provided, as well as an indication of equipment performance to the manufacturers. Briefly the programme included;

4.3.1 Seismic testing

The National Engineering Laboratory and GEC Research have carried out RIM testing of four-inch parallel slide valves from two suppliers to explore the ANSI B16.41 testing route.

Using a triaxial shaker table, NEL conducted multi-frequency testing of two types of storage batteries from two independent suppliers under 'Sizewell specific' and 'all sites' test conditions.

Although not strictly qualification testing, but an extension of it, fragility testing of a complete motor control centre, its various sub-assemblies and individual components was carried out by NEL in conjunction with NNC. These tests, to determine the ultimate capability of the equipment to withstand seismic excitation, ranged up to 150% of the applicable 'all-sites' response spectra.

4.3.2 Harsh environment testing

The three harsh environment facilities have carried out tests on several items of C&I equipment.

(i) Pressure transmitters from two suppliers.
(ii) Resistance temperature detector.
(iii) Limit switches from two suppliers.
(iv) Various cable seals, connectors, feedthroughs and terminations.

The tests, some involving prototype equipment, have provided valuable design information to the manufacturers. Tests on some previously qualified items, whilst not revealing serious shortcomings, nevertheless indicated potential problem areas.

4.3.3 Materials evaluation

Data to support the use of non-metallic materials is a necessity for qualification. Where suitable information is not available, from sources such as the Electrical Power Research Institute EQ Data Base to which CEGB subscribes, specific testing may be necessary. This has so far been undertaken to assess;

(i) Ageing/irradiation performance of flexible graphite-based gaskets.
(ii) Ageing/irradiation effects on the operability of elastomer diaphragm valves.
(iii) The ability of aged and irradiated coatings, for the reactor building steelwork and concrete, to withstand LOCA conditions.

5 IMPLEMENTATION OF EQ ON CONTRACTS

5.1 Preparation of enquiry specifications

All safety classified equipment for the station requires qualification and thus EQ requirements are included in the relevant equipment specifications and these detail the required safety function, the applicable faults and hazards, and the time required for the safety function to be accomplished following the event.

If the location of the equipment is not known at the time of preparing the specification, then the environmental conditions must be specified to envelop all possible locations. It is also possible that the same equipment may be provided in several contracts. In such cases, the qualification requirements for one contract are specified to cover subsequent contracts and thus avoid the need for duplicating the qualification.

5.2 Contractor's responsibilities

Except in special circumstances, responsibility for carrying out the equipment qualification rests with the contractor, with the following steps being required.

(i) A statement of compliance with the specifications and an outline EQ plan must be submitted with the tender which contains a description of the proposed qualification method and programme in sufficient detail to determine acceptability. Proposals for the maintenance of a 40 year qualified life are also required.

(ii) Following contract award, a detailed EQ plan must be submitted. This contains specific qualification methods and test procedures if applicable. Qualification plans are required to be approved before work commences to ensure that correct and justifiable procedures will be implemented and to avoid costly abortive work. Of particular interest are the proposals for age-conditioning. It is essential that ageing conditions are agreed at the outset otherwise an unacceptably short qualified life may be established, with little recourse to correct it during the test programme apart from starting again.

Where qualification is to be achieved by analysis, it is considered as part of the normal engineering process.

(iii) Upon completion of qualification activities a qualification report is submitted, providing a detailed description of the work to establish qualification, including a complete justification for all deviations and anomalies. The maintenance and surveillance programmes to support a 40 year qualified life are also presented at this time.

(iv) Before despatch of equipment to site the contractor must provide certification that the delivered equipment meets the specification requirements. This certification includes traceability of the installed equipment to the test samples.

6   STATUS OF SIZEWELL EQ PROGRAMME

Considerable progress has been made with the implementation of the Sizewell 'B' EQ programme for contract supplied equipment. Qualification programmes have been completed for several items of equipment and many others are now underway. In total it is expected that nearly 300 EQ programmes will be undertaken for the project, with approximately half of these programmes involving type testing. Some of the more illustrative and significant progress to date is discussed below.

6.1 Cables

Because a wide range of cables types and sizes from several manufacturers is required for Sizewell 'B', the qualification of cables has been undertaken by CEGB and is now essentially complete.

By 1982 it was recognised by CEGB that there was a need to develop non-polyvinyl chloride (PVC) cables, for which the toxic and smoke emissions in a fire would be considerably reduced, but which would withstand the rigours of the post-fault in-containment environments of the PWR. The CEGB established the design requirements for the cable range necessary for Sizewell 'B' and subsequently, in conjunction with the principal UK cable manufacturers, new non-PVC cable designs were produced for type testing. A wide range of tests and trials to prove the designs was undertaken with environmental qualification testing being part of the overall programme, which included fire resistance testing.

Specifically the qualification tests considered the cable materials' degradation due to temperature, irradiation, and time, mechanical damage during installation, and voltage/current withstand capability. For testing the cables were wound on to mandrels and thermal ageing was simulated, using Arrhenius methodology, based on the mean conductor temperature over a 40-year life. The specimens were then irradiated to 5×10^5 Gray in an ambient temperature of 90°C, using a gamma dose-rate not exceeding 3000 Gray/hour. For harsh environment qualification, the aged cables were exposed to the Sizewell 'B' in-containment pressure temperature profile whilst energised at rated voltage and current.

The harsh environment conditions specified for the test provided the equivalent of one year post-fault operation based upon Arrhenius methodology and accounted for conductor self-heating effects. The harsh environment tests were conducted on both aged and unaged specimens, to account for the potential that cross-linking or hardening of polymers during thermal and irradiation ageing, may benefit performance. Following harsh environment testing the cable specimens were visually inspected, unwound from their mandrels, then wound backwards on other mandrels of the same size. The cables were then subjected to insulation resistance and voltage withstand tests both in air and whilst submerged in water. Testing of the cables has been successful, the only problems being with some exposed cable cores and cores which had short lengths of insulation conservatively removed as part of the test.

6.2 ASME pump sets

The method being used by Weir Pumps Ltd to qualify the pump sets is a combination of test and analysis, although the emphasis has been on analysis. Seismic qualification used 'all-sites' spectra with the pressure retaining parts of the pump being seismically qualified by analysis through adherence to the ASME code. This analysis also covered the pump baseplate, bolting, couplings etc. It was decided however that the lubricating system was too complex to be qualified by analysis, and thus full scale shaker table tests were conducted on a complete lubricating system, including oil reservoir, pumps, pipework, filters, and valves.

Environmental qualification of the pumps was performed entirely by analysis. Operability of the pump was confirmed by calculations of lateral critical speed, wear ring clearances, bearing loads, pump shaft fatigue, and misalignment of mechanical seals, bearings, and couplings.

Seismic qualification of the 3.3 kV drive motors, provided by Laurence, Scott and Electromotors Ltd, was performed by analysis. A finite element model of the motor was created to calculate the natural frequencies, stresses, and deflections of the motor when subjected to the required combination of loads i.e. seismic, gravitational, normal operational and faulted nozzle loads. The resulting deflections and stresses were compared to allowable levels.

Environmental qualification of the drive motors was achieved by a combination of test and analysis and was based on IEEE Std 334 (4). In general, inorganic material components were evaluated against existing data but components made of organic materials were subject to lifetime evaluation testing, particular attention being given to the stator winding insulation. To establish an activation energy and qualified life for the insulation system, formettes were manufactured and exposed to cycles of elevated temperature, moisture, vibration, radiation and electrical stress. Tests were conducted on three groups of formettes at three test temperatures and were continued until the formettes failed. A qualified life was established by extrapolating a line through the mean calculated life for each test temperature at the 95% confidence limit. As the temperature intercept of this line at 40 years, taking service factors into account, was greater than the maximum operating temperature of the motor, a qualified life considerably in excess of 40 years was established.

6.3 P20 control equipment

The P20 Controbloc control equipment provides a data acquisition and control function for the Sizewell station and is being supplied by GEC Power Instrumentation and Control Ltd and CGEE Alsthom. The equipment is essentially identical to that used for the Chooz 'B' power station and was in the process of being qualified by Electricite de France (EDF) for use in the French nuclear programme. Consequently maximum use is being made of this testing programme to achieve qualification for Sizewell 'B', through the merging, as much as possible, of CEGB and EDF requirements.

The EDF qualification programme does not include a determination of qualified life but, as the P20 equipment is situated in mild environment locations, this is also not necessary for Sizewell 'B'. Ageing of the P20 equipment will be addressed by a comprehensive surveillance and maintenance document for each type of equipment supplied.

Functional testing is being undertaken at the specified limits of ambient temperature, supply voltage and humidity, and environmental tests will include mechanical vibration, rapid changes in temperature, and humidity cycling. Endurance testing will consist of operating the equipment continuously for 1000 hours whilst at maximum nominal voltage and ambient temperature.

The seismic testing procedures used by EDF are quite similar to those required by CEGB. A cubicle of representative P20 components will be subjected to broad-band random motion excitation on a biaxial shaker table. The equipment will be subjected to five tests at 50% of the SSE level prior to testing at the SSE level. Biaxial motion is to be applied in the longitudinal and vertical directions simultaneously and will then be repeated in the transverse and vertical directions. The French 'all-sites' SSE is less severe than the UK 'all-sites' SSE, but it does envelop the 'Sizewell specific' SSE and thus qualification for Sizewell 'B' will be achieved. The means by which the qualification can be extended to meet the CEGB 'all-sites' criteria is currently being assessed.

6.4 Essential diesel generator systems

The essential diesel generator sets supply power for the operation of various safety systems, used for safe shutdown of the nuclear reactor, which must remain operable following a seismic event. The scope of the equipment, and hence qualification, is such that it has been found convenient by the contractor, Mirrlees Blackstone (Stockport) Ltd, to split it into ten work packages which are further subdivided into environmental and seismic qualification.

As the diesel generators are located in a mild environment the environmental qualification lends itself to analysis. This draws on information from the manufacturer and component suppliers and material properties from recognised databases providing traceable references. The potential ageing mechanisms which require assessment include radiation, temperature, pressure, humidity, corrosion, weather, vibration, mechanical and electrical wear. In some cases it can readily be determined that age-related deterioration will not occur and thus a detailed component ageing analysis is unecessary. The object of the assessment is to identify potential weak-link components in the design and address the applicable ageing mechanisms in considerable detail.

Seismic qualification of most equipment associated with the diesel generators will be achieved by analysis. Finite element modelling techniques will be used to verify that allowable stresses in equipment and holding-down bolts are not exceeded by the combined deadweight and operational loads, and deformations will not prevent operation. For some of the equipment sub-assemblies it is more practical to carry out seismic testing than analysis. Consequently, for the radiator fan and motor assembly, diesel generator controls and instrumentation, shaker table testing will be used to demonstrate functional performance.

6.5 Pressuriser relief valves

The pilot-operated relief and protection valve systems to be fitted to the Sizewell 'B' pressuriser are being supplied by SEBIM under the CEGB/Westinghouse primary circuit contract. Such systems have been extensively developed and functionally tested by EDF for its range of PWR stations and were expected to be formally qualified by EDF against French requirements. However, as the start of the EDF qualification was delayed, the opportunity was provided to CEGB for a joint programme to be arranged via the CEGB/EDF Technical Exchange Agreement.

The differences between the EQ requirements of the organisations were resolved by adopting the upper bound conditions, where applicable, enabling a common test specification to be produced. In addition, to enable the costs of the work to be shared, a two part programme was agreed with,

(i) the comprehensive functional peformance/characterisation tests, thermal/mechanical ageing and irradiation testing being undertaken by EDF using its facilities
(ii) pressurisation and vibration ageing followed by seismic and harsh environment testing being carried out by NEI-IRD on behalf of CEGB.

Currently the work is proceeding to programme and the few anomalies which have arisen in the course of testing have been satisfactorily and jointly resolved. Although unusual, the arrangements described above have enabled CEGB to benefit directly from EDF's experience with the equipment and commence the qualification programme on an otherwise unachievable timescale.

7   CONCLUDING REMARKS

The evolution of qualification requirements, applied to safety classified equipment installed in the CEGB's nuclear power stations, is such that for Sizewell 'B' new challenges were presented and are being met by the UK nuclear industry. The EQ methods have been established and specialised testing facilities and expertise developed. This, together with the participation of equipment suppliers in the EQ development programme, has provided the basis for the contract equipment test and analysis programmes which are now being undertaken and successfully completed.

8   ACKNOWLEDGEMENTS

This paper is published with the permission of the Central Electricity Generating Board and Bechtel Ltd.

REFERENCES

(1)   CEGB. Attachment specification for environmental qualification of equipment. SXB-IP-020910X(Q)/4, 1987.

(2)   CEGB. Attachment specification for seismic qualification of equipment. SXB-IP-020900X(Q)/4, 1987.

(3)   IEEE Std 382-1985. IEEE Standard for Qualification of Safety-Related Valve Actuators.

(4)   IEEE Std 334-1974. IEEE Standard for Type Tests of Continuous Duty Class 1E Motors for Nuclear Power Generating Stations.

(5)   IEEE Std 317-1983. IEEE Standard for Electrical Penetration Assemblies in Containment Structures for Nuclear Power Generating Stations.

(6)   ANSI B16.41-1983. Functional Qualification Requirements for Power Operated Active Valve Assemblies for Nuclear Power Plants.

(7)   BS 5882 : 1983 British Standard Specification for a total quality assurance programme for nuclear installations.

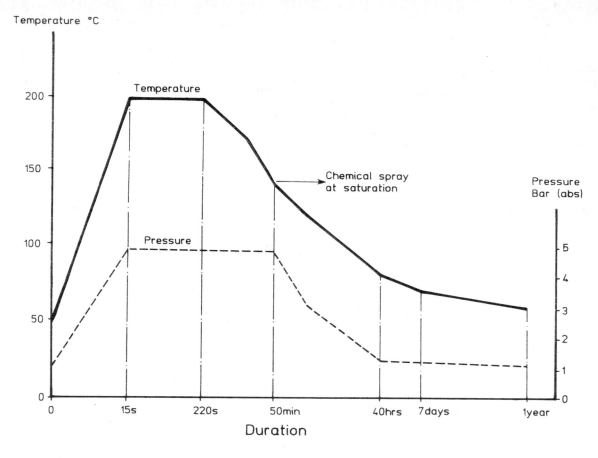

Fig 1   Temperature and pressure profiles for DBF environment simulation

Fig 3   NEI—IRD harsh environment test facility (courtesy NEI—IRD)

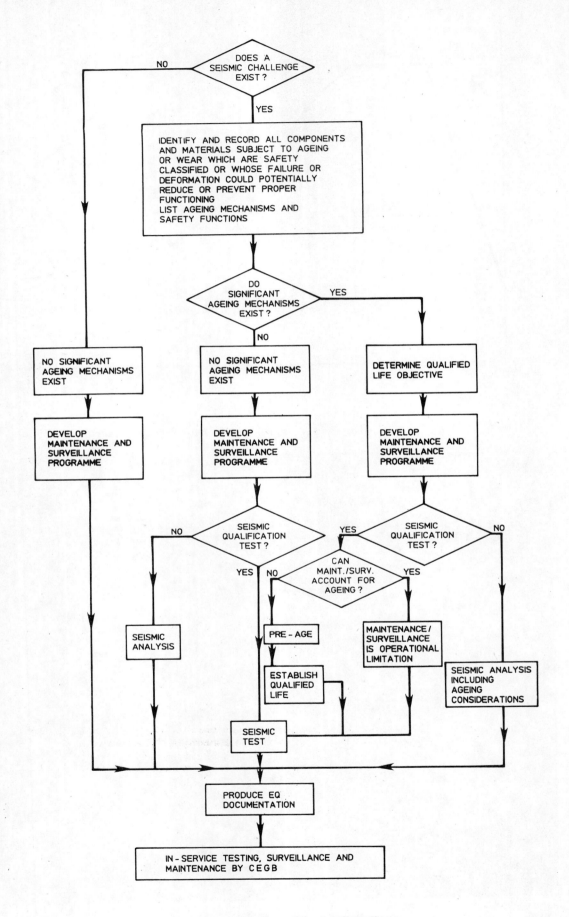

Fig 2   Mild environment qualification flow diagram

Application of seismic requirements to the Sizewell 'B' nuclear power station

D J SHEPHERD, BSc, CEng, MIMechE and **C R SMITH**, BSc
National Nuclear Corporation, Knutsford, Cheshire
R M WHITE, BSc
PWR Project Group, National Power Division of CEGB, Knutsford, Cheshire

SYNOPSIS The paper describes how seismic requirements have been applied to the design of the Sizewell 'B' nuclear power plant. Topics discussed include the characterisation of the specified Safe-Shutdown Earthquake, the analysis of the response of the main structures and the qualification of plant. Additional studies to assess the possible effects of more severe earthquakes are also described. Finally, the paper discusses how the requirements for Sizewell 'B' are being developed for future nuclear power stations in the UK.

INTRODUCTION

Historically the design of nuclear plants to withstand seismic events has been achieved through the specification of a design event, the Safe Shutdown Earthquake (SSE). The designer is required to demonstrate that the plant can be safely shut down during or following this event with a degree of confidence consistent with the overall safety targets of the power station.

For those nuclear power plants in the United Kingdom for which a seismic capability has been required, the SSE description has been based on a free-field peak ground acceleration (pga) of 0.25 g. This acceleration has been assessed to be a conservative representation of the ground motion level which will be exceeded at the site with a probability of 10 to-the-minus 4 in any year. The plants for which this SSE has been specified are the recently completed Heysham 2 and Torness stations and the Sizewell 'B' station which is presently under construction.

The determination of the ground motions which define the SSE is decribed by Irving (1), (2). These motions are supplied to the designer in terms of horizontal and vertical free-field peak ground accelerations with the frequency content described by representative accelerograms or by elastic response spectra.

This paper described the procedures being adopted for the Sizewell 'B' project by which a design is achieved which meets the safety criteria under the specified ground motion loading, and the studies which are carried out to demonstrate the adequacy of the adopted procedures.

DESIGN OBJECTIVES AND APPROACH

The objective of the seismic design process is to achieve a design which can be shut down safely and reliably during or following an SSE without exceeding permission levels of release of activity at the site boundary. Although the SSE has an annual probability of being exceeded of 10 to-the-minus 4, the overall safety objectives are such that the probability of a large uncontrolled release of activity due to a seismic event should be at least three orders of magnitude less than this. It is therefore essential that a conservative design process is employed, both to obtain a high degree of confidence that the plant will withstand the SSE and also to ensure that the plant has the capacity to survive the more onerous seismic loads that would be expected to occur with an annual probability less than that of the SSE.

The seismic design process is divided into two broad phases. The first of these concerns the analysis of the overall response of the main structures to determine the seismic loads, in terms of accelerations, response spectra and displacements, which will occur within the structures. The second phase concerns the qualification, under the loads calculated in the first phase, of structures and equipment which are required to survive the SSE.

DESIGN GROUND MOTIONS

For previous projects seismic motions were defined by two accelerograms, based on the Temblor and Parkfield 5 records from the Parkfield 1966 event, considered to be representative of UK events (1), (3). For the Sizewell 'B' PWR station the ground motion description is based on design response spectra presented in (2), for three site soil categories (hard, medium and soft). The spectrum for soft sites is used for Sizewell and is shown in Fig 1.

The response of the structures is calculated using artificially generated accelerograms whose spectra match the design spectra within required criteria defined by US Nuclear Regulatory Commission.

SELECTION OF PLANT TO BE SEISMICALLY QUALIFIED

There are two categories of plant for which a capability to withstand the SSE must be rigorously demonstrated. Plant in the first category is required to function so as to ensure that the safe shutdown objectives can be met. This category includes those structures which contain or support seismically qualified equipment. Plant in the second category comprises items which are not themselves required to function but whose failure could imperil other plant of the first category, which has a requirement to function.

In addition there is a third category of equipment for which successful operation during an earthquake is not essential to the safety case but nevertheless provides a significant contribution to safety. This third category of equipment is not subject to the rigorous qualification procedures discussed below but is assessed using experience based design guidelines or very simple equivalent static analysis procedures.

It should be noted that some plant is not qualified. Firstly, since there is no requirement to ensure that the power station continues to operates during or following the SSE, plant required for operation but not for normal shutting down does not have to be qualified. Secondly, not all plant provided to assist in shutting down is qualified. For some safety functions an extremely high reliability is achieved through diverse provisions with the specific purpose of giving protection against faults which are more frequent than the SSE. The degree of reliability required to protect against rarer events, such as earthquakes, is less and hence it may not be necessary to qualify all diverse plant. For Sizewell 'B', major items excluded are turbines, the main seawater cooling systems, certain electrical systems and the electrical transmission grid.

DERIVATION OF IN-STRUCTURE LOADS

Loads within the main structures are determined through a dynamic response analysis, referred to as a soil-structure interaction analysis, of the structure and adjacent soil. There are two types of approach to this analysis which are known as the direct and the sub-structure methods. In the direct approach the motion of the ground at depth (bedrock) is determined first. The response of the combined soil and structure to the bedrock motion is then calculated in a single step using a purpose-written computer program of which FLUSH (4) and PRESS (5) are examples. In the sub-structure approach the soil is first analysed separately to determine compliances in the form of springs and viscous dampers which represent the reaction forces imposed on the structure due to displacement and velocity distortions of the soil relative to the free-field surface motion. These springs and dampers are then added to a finite element model of the structure for the analysis of the complete system. This approach may utilise either a standard structural analysis program or a purpose-written program, e.g. CLASSI (6).

Despite the steady flow of enhancements to soil-structure interaction analysis techniques and computer programs over recent years, the fact remains that there is no single analysis approach that adequately models all effects which might have a significant influence on the response of the structures. For this reason the approach has been to divide the analysis into two parts. The first part consists of a soil-structure interaction analysis which uses the best available method, i.e. that available method which the analyst judges will best represent the response of his particular soil/structure system. Appropriate margins are then added to the calculated response to ensure that the derived floor response spectra are sufficiently conservative to cover uncertainties. In the second part of the process parametric studies are carried out to assess uncertainties and those aspects which might be considered not to be represented adequately in the first analysis, using whatever techniques are necessary. These studies are used to demonstrate that the responses calculated in the principal analysis are adequately conservative.

At the start of the Sizewell 'B' project it was recognised that some of the major structures was were highly asymmetric and thus the response, event to a unidirectional input, would be significantly three-dimensional. It was therefore considered that the sub-structure approach, incorporating representation of irregular basemat shapes and the variation of soil properties with depth, would be more suitable than the direct approach for which available programs were two-dimensional and hence not able to model real three-dimensional responses.

To calculate the compliances for the Sizewell 'B' basemats, the front end of the CLASSI program was used. For this analysis the basemat plan shape is discretised to obtain a mesh such as that shown on Fig 2 for the auxiliary and control building. Low strain soil properties which vary with depth, were obtained from the site investigation interpretation report and then adjusted to be appropriate to the strain levels to be expected in the soil during the SSE. The output from CLASSI is the spring stiffnesses and viscous damping constants for each of the six degrees of freedom of the rigid basemat. These parameters, as calculated by CLASSI, vary with the frequency of the basemat motion. Typical variation, as calculated for the auxiliary and control building, is shown on Fig 3. For the structure response analysis discussed below a single frequency-independent value is required for each parameter. The values appropriate to the first mode natural frequency of the soil-structure system in each degree of freedom were used.

The soil-structure interaction analysis was carried out using the finite element structural analysis program MSC/NASTRAN (7). The details of how this analysis was performed are given by Parris (8) who describes the beam modelling of the structures, the automation of the calculation of the beam section properties using direct digitisation from drawings and the SDRC/SUPERTAB finite element modelling system, the manner in which NASTRAN was organised to allow representation of both structural and viscous damping, and the calculation of structural response and floor response spectra.

Figure 4 shows a typical horizontal design spectrum derived from the above analysis. The spectra are biased towards low frequencies because the site is soft. Broadening of the spectra has been introduced following the response analysis because of uncertainties in the strain-reduced soil properties to which the response frequencies of the soil-structure system are sensitive. For firmer sites, the spectra would be shifted to higher frequencies, but, since soil-structure interaction would be less significant, it would not be necessary to broaden spectra to the same extent.

The use of simple beam models is generally acceptable for the calculation of the global response of the structures, particularly when the site is relatively soft, as at Sizewell, so that most deformation occurs in the soil rather than in the structures, and when the structures have a relatively regular shear wall construction so that distortion of the beam sections is minimal. However there are some structures for which simple beam models are inadequate because there are significant proportions of the overall structure mass which respond flexibly. The Sizewell 'B' auxiliary and control building is typical of these where substantial areas of floors have natural frequencies within the range which amplifies the free-field input as indicated in Fig 5. The approach adopted is to model such areas explicitly using plate or beam elements in order to remove any unnecessary conservatism arising from a decoupled approach. Even so, a significantly enhanced vertical response is found in those areas at the frequencies or resonance. Flexible areas having less significant mass, are analysed separately as discussed later.

SUPPORTING SOIL-STRUCTURES INTERACTION STUDIES

The structural response analysis described above used an approach which is known not to represent a number of soil-structure interaction effects which might be considered significant. The paragraphs below give a brief review of the most important aspects which are being addressed for Sizewell 'B' and the methods which are being employed.

In each study the analysis concentrates on a single aspect. The models in other respects (e.g. structural modelling) are simplified. Comparisons are always on like-with-like basis in that, for a single modelling aspect, the model assumed in the main response analysis is compared with more representative models while other variables are kept constant.

Frequency-dependency of soil compliances

Although the calculated compliances are frequency-dependent, a single frequency-independent value is used for the structural response analysis. This approximation is evaluated using a frequency domain analysis which can represent both cases. An internal NNC Limited program, SASSIF, has been used. Preliminary results show that the effect of the approximation is small. This is because the compliances are accurate for the lower building response modes while for higher modes, the response is less sensitive to the compliance values.

Inclined and surface waves

The main response analysis assumes that seismic waves arrive vertically at the site surface so that all points on the surface move in phase. Body waves, arriving at other angles or surface waves could lead to enhanced rocking. To analyse this effect, an additional stage is introduced into the analysis in which the motion of a rigid massless foundation is calculated. This is the same as the free-field motion in the case of the vertically incident wave. The calculated foundation motion is then input to the soil-structure interaction model. The effective filter which is applied in this stage of the analysis is dependent on the wave length of the surface motion and is thus frequency-dependent so that a frequency domain analysis is again necessary. The parameters of the filter may be approximated by the solutions for different wave types given by various papers including those by Luco and Westmann (9), Wolf (10) and Lam and Scavuzzo (11). Using these procedures it has been shown that non-vertically incident waves could lead to some increased response a higher levels in the structures. However analyses of surface wave transmission and of refraction of body waves have shown that the contribution to ground motion from other than vertically incident waves will be vary small. No additional margins have therefore been added to allow for their effects.

Adjacent structures

The response of an individual structure can be influenced by the presence of an adjacent structure. To study this effect the methods given by Wong and Luco (12) have been used in a preliminary study. Two adjacent basemats were discretised into subregions in the manner shown for a single raft in Fig 2. Coefficients which relate stresses and displacements of those subregions were then derived, from a complex stiffness matrix linking the displacements of the two rafts and the free-field motion were obtained. A two-structure response analysis was then carried out, the results showing that the influence of one structure on an adjacent structure will not be great. This preliminary study is currently being confirmed using a multi-building sub-structure approach which can include the effect of building to building interaction arising through embedment.

Embedment

In the main response analysis the effect of the embedment of the principal structures is represented by increased soil-structure interaction stiffnesses. The influence of enhanced radiation damping and reduced free-field motion at depth were neglected. Further studies will consider these effects and also review the sensitivity of the response to the effectiveness of the lateral connection between the structures and the soil.

Basemat lift-off

The normal analytical assumption that the basemat is directly coupled to the soil may be inadequate for predicting structural response if significant separation occurs when the structure rocks. A number of simple methods are available to predict whether this effect is significant. On the basis of the method proposed by Tseng and Liou (13), it has been inferred that the structural response will not be sensitive to lift-off. It is planned that this will be confirmed by a non-linear response analysis at a later date.

Non-linear soil properties

Soil-structures interaction analyses involve soil non-linearity arising from the passage of shear and compression waves through the soil (primary non-linearity) and due to enhanced strains caused by soil-structure interaction, which arise primarily at the foundation/soil interface (secondary non-linearity). For the calculation of compliances, equivalent-linear properties appropriate to the seismic stress level have been used which account for the primary non-linearity. Typically, effective shear moduli under SSE loading are found to be of the order of 50% to 60% of the low-strain values. Primary non-linearity is therefore significant. It is generally recognised that in circumstances similar to those at Sizewell the equivalent-linear approach is not adequate to predict the response of a simple soil column, and comparisons between results using equivalent-linear and non-linear methods for this type of problem have confirmed that this is indeed the case at Sizewell. However, a complete soil-structure interaction problem either includes, or effectively includes, both a deconvolution analysis to determine motion at depth and a convolution analysis to obtain surface and structure motion. It is clear that to some extent the errors introduced in the first part of the process will be cancelled by those of the second part, so that the method may still give acceptable results. A preliminary check, using a one-dimensional soil model with a lumped mass to represent the structure, has shown this to be the case. However, since this model is not strictly representative, further studies are planned to check the use of the equivalent non-linear methods and to confirm that secondary non-linearities need not be considered for the calculation of overall response.

QUALIFICATION OF STRUCTURES AND EQUIPMENT

The demonstration that structures and equipment can withstand the loading which is imposed on them during the SSE is carried out using test and analysis procedures in line with internationally accepted standards. The principles of the approaches adopted for the Sizewell 'B' plant are discussed briefly below for structures and equipment respectively.

Structures

Structures are assessed by analysis. To meet a general requirement that the plant must be licensable in its country of origin, acceptance criteria are based on US standards, viz. ASME III Division 2 for the containment shell and ACI 349-80 for other concrete structures. For steelwork, British Standards are used with allowable stresses under seismic loading chosen to be consistent with US practice. The above

requirements lead to structures responding in a generally elastic manner under SSE loads. The SSE loads have been combined with Loss Of Coolant Accident (LOCA) loads for the civil structures and RCS.

For the main structures the seismic analysis procedure has been simplified by neglecting the effects of soil-structures interaction in determining building dimensions. To derive gross loads the ground motion is applied directly to the basemat, this procedure being shown to be conservative by comparison with the global soil-structure interaction analysis at a later stage. The important effects of soil-structure interaction are an increase in damping due to seismic wave radiation damping and a reduction in natural frequencies of important modes of response. Both of these effects indicate that a fixed-base response spectrum analysis is conservative. Civil design has proceeded independently of the soil-structure interaction analysis. For the design of reinforcement this procedure is over-conservative and it is now proposed that soil-structure interaction will be taken into account for this purpose.

The same global structural models are used for the civil structure assessment as for the main soil-structure interaction analysis, excepting where details of load distribution are required for the demonstration of structural integrity, in which case models which are locally more complex may be used.

Locally flexible areas of the concrete structures and steel structures, are analysed separately using seismic floor response spectra derived in the soil-structure interaction analysis.

Equipment

Equipment is qualified to standards equivalent to those given by IEEE-344 (1975). Mechanical plant is generally qualified by analysis using acceptance criteria given by ASME for faulted loads. Elastic analysis is normally employed, with stress limits appropriate to this type of analysis, to avoid the complexity of non-linear analysis. Since these stress limits permit a degree of inelastic movement, stresses must be limited further where it is necessary to guarantee operation of moving parts. In these cases the ASME normal operating seismic limits are utilised.

Electrical equipment is normally qualified by shaker table testing. Well developed international practices, again based on IEEE-344, have been adopted for UK practice as discussed in (14). In order to demonstrate compliance that the response to events greater than the SSE is acceptable (see below), wherever practicable, testing is carried out to regional spectra normalised to a peak ground acceleration of 0.4 g.

CONSIDERATION OF EVENTS GREATER THAN THE SSE

It has been noted earlier in this paper that, although the SSE design ground motion has been estimated to have a nominal annual probability of being exceeded of 10 to-the-minus 4, the overall safety objectives for UK nuclear power stations require the probability of an active release due to seismic events to be considerably less than this. The safety case therefore depends upon the seismic design approach described in previous sections being conservative to ensure that the plant has a capability to withstand events greater than the SSE.

In recent years studies have been undertaken, mainly in the USA, to quantify the margins in the design process through seismic Probabilistic Risk Assessments (PRAs). These studies, which have the primary objective of determining the probability that seismic events will lead to release of activity, have followed two routes. firstly, there have been industry-sponsored assessments, for which a relatively simple approach has been used. Secondly, the USNRC has sponsored the development of more complex procedures under the Seismic Safety Margins Research Program. Both approaches are described in a USNRC document (15).

For the Sizewell 'B' plant a preliminary seismic PRA assessment has been carried out using the simpler approach. This gave a best-estimate probability of release of activity due to earthquake of 7.5 times 10 to-the-minus 7 per annum.

The industry-sponsored studies in the USA have been generally accepted as giving a reasonable estimate of the order of magnitude of seismic risk at the plants included in the studies. However, the confidence bounds on the results of the US studies and the Sizewell 'B' preliminary study are wide and there are a number of areas of uncertainty whose significance can be highly plant-dependent. For the Sizewell 'B' preliminary study, the problems were exacerbated by uncertainties arising from the preliminary state of the design at the time of the study (US studies have been concerned with existing plant) and doubts on the applicability to UK plant of sparse US data on equipment seismic capacities (fragility data). In addition, the seismic risk levels which have to be achieved in the UK are lower than those calculated in the US studies. UK studies will thus be more sensitive to the highly uncertain tails of the hazard and fragility probability distributions.

Work is now in hand to obtain a more accurate assessment of seismic risk. In particular this reassessment will take account of more recent design information, results from fragility tests on UK equipment now in progress and non-linear response effects discussed below. Results from fragility tests to date, which cover motor control centres plus some exploratory tests on batteries and racks, are encouraging in that UK specific equipment has been shown to have capacity to withstand events well beyond the SSE level. It is therefore confidently anticipated that the reassessed seismic risk will be significantly less than that determined in the preliminary study.

The Sizewell 'B' project was asked to provide an early demonstration that there is no sudden loss of seismic capacity for events in the range immediately beyond the SSE. Because of the considerations discussed above the preliminary PRA study was not used for this purpose. Instead, 'cliff-edge' studies were carried out to assess how the site and plant might respond to more severe events than the SSE. A nominal level of 0.35 g was considered.

An important facet of the cliff-edge studies was a site response assessment which investigated the behaviour of the Sizewell site under increasing seismic load. It was assumed that the input motion used for design was applicable at a hypothetical outcrop of the bedrock adjacent to the site but not at the site itself since the site properties were not considered in the hazard assessment which defined the SSE design level. Then as shown on Fig 6, the motion at the bedrock depth was calculated and from this, using a non-linear model and actual Sizewell soil properties, the motion at the site surface was calculated. Figure 7 shows the results in terms of site horizontal peak ground acceleration as a function of the same parameter at the outcrop. The upper straight line shows that, if linear properties were assumed, the site would amplify the response. When the non-linear properties are represented the site surface motion is much lower, the two curved lines showing site response for upper and lower bound soil properties. The lines of Fig 6 were generated assuming an artificial time-history at the outcrop which matches the broad-band design spectrum. The points on the figure show the site response for real events assumed at the outcrop and show that the results are much the same as for the broad-band input. Similar site response has been shown to have occurred in the 1979 Imperial Valley earthquake by Mohammadioun and Pecker (16). It was concluded from this study that the Sizewell site has a limited capability to transmit horizontal motion, and that there is therefore no need to enhance qualification levels to protect against events greater than SSE. However it must be noted that this demonstration is highly specific to the Sizewell site.

DISCUSSION

The procedures which are being adopted for the seismic design of the Sizewell 'B' PWR power station have been described. In addition short-term and long-term exercises aimed at showing the capacity of the plant to withstand events greater then the SSE have been summarised.

The procedures are based on state-of-the-art methods and are judged to ensure that the design is extremely safe with regard to seismic events. Nevertheless, as analysis methods and understanding of the physical processes develop, changes in the existing approaches are inevitable. Three areas where it is judged that developments might lead to a reassessment of seismic design requirements for future plants are the elimination of the unnecessary over-conservatisms which current procedures encourage in certain areas, notably pipework design, seismic PRA studies, and the definition of the input spectrum.

The difficulties in validating and carrying out non-linear response analysis for the large quantity of piping in a nuclear power station have made it generally impractical to qualify pipework other than through the ASME elastic analysis route with its inherently restrictive criteria. This in turn has led to the use of large numbers of snubbers even though the pipework could probably withstand the applied seismic load without them. Work is in progress in the USA, co-ordinated by the Electrical Power Research Institute and the Pressure Vessel Research Committee of the Welding Research Council, to develop new criteria which allow pipework to be designed more flexibly. Tests and analysis to investigate inelastic response are also in hand in the UK at the Central Electricity Generating Board's Berkeley Nuclear Laboratories (and via exchange agreements at the HDR facility in Germany), and within the NNC Limited. It is hoped that these activities will lead to less conservative pipework analysis procedures which are both relatively simple, so that savings in hardware are not lost through additional design and analysis expense, and soundly based, so that they can be justified.

Concerning seismic risk, it is considered likely that for future nuclear power stations seismic PRA assessments will be required to quantify the conservatisms in the seismic design process. Given that such studies are carried out, it is probable that they will, in the longer term, lead to some rationalisation of design requirements, focusing attention on risk-sensitive areas of the plant and permitting simpler approaches to be adopted for plant which is less critical to safety. In particular there is already clear evidence, from analysis in support of risk studies, that the present spectra are exceptionally onerous at low frequencies (e.g. see Fig 8). Hence it would be advantageous, and justified, to develop a more balanced input specification.

ACKNOWLEDGEMENTS

This paper is published with the permission of the NNC Limited and the Central Electricity Generating Board.

REFERENCES

(1) IRVING, J. Earthquake hazard. CEGB report C/JI/SD/152.0/R019, December 1982.

(2) IRVING, J. Seismic hazard in the United Kingdom. Proceedings of the Institution of Mechanical Engineers, Seminar on seismic qualification of the safety related nuclear plant and equipment, April 1984.

(3) MALLARD, D.J., IRVING, J. and CORKERTON, P.A. The assessment of seismic design criteria for nuclear power stations in England and Wales. Proceedings of the CSNI specialists meeting on anti-seismic design for nuclear installations NEA-OECD, Paris, December 1975.

(4) LYSMER, J. et al. FLUSH. A computer program for approximate 3-D analysis of soil-structure interaction problems. Report EERC 75-30, 1975.

(5) KUNAR, R.R. An explicit method in non-linear soil-structure interaction analysis Transactions of the 6th International Conference on Structural Mechanics in Reactor Technology, Paris, August 1981, Paper M7/1.

(6) ASD INTERNATIONAL, INC. CLASSI/ASD, Computer program for three-dimensional soil/multiple-foundation interaction analysis. ASD International, Inc., San Francisco, California, January 1984.

(7) MSC/NASTRAN. Macneal-Schwendler Corporation, Los Angeles. Version 65, November 1985.

(8) PARRIS, R.A. Aspects of seismic analysis using MSC/NASTRAN. Proceedings of the MSC/NASTRAN European users' conference. Munich, June 1983.

(9) LUCO, J.E. and WESTMANN, R.A. Dynamic response of circular footings. Journal of the Engineering Mechanics Division, ASCE, No. EM5, Proc., Paper 8416, October 1971, 1381-1394.

(10) WOLF, J.P. Seismic response due to travelling shear wave including soil-structure interaction with basemat uplift. Earthquake Engineering and Structural Dynamics, 1971, Vol. 5, 337-363.

(11) LAM, P.C. and SCAVUZZO, R.J. Lateral-torsional structure response from free-field ground motions. Nuclear Engineering and Design 65, 1981, 269-281.

(12) WONG, H.L. and LUCO, J.E. Dynamic response of rigid foundations of arbitrary shape. Earthquake Engineering and Structural Dynamics, 1976, Vol. 4, 579-587.

(13) TSENG, W.S. and LIOU, D.D. Simplified methods for predicting seismic basemat uplift of nuclear power plant structures. Transactions of the 6th International Conference on Structural Mechanics in Reactor Technology, Paris, August 1981, Paper K3/6.

(14) CEGB Specification IP-020900X(Q). Seismic Qualification of Equipment, Issue 4, 1987.

(15) USNRC. PRA Procedures Guide. NUREG/CR-2300, January 1983.

(16) MOHAMMADIOUN, B. and PECKER A. Low-frequency transfer of seismic energy by superficial soil deposits and soft rocks. Earthquake Engineering and Structural Dynamics, 1984, Vol. 12, 537-564.

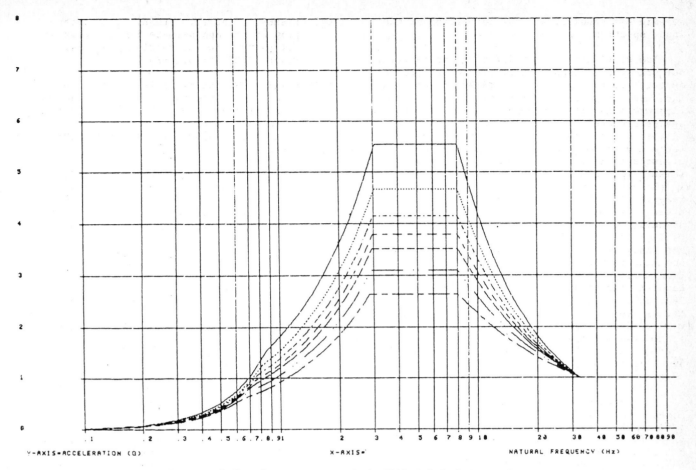

Fig 1   PML defined spectra — soft site (SA); 1, 2, 3, 4, 5, 7 + 10% damping

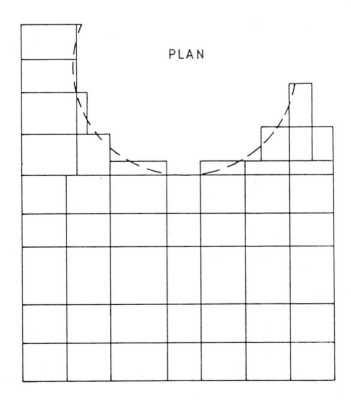

PLAN

Fig 2   Discretization of auxiliary and control building basement

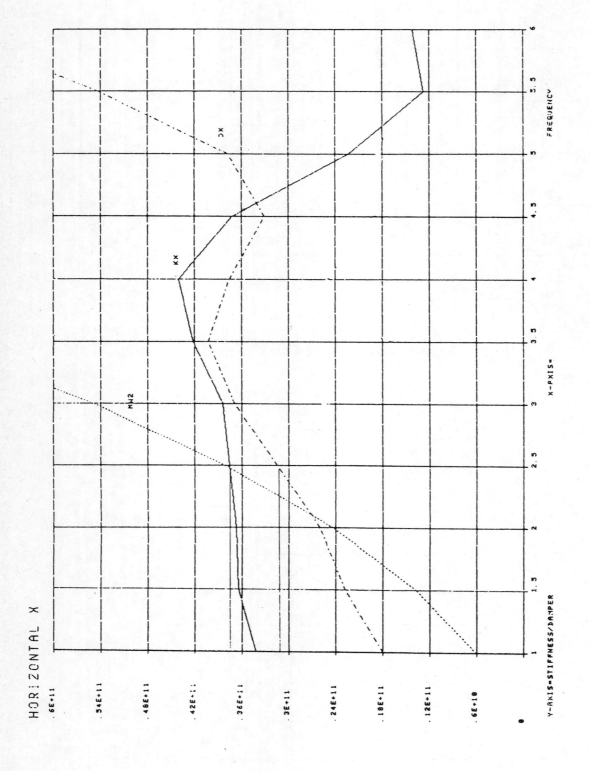

Fig 3   Auxiliary and control building compliances

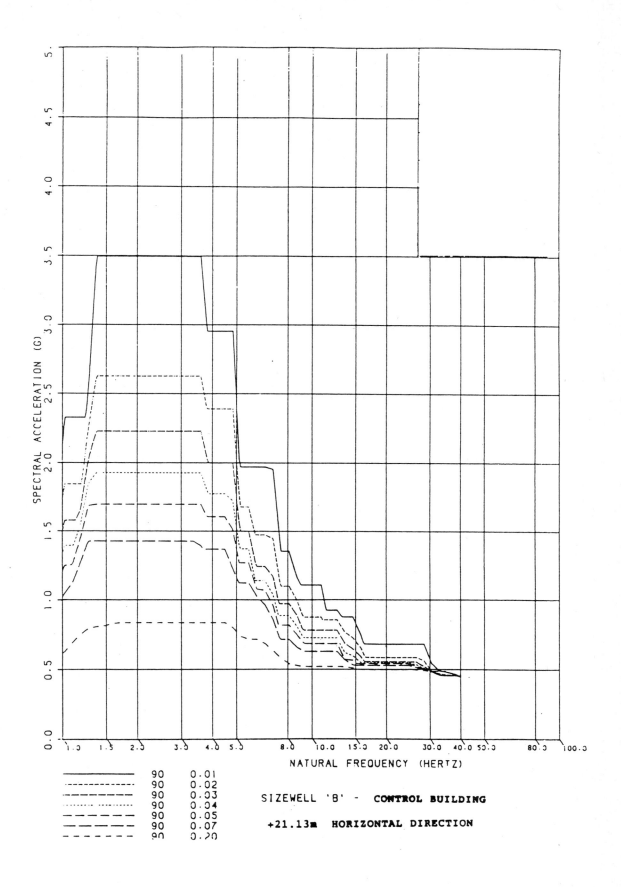

SIZEWELL 'B' - **CONTROL BUILDING**

+21.13m **HORIZONTAL DIRECTION**

——————	90	0.01
— · — · —	90	0.02
— — — —	90	0.03
·············	90	0.04
— — — —	90	0.05
— — — —	90	0.07
- - - - -	90	0.20

Fig 4   Horizontal design spectrum

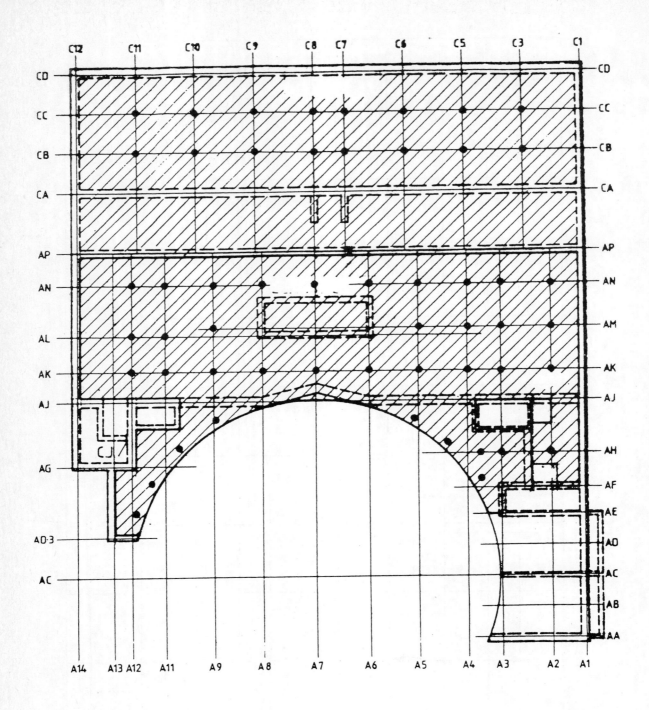

 —FLOOR AREAS FOR WHICH FLEXIBLE AREA
SPECTRA ARE APPROPRIATE.

—FOR ALL OTHER LOCATIONS RIGID AREA
SPECTRA ARE APPROPRIATE.

21·13m LEVEL

Fig 5   Sizewell 'B' auxiliary and control building location of flexible
floor spectra

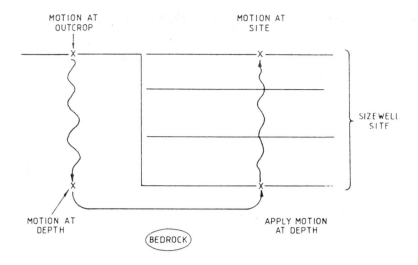

Fig 6   Model for site response analysis

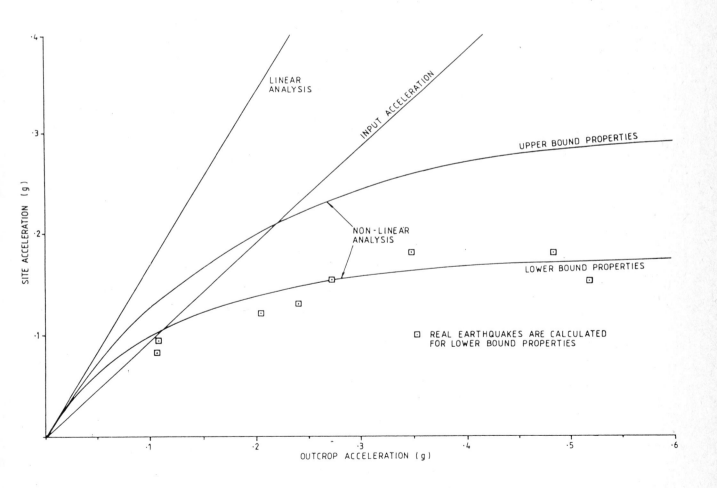

Fig 7   Site response for different levels of outcrop acceleration

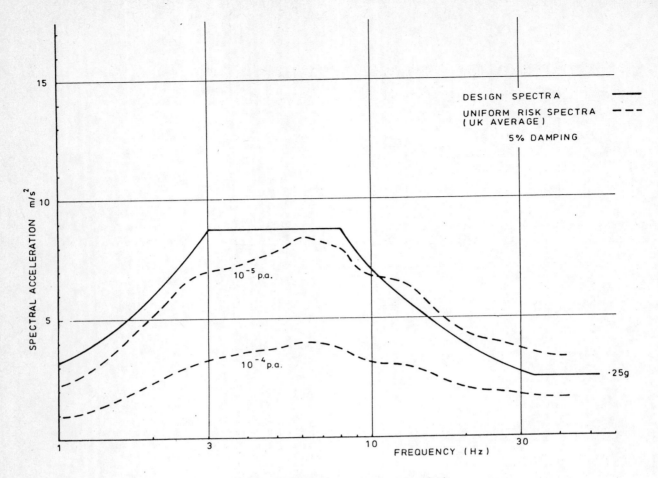

Fig 8   Ground response spectra soft site

C388/037

Development of the environmental qualification profile for Sizewell 'B'

K T ROUTLEDGE, BA and **D B UTTON**, BSc, PhD
National Nuclear Corporation, Knutsford, Cheshire

SYNOPSIS   Safeguards equipment and the associated instrumentation are
required to operate in a potentially hostile environment, following a range of
faults considered in the safety assessment of the Sizewell 'B' reactor. With
regard to pressure and temperature, the method of specifying the limiting
conditions is via the development of Environmental Qualification (EQ)
profiles. These profiles are based on the results of computer code
predictions of the heat up and pressurisation of the reactor building, and
associated buildings, following a range of faults.

The paper outlines the approach adopted for the development of the EQ profiles
for Sizewell 'B' and the way these correspond to US practise.

1.0   INTRODUCTION

To demonstrate that the potential
environmental risk to the public of
the Sizewell 'B' power station is
acceptably low, a wide range of faults
is considered in the safety case which
is presented in the Pre-Operational
Safety Report (POSR). These faults
cover a very comprehensive range of
initiating events, coupled with
assumed failures in the equipment and
instrumentation provided to safeguard
the plant. In some of the faults
considered there is a heat-up and
pressurisation of the atmosphere
surrounding the equipment and
instrumentation, which has the
potential to degrade performance.
Consideration must also be given to a
potentially adverse radiation
environment. It is a requirement of
the safety case to show that the
safety related equipment claimed to
operate, based on a probabilistic
assessment, can limit the consequences
of the fault to within defined limits,
inspite of the hostile environment.
To demonstrate this, an estimate of
pressures, temperatures (and radiation
levels) is made for the various
faults, and this information is used
to define environmental qualification
(EQ) profiles to which the equipment
must be shown to be tolerant by test.

The Sizewell 'B' reactor is based on a
U.S. design and, where appropriate,
U.S. practice has been adopted in
determining the approach to the
qualification of equipment. However,
there are a number of detailed
features of the plant which are
different, such as in the provision of
safeguards equipment, because of the
different UK licensing approach. The
design of safeguards equipment can, in
turn, affect the histories of pressure
and temperature experienced by the
equipment, and thus must be taken into
account in the specification of the
levels to which the equipment is
tested. Thus the whole basis of the
approach to the qualification has been
re-examined in the context of the
Sizewell 'B' design and this paper
outlines some of the aspects that were
considered in developing appropriate
test envelopes.

2.0   OTHER ENVELOPES

The approach to the qualification of
equipment in the USA for potentially
hostile environments was developed in
the mid to late 70s and focused in
particular on two postulated faults; a
guillotine failure of one of the main
coolant loop pipes (a large loss of
coolant accident (LOCA)) or one of the
secondary side steam pipes (a
steamline break (SLB)). These faults
result in a rapid pressurisation of
the reactor building (containment) and
high temperatures.

In some projects the assessment of qualification considered the potential pressure/temperature transients that might be calculated for those individual faults. In other projects the concept of profiles was developed which encompassed the worst features of both the transients considered, even though, realistically, the resulting conditions were more onerous than could be seen in either individual fault.

The preferred approach to qualification was to test individual pieces of equipment to specified profiles in demonstration tests. However, because plants were being built as the required standards were being determined, it was sometimes necessary to qualify equipment by a combination of testing and calculation.

It is apparent from a study of the EQ literature that there is a multitude of test envelopes for water reactor power stations. The form of the calculated temperature and pressure transients is dependent on the station characteristics and thus the variety of designs meant a variety of envelopes.

The Sizewell 'B' design is based on a Westinghouse Nuclear Steam Supply System (NSSS) with similar Balance of Plant features to the Standarised Nuclear Unit Power Plant System (SNUPPS) series of plants in the U.S. The SNUPPS plants are also some of the most recent plants to be licensed, so that they provide particularly relevant data with regard to EQ. A feature of the organisational arrangements in the U.S. is that the responsibility for defining conditions to which equipment must be qualified is split between two organisations. The vendor, in this case Westinghouse, is confined to the qualification of the NSSS and any equipment directly attached to it. All other equipment, including the containment structure itself, is qualified by the architect engineers for the plant.

The licensing requirements for equipment qualification at the time of the SNUPPS project are set out in published documents by the US Nuclear Regulatory Commission (NRC) (Ref 1 & 2). They state that it is preferable that testing is done to a combined SLB/LOCA profile but that it is acceptable if separate SLB and LOCA profiles are used. Furthermore a test to LOCA conditions alone was considered to be acceptable if it could be demonstrated by analysis that the equipment surface temperature would be no greater if subjected to a SLB profile. In the latter case, the calculational method, including the heat transfer correlations to be used, was prescribed. The transient

calculations for SNUPPS equipment, excluding the NSSS, were not used to derive a universal test envelope, but instead it was sufficient to demonstrate that their equipment was qualified to those conditions. The current licensing requirements in the US specifically pertaining to qualification of certain electrical equipment important to safety which is located in a harsh environment, are contained in 10CFR50.49 (Ref. 3). US NRC Regulations Guide 1.89 (Ref. 4) describes a method acceptable to the USNRC for complying with 10CFR50.49 based on the requirements of IEEE Std 323 (1974).

Westinghouse has specified generic envelopes to encompass the transients resulting from a spectrum of reactor designs, break sizes and locations and differing containment designs (Ref. 5). It is stated that this includes preliminary containment analyses completed by architect-engineers for Westinghouse NSSS plants committed to qualify equipment to IEEE-Std 323 (1974). They add that if the calculations are found to be conservative then the envelope can be reduced, as appropriate, to bound the final calculations. IEEE-Std 323 (1974) recommends that margins be applied to transient envelopes to account for normal variations in commercial production of components (i.e. irrespective of the analysis itself). The recommendation is translated by Westinghouse into a margin of 8ºC (15ºF) on temperature and 0.69 bar (10psi) on pressure. This procedure has resulted in the Westinghouse test envelopes which were used to qualify, for example, pressure transmitters.

3.0   REVIEW OF COMPUTER CODES AND CALCULATIONS

Computer codes are used to calculate the thermal hydraulic transients in the reactor building for severe faults. Due to the organizational arrangements discussed above there are two potential calculational methods for SNUPPS. However, in practice, any contrast is not as great as it may first seem. The architect engineer (Bechtel) use the code COPATTA (Ref. 6) for their calculations, whilst Westinghouse use COCO (Ref. 7), which is also the code used by NNC for Sizewell 'B' PCSR containment calculations. Examination of the details of the two codes reveals that they have much in common, and despite their differences, both codes have been approved for use in licensing calculations by the USNRC.

A detailed comparison of COPATTA and COCO has been made and in general, it has been found that the codes differ mainly in their detailed treatment of heat transfer between the atmosphere and the surrounding steel and concrete structures.

There are differences between the SNUPPS stations and Sizewell 'B', which will influence the predictions for the pressure and temperature transient within the containment. In particular, the SNUPPS containment volume is approximately 15% less than Sizewell 'B', the sprays are activated when the containment pressure rises to 3.07 bar (30 psig) as compared with 2.38 bar (20 psig) currently assumed for Sizewell 'B', and the safeguard provisions are different. These features, on balance, will tend to cause pressures and temperatures for SNUPPS to be higher, but in practice there is a somewhat more conservative treatment of the heat transfer model in COCO compared with COPATTA, with the result that the temperature calculations are quite similar for the two stations. Notwithstanding the differences in details of the calculations, it is possible to discern significant features which are common.

(i) LOCA

For loss of coolant accidents the containment atmosphere for most of the transient is not significantly superheated, that is, the temperature is usually within a few degrees of its saturation value. This confirms what is expected from simple physical arguments, so that it can be concluded that, for a LOCA, the atmosphere should remain effectively saturated.

(ii) SLB

For a main steam line break there is an initial period when the atmosphere is calculated to be superheated. This period is always terminated when the containment sprays are activated with the transition to saturation conditions taking up to a few minutes. The predicted rate of change depends on the details of the heat transfer model between spray and atmosphere. This transition is relatively short in qualification terms, compared with the total duration of the transient, so that its precise duration for any one transient is not a critical parameter.

For SNUPPS a whole series of SLBs were analysed, varying the break size, amongst other parameters, since it was not clear what would be the most onerous transient for EQ purposes. Energy input from the break to the containment is greatly reduced when the steam generators are calculated to empty. Steam line breaks of a smaller size than assumed for a guillotine failure with minimum safeguards equipment available give rise to peak values of temperature and pressure which occur later, since the spray will be actuated at a later time and the steam generators will take longer to empty. These breaks give rise to a family of limiting transients which define the envelope in the period 100s to 2000s.

Details of the temperature and pressure transients are in the appropriate safety reports (for SNUPPS the Formal Safety Report (FSAR), whilst for Sizewell 'B' the PCSR).

While qualification usually concentrates on large LOCAS and SLBs, it is recognised that there are a wide variety of lesser and different transients, which will input mass and energy to the containment at a lower rate than the large primary or secondary side breaks, but for which the discharge can occur over extended periods. In addition, the different (probabilistics) approach adopted in presenting the safety case in the UK leads inevitably to a greater number of transients being analysed, with a wider variety of assumptions about systems availability and the actions of the operator. Thus while envelopes, including those considered here, are dominated by LOCA and SLB transients, the transients for these other faults must be included in any assessment of the adequacy of the envelopes.

4.0   THE SIZEWELL 'B' ENVELOPES

4.1   Background

By their very nature envelopes cannot accurately represent all the features of the individual transient calculations. It follows that the creation of an envelope for equipment qualification involves judgements on the relative importance of different features, and assumptions about the ageing and degradation mechanisms of equipment. This is illustrated by the common practice of specifying only the environmental pressure and temperature without any reference either to heat transfer coefficients between the environment and the equipment or, for example, to the air content of the environment. These are clearly inadequate specifications in their own right and care needs to be taken in the qualification process to ensure that the actual detailed test conditions correspond in an appropriate manner to the desired conditions. Thus it is considered necessary to undertake analysis of qualification test conditions in order to ensure that the calculated conditions are suitably consistent with the calculated containment conditions. It is also noted that, if the thermal degradation mechanisms are understood, then reproduction of absolute temperature transients long term is not necessarily required since an appropriate theory can be used to derive equivalent ageing at other (elevated) temperatures. The Arrhenius model is commonly used to derive appropriate ageing methods.

This model assumes that the ageing mechanism is governed by a single chemical reaction (identified via an activation energy), the rate of which is dependent on temperature alone. The production of absolute temperatures may be important if it is known that the Arrhenius equation is inadequate due to, for example, phase changes or other phenomena dependent on absolute temperature changes e.g. thermal expansion. The current approach to the specification of environmental conditions is to assume that absolute values of peak temperature and pressure are important, but that lower temperatures at later times in the transient can be simulated by higher temperatures for shorter periods by using the Arrhenius relation. This is not straightforward when equipment contains several materials, each with different degradation mechanisms. In these circumstances the calculations are usually based on the material with the lowest activation energy, but it must be recognised that there is uncertainty associated with the specification of this parameter.

From the viewpoint of EQ methodology, it is important to recognise that the pressure and temperature are coupled when the atmosphere is saturated. In general, the EQ environmental atmosphere should be in the same (or more conservative) state as that calculated for the individual transients. This cannot be achieved at all times in the transient but the aim should be borne in mind when constructing an envelope. In addition the practical difficulties that might occur in attempting to achieve the conditions in an EQ test rig need to be considered.

4.2 Uncertainties

It is inevitable that there will be uncertainties associated with the development of equipment qualification test profiles. Calculation of the temperature and pressure transients within the reactor building requires assumptions about the availability and performance of engineered safeguards systems. As a general rule the transients within the reactor building will be most severe when the safeguards systems are modelled by their minimum specified performance.

The major sources of uncertainty are in the calculational methods used to predict the transients within the reactor building. Discharges of the pressurised coolant during a LOCA, or secondary side fluid due to a steam line break, are influenced by a variety of complex thermo-hydraulic phenomena and by the response of the reactor coolant system. In practice it is necessary to perform a series of sensitivity calculations to determine the most onerous set of assumptions for the calculation of the mass and energy releases into the reactor building.

The COCO code models the entire reactor building as a single volume with a vapour region and a water region. This simplification is widely recognised to have limitations since any non-uniformity of conditions due to, for example, stratification and incomplete mixing of the atmosphere, cannot be accounted for explicitly. The calculations compensate for this, and other simplifications, by deliberately incorporating conservatisms into the data and into various models such as the treatment of fluid energies and of heat transfer. Further work is ongoing to quantify the magnitude of these conservatisms.

It is noted that there is sufficient redundancy of safety related equipment that the reactor can be brought to a safe shutdown condition despite the loss of equipment adjacent to the break. In addition there is potential uncertainty in the calculated conditions due to the impact of the operator. If he switches off key safeguards systems then the calculated conditions following any specific fault can be made more onerous. No claim is made for operator action within 30 minutes of the fault being detected but, nevertheless, the potential effects of possible operator action following a range of initiating events is undergoing continuing analysis. While the effect has been assessed to be limited, some allowance for these effects has been part of the philosophy in specifying the current EQ envelope.

It is the recommended practice in the US to include margin between the calculated most severe conditions and the conditions used in testing to account for normal equipment variations and errors in measuring performance (IEEE Std 323 (1983)). This can be done by adding the assessed temperature and pressure uncertainties to the maximum calculated values from the transient analysis. Alternatively the equipment can be subjected to an additional pressure and temperature transient which reproduces the peak calculated values. It was decided to recommend the second option for Sizewell 'B'.

4.3 The Envelopes

The environmental qualification profile for Sizewell 'B', defined by the following table, is based on calculations for a spectrum of LOCA's and MSLB's, and included a series of less severe transients.

Time After Start of Fault	Absolute Pressure (Bar)	Temperature ($^{\circ}$C)
0	1.0	50
15 seconds	4.9	200
220 "	4.9	200
20 minutes	4.9	170
50 minutes	4.9	140
165 "	3.2	120
40 hours	1.6	82
7 days	1.4	71
1 year	1.2	60

Figure 1 depicts the initial 10^6 seconds of the profile. The temperature varies linearly with the logarithm of time up to 165 minutes and linearly with time thereafter.

The rate of increase of temperature and pressure in the initial 15 seconds are characteristic of large break LOCAs which are responsible for the greatest rate of mass and energy release into the reactor building during the rapid depressurisation of the reactor primary circuit. However, the peak temperature of 200°C, which corresponds to a superheated atmosphere, is required to envelope the maximum temperatures associated with a break of the main steam line from a steam generator. Limited steam line breaks give rise to peak values of temperature and pressure which occur later and are responsible for the form of the envelope up to the time when the spray is initiated and the atmosphere becomes saturated.

The peak pressure of 4.9 bar exceeds the containment design pressure of 4.46 bar and significantly exceeds the calculated pressures from the transient analysis (which are less than the design

pressure). The reason for this higher test pressure is related to the achievement of a saturated atmosphere after 50 minutes. If the test pressure is reduced to 4.46 bar, then the superheated phase would persist for approximately another 15 minutes. It was judged that there is adequate conservatism in the envelope by maintaining a superheated atmosphere for 50 minutes and that to prolong the period of superheat for an additional 15 minutes would be unnecessarily onerous.

The choice of the time at which spray is initiated is not straightforward because it is different for every transient. However, in all cases the spray removes superheat from the atmosphere and brings it to saturated conditions. An envelope which had a superheated atmosphere in the presence of a spray would be unrepresentative and also virtually impossible to achieve in practice. Accordingly the spray initiation time of 50 minutes was chosen since it marks the end of the period of superheated conditions due to the limited steam line break transients. It is also noted that the delay to initiation is a small fraction of the time period for which the spray is activated.

The remainder of the envelope is determined by the long term cooldown following a LOCA and extends for one year.

Within the design basis, the reactor containment leakage rate is specified to be less than 0.1% of its volume per day. This leakage rate is sufficiently low that, for EQ test purposes, the containment can be considered to be leak tight. It follows that it is desirable that the test chamber always contains a mass of air equal to that in the chamber at normal starting conditions.

The presence of air in the test chamber atmosphere will influence the behaviour of equipment in two ways. Condensation heat transfer coefficients are strongly dependent on the air-to-steam ratio (being greater when less air is present). These coefficients determine the thermal response of equipment during the heat-up period in the early part of the test transient. On the other hand, the presence of air can be expected to affect some of the chemical degradation processes that may occur during the test. It is judged that the requirement for the presence of air can be relaxed during the initial superheated phase of the envelope, which is of relatively short duration, if it creates excessive problems in the implementation of the envelope.

In summary, the envelope is specified based on specific Sizewell 'B' transient analysis, which covered a wide spectrum of faults. Each of the main parameters in the specification was considered in determining the adequacy of the envelope. Uncertainties in the approach and methods used were recognised, and it is judged that these uncertainties can be covered by the overall conservatism of the approach, and the specific conservatism in some aspects of the modelling.

5.0 CONCLUSIONS

Temperature and pressure profiles for the qualification of equipment have been developed on the basis of four main considerations; namely, the review of previous EQ envelopes for other LWR stations, the review of transient calculations for Sizewell 'B', the adoption of the IEEE-Std 323 (1983) recommendations for the inclusion of margins, and finally, the practical difficulties in achieving the presently required conditions in an experimental test facility.

It is concluded that the envelopes reflect the Sizewell 'B' transient calculations but at the same time are also broadly consistent with calculations for other stations. The envelopes also avoid some of the practical difficulties associated with the adoption of previous envelopes.

References

1. Interim Staff Position on Environmental Qualification of Safety-Related Electrical Equipment NUREG-0588, December 1979.

2. Standard Review Plan for the Review of Safety Analysis Reports for Nuclear Power Plants NUREG-0800 (LWR Edition), July 1981.

3. Environmental Qualification of Electrical Equipment Important to Safety for Nuclear Power Plants Code of Federal Regulations 10CFR50.49.

4. Environmental Qualification of Certain Electrical Equipment Important to Safety for Nuclear Power Plants United States Nuclear Regulatory Commission Regulations Guide 1.89, June 1984.

5. Methodology for Qualifying Westinghouse supplied NSSS Safety-Related Electrical Equipment Westinghouse WCAP 8587, January 1981.

6. Performance and Sizing of Dry Pressure Containments Bechtel BN TOP-3, October 1977.

7. Bordelon F.M. and Murphy E.T. Containment Pressure Analysis Code (COCO) Westinghouse WCAP 8326, July 1974.

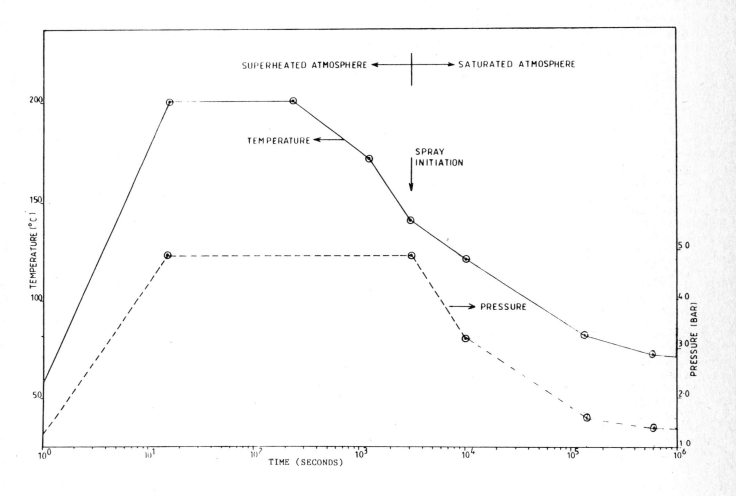

Fig 1   Temperature and pressure profiles for equipment qualification

Sizewell 'B' PWR—structural design of the primary containment

R CROWDER, BSc, ACGI, CEng, MICE
Nuclear Design Associates, Knutsford, Cheshire
D W TWIDALE, BSc, CEng, MICE
PWR Project Group, National Power Division of CEGB, Knutsford, Cheshire

SYNOPSIS:- This paper sets out to illustrate the primary containment structure resulting from a number of years of design development by the Central Electricity Generating Board's Project Management Team (PMT) and their design consultants Nuclear Design Associates (NDA). The paper traces the development of the design rules for the first U.K. PWR primary containment and highlights the main differences from other codes in common use. The principal loads and loading combinations for which the structure is designed are also defined.

A review is provided of the key static, dynamic and non linear analyses performed on the containment structure which for licensing purposes formed part of the necessary 'design report'. The essential validation procedures for such analyses are also described. The paper concludes with the influence of the analysis on the final design.

1.0 INTRODUCTION

Development of the PWR has been active in the UK since 1979. It was decided at an early stage that the UK PWR should be based upon a fully proven primary circuit plant system and to this end the Westinghouse 3425 MW (thermal) 4 loop nuclear steam supply system (NSSS) was selected. After some abortive effort to develop a UK style of PWR station, the decision was taken in 1981 to adopt the standard nuclear unit power plant system (SNUPPS) concept developed in the States by Bechtel and Westinghouse (W), with prototype plants built at Calloway (Missouri) and Wolf Creek (Kansas). SNUPPS introduced a number of features which are retained for the UK PWR, in particular the distinctive shape of the reactor containment with its hemispherical dome.

From the very early days it was a condition of using the W plant that the UK adaptation of the system should be "licensable in the country of origin". The UK licensing authority, the Nuclear Installations Inspectorate (NII) therefore required that the design and construction rules for the primary containment should be broadly based on U.S. codes with particular reference to the ASME Boiler and PV code Section III Division 2.

The Sizewell PWR primary containment is defined as the outer shell structure of the reactor building and comprises a superstructure of a prestressed concrete cylinder with hemispherical dome supported by a reinforced concrete base. The containment is designed for a life of 40 years (as are the other major structures of the PWR). It must be competent to fulfil a number of important structural functions during this timespan whilst subjected to a variety of loads and loading combinations as defined under section 5.0.

Because of the key significance of the primary circuit plant housed within the reactor building, the primary containment is arguably the most important structure of the PWR station. The containment is the last principal barrier between a possible (but highly unlikely) reactor accident and the outside environment. It is therefore essential that in the public perception, this structure should be identified as one which is subject to the highest quality of design and construction. To this end the primary containment is classified as a seismic category 1 structure which is capable of withstanding a safe shutdown earthquake (SSE). The safe shutdown earthquake definition derives from the requirement that it must be possible to safely shutdown and cool the reactor after the occurrence of this seismic event. Concurrent with the SSE, the structure must also be capable of withstanding and containing the effects of a design basis accident within.

2.0 CONTAINMENT FUNCTIONS

The principal functions of the primary containment can be set out as follows:-

2.1 To protect the reactor and primary circuit plant from external hazards.

2.2 To provide support to structures carrying the primary circuit plant, and to support the polar crane.

2.3 To withstand the pressures and temperatures generated in a design basis accident.

2.4 To restrict the release of fission products to the atmosphere to specified levels under normal operating and accident conditions.

2.5 To contain fluid discharged from the primary circuit under accident conditions.

2.6 To act as biological shielding to plant within the containment structure.

3.0 CONTAINMENT DESCRIPTION

The primary containment takes the general form depicted in Fig 1, with a prestressed concrete cylinder and dome founded on a reinforced concrete base. The cylinder shell is of 45.7 m ID with a wall thickness 1.3 m and it is surmounted by a hemispherical dome of 1.0 m thickness. The reinforced concrete base of some 3.85 m thickness is essentially unpenetrated but has a central depression to accommodate reactor instrumentation lines, and around the periphery of the underside of the base is an annular prestressing gallery. The containment is sized so that the net free volume is such as to limit the pressure rise inside to a design pressure of .345 MPa (accident pressure +10% margin).

The cylinder of the containment is where the major penetrations occur, and prestressed concrete is therefore used to preserve this part of the structure and the dome in a state essentially free from through cracks under accident conditions.

Prestress is applied in the meridional direction by 74 No. "up and over" tendons each of 11.1 MN ultimate capacity. These are anchored equi-spaced on the underside of the base, run vertically up the wall and cross the dome on "small circles" forming an orthogonal pattern. Hoop prestress is applied by 107 No. hoop tendons starting near the bottom of the cylinder wall and extending to a 45° angle up the dome. The hoop tendons are anchored on vertical buttresses of which there are 3 equi-spaced at 120°, with each tendon passing through 240° between the anchored ends.

The prestressing system employed is the Freyssinet/PSC 37 K 15, in which each tendon comprises 37 No. 15.2 mm diameter "compacted" strands. Anchorage is achieved by the use of tapered wedges with teeth to grip the strands located in similar shaped holes in a special bearing plate. The tendons are housed in mild steel (ungalvanised) ducts of spirally wound construction and 130 mm internal diameter. Corrosion protection is provided by a combination of oil and grease compounds on the various elements. This arrangement is preferred to cement grouting as it provides the opportunity to periodically inspect sample tendons for corrosion or to remove and replace them completely. It also allows load checking and load adjustment of the tendons to be carried out as required during the life of the structure.

The tendon pattern is modified as necessary to accommodate the large number of penetrations through the containment wall. The largest of these is the 6.1 m diameter equipment access hatch. Two 3.25 m diameter penetrations provide for personnel access. Numerous other smaller penetrations cater for electrical, control and instrumentation, steam and feed penetrations to the boilers, as well as penetrations for the reactor safety systems. Closures are provided to the main hatch and access penetrations of steel plate construction.

The inside surface of the primary containment is covered by a nominal 6 mm thick mild steel liner which is anchored to the structural concrete by a series of stiffener angles, though for fabrication purposes parts of this may be 12 mm thick. The liner serves as a gas-tight membrane during the life of the structure and has the secondary function of providing an internal shutter against which the concrete of the cylinder and dome can be cast. Overlying the liner on the base of the primary containment is a 600 mm layer of topping concrete.

In addition to the prestress, bonded reinforcement is provided in the walls and dome of the structure for general crack control purposes and to cope with local highly stressed zones. The bonded reinforcement unlike the liner, is also taken into account in assessing the ultimate load capability of the structure.

Though not specifically the subject of this paper, a secondary containment structure surrounds the primary containment with a nominal 3 m interspace. The objective is that in the event of a design basis accident the interspace pressure is reduced to below atmospheric so that any leakage occurring is generally from the outside in, not vice-versa. The secondary containment structure is of 0.3 m thick lightweight concrete and the dome portion of it is supported on cantilevers which project from the primary containment near the top of the cylinder wall. These cantilevers are designed as discrete elements with radial joints so that a massive hoop stiffening element at this location on the primary containment is avoided.

4.0 DOCUMENTATION

The importance of the containment function and its design complexity has led to a number of licensing, management and specialist design and contractor organisations being involved. These include:-

1) Nuclear Installations Inspectorate (NII) - Responsible for all licensing matters to Secretary of State for Energy.

2) Central Electricity Generating Board (CEGB) - Owner and Licensee of the PWR station with separate companies/departments having specific assigned responsibilities:-

. Project Management Team (PMT) - Designer/Constructor of the PWR.

. Health & Safety Dept (HSD) - Responsible for all project interfaces with the NII.

. Engineering Services Dept (ESD) - Offsite inspection

3) <u>Independant Inspection Authority (IIA)</u> - Reviews the primary containment design and witnesses construction.

4) <u>National Nuclear Corporation (NNC)</u> - Liner design consultant to PMT.

5) <u>Nuclear Design Associates (NDA)</u> - Structural design consultant to PMT.

6) <u>John Laing Construction (JLC)</u> - Main civil contractor on site.

7) <u>Cleveland Bridge and Engineering (CBE)</u> - Liner fabricator and erector.

The interaction of these various organisations is broadly as shown in Fig 2.

With such organisational complexity it was deemed necessary to have documentation defining the basic design and construction requirements together with responsibilities and inter-relationships of the various bodies involved. Furthermore this also provides a framework within which the organisational precepts of Q.A. can be satisfied.

The intent has been to derive a "stand alone" set of generic documents which would apply not only to Sizewell, but to all PWRs in the "first family". These are supplemented by further documents defining parameters specific to Sizewell. The salient documents include:-

. <u>SXB-IC-096023</u> - Design and Construction Rules for PWR Primary Containment.

This effectively is the "design bible" for the primary containment basically derived from ASME III Division 2 (Subsection CC) and has been under development for a number of years (1). It is intended to serve as the design document for all U.K. PWRs. The document comprises three parts:-

- Part 1 covers definitions, loads to be considered, loading combinations, and design allowables.

- Part 2 is the technical specification for main structural components viz concrete, prestress, reinforcement.

- Part 3 shows how ASME has been changed in arriving at the U.K. equivalent.

The principal differences between ASME and the UK D&C rules are:-

1) The definitions are more in line with the UK pre-stressed concrete pressure vessel code BS4975.

2) Again in line with BS4975, an ultimate load requirement is specified for the containment.

3) Design allowables are expressed in UK terms e.g. concrete as 28 day cube strength, and reinforcement yield for UK steel.

A most important requirement of the D&C rules is that the designer must produce a "design report" addressing effects of the salient loads and loading combinations applied to the primary containment and the consequences of credible failure of components. This report is required to be approved by the NII as part of the licensing documentation before construction commences.

. <u>SXB-IC-020051</u> - Design Specification for the Primary Containment Structure.

This document is to be read in conjunction with the D&C rules turning a U.K. generic document into one specific for Sizewell. Where loadings are referred to in general terms in the D&C rules, the design specification gives absolute values to be used for Sizewell. For each of the other sites another unique design specification will be necessary.

The design specification also contains the safety design bases and other matters referred to in the pre-construction safety report (PCSR). This latter document sets out all issues which the NII require to be addressed as a condition of granting a construction license.

. <u>SXB-IP-020906</u> - Attachment Specification for Adaptation of ASME Code Section III.

The main purpose of this document is to provide a certification route in the UK which is compatible with ASME code requirements. In broad terms ASME requirements are specific to USA and Canada and certain changes are needed to allow proven UK practises to be used. The document provides sample proformas for certificates to be signed off for various design and construction matters.

. <u>SXB-IC-020055</u> - Interface and Communication Arrangements for the Organisations Involved in the Design, Construction and Testing of the Primary Containment Structure.

This document provides the detailed interrelationship between the various bodies set out on Fig 2.

5.0 LOADS AND LOADING COMBINATIONS

The behaviour of the primary containment is required to be assessed under the action of some 20 loads as defined in Fig 3, arranged in 13 loading combinations, with appropriate load factors also given in Fig 3.

The loading combinations divide into 4 categories:-

- Construction - this warrants separate treatment because of the temporary nature of the loads, and "non-nuclear" consequences.

- Normal - These combinations represent conditions which are permanently applied to the structure or which may occur at least once in the life of the plant (e.g test conditions) and for which the plant must remain operational.

- Exceptional - These are combinations which include loads which have low probability of occurrence and for which it must be demonstrated that the reactor can be safely shut down and cooled.

- Ultimate - For purposes of defining the ultimate load capability of the primary containment, a factor (K) of 2 is applied to design pressure. The structure must be shown to be capable of carrying K x design pressure without significant structural failure. In this analysis it is assumed that the liner remains intact.

Normal loads to which the containment is subjected include dead, live, wind, plant, pre-stress and operating temperature and pressure loads:-

Prestressing loads are determined taking account of short and long term losses due to tendon relaxation and elastic shortening in the concrete, as well as creep and shrinkage. Tendon loads are based on achieving an initial jack force of 80% specified characteristic ultimate tensile strength (SCUTS) with a friction coefficient μ =0.2 and an anchor draw-in of 6 mm.

Temperature loads arise as a result of differences between internal and external ambient conditions. An onerously low temperature of -13°C is taken external to the primary containment with an internal operational temperature of 50°C. Some 16 steady state cases and 19 transient cases have been examined.

In addition to the normal loads there are a number of exceptional loads which the containment design must accommodate. Such loads are defined as having a low probability of occurrence. For Sizewell this corresponds to a probability of exceedance less than 10^{-4} per annum and specifically this applies to the occurrence of the safe shutdown earthquake, and the design basis fault (accident) pressure.

The safe shutdown earthquake (SSE) is defined as having a peak horizontal acceleration in the free field of 0.25 g and resulting loads on the structure are obtained by dynamic analysis. Response spectra appropriate to the "soft" Sizewell site are provided for input into the dynamic analysis, and vertical accelerations are taken as 2/3 of the horizontal.

The design pressure P is set at a level some 10% above the peak pressure resulting from a design basis accident. For Sizewell the design pressure is .345 MPa (50 psig). A factor of 1.15 is applied to the design pressure for structural over pressure test conditions.

No specific allowance is made in the the design of the containment to cater for aircraft impact. However an assessment has been made of the consequences of a Cessna 210 impact and model testing has shown that a 600 mm thick reinforced concrete wall can resist such an aircraft, (c.f. the minimum shell thickness of 1.0 m provided).

6.0 ANALYSIS

The behaviour of the primary containment under specified loadings has been the subject of a number of different analyses. The results of one or more of these are appropriately combined to yield specific stress or deformation behaviour for particular zones of the structure. Some thirty different analysis reports for global or local areas of the primary containment made up the design report submitted to the NII. The bulk of the structural analyses are performed using four computer codes as set out in the following table:

Scope \ Type	Elastic	Dynamic	Non-Linear
Axisymmetric	Pafec		Adina
3D	Pafec	MSC/Nastran	
Settlement	Setmod		

It should be noted that the structural analysis with the PAFEC code takes no material account of reinforcement or prestressing tendons, whilst the ADINA code does.

In establishing the design requirements of the containment the principal strength member, the prestressing, had been determined from past U.S experience. The designated number of hoop and meridional tendons is provided to impose a prestress "pressure" of 1.2 x design pressure at the mid buttress and dome apex positions where friction losses, are a maximum, and at containment late life when other losses would be at a maximum. The various elastic analyses then carried out sought to justify that with this amount of prestress, the global stress conditions in the structure would be satisfactory and that reinforcement could be included in appropriate quantities to control cracking and satisfy local stress conditions.

Dynamic Analysis

The dynamic analysis relates particularly to seismic analysis and is carried out using the code MSC/NASTRAN. The analysis model (83/87) used to derive the seismic loads which are then combined into other analyses, comprises a lumped mass beam representation of the containment base raft, the mass concrete below, and the internal structures. The shell is represented as a super element (Fig 4a). The secondary containment is represented by adding lumped mass/inertia to selected nodes of the shell.

For the purposes of structural design, the seismic analysis has been carried out assuming a fixed base. However for the stability analysis where conditions of bearing capacity failure together with the containment overturning and sliding on the supporting soil are considered, it was appropriate that soil structure interaction effects should be considered.

Although a more refined seismic analysis model is now available with the secondary containment modelled as 2D plate elements (Fig 4b), the 83/87 original model gave more onerous results, so these have been used for the final design.

Shell Analysis (Elastic)

A global elastic shell analysis has been performed using the finite element code PAFEC with an axisymmetric model as shown in Fig. (5a). This is described in more detail in (2). This model extends into the ground to a depth greater than 50 m below the containment base with the soil split into 6 discrete bands according to properties, the first band embracing the mass fill concrete on which the containment base sits. The internal structures are represented by a small number of elements at the top of the base and the base topping slab is represented by material of low modulus so as not to add unduly to the base stiffness.

The penetrations are omitted from this global model as are the effects of the secondary containment, both these matters being the subject of further local analysis. In the base, the asymmetric reactor cavity/instrumentation tunnel is necessarily simplified for the axisymmetric analysis.

Symmetrical mechanical and thermal loads are applied directly to the model. However horizontal seismic loading is applied using a first harmonic Fourier series to simulate the asymmetric loading generated by the earthquake.

The axisymmetric model was used particularly to analyse the stress situation at the wall/base junction. At this location, the wall inner face is controlled by the design basis fault load case 8a which includes a factor of 1.5 on accident pressure. The outside face, where concrete compression is critical, is controlled by structural over pressure test conditions (1.15P). Higher up the barrel, the design is controlled by the loading combination involving accident pressure (1.0P) combined with SSE. Beyond some 20m height from the base and over the containment dome current expectations are that only nominal reinforcement is required, .21% each way each face.

Assessment of local effects, for example in the stiffened area around the equipment access hatch, was achieved by 3D FE analysis. In the first instance a coarse finite element mesh

covering an arc of 180° was analysed. From this, boundary conditions for a "fine" model were derived; the comparative models being as depicted in Figs 6a and 6b. The finite element analysis on this fine mesh indicated that the design basis fault loading combination 8a principally controls the local reinforcement.

Base Analysis (Elastic)

A detailed account of this is given in (3). The effects of symmetric mechanical loads and temperature on the base were generally determined from the same global axisymmetric model as used for the shell. However to avoid over-stiffening the base, a change was made to the elements in the mass concrete zone immediately below the foundation to allow vertical transfer of load but with no hoop or flexural stiffness.

It was considered that the axisymmetric model would not suffice to assess the effects of asymmetric loads on the structure, nor provide a realistic assessment of local stresses in the reactor cavity and instrumentation tunnel, the major discontinuities in the base. Furthermore, the axisymmetric model was not capable of analysing the influence of the instrumentation tunnel on the stress situation in the adjacent base. For asymmetric loads, a 180° 3D model of the base and soil was first assessed with the shell and dome represented by 2D plate elements and with the base itself simplified to a flat circular plate (Fig 7a). Certain modelling features were included to simulate the influence of structural discontinuities. Under loading conditions which included the translational SSE loads, the effect of uplift could be assessed and the minimum contact area between the soil and base determined. The results from this model were then used to derive pressure and spring constants at the base/soil interface for asymmetric loads for use on further 3D models without soil representation. Such constants for axisymmetric loads were derived from the global axisymmetric analysis.

Two such further models of 180° extent were developed. Both included the shell wall up to approximately mid-barrel height only, but with a full representation of the prestressing gallery and instrumentation tunnel. The continuity of the barrel and associated loads above mid-height were represented by boundary conditions at the cut surface. One of the models had its axis of symmetry on the centre line of the instrumentation tunnel, Fig 7b, and the other was normal to this. These models were analysed for the load cases selected as likely to be the most onerous. In general terms, it was found that the upper and lower mats of reinforcement in the base are controlled by the loading combination of DBF + SSE as is the reinforcement in the walls of the prestressing gallery and reactor cavity. This proved to be a significantly severe loading condition yielding a base reinforcement density of around 250 kg/m^3 of concrete but with local parts of the below base structures being as high as 650 kg/m^3. Figs 8 and 9 give some idea of the resulting complexity for site construction.

Non-Linear Analysis

In order to determine the ultimate load behaviour of the primary containment and the ultimate load factor on design pressure, a non-linear analysis (materially non-linear rather than geometrically non-linear) was carried out using the code ADINA-TW. Two axisymmetric models were evolved as depicted in Fig 10. The first model (Fig 10a) had two principal concrete elements through the walls of the shell and dome and omitted the prestressing gallery. The second more refined model (Fig 10b) had twice the number of concrete elements in both the walls and the base and also included the prestressing gallery. Both models omitted significant asymmetric features of the containment such as penetrations, prestressing buttresses, the secondary containment cantilevers and the internal structures. It should be also noted that ADINA-TW modelled not only the structural concrete but contained elements representing the principal reinforcement mats and prestressing. Despite being a significant strength member, the containment liner was conservatively omitted from this analysis.

The analysis initially carried out on the simpler model indicated an ultimate structural condition determined by hoop tendon failure (the tendon having reached its defined ultimate limit of 1% strain) at approximately mid height of the cylindrical shell wall. The 1% strain figure was reached at a pressure of 0.72 MPa giving a factor of 2.09 on design pressure.

This failure is characteristic of membrane tension failure which is a ductile mode preceded by significant deformation, and is more desirable than sudden failure with little deformation associated with a shear mechanism.

Parametric studies were then carried out to determine the sensitivity of the ultimate condition to changes in a number of factors. Various fixity conditions were examined for the base and these were found not to change the ultimate load factor or the failure location. Similarly lowering the percentage of reinforcement in the base to 0.5%, also had no effect. It was of particular concern to see whether the structure had an "incipient" shear failure characteristic. To this end the model was run with levels of reduced reinforcement at the wall base junction, the most likely place for shear failure to occur. Again it was found that this change had no significant effect on the ultimate load factor or failure load location.

Finally the analysis was re-run on the refined model Fig 10b containing "probable" quantities of reinforcement and this again confirmed the ultimate load factor and location of failure. The results of the refined model analysis were also useful in establishing the build up of cracking in tensile zones and provided further justification for reinforcement disposition.

Hand calculations performed on a force balancing basis had previously shown that the quantity of prestressing material provided on the 1.2 P basis would be adequate for an ultimate load factor of 2. This result was confirmed by the ADINA analyses.

Settlement Analysis

Settlement analyses were conducted using the code SETMOD on a number of different models. Broadly SETMOD allows for a building foundation to be represented by a plate of defined stiffness sup-ported on soil. The depth of soil on the Sizewell models was taken down to some 115 m below the containment foundations and soil properties were ascribed to 7 defined bands of material. Conditions examined in the analyses included immediate settlement of the reactor base as an isolated structure, immediate settlement including the influence of adjacent foundations and long term settlement also including the effect of adjacent foundations.

As an isolated structure the reactor has an immediate average settlement of some 40 mm with hardly any tilt. The settlement is increased to around 57 mm taking account of adjacent foundations and because of the non-uniform nature of the load from these, a tilt of 17 mm is induced across the base. Taking account of consolidation effects, the total settlement of the base at the centre is increased to 115 mm and the tilt is increased to 54 mm. These settlement values, both immediate and long term are not a problem for the containment structure itself. However plant installed within the structure must be designed to accommodate the tilt, and services which connect through to adjacent buildings are designed to cope with resulting differential settlements. To service this aspect of design, additional analyses were performed to derive reactor building settlements for a number of incremental load cases representing discrete phases of the construction programme. Monitoring points have been designated in the structures so that actual settlements can be compared with predictions during the construction and commissioning period.

7.0 CODE VALIDATION

To accord with the high level of Quality Assurance ascribed to the Sizewell 'B' primary containment it was necessary to demonstrate, as far as possible, that the computer codes and modelling techniques used for the main structural analyses of the primary containment were appropriate. This has been done in part by a process of verification and in part by a process of validation. In this context, it is of note that in the United States a retrospective process of examination of the ultimate load behaviour of containments has been put in hand using physical models. This is being conducted by SANDIA Laboratories on behalf of the Nuclear Regulatory Commission (NRC) and so far has dealt with the testing of steel model containments and most recently a 1/10th scale reinforced concrete model with a hemispherical dome.

For the seismic analysis, the NASTRAN code was verified by comparing the results for a similar model of the primary containment, dynamically analysed firstly using NASTRAN and secondly PAFEC. For fixed base analysis the significant lower modal frequencies are predicted by the two codes to within 2% and the horizontal and vertical responses for these modes are within 5%. Taking account of soil structure interaction, the dominant modes are predicted within 5% and the horizontal and vertical responses agree to within 15%.

For elastic analyses carried out using the code PAFEC, a part validation, part verification process was performed some time ago. In the first instance, a PAFEC analysis was made of a containment shape with a known classical solution (a pure sphere). For purposes of further comparison, results of this analysis were also obtained using codes ASHSD2 and ANSYS. Both PAFEC and ANSYS gave results within 1% of the classical solution for the sphere shell stresses and deformations.

A containment model comprising a cylinder and torispherical dome were then analysed using the same three codes and good agreement between PAFEC and ANSYS was obtained for hoop and meridional stresses on both the inside and outside faces of the structure though ASHSD2 did not compare so well. More recently a complete containment model including a base and hemispherical dome (in fact the Sandia 1/10th reinforced concrete model) was analysed using PAFEC and ADINA-TW (elastic). Again both stress and deformation results gave good correlation with an average difference of less than 2% between the two codes.

The purpose of correlating PAFEC and ADINA-TW is that this latter code is in the process of being fully validated against physical models. In the first instance ADINA-TW has been validated against the SANDIA 1/10th scale reinforced concrete model in both the elastic and non-linear phases. This model had been instrumented and subject to internal pressurisation, and strain and deformation measurements were recorded for each pressure stage. Particularly good agreement between ADINA-TW predictions and model results were obtained at barrel mid-height where the global type failure is predicted to occur at Sizewell.

As the final piece of validation of the ADINA-TW code a 1/10th scale physical model of the actual Sizewell 'B' primary containment is being constructed at the Southall laboratories of Taywood Engineering Ltd. The philosophy behind this model is discussed in (4) and (5). It differs from the SANDIA model in that it contains prestress. All the main geometric structural features of Sizewell 'B' primary containment are included in the model, though the base is simplified to a flat slab. The prestressing tendons are individually modelled though to achieve the scaled area it is necessary to use a mix of 8 mm and 12 mm strands as model tendons. The reinforcement bars are not individually modelled, but the scale area (^{1}/100) is represented by fewer bars of larger size. Fig 11 shows the state of construction of the model with all barrel and dome reinforcement and prestressing tendons in place prior to concreting. The liner is not represented in the model as the intent is to determine the structural ultimate load rather than leakage failure. Pressure is therefore applied within the model containment via an internal rubber bag. It is intended to carry out the pressure test under ambient temperature conditions. The expected good correlation between strains/deformations predicted by the ADINA-TW analysis and model measurements will demonstrate the validity of applicability of this code to the full size structure.

8.0 CONCLUSIONS

From the foregoing the following conclusions can be drawn:-

1) Although the PWR is new in the U.K., the primary containment has been under design and development here for the past 10 years. The concept is based upon designs which have been working successfully in the U.S. for a number of years.

2) Comprehensive documentation has been evolved covering the requirements for design and construction of the primary containment. In certain instances the design requirements for the primary containment in the UK are more onerous than what is required elsewhere in the world.

3) All the principal detailed analyses of the primary containment are complete and the results have been reported to the Licensing Authority prior to construction being commenced. The analysis results are such that it is possible to justify global and local stress situations arising within the structure, and control these as necessary with a combination of prestress and bonded reinforcement.

4) The analysis techniques have or are being fully verified/validated as appropriate, and this process involves the testing of physical models of the containment.

5) It is considered that the development and design process to which the primary containment of the first of the UK PWR power stations has been subjected will ensure a fully safe and reliable structure capable of withstanding and protecting the public from the consequences of beyond design basis accidents which occur at a level of extremely low probability.

REFERENCES

(1) CROWDER R, CHALMERS A.G., HUNTER I, & IRVING J. J1/3 Proposed Design Specification for the UK PWR Primary Containment. SMiRT 6, Paris 1981.

(2) HINLEY M.S. & NESS D. Finite Element Linear and Non-linear Analysis of Sizewell 'B' PWR Containment Building. Nuclear Containment Conference, Cambridge 1987, Pages 114-117, C.U.P.

(3) ROBERTS A.C. & HOPKIN I.B. Sizewell PWR Reactor Building Primary Containment Foundation Design. Nuclear Containment Conference, Cambridge, 1987 Pages 139-152, C.U.P.

(4) CROWDER.R. Ultimate Load Model Test for Sizewell 'B' Primary Containment. Nuclear Containment Conference, Cambridge, 1987, Pages 5-19, C.U.P.

(5) SMITH J.C.W. The Design of a ^{1}/10th Scale Model of the Sizewell 'B' Primary Containment. 4th Conference on Containment Integrity, Washington 1988.

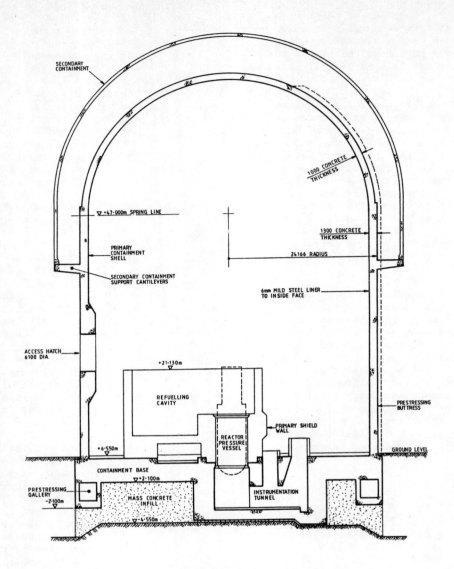

Fig 1   Vertical section through primary containment

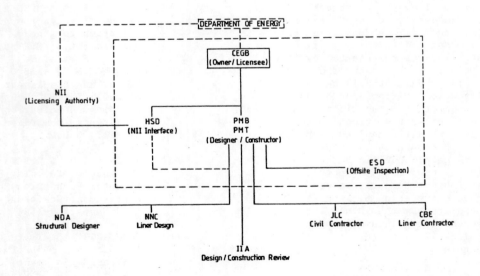

Fig 2   Relationship between organisations involved on primary containment

LOAD COMBINATIONS		CONSTRUCTION	NORMAL	EXCEPTIONAL	ULTIMATE	D	L	F	W	V'	E	E'	P₀	T₀	P	T	P₂	T₂	R₀	R₁	R₂	Rₑ	Rₑ'	Y	Z
1	CONSTRUCTION	✶	–	–	–	1.0	1.0	1.0	0.67	–	–	–	–	–	1.0	–	–	–	–	–	–	–	–	–	–
2	STRUCTURAL OVERPRESSURE	–	✶	–	–	1.0	1.0	1.0	–	–	–	–	–	–	1.0	1.15	–	–	–	–	–	–	–	–	–
	INTEGRATED LEAK RATE	–	✶	–	–	1.0	1.0	1.0	–	–	–	–	–	–	1.0	1.0	–	–	–	–	–	–	–	–	–
3	NORMAL OPERATION	–	✶	–	–	1.0	1.0	1.0	–	–	–	–	1.0	1.0	–	–	–	–	1.0	–	–	–	–	–	–
4	NORMAL OPERATION + NORMAL CLIMATIC	–	–	✶	–	1.0	1.3	1.0	1.5	–	–	–	1.0	1.0	–	–	–	–	1.0	–	–	–	–	–	–
5	NORMAL OPERATION + OPERATIONAL SHUTDOWN EARTHQUAKE (OSE)	–	–	✶	–	1.0	1.3	1.0	–	–	1.5	–	1.0	1.0	–	–	–	–	1.0	–	–	1.0	–	–	–
6	NORMAL OPERATION + EXCEPTIONAL CLIMATIC	–	–	✶	–	1.0	1.0	1.0	–	1.0	–	–	1.0	1.0	–	–	–	–	1.0	–	–	–	–	–	–
7	NORMAL OPERATION + SAFE SHUTDOWN EARTHQUAKE (SSE)	–	–	✶	–	1.0	1.0	1.0	–	–	–	1.0	1.0	1.0	–	–	–	–	1.0	–	–	–	–	1.0	–
8	DESIGN BASIS FAULT a	–	–	■	–	1.0	1.0	1.0	–	–	–	–	–	–	1.5	1.0	–	–	–	1.0	–	–	–	–	–
	DESIGN BASIS FAULT b	–	–	■	–	1.0	1.0	1.0	–	–	–	–	–	–	1.0	1.0	–	–	–	1.25	–	–	–	–	–
	DESIGN BASIS FAULT c	–	–	■	–	1.0	1.0	1.0	1.25	–	–	–	–	–	1.25	1.0	–	–	–	1.0	–	–	–	–	–
9	DESIGN BASIS FAULT + SAFE SHUTDOWN EARTHQUAKE	–	–	✶	–	1.0	1.0	1.0	–	–	–	1.0	–	–	1.0	1.0	–	–	–	1.0	–	–	1.0	–	–
10	NORMAL OPERATION + PIPE RUPTURE OTHER THAN DBF	–	–	✶	–	1.0	1.0	1.0	–	–	–	–	–	–	–	–	1.0	1.0	–	–	1.25	–	–	–	–
11	NORMAL OPERATION + MISSILES	–	–	✶	–	1.0	1.0	1.0	–	–	–	–	1.0	1.0	–	–	–	–	1.0	–	–	–	–	1.0	–
12	NORMAL OPERATION + OTHER HAZARDOUS LOADS OR MALFUNCTIONS	–	–	✶	–	1.0	1.0	1.0	–	–	–	–	1.0	1.0	–	–	–	–	1.0	–	–	–	–	–	1.0
13	ULTIMATE PRESSURE LOAD	–	–	–	✶	1.0	–	1.0	–	–	–	–	–	–	K	–	–	–	–	–	–	–	–	–	–

SYMBOLS USED ON THIS DRAWING

D DEAD LOADS (PERMANENT GRAVITY LOADS)
E EARTHQUAKE LOADS (O.S.E.)
E' EARTHQUAKE LOADS (S.S.E.)
F PRESTRESSING LOADS (CALCULATED AT ALL RELEVANT TIMES TO BE CONSIDERED)
L LIVE LOADS (IMPOSED LOADS)
P DESIGN PRESSURE
P₀ OPERATING PRESSURE
P₂ INTERNAL PRESSURE LOADS DUE TO ACCIDENT CONDITIONS OTHER THAN DBF

Rₑ LOCAL LOADS DUE TO EARTHQUAKE (O.S.E.)
Rₑ' LOCAL LOADS DUE TO EARTHQUAKE (S.S.E.)
R₀ LOCAL LOADS UNDER NORMAL OPERATION
R₁ LOCAL LOADS DUE TO PIPE RUPTURE UNDER DBF CONDITIONS
R₂ LOCAL LOADS DUE TO PIPE RUPTURE OTHER THAN THAT CAUSED BY DBF CONDITIONS
T DBF TEMPERATURE DISTRIBUTION
T₀ OPERATING TEMPERATURE DISTRIBUTION

T₂ INTERNAL TEMPERATURE LOADS DUE TO ACCIDENT CONDITIONS OTHER THAN DBF
W WIND LOADS (NORMAL)
V' WIND LOADS (EXCEPTIONAL)
Y LOCAL LOADS DUE TO MISSILES
Z LOADS FROM ANY OTHER HAZARDS OR MALFUNCTIONS TO BE CONSIDERED

Pu=KxP ULTIMATE PNEUMATIC PRESSURE TO BE DETERMINED FOR ULTIMATE LOAD ANALYSIS

Fig 3   Table of loads and loading combinations

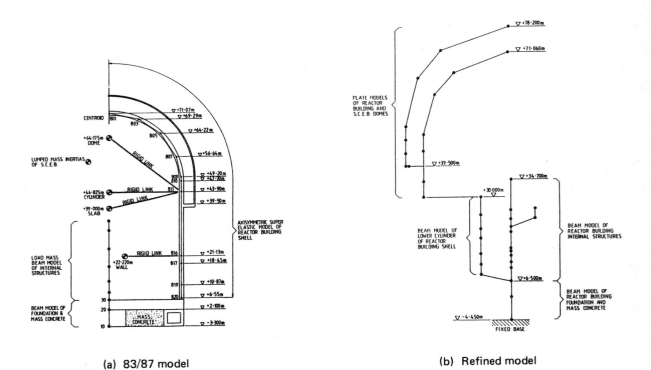

(a) 83/87 model

(b) Refined model

Fig 4   Models for seismic analysis of primary containment

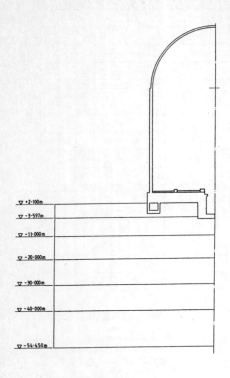

(a) Global model

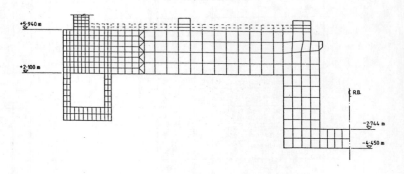

(b) Detail model of base

Fig 5   Elastic analysis axisymmetric model

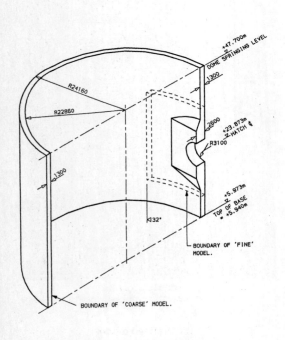

(a) 180° shell arc coarse model

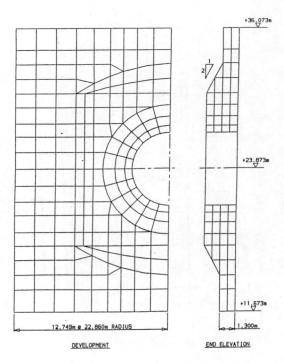

DEVELOPMENT   END ELEVATION

(b) Fine mesh model around hatch

Fig 6   3D elastic analysis of equipment hatch

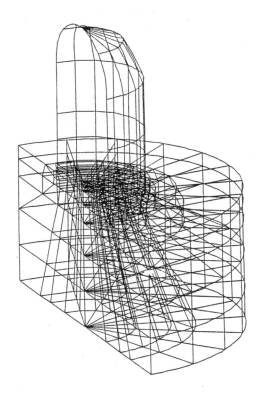

(a) Global 3D model of base and soil

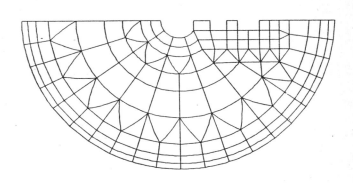

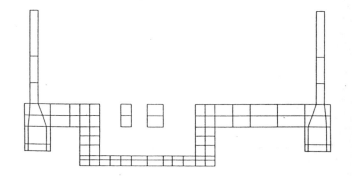

(b) Detailed 3D model (180°) of base

Fig 7   Base analysis models

Fig 8   Reinforcement in prestressing gallery base and wall

Fig 9   Reinforcement in walls of instrumentation tunnel

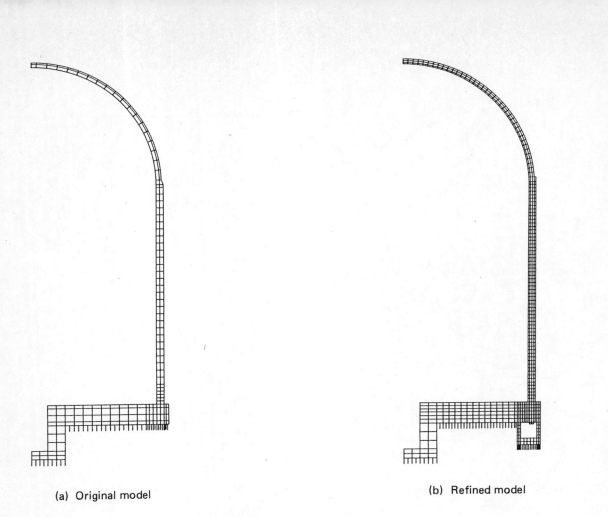

(a) Original model   (b) Refined model

Fig 10   Non-linear analysis model (ADINA-TW)

Fig 11   One tenth scale model of primary containment under construction

C388/022

Design and analysis of the containment liner

J B SHAW, BSc, CEng, MIMechE
National Nuclear Corporation Limited, Knutsford, Cheshire

SYNOPSIS The steel liner of the PWR concrete containment building is a high-integrity component which is required to form a leak-tight membrane during all normal reactor operating conditions and also during and after any postulated accident events. The many penetrations through it, for process pipework, personnel access, electrical services, and for structural embedments into the concrete, present local design and analysis problems which are often very different from those encountered in pressure vessels and other structures.

The paper describes the fundamental design approach to the containment liner and discusses the development of appropriate design code rules. Their application is illustrated by reference to the programme of stress analysis work which has been put in hand to demonstrate the integrity of the liner.

1 INTRODUCTION

The containment liner forms a continuous steel membrane covering the inner surface of the reinforced post-tensioned concrete reactor containment building. Its function is to provide an impermeable barrier to contain any radioactive fluids and aerosols which may be released from the reactor system either during normal operation or fault situations. Since the steel liner is backed by concrete it is supported against internal pressure loading but suffers strains as the vessel distorts under pre-stress, shrinkage, internal pressure, thermal and seismic loading. The liner material is also subject to significant strain whenever its temperature changes relative to that of the bulk concrete, in particular during the thermal transient which may accompany a large loss-of-coolant accident (LOCA) or main steam line break.

To ensure that the liner will remain leak-tight under all conditions, including in the longer term following any postulated accident event, requires a high standard of construction and sufficient detailed analysis to demonstrate that the strains will not exceed acceptable levels. It must also be recognised that the liner will act as shuttering to support the wet concrete during construction of the building and care must be taken to avoid any damage or initial over-straining of the liner at that time.

2 GENERAL DESIGN FEATURES

The liner is constructed of 6mm thick, butt-welded mild steel plate. It is anchored to the concrete in different ways in various parts of the building. On the base slab there is an array of grillage beams set into the concrete and the floor liner plates are welded directly to the exposed upper flanges of these beams. On the side wall (Fig 1) the liner plates are provided with angle sections welded to their outer surfaces at 345mm pitch and subsequently cast within the concrete wall. These angle sections are aligned vertically to facilitate placement of the concrete. Circumferential channel sections are also provided to hold the panel in shape and to stiffen the liner during construction of the building. In certain areas the anchorage of the liner is improved by adding headed studs (not shown in Fig 1), resistance-welded to the back of the angle sections at about 150mm spacing. The dome liner is backed by an orthogonal grid of tee and angle sections which, in addition to providing anchorage for the liner, also give sufficient stiffening to support the wet concrete as the dome is constructed.

Various penetrations are provided through the walls of the reactor building. These are for the pipework associated with the feedwater and steam lines to and from the steam generators, for the many other piping systems and for ducting of electrical cables. Every one of these penetrations must be reliably sealed to the liner to ensure containment and, where the piping system operates at high temperature, must be designed to limit heat transfer to the concrete wall. This is generally achieved by one of the arrangements illustrated in Fig 2. Hot penetrations have thermal sleeves of adequate length to accommodate any difference in temperature between the wall of the pipe and the liner. For high integrity process systems these are connected to the pipes by means of forged flued heads. The annular spaces between the penetration sleeves and the process pipes, cooled by natural circulation of air, serve to control the concrete temperatures within acceptable limits.

There are also three major access hatches into the building, two manways and a larger one for equipment access. The manways are fitted with airlocks having double-door sealing arrangements. The equipment hatch is for use during plant construction and maintenance and has a single door with a double 'O' ring seal. All three hatch closures are sealed to penetration sleeves which form the opening in the concrete wall and which are welded to the liner to ensure a continuous containment boundary.

The various floors, structures, piping systems, etc inside the building are supported on embedments which pass through the liner and transfer their loads directly into the concrete. In principle no mechanical loading is allowed to be taken directly on the liner, but to ensure a continuous containment boundary each embedment is fabricated complete with a thickened insert plate which is then butt welded to the surrounding liner plate. The insert plate is designed to have sufficient flexibility to absorb any relative movement between the embedment and the concrete without locally overstressing any of the containment welds. A similar approach is adopted in the vicinity of penetrations which are required to take mechanical loadings from attached piping, where all efforts are made to transmit the forces directly to the concrete through penetration sleeve anchorages, and thickened insert plates are provided around the penetrations, butt-welded to the liner and having adequate flexibility to absorb any relative movement between the penetration sleeves and the concrete. Where there are multiple penetrations, eg as in the case of the main steam penetrations, a single insert plate is fabricated together with the required number of penetration sleeves.

Exceptions to the general rule are certain lightly loaded embedments, where a thickened insert plate is provided, with an attachment point on its inner surface and an array of headed studs welded on the outside. In this case the load is transmitted through the thickness of the insert plate so that the allowable stresses are reduced accordingly and the insert plate is tested for laminations. Again, in areas where there are clusters of such embedments, a large insert plate is provided, with several identified and studded attachment points.

3 SUBSTANTIATION ANALYSIS

Although generally free from significant loading under normal plant operating conditions the reactor containment building is designed to withstand any increase in internal pressure and temperature which may arise due to failure within the reactor system. The duty of the liner under these conditions is to remain leak tight, so it must have sufficient ductility to strain with the concrete as the building distorts and also to absorb any differential expansion between itself and the concrete as the internal temperature rises. Similarly if an earthquake were to occur the liner would be required to strain with the building.

The most significant loading specified on the liner is the rise in temperature following the most severe postulated fault. An upper bound for the maximum transient temperature of the internal environment, occurring as a result of a main steam line break, has been established as 200°C. It should be emphasised here, however, that this is considered as a one-time hypothetical occurrence of extremely low probability.

Since the 1.3m thick concrete walls will not respond as rapidly as the steel liner to the temperature transient and since the liner is fully constrained by the walls, then general areas of liner plate will suffer an equibiaxial thermal strain, which may be expected to exceed the yield strain. Under these conditions the anchors into the concrete would carry no shear forces. As a general indication a 200°C rise in temperature will give a strain of 2500$\mu\epsilon$. To this must be added initial strains due to pre-stressing of the building, about 300$\mu\epsilon$, plus an allowance of 400$\mu\epsilon$ for shrinkage of the concrete during construction and service, giving a total compressive strain of 3200$\mu\epsilon$. Upon cooling down, if compressive yielding has taken place then the liner would develop a residual tensile strain, which clearly must not be sufficient to give rise to any danger of rupture. Assuming the pre-stressing and shrinkage strains to remain then on a very simple basis (Fig 3), with a material yield strain of 1000$\mu\epsilon$, the final state may be expected to be represented by point 'D' on the figure. For design code assessment we may define the final 'strain' to be that associated with the residual tensile stress in the liner, of the order of 1500$\mu\epsilon$. Based on this simple scenario, a value of 3000$\mu\epsilon$ has been selected as a workable tensile strain limit and is embodied in the design and construction rules, the development of which is discussed in more detail below. Clearly this limit will give a very substantial margin against any possibility of general liner tearing provided that the material has normal levels of ductility.

The maintenance of this uniform compression or tension within the steel membrane, with little or no shear on the anchors, requires that at any internal corners, for example the floor-to-wall junction and the vertical corners of the various rectangular openings in the floor, suitable bearing plates should be provided to transmit the expansion forces into the concrete. In the interests of keeping these forces within reasonable bounds, it can also be seen that it is advantageous to have a thin liner, constructed of material with a low yield strength. For the Sizewell B liner, a maximum permitted yield of 325 MN/m^2 is specified for the plate material.

In some situations, for example if during the compressive thermal loading an individual liner panel, between angle stiffeners, were to buckle away from the concrete, so losing its ability to transmit the tangential membrane thrust, then in the limit the full expansion force would have to be resisted by the adjacent anchors. The ability of the anchors to carry this load has been investigated by testwork. Full-scale sections of liner plate with anchors, mounted in concrete blocks, have been tested to determine their force-deflection relationship (Fig 4) up to complete shear failure of the anchorage. This non-linear characteristic has then been used in a special-purpose computer program, which carries out a flexibility analysis, by considering a group of anchors adjacent to a failed panel, to determine the force carried by each anchor under a given initial strain and thermal expansion. Sufficient anchors are included to ensure that the anchor forces eventually reduce to negligible values away from the failed panel. The maximum anchor force and displacement, occurring immediately adjacent to the failed panel, are then determined and compared with the maximum load capacity and the failure deflection obtained from the test. The design and construction rules require that the calculated values should be within the test values by a specified margin.

A special case also occurs near the horizontal top edges of the openings in the base. Here, the angle sections on the walls of the instrument tunnel for example are vertical so that they cannot fully resist vertical thermal expansion. If the wall were free to expand then the local bending strain in the floor plate, at its junction with the instrument tunnel wall, would be unacceptably high. However, the angle sections are provided with studs which will resist vertical movement. Again, the non-linear characteristic of these studs has been used in a finite element analysis to confirm the stud integrity and to determine the reduced upward deflection of the top edge and hence the local bending strains in the floor plate. These bending strains are limited by the design rules to 1.0%, and some flexibility has been provided at this connection in order to achieve this.

In addition to these general problems of liner integrity there are many local areas which must be examined to demonstrate that no failure will occur. Fig 5, for example, shows a three-dimensional finite element model of a corner detail on the instrument tunnel liner. Again the anchorage system has been represented by non-linear restraints and the angle sections have been included in order to take account of the temperature difference between them and the liner plate.

All major penetrations and access hatches have been addressed by finite element analysis. In the case of process pipe penetrations, connected to the liner by means of thermal sleeves, the worst thermal stresses may occur during normal operation, when the pipe may be hot. This is likely to be a cyclic condition as the plant starts up and shuts down, so the possibility of fatigue failure must be considered. Fig 6 shows a model of a typical penetration, in this case one which can be adequately represented as axisymmetric. The concrete is modelled with non-linear material properties determined from tests on Sizewell-specific materials, and the effects of pre-stress and shrinkage are included. At the interface between the steel and the concrete, 'gap' elements are used so that the two surfaces can slide or separate freely. The results show that under fault conditions the steel sleeve will expand axially inwards from the keying ring so that a degree of flexibility is required in the insert plate, whilst the constraint of its radial expansion by the surrounding concrete will result in severe compressive hoop strains. Temperature gradients along the extended part of the sleeve will give rise to thermal stresses at both ends, which, together with the requirement to maintain the local concrete temperature below 95°C, determines the required length of the thermal sleeve. Mechanical loads from the attached pipework also arise, and these stresses must be superimposed on those from thermal loadings. The most severe mechanical loadings are due to seismic effects and reaction forces resulting from pipe rupture.

The various embedments in the walls and floor of the building are designed so as not to impose loads directly on to the liner, but where embedments pass through the liner additional analysis is necessary, for example of deflections at the concrete face to demonstrate the integrity of the sealing weld and of heat transfer into the embedment to confirm the acceptability of local concrete temperatures.

The analysis of the embedments themselves is carried out in accordance with conventional structural design techniques, augmented by detailed finite element analysis where appropriate. These analyses address stresses in both the steel components and the surrounding concrete.

Other specific problems also need to be analysed. For example many of the internal structures are susceptible to pipe whip and suitable restraints are provided, but this exacerbates the possibility of sustained jet impingement which may give rise to local over-heating of the liner and the concrete behind it. Analysis has been carried out to demonstrate that this will not prejudice the integrity of the containment. A second example is the occurrence of very high forces on the embedments supporting the thimble tube restraint frames due to the pressure transient which may result from a LOCA. Here the attachments have been specially designed to ensure that only direct compressive loads are imposed on the embedments.

4 DESIGN AND CONSTRUCTION RULES

A special-purpose design code has been developed for the containment building and its liner. In general approach, it is similar to ASME III, Division 2, but insofar as the structural analysis is concerned there are some differences in detail.

Firstly, in order to ensure a sufficient margin on anchor failure in terms of thermal loading, the analysis is considered in two ways. On the one hand the anchor forces and deflections are calculated using the predicted upper bound temperature loading, with the condition that the latter must not exceed 50% of the experimental maximum failure deflection, whilst on the other hand the predicted temperature difference is doubled, whereupon the calculated deflections must not exceed the experimental maximum. This ensures sufficient margin whilst allowing for the non-linear temperature-force-deflection relationship. In this assessment the ASME code gives no guidance on the statistical interpretation of the test results, which exhibit a considerable degree of scatter. In the Sizewell B analysis the typical load-deflection relationship for each anchor type is defined as being the mean curve obtained from at least six tests, and the failure deflection is that at which the measured anchor force has dropped to 80% of its maximum value.

Secondly, strains in the liner itself are predominantly compressive so that no rupture may be expected under fault conditions. However, the integrity must also be preserved during cooling down in the longer term, when there is a possibility of a residual tensile stress. Therefore the design and construction rules for Sizewell B put the emphasis on limiting the tensile strain. The compressive strain limits of ASME III, Division 2 have, however, been retained as a useful screening criterion to identify possible problem areas without a full cyclic inelastic analysis.

The design and construction rules have been further extended to allow for higher strains in very localised areas and to provide guidelines for fatigue analysis. Cyclic loading is not, however, a significant problem in most parts of the containment liner since its prime duty is to provide protection against events having an extremely low probability of occurrence. Exceptions to this rule are the process penetrations, where thermal stresses may be cyclic and certain embedments which may carry variable loads.

The assessment of those parts of the penetrations not immediately backed by concrete is based on stress limits rather than strain limits and is carried out in accordance with ASME III, Subsection NE, for Class MC components. This requires the evaluation of primary, secondary and peak stress intensities as appropriate, under normal and design basis fault (level A & B) conditions, safe shutdown earthquake (level C) conditions and pipe rupture loadings (level D).

The design and construction rules also provide for the assessment of the local concrete stresses around embedments and penetrations to demonstrate that the applied mechanical loads can be adequately supported.

5 MANUFACTURE AND CONSTRUCTION

The liner is fabricated from carbon steel plates formed to cylindrical or spherical shapes as required. After attachment of the anchors, using staggered intermittent fillet welds, the plates are assembled on site and butt-welded together. The anchors, vertical on the sidewall and circumferential on the dome, are augmented by circumferential channel stiffeners on the sidewall and meridonial tees on the dome to provide sufficient stiffness to support the wet concrete loading. The thickened insert plates for penetrations and embedments are tapered on their outer edges before being butt-welded into apertures cut into the assembled liner, or in some cases into individual panels before assembly.

The selection of weld details at the wall-base junction, penetration connections and at embedments is restricted by the design and construction rules to a small number of high integrity types. The joints in the liner floor, made by means of full-penetration butt-welds designed to give fusion also to the supporting joist flanges, are provided with a leak-chase system for testing them. This consists of inverted channel sections fillet-welded over the joints, divided into isolatable lengths of about 30m, fitted with pipe connections through which the contained space can be pressurised. This leak-chase system remains in place when the overlay slab of protective concrete is placed on the floor.

Tolerances on plate distortion during forming, welding on of the anchors and subsequent assembly are carefully controlled to ensure that there is no unacceptable degree of misalignment at the butt welds.

Material quality and traceability and welding procedures are controlled by quality assurance arrangements which comply with BS5882, with the total manufacturing and construction process being covered throughout by comprehensive quality plans.

All butt welds in the sidewall liner plate are leak tested locally using a vacuum box method, and a proportion of their length is subject to radiographic examination. The butt welds around penetrations and insert plates are fully radiographed. The fillet welds attaching the anchors are examined visually, with a proportion subject to magnetic particle inspection. Stud welding procedures are tested regularly during production by bend testing samples.

Prior to laying the base overlay concrete the floor welds are fully tested by pressurising sections of the leak-chase system and detecting any decay of pressure. Finally the complete building is subject to an overpressure test, monitored for any leakage through the liner and the penetration closures.

Periodic integrated leak rate tests are carried out on the liner during service. If excessive leakage is indicated then all welds can be individually tested either directly or by use of the leak chase system.

6 CONCLUSION

The containment building liner is a high integrity structure for which a very low probability of leakage has been demonstrated. This has been achieved by a combination of high quality design and manufacture, together with detailed structural analysis. The fundamental requirement is that it must retain its integrity and prevent leakage from the containment during and after the most severe postulated accident conditions. Its ability to do this must not be impaired by loadings which may occur during normal plant operation. Analysis of the liner has shown that the design meets these requirements when judged by criteria which are consistent with, or more stringent than established design codes.

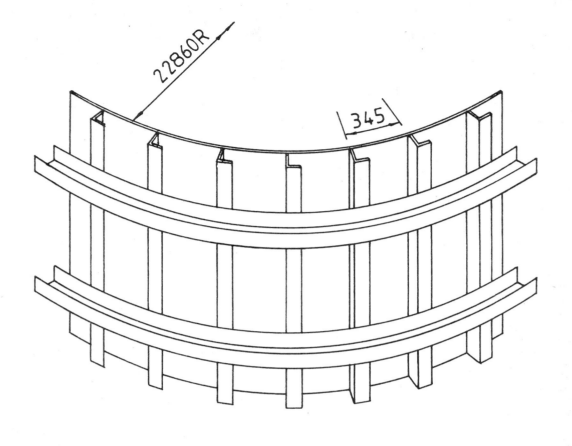

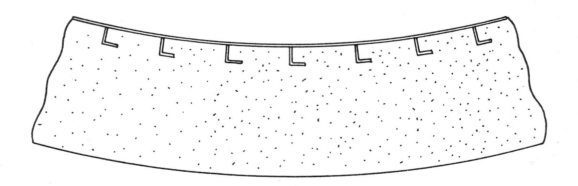

Fig 1   Arrangement of anchors and stiffeners on the side wall liner

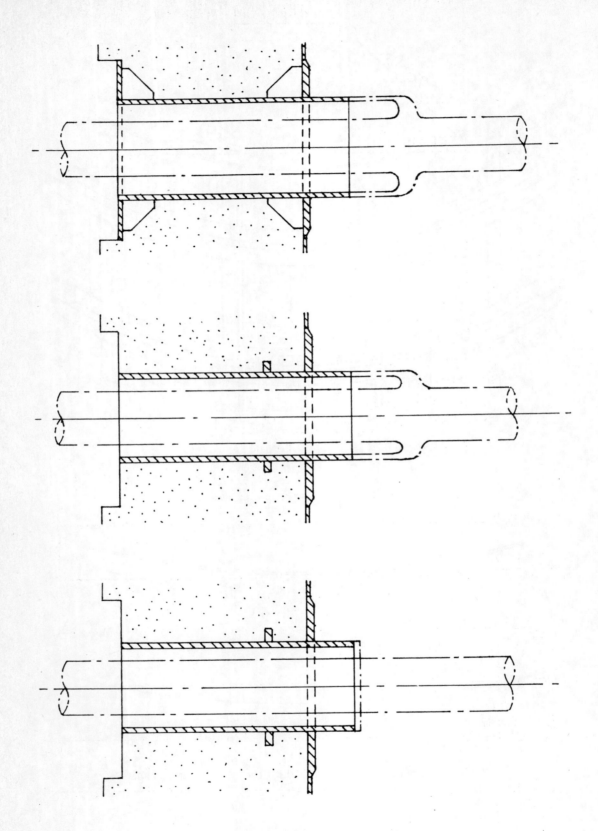

Fig 2   Arrangements for penetrations

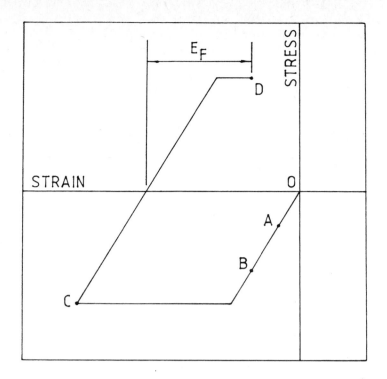

O-A : PRE-STRESSING STRAIN
A-B : SHRINKAGE STRAIN
B-C : THERMAL STRAIN - HEATING
C-D : THERMAL STRAIN - COOLING
E_F : FINAL 'TENSILE' STRAIN

Fig 3   Simplified loading cycle

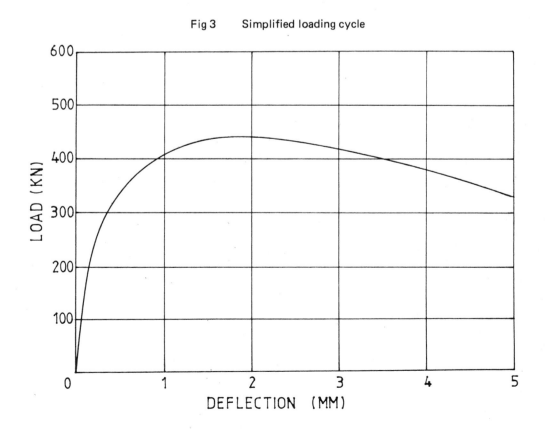

Fig 4   Typical anchor load—deflection relationship

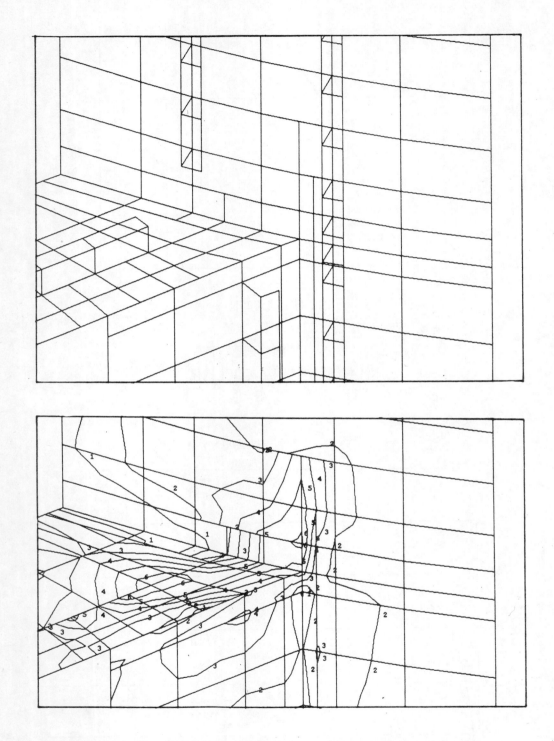

Fig 5   Finite element model and strain contours for instrument tunnel
         corner detail

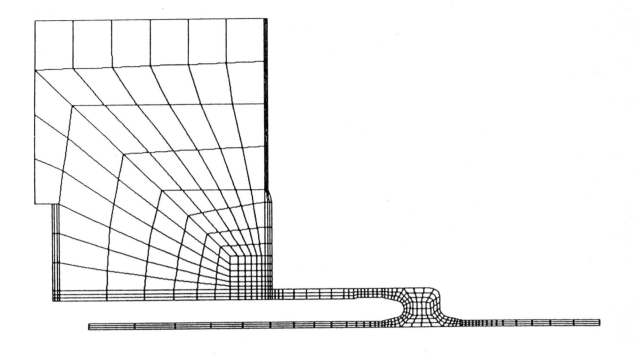

Fig 6   Typical axisymmetric penetration model

The Sizewell 'B' containment airlocks

S C DAVIS, P LESLIE, BSc, CEng, MIMechE and **W O LIVSEY**, CEng, MIMechE
GEC Alsthom Energy Systems Limited, Whetstone, Leicester

SYNOPSIS This paper describes the design and analysis of the Personnel Access Airlocks for the Sizewell 'B' Power Station. Airlocks are incorporated as an integral part of the containment liner to provide a means of personnel entry which does not compromise the integrity of the Primary Containment enclosure.

1.0   INTRODUCTION

The Sizewell 'B' Reactor Building is in the form of a pre-stressed concrete containment vessel with a carbon steel liner.

The liner is required to prevent escape of fission products, which may have been released due to a postulated fracture of the primary circuit, which in turn is postulated as the result of internal or external faults or abnormal conditions including earthquakes.

Personnel entry to the reactor building during normal operation requires a means of entry which will permit personnel access while still maintaining the integrity of the primary containment.

This requirement is met by providing Personnel Airlocks at two locations in the Reactor Building.

When the decision was taken to build the first U.K. PWR at Sizewell there was limited experience in the U.K. of supplying mechanical plant and equipment to PWR installations. GEC ESL had previously supplied the balance of primary plant and erection services for the KORI 1 PWR in Korea. This contract included design and erection of the steel containment vessel which incorporated personnel and equipment access airlocks.

These airlocks, which were constructed in accordance with the then current edition of ASME codes, were designed to meet the specific requirements of that customer and reflected the type of equipment generally used for this application.

A design to meet the current requirements of ASME and the safety and operational requirements for a UK PWR involved significant changes from the previous design.

Security methods have been included in the design of control devices to ensure unauthorised persons cannot gain access or defeat the integrity of the Airlock without impeding the needs of staff during normal or emergency operations.

2.0   PLANT DESCRIPTION

2.1   General

All parts of the airlock are designed to withstand reactor building design, test and fault conditions with either airlock door in the open condition.

Interlocks are provided to prevent the pressure-equalising valves and doors being opened in such combinations as to provide a direct leakage path through the airlock.

Doors are provided with two sealable boundaries in series incorporating leak checking facilities. Door actuation is achieved by either power or hand-drive.

The airlock electrical interlocking is implemented using a programmable controller (PC). Processing of the interlock logic forms only part of the PC function, its other activities include sequence control of the door seal leak tests, handling control panel input signals, indication and annunciation of alarms.

2.2   Vessel Design and Construction

The airlock is classified as a pressure vessel and is designed and constructed in accordance with the requirements of ASME III Sub-Section NE class MC components.

The airlocks, which are cylindrical in form, are structurally supported by welding a flange at the inboard end of the airlock to a concentric penetration sleeve, which is anchored into the containment vessel. The penetration sleeve is in turn welded to the liner plate to complete the integrity of the complete pressure retaining boundary (see fig.1).

The vessel body is rolled 13mm thick steel plate with thick plate bulkheads bolted to the end flanges. Rectangular doors are mounted in an opening in each bulkhead. The adoption of a thick plate bulkhead concept gives maximum freedom in locating the door hinges, operating mechanisms etc, which are not restricted by pre-determined stiffening web positions. Equipment mounting is achieved by tapping directly into the bulkhead.

Both doors are positioned to open inwards, ie the inner door swings into the reactor building and the outer door into the airlock (see fig.2). With this mode of mounting the fault pressure differential assists the door locking mechanism to provide the door sealing force even though the design basis has to assume that the pressure forces oppose door sealing, as under test conditions.

The door seal is carried in a groove set into the face of the door.

2.3   Door Operation

The door is required to be operated by an electro-mechanical system normally, and by mechanical means without power assistance in the event of power supply failure.

The operation of the doors can be accomplished from any one of the three control stations located as follows:-

i)   Inside the reactor building
ii)   Outside the reactor building
iii) Inside the airlock.

To engage the door drive mechanism the operator must select the required door by operating the door drive selector lever. This action also opens a pressure balance valve in the selected bulkhead and closes an identical valve in the opposite bulkhead.

An electric motor/gearbox mounted on the outside of the outer bulkhead drives the input shaft which is extended through the interlock box and the inner bulkhead. This shaft can also be driven manually by a handwheel at each control position. During normal operations the hand-drives are withdrawn and disconnected from the drive shaft. When the hand-drive is engaged with the drive shaft a micro-switch isolates the electric supply to the motor drive.

The door closing and locking mechanisms are driven by a series of geared shafts as illustrated diagrammatically in figure 3.

When extended, the door locking bolts engage in sockets incorporated in the vessel door frame. Correct bolt engagement is monitored by micro-switches located in the sockets which alarm a "door not closed" condition.

2.4   Interlock Philosophy and Implementation

The required integrity of the containment dictates that the following conditions are met within the airlocks:-

i)   Each door is mechanically interlocked such that one door cannot be opened unless the opposite door and balance valve are closed.

ii)   Each balance valve is interlocked such that only one valve can be opened at a

time and only when the opposite door is closed and locked.

iii) Valve opening is prevented when a differential pressure across the bulkhead excess 0.35 bar.

iv)   Door opening is prevented when a differential pressure across the bulkhead exceeds 0.14 bar.

Protection against inadvertently having both doors or pressure balance valves open at the same time is achieved by having a single door selector lever. Selection of a door drive is prohibited by a mechanical interlock unless the opposite door and pressure balance valve are fully closed.

The overpressure interlock is achieved by pressure switches controlling solenoid locking pins which inhibit the airlock sequence during an electrical failure or overpressure condition.

All interlocks are grouped in a common selector box located within the airlock.

In certain circumstances, such as in the event of loss of electrical power or when the airlock is required for special activities during reactor maintenance outages, it may be necessary to override the interlocks. A means of overriding the interlocks is incorporated into the design but this function can only be implemented using an administratively controlled key. All door movements whilst the interlocks are overridden must be achieved manually.

The interlock arrangement is shown schematically in figure 4.

2.5   Door Sealing

Door sealing is achieved by a profiled sealing strip mounted on the airlock bulkhead which seats into a neoprene seal located in the door. When the door is closed a small interspace is formed by the profiled strip. A section through the door seal is shown in figure 5.

It is an operational requirement that a door seal leak test is carried out every time an airlock door is closed. This test is manually initiated from any of the three control stations and involves pressurising the seal interspace and monitoring the pressure decay.

Local indication/alarm of the test result is provided at each control station.

2.6   Control and Instrumentation

The principal design functions of the control and instrumentation system are as follows:-

i)   Differential pressure interlocks
ii)   Powered door operation
iii) Door seal leak testing
iv)   Indications and alarms
v)   Airlock lighting

All of these functions, with the exception of airlock lighting, are supervised by a programmable controller.

For control purposes the airlocks are provided with three control stations. Each position is equipped with an electrical control panel which provides the operator with various indications, alarms and pushbuttons. The control panels also act as marshalling points for the local plant sensor switch signals. These switch signals together with the control panel signals are transmitted to and from the programmable controller via multipair cables. Where these signals need to pass through the airlock bulkheads, this is achieved by utilising multipin connectors qualified to IEEE standard 317.

The programmable controller equipment is located in a free standing cubicle in an area outside of the reactor building adjacent to the power cubicle.

The airlocks are designed to be manually operated following a loss of electrical power. In this situation power door operation door, seal leak testing and indicator/alarm functions will be lost.

The airlock lighting will be maintained at a reduced emergency level by means of battery support.

2.7 Communication and Safety Equipment

In the event of personnel encountering difficulties within the airlock, communication is provided by a local intercom system which connects with the inner and outer control stations. A telephone link to the Main Control Room is also installed in the vessel.

A general station tannoy, suitably muted, is located within the airlock.

A connection in the outer bulkhead allows an emergency breathing air supply to be provided in the event of entrapment.

3.0 STRESS ANALYSIS

3.1 Boundary Conditions

Although the containment vessel is post-tensioned concrete, the airlock vessel is metal and hence comes within the scope of metal containment. The point of demarcation from concrete vessel to steel vessel is where the steel liner for the penetration is not backed by concrete. Strains in the concrete due to various loadings affect the stresses in the air lock vessel. It follows that at least part of the containment vessel proper must be considered in the stress analysis of the steel airlock vessel. Figure 1 shows the geometry considered for the upper personnel airlock which is perpendicular to the vessel wall and designated 'radial'. Figure 2 shows the geometry of the lower personnel airlock which is inclined towards the vessel tangent and is designated 'non-radial'.

Only the analysis of the radial airlock is discussed in this paper.

3.2 Loadings

Containment vessels in normal reactor operation are subject to modest loadings only. These are primarily self weight, slowly changing concrete strains due to post tensioning and day to day fluctuations in temperature and pressure, arising from atmospheric conditions plus the effect of reactor operating temperature. The design condition is that of a breached reactor pressure circuit resulting in an elevated pressure and temperature regime within the containment.

A safe shutdown earthquake condition is considered as a faulted case.

From such considerations five loading combinations are chosen as follows:-

(a) $D + L + Pt + To + F$

(b) $D + L + To + F$

(c) $D + L + T + 1.5P + F$

(d) $D + L + To + Pe + F + E'$

(e) $D + L + T + P + F + E'$

The loading associated with each of the above designations is given below.

D	Dead load
L	Static and live loads
Pt	Reactor building test pressure
To	Thermal conditions during normal reactor operation or shutdown
E'	A safe shutdown earthquake.
Pe	Design external pressure.
T	Thermal conditions due to reactor faulted conditions.
F	Loading due to concrete strains
P	Design pressure.

3.3 Assessment

The assessment was carried out using the Finite Element Program ANSYS. Three models were used in the analysis; an axisymmetric model for the concrete vessel and liner, a three-dimensional model of the metal airlock and a detailed model of the flat bulkhead door and seal.

The first model was not truly axisymmetric because of the curvature of the containment vessel wall, but it was considered sufficiently accurate for the purpose, which was to determine the effect of concrete strains and thermal expansion on the metal airlock. In this model the rectangular door frame was replaced by a round one with the same periphery. Concrete strains were made up of load transfer from the post-tensioning cables, shrinkage, creep and seismic loading. Since some of these have time-dependent values, the early and late life of the plant were considered.

Sensitivity studies were carried out to consider the effect of the radius of the model boundary in the concrete and also the effect of simulating shrinkage by an assumed temperature input rather than as a strain, since these are different in effect.

The second model was terminated at the concrete vessel and was similar in scope to the geometry of figure 1 with the door being modelled as a more simple mass. This model was necessary for the seismic analysis. Two versions were considered, one with the door open and the other with the door closed.

The third model of the bulkhead was necessary to consider the adequacy of the door seal and detailed stresses in the bulkhead plate. In the design base faulted condition the internal containment vessel pressure tends to close the door on to its seal. However, the seal must be demonstrated to function during the pressure tests which tend to open the gap. Near the periphery, a ring of bolts secures the flat bulkhead plate to the cylindrical part of the airlock. Both the door to door frame and bulkhead to cylinder joints are modelled using special "gap" elements by which gaps may open up when loaded to tension.

Each type of loading was analysed individually so that the correct loading combination could be post-processed as required by the program. Where a model which is only part of the whole geometry under consideration was assessed, the displacements and rotations from the adjacent model were input at the boundary.

The seismic analysis was carried out using the dynamic capability of the ANSYS program.

Response spectra for the containment vessel at the appropriate elevation were provided for the analysis in each of three perpendicular planes, one of which was the airlock vessel axis. All modes within the range 0.1 to 40 Hertz were computed and the resulting stresses summed by the SRSS method. This is a standard procedure for the modal combination of stresses in which the square root of the sum of the individual squares of stress for each mode is taken to be the approximate total stress. These stresses were then combined with those from other loadings in order to obtain the overall maximum stresses.

The limit on stress is in line with ASME III requirements where limits are set on the level of general membrane stress, local membrane stress, bending plus local membrane stress, secondary stress and peak stress (no limit). There are no limits on secondary stress for faulted conditions.

3.4 Results

The results of all stress combinations were analysed and the highest level of stress for each loading case are given in table 1 for a typical area, together with the permissible maximum stress.

A typical plot of stress contours for two load cases are shown on figures 6 and 7. These are static plus seismic loading.

Stresses in bolts and local fixing details such as door hinges, brackets carrying loads etc., were assessed by means of hand calculations from computed forces and moments where necessary. Stresses in welds were also calculated where the detail was other than

			COMPONENT: CYLINDER							
			PRIMARY STRESSES N/mm²						PRIMARY PLUS SECONDARY STRESSES N/mm²	
LOAD COMBINATION NUMBER	DESCRIPTION OF LOAD COMBINATION		GENERAL MEMB. Pm		LOCAL MEMB. Pl		BENDING PLUS LOCAL MEMB.			
			Permissible	Actual	Permissible	Actual	Permissible	Actual	Permissible	Actual
a	D + L + Pt + To + F		236.3	47.4	328.3	173.5	328.3	185.3	400.0	182.0
b	D + L + To + F		133.4	7.6	200.0	7.3	200.0	9.3	400.0	12.0
c	D + L + T + 1.5P + F	INT	262.4	59.5	393.9	244.1	393.9	239.6	-	255.6
		NOT INT								
d	D + L + To + Pe + F + E'	INT	262.4	13.6	393.9	13.3	393.3	17.5	-	20.2
		NOT INT								
e	D + L + T + P + F + E'	INT	262.4	48.2	393.9	157.8	393.9	171.0	-	187.9
		NOT INT								

INT: Integral and Continuous
NOT INT: Not Integral and Continuous

TABLE 1 ASSESSMENT OF STRESSES IN THE CYLINDER

simple butt welding or other integral connection.

The loss of contact at the door to door frame was determined and the adequacy of the seal with a partial loss of compression was assessed.

Mode shapes are not easy to visualise from a still picture. To assist in understanding the mode behaviour under dynamic conditions, a computer software package which animates the display was written. In this way, both deformations due to loading and vibratory modes shapes can be viewed on a VDU. This is particularly useful in seeing the actual modes of vibration and also affords an excellent check on the model constraints.

A fatigue analysis was carried out for the cyclic loadings which includes those stresses caused during works and in situ pressure testing.

It is concluded that all stresses in all load combinations considered are within requirements. All localised stresses, bolts and weld details are also acceptable. The reduction of door seal compression at the worst conditions is also acceptable.

4.0 AIRLOCK TESTING

The airlocks will be subject to four main areas of test as follows:-

i)   Airlock vessel proof pressure test.
ii)   Sub-assembly function testing.
iii) Works performance testing.
iv)   Site performance testing.

Proof pressure testing is performed after vessel fabrication to prove its safe construction. The vessel pressure boundary components are assembled and subjected to a test pressure in accordance with ASME III sub section NE 6000.

The airlock has been designed in modular form to permit individual functional testing of the components before incorporating into the complete unit for works testing.

After completion of works build and setting-to-work operations performance testing will be conducted comprising:-

i)   Vessel leak rate check.
ii)   Vessel decompression rate via pressure balance valves.
iii) Door seal leak tests.
iv)   Airlock penetration seals leak check.
v)   Interlock testing.
vi)   Operational testing.

Following installation of the airlocks, site performance testing will be carried out which repeats the works performance test routine. After successful completion of performance testing, the PC program will be converted to EPROM in order to maintain a non-corruptible memory.

An additional integrated leak check will be carried out to confirm the integrity of the complete reactor building liner.

5.0 CONCLUSION

The resulting design incorporates considerable design margins, a high standard of interlock protection and meets stringent Quality Assurance standards.

The design is now essentially complete; manufacture is scheduled for completion during 1989 and site installation will commence during 1990.

6.0 LIST OF FIGURES

Fig.1 Cross Section Through Airlock, Penetration Sleeve and Liner Plate.

Fig.2 Cross Section Through Airlock Showing Doors in Open Position.

Fig.3 Schematic Diagram of Door Operating Mechanism.

Fig.4 Schematic Diagram of Interlock Arrangement.

Fig.5 Section Through Door Seal

Fig.6 Door & Bulkhead Model (radial airlock).

Fig.7 Plot of Stress Contours.

Fig.8 Plot of Stress Contours.

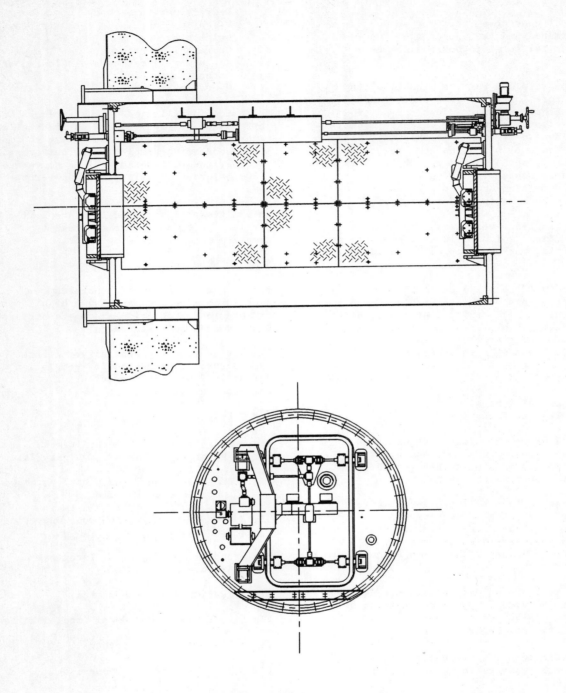

Fig 1   End elevation and cross-section through airlock, penetration
sleeve and liner plate

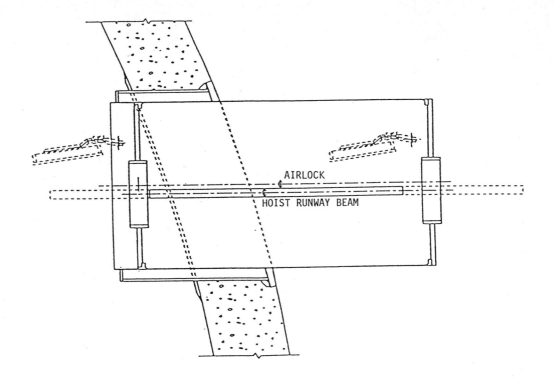

Fig 2   Cross-section through airlock showing doors in open position

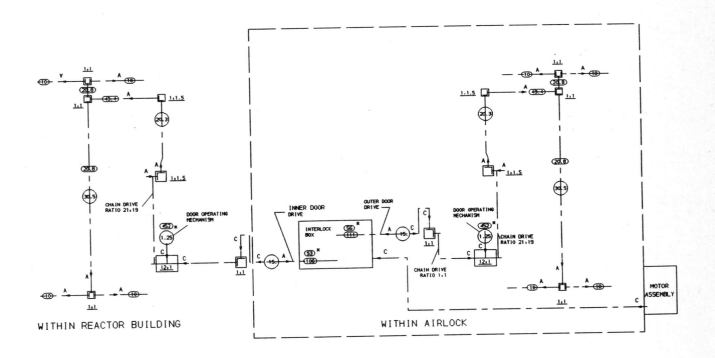

Fig 3   Schematic diagram of door operating mechanism

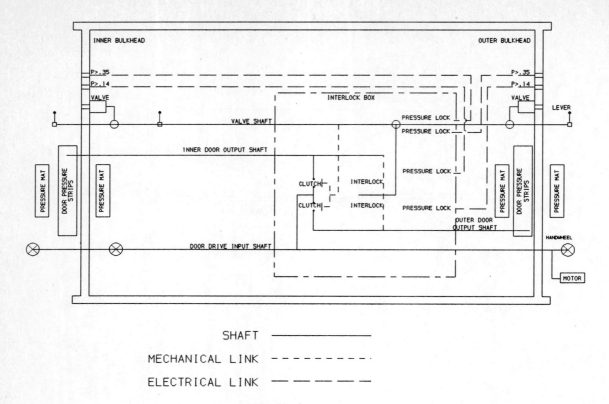

SHAFT ————————

MECHANICAL LINK - - - - - - - - -

ELECTRICAL LINK — - — - — - —

Fig 4   Schematic diagram of interlock arrangement

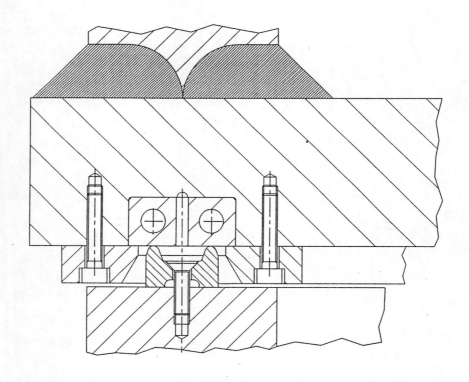

Fig 5   Section through door seal

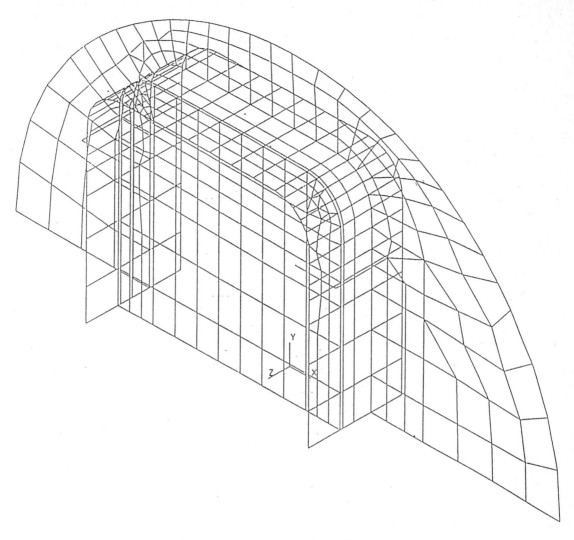

AIRLOCK INTERNAL PRESSURE CASE. BOLT C/L = 725MM. P=1.15P
SPA210.T33

Fig 6   Bulkhead geometry

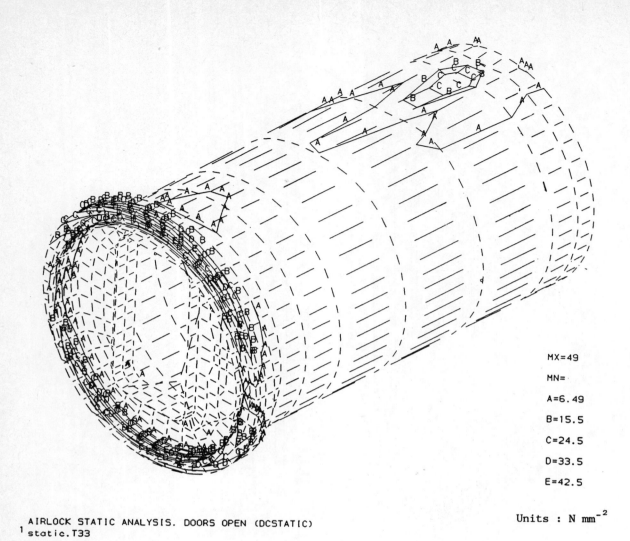

MX=49

MN=

A=6.49

B=15.5

C=24.5

D=33.5

E=42.5

Units : N mm^{-2}

AIRLOCK STATIC ANALYSIS. DOORS OPEN (DCSTATIC)
1 static.T33

Fig 7   Stress intensity distribution on the whole structure — static
loading only

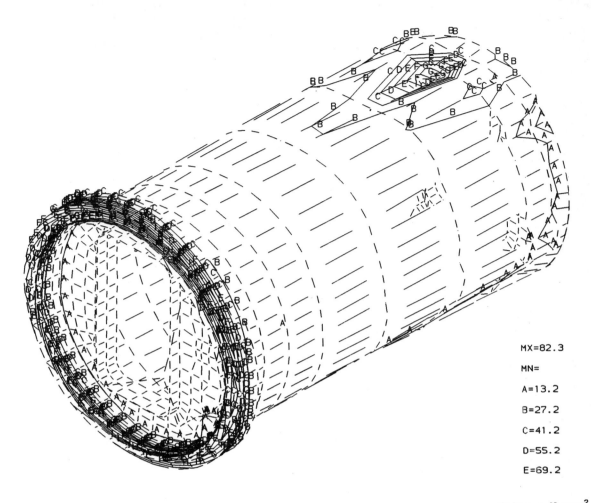

MX=82.3

MN=

A=13.2

B=27.2

C=41.2

D=55.2

E=69.2

Units : N mm^{-2}

AIRLOCK SEISMIC ANALYSIS. DOORS OPEN (DCSEISMIC)
[1] al3dseis2.T33

Fig 8   Stress intensity distribution on the whole structure — static
plus seismic loading